The Cambridge Companion to English Lite

This volume offers an introduction to British literature that crosses the traditional divide between eighteenth-century and Romantic studies. Contributors explore the development of literary genres and modes through a period of rapid change. They show how literature was shaped by historical factors including the development of the book trade, the rise of literary criticism, and the expansion of commercial society and empire. The first part of the volume focuses on broad themes including taste and aesthetics, national identity and empire, and key cultural trends such as sensibility and the gothic. The second part pays close attention to the work of individual writers including Sterne, Blake, Barbauld, and Austen, and to the role of literary schools such as the 'Lake' and 'Cockney' schools. The wide scope of the collection, juxtaposing canonical authors with those now gaining new attention from scholars, makes it essential reading for all students of eighteenth-century literature and Romanticism.

THE CAMBRIDGE
COMPANION TO
ENGLISH LITERATURE
1740–1830

EDITED BY

THOMAS KEYMER
University of Oxford

and

JON MEE
University of Oxford

CAMBRIDGE
UNIVERSITY PRESS

PUBLISHED BY THE PRESS SYNDICATE OF THE UNIVERSITY OF CAMBRIDGE
The Pitt Building, Trumpington Street, Cambridge, United Kingdom

CAMBRIDGE UNIVERSITY PRESS
The Edinburgh Building, Cambridge, CB2 2RU, UK
40 West 20th Street, New York, NY 10011–4211, USA
477 Williamstown Road, Port Melbourne, VIC 3207, Australia
Ruiz de Alarcón 13, 28014 Madrid, Spain
Dock House, The Waterfront, Cape Town 8001, South Africa

http://www.cambridge.org

First published 2004

Printed in the United Kingdom at the University Press, Cambridge

Typeface Sabon 10/13 pt.   *System* LATEX 2$_\varepsilon$ [TB]

A catalogue record for this book is available from the British Library

ISBN 0 521 80974 6 hardback
ISBN 0 521 00757 7 paperback

The publisher has used its best endeavours to ensure that the URLs for external websites
referred to in this book are correct and active at the time of going to press. However, the
publisher has no responsibility for the websites and can make no guarantee that a site will
remain live or that the content is or will remain appropriate.

CONTENTS

Part II Writers, circles, traditions

ILLUSTRATIONS

CONTRIBUTORS

BARBARA M. BENEDICT is Charles A. Dana Professor of English at Trinity College, Hartford. She is the author of *Framing Feeling: Sentiment and Style in English Prose Fiction, 1745–1800* (AMS Press, 1994), *Making the Modern Reader: Cultural Mediation in Early Modern Literary Anthologies* (Princeton University Press, 1996), and *Curiosity: A Cultural History of Early Modern Inquiry* (University of Chicago Press, 2001).

JOHN GOODRIDGE is Professor of English at Nottingham Trent University. He is general editor of the *English Labouring-Class Poets* series (Pickering and Chatto, 2003–4), and has edited the *John Clare Society Journal* since 1991. His books include *Rural Life in Eighteenth-Century Poetry* (Cambridge University Press, 1995), selections of verse by Robert Bloomfield and John Dyer, and a forthcoming monograph about Clare and trespass.

SIMON JARVIS is Gorley Putt Lecturer in English Literary History at the University of Cambridge. He is the author of *Scholars and Gentlemen: Shakespearean Textual Criticism and Representations of Scholarly Labour, 1725–1765* (Clarendon Press, 1995) and *Adorno: A Critical Introduction* (Polity, 1998), and is currently completing a study of Wordsworth.

BRIDGET KEEGAN is Associate Professor and Chair of English at Creighton University. She has edited the 1740–80 volume of *Eighteenth-Century English Labouring-Class Poets* (Pickering and Chatto, 2003) and, with James McKusick, *Literature and Nature: Four Centuries of Nature Writing* (Prentice Hall, 2001). She is writing a monograph on eighteenth-century British labouring-class writing about nature, landscape, and environment.

THOMAS KEYMER is Elmore Fellow in English at St Anne's College, Oxford, where he currently holds a Leverhulme Major Research Fellowship. His books include *Richardson's Clarissa and the Eighteenth-Century Reader* (Cambridge University Press, 1992), *Sterne, the Moderns, and the*

Novel (Oxford University Press, 2002), and numerous editions of eighteenth-century fiction, journalism, and travel writing.

GREG KUCICH is Associate Professor of English at the University of Notre Dame. He is the author of *Keats, Shelley, and Romantic Spenserianism* (Pennsylvania State University Press, 1991), and is completing a study tentatively entitled *British Romanticism and Women's Historical Writing*. With Keith Hanley, he co-edits *Nineteenth-Century Contexts: An Interdisciplinary Journal*.

PAUL MAGNUSON is Professor of English at New York University. He is the author of *Coleridge's Nightmare Poetry* (University Press of Virginia, 1974), *Coleridge and Wordsworth: A Lyrical Dialogue* (Princeton University Press, 1988), and *Reading Public Romanticism* (Princeton University Press, 1998).

SAREE MAKDISI is Professor of English and Comparative Literature at the University of California, Los Angeles. His work on Romantic period writing includes *Romantic Imperialism: Universal History and the Culture of Modernity* (Cambridge University Press, 1998) and *William Blake and the Impossible History of the 1790s* (University of Chicago Press, 2003).

SUSAN MANNING is Grierson Professor of English Literature at the University of Edinburgh. Her books include *The Puritan-Provincial Vision* (Cambridge University Press, 1990), *Fragments of Union: Making Connections in Scottish and American Writing* (Palgrave, 2002), and numerous editions of British and American eighteenth and nineteenth-century writing.

JON MEE is Margaret Candfield Fellow in English at University College, Oxford. His books include *Dangerous Enthusiasm: William Blake and the Culture of Radicalism in the 1790s* (Oxford University Press, 1992), *Romanticism, Enthusiasm, and Regulation: Poetics and the Policing of Culture in the Romantic Period* (Oxford University Press, 2003), and the recent Oxford World's Classics edition of Keats's *Selected Letters* (2002).

JUDITH PASCOE is Associate Professor of English at the University of Iowa. She is the author of *Romantic Theatricality: Gender, Poetry, and Spectatorship* (Cornell University Press, 1997) and has edited Mary Robinson's *Selected Poems* (Broadview, 2000). Her current project is a book-length study of Romantic era collectors.

MURRAY PITTOCK is Professor of Scottish and Romantic Literature at the University of Manchester. Among his books are *Celtic Identity and the British Image* (Manchester University Press, 1999), *Poetry and Jacobite Politics in Eighteenth-Century Britain and Ireland* (Cambridge University Press, 1994), and an edition of James Hogg's *The Jacobite Relics of Scotland* (Edinburgh University Press, 2002–3). He is editing Boswell's political correspondence in the Yale series.

GILLIAN RUSSELL is Senior Lecturer in English at the Australian National University. She is the author of *The Theatres of War: Performance, Politics, and Society, 1793–1815* (Oxford University Press, 1995) and editor, with Clara Tuite, of *Romantic Sociability: Social Networks and Literary Culture in Britain, 1770–1840* (Cambridge University Press, 1995). She is completing a book on sociability and theatre in Sheridan's London.

PETER SABOR is Canada Research Chair in Eighteenth-Century Studies and Director of the Burney Centre at McGill University. His publications include editions of Richardson's *Pamela* (Penguin, 1980) and Sarah Fielding's *David Simple* (University Press of Kentucky, 1998) and *Ophelia* (Broadview, 2004). He is general editor of *The Court Journals of Frances Burney* (Oxford University Press) and, with Thomas Keymer, *The Cambridge Edition of the Works and Correspondence of Samuel Richardson*.

MICHAEL SCRIVENER is Professor of English at Wayne State University. He is the author of *Radical Shelley* (Princeton University Press, 1982), *Poetry and Reform: Periodical Verse from the English Democratic Press, 1792–1824* (Wayne State University Press, 1992), and *Seditious Allegories: John Thelwall and Jacobin Writing* (Pennsylvania State University Press, 2001).

KATHRYN SUTHERLAND is Professor of Bibliography and Textual Criticism at the University of Oxford. Her work on Austen includes editions of *Mansfield Park* (Penguin, 1996) and J. E. Austen-Leigh's *A Memoir of Jane Austen and Other Family Recollections* (Oxford World's Classics, 2002), and she is completing a textual study of the novels. She has also edited *Adam Smith: Interdisciplinary Essays* (Manchester University Press, 1995) and *Electronic Text: Investigations in Method and Theory* (Clarendon Press, 1997).

JAMES WATT is Lecturer in English at the University of York. His publications include *Contesting the Gothic: Fiction, Genre, and Cultural Conflict, 1764–1832* (Cambridge University Press, 1999) and the Oxford World's Classics edition of Clara Reeve's *The Old English Baron* (2004). He is currently working on British orientalisms between 1700 and 1850.

PREFACE

The Cambridge Companion to English Literature, 1740–1830 introduces a period of rapid change and great achievement – a period in which literature was self-consciously offered as a token of Britain's ascendancy as an enlightened nation, yet looked to as a place in which human values under threat from modernity or 'progress' could still be discovered and nourished. This phase of literary production is still often defined as the 'Romantic' period, though later inaugural dates have conventionally been used (with reference to political events such as the outbreak of revolution in America or France, or to early publications by Wordsworth and others). Among the advantages of the less restricted time-frame explored in this Companion is that it enables an understanding of longer processes now increasingly seen as central to the formation of Romantic culture; acknowledges the survival into the early nineteenth century of characteristically eighteenth-century modes and discourses; and avoids marginalization of the many 'Romantic period' writers who for one reason or another resist explanation in terms of the idioms or ideology of 'high' Romanticism. This broader chronological focus, with corresponding attention to the continuities and developments of eighteenth-century literary culture into the nineteenth, distinguishes our volume from Stuart Curran's *Cambridge Companion to British Romanticism*, the intention being to complement and augment the emphases of this earlier Companion. While Curran's volume was far from being defined by a rigid adherence to the canonical texts of Romanticism, its concerns were necessarily focused on a narrower range of writing, and the bulk of its attention was given to aspects of British culture more easily assimilated to the (still much contested) -*ism* than to the more obvious diversity of the century from which this -*ism* emerged.

The extended period needs little justification in the case of the novel. The *Pamela* controversy of the early 1740s continues to be seen as the defining moment of innovation and elevation in the novel genre, and the achievements of later writers such as Burney and Austen involve a conscious development and fusion of techniques inherited from Richardson, Fielding and (as is increasingly being recognized) mid-century women novelists such as Sarah Fielding. Even the psychosexual recesses probed by Gothic novelists in the 1790s have origins in Richardson's explorations, while the socio-political sweep of Scott's fiction extends territory previously broken by Fielding and Smollett. Scholars of poetry have been more used to thinking in terms of a distinctive Romantic period beginning around 1790, but revisionist studies have rightly challenged this periodization with reference to the poetic innovations that followed the deaths of Pope and Swift in the 1740s, as well as to influential aesthetic treatises of the 1750s by Edmund Burke and Edward Young. A mid-century tradition of poetic enthusiasm emerged strongly in the verse of Collins, Gray, Smart and others, for which the term 'early Romantic' is now commonly used (alongside the older 'pre-Romantic', a category reanimated and refined in Marshall Brown's study of 1991, *Preromanticism*). By taking the extended period as its range, this Companion helps to plot the relationship between these mid-eighteenth-century forbears and the major canonical Romantics, while also registering the interaction between both categories of poet and broader cultural movements such as the pervasive sensibility vogue.

In drama, the period is often considered a desert, especially where the antitheatrical prejudices of influential Romantic writers continue to hold sway. Yet the theatre remained a key cultural institution throughout these years, and old assumptions that the Stage Licensing Act simply froze creativity for decades have given way to serious investigation of the new directions forced on managers and dramatists by the legislation of 1737. As a whole, the period witnessed the talents of playwrights such as Goldsmith and Sheridan, theatre critics of the calibre of Lamb and Hazlitt, and the emergence of star actors such as Garrick and Siddons. Just as the 1740s saw radical change in poetry and fiction, so drama was enduringly conditioned (not least in its strategies for accommodating and circumventing censorship) by a new generation of actor-dramatists who cut their teeth in the early post-licensing years. In all three genres, of course, important lines of continuity also cross the chronological bounds of this Companion, in ways registered by several contributors. All are valuably illuminated by the longer view, however, and by consideration of their development across an extended period in which rapid change and innovation coincide with attempts to find stability and permanence amid revolutionary times.

The period also gains definition and coherence from a series of cultural, social, and political developments which, it could be argued, mark the birth of the modern British cultural landscape. It begins with Pope railing in *The Dunciad* against the impoverishment of a literary marketplace in which hack writers feed middle-class readers with cheap, fugitive print; it ends in the prospect of mass readerships and democratic culture with which Victorians such as Arnold were to wrestle. As a whole, the period is central to the emergence of what scholars have come to call the 'public sphere' (a term originating in Jürgen Habermas's influential study of 1962, *The Structural Transformation of the Public Sphere*). Literature gained a key role in the process whereby public opinion came to be identified not with the state authority of court or ministry but with the rational debates of private individuals, as expressed in the more diffuse field of print and other mechanisms and spaces of urban culture. With the lowering of political temperatures that followed the fall of Walpole in 1742 and the conclusive defeat of the Jacobite challenge in 1745–6, the Hanoverian regime became firmly established, inaugurating a period of relatively settled institutions and structures that is traditionally seen as closing with Reform in 1832. The creation of a coherent though flexible British national identity, in which Welsh, Scottish, and Irish writers played a key role, moved to the centre of cultural production. The phenomenon of James Macpherson's Ossian poems, for instance, represents a rewriting of Gaelic tradition for a metropolitan audience, even though the poems and surrounding commentaries also mourned the loss of a primitive heroic culture and seemed to deplore the emergence of the modern nation for which they were written. After the Seven Years War of 1756–63, from which vast territorial gains accrued, Britain's status and identity as an imperial power were also being cemented. What was less certain – as Linda Colley has suggested in *Britons: Forging the Nation 1707–1837* (1992) – was how writers and readers understood their own identities in relation to this emerging power. Empire becomes a given in writing of this period, either by directly providing the material for forays into the exotic or the primitive, or, in more displaced ways, by procuring the transformations of fortune on which domestic narratives depended (as in the recently controversial case of *Mansfield Park*). For all the growing familiarity of the exotic, however, imperial expansion and its consequences still involved widespread anxiety, and even – as in the case of the broad-based abolitionist movement of the period – extensive outright opposition.

Internally, political opposition ceased to be driven by the predominantly Tory satire of the Walpole era, though Johnson and Austen are among the later writers in whom Pope's critique of Whig political and socio-economic corruption continues to echo. Opposition developed around issues of parliamentary reform, from the Wilkesite agitations of the 1760s to the popular radical movement of the 1790s and beyond, in ways that begin to look familiar to readers in a democratic society. In this context, the identity of 'the public' for literature, as for society more generally, became a contested matter. The wealth being generated from industry, trade and empire was fuelling, among much else, a rapid expansion of the publishing industry, and a middle-class reading audience was coming into its own. This growing audience sustained the development of the novel, fed elite fears about taste and its relationship to the marketplace, and encouraged (with the mid-century establishment of the *Monthly* and *Critical* reviews) an associated proliferation of periodicals that served to mediate and police literary culture to an expanded readership. After the French Revolution, the situation was complicated further by the spectre of a plebeian reading public, much to the alarm of figures such as Coleridge, and by fears that literature would become the servant of ignorance. Yet this explosion of print culture, and the powerful cultural paradigm of the republic of letters, also encouraged writers from below such as Blake and Clare to lay claim to a public voice on the basis of talent or inspiration alone. The culture of sensibility that gained sway from the mid eighteenth century likewise encouraged writers and readers, especially women, to believe that it was sufficient to feel to experience literature, even as it worked to protect cultural value by insisting that authentic feeling was far from ubiquitous. Those who contributed to the period's remarkable efflorescence of literary production were often divided within themselves as to whether they were participating in a cultural renaissance or witnessing, on the other hand, a fatal erosion of fundamental values.

Many writers reacted with alarm, in particular, at the emergence of modern urban and industrial culture. The development of a historical imagination from the Gothic novel through to Scott went hand in hand with primitivist nostalgia for a pre-commercial past, most closely associated with the name of Rousseau, and with an anti-urban poetry of retirement into nature that culminates with Wordsworth and Coleridge but finds significant expression from the start of the period. This reflex could serve as a radical critique of modern commercial society, but also sustained conservative longings for more feudal and organic social hierarchies of the kind famously articulated in Burke's *Reflections on the Revolution in France*. In poets as dissimilar as Keats and Clare towards the close of the period, nostalgic evocations of harmonious rural community accompany more or less explicit protest at the dislocations and losses entailed by agricultural and industrial 'improvement'.

The aim of this Companion is to provide a clear and accessible introduction to these complex cultural trends, and to the literature that sprang from, responded to, and in turn conditioned their emergence. The first part is concerned with matters of literary genre and cultural context as they unfolded across the period; the second is more directly focused on individual writers, but in ways that reflect the often collaborative or interactive nature of literary production at the time, whether in terms of circles of mutual influence or lines of putative tradition. The writers covered here include both the major canonical figures and others, especially women, who have recently gained fresh attention from scholars and critics. For the editors, the sense of richness and diversity in the period that has been such an important part of recent scholarship has been reaffirmed by collecting these essays, which in themselves display a rich diversity of approaches and stances. We hope that readers will also experience the volume as an opening out of one of the great periods of literary culture in Britain.

THOMAS KEYMER AND JON MEE

I

CONTEXTS AND MODES

I

BARBARA M. BENEDICT

Readers, writers, reviewers, and the professionalization of literature

'Reading is to the Mind, what Exercise is to the Body', wrote Richard Steele in his periodical paper, the *Tatler*, in 1710.[1] By the middle of the eighteenth century, readers of all classes and kinds were plentiful, and were growing in both wealth and influence. Men and women, gentry and professionals, merchants and urban servants read all kinds of printed works, from scientific treatises and travelogues to jest books, sentimental plays, advertisements, collections of poetry, periodical journals and, in increasing numbers, novels. They read for information, for entertainment and for profit, but as the period wore on they were increasingly reading for a further reason: moral improvement. Reading had become a route for the development of the individual into a fully formed member of society. Thus, what people read, as well as how and where they read it, could be seen to indicate much about them. 'Miss Eliza Bennet . . . despises cards', sneers Caroline Bingley in Jane Austen's *Pride and Prejudice* (1813), as Elizabeth picks up a book: 'she is a great reader and has no pleasure in any thing else.'[2] To this shallow and jealous upstart, Elizabeth Bennet's love of reading proves her a dangerous rival for the aristocratic Darcy's affection, for it denotes Elizabeth's natural refinement. By now, reading shows both social and moral merit.

Austen does not tell us what Elizabeth is reading, but it is certainly some form of imaginative literature, and the chances are that it is either a novel or a volume of history or travels. These long prose genres burgeoned in the eighteenth century, especially after 1770, fed by cheap print, hopeful authors, and eager audiences, themselves stoked by newly efficient booksellers and publishers who understood how to profit from literature. Moreover, such genres were produced by a growing class of writers who considered themselves professionals, and vetted by another new type of professional, the literary critic. These emergent professions of writer and critic arose from yet another kind of professionalization: the systematization of the entire process of making and selling books. Together, printers, publishers, booksellers, writers, readers, and critics transformed literature in the eighteenth century from a rarified pleasure tasted by an elite and leisured gentry into a ubiquitous consumer product.

The rise of reading as a sign of internal merit also reflects the rise of a new category for printed works of learning and imagination: the category of 'literature' itself. In his *Dictionary* of 1755, Samuel Johnson had defined literature as 'learning, skill in letters', but by the century's close it had come to mean a material product and a profession. The *OED* defines the term as 'literary work or production; the activity or profession of a man of letters', and, by 1813, as 'the body of writings produced in a particular country or period'. This revolutionary idea of literature reflects four key and intertwined changes in literary culture that gained pace in the period. The first is the evolution of the book trade from a relatively haphazard, loose-knit craft into a professional, profit-seeking industry. The second is the corresponding transformation of writers from gentlemen dilettantes into professional authors. These changes reflect and propel a change in who was reading: the reading public expanded from the small, traditional groups of leisured gentry and practical businessmen into a widespread national audience of both genders and all classes. In turn, readers understood themselves as participants in public culture. Finally, imaginative literature itself was redefined: no longer a luxury of the wealthy and learned, it was conceived as a commodity fit for all palates.

Who was this audience, and how much did they really read? Although the number of different titles produced annually at the beginning of the eighteenth century was below two thousand, this annual figure had risen to about six thousand by 1800, and literacy rates continued to increase.[3] By the middle of the century, at least 40 per cent of women and 60 per cent of men could read and write (albeit with varying levels of competence), out of a total population that more than doubled in England alone from a base of 5.6 million in 1741 to 13.3 million in 1831.[4] Such a large proportion of literate people meant that those who considered themselves readers belonged not merely to the traditional elite, but to all classes of professionals, merchants, farmers, tradespeople and skilled artisans, together with many servants and labourers and, of course, women of all ranks.

In the expanding readership of the period, these last categories were of new importance. By 1768, 107,000 copies of an astrological almanac aimed at labouring-class readers, *Moore's Vox Stellarum* (generally known as *Moore's Almanack*), were printed annually, whereas the more self-consciously polite periodical the *Gentleman's Magazine* (subtitled *Trader's Monthly Intelligencer* on its launch in 1731, but increasingly aimed thereafter at a genteel readership) crested at 10,000. By 1800 the print order for Moore's stood at 353,000, peaking at of 560,000 in 1839.[5] Despite these differences, publishers continually aimed at crossover genres. The other newly ascendant audience was women. As readers, writers, topics and targets in literature, women and female concerns leapt into the forefront of literary culture. As the century wore on, literary ventures aimed at women burgeoned. Periodicals such as Henry Mackenzie's *Mirror* (1779–80) anatomized feminine manners, education, and expectations; plays such as Richard Sheridan's *The Rivals* (1775) satirized adolescent maidens' appetite for hot novels; and both women and men, some using female pen-names, themselves wrote fiction for this hungry new audience. On the bustling streets of late eighteenth-century British cities, shops and circulating libraries bulged with sentimental novels, monthly periodicals containing serialized stories, gift books, poetical miscellanies, and conduct books, all directed at middle-class female readers.

Printing had always been a risky business. Official restrictions on the publication of political or erotic material were punitive, and few printers operated because the government controlled their numbers and charged heavy fees for licences. Bankruptcies throughout the seventeenth and eighteenth centuries remained high, as inexperienced printers took risks on unknown authors or expensive editions. One melancholy instance involves Richard Chandler, an entrepreneurial printer-bookseller of London and York, who rose rapidly from lowly apprentice to master bookseller before reaching twenty, and published a successful though meretricious continuation of Richardson's *Pamela*, John Kelly's *Pamela's Conduct in High Life*, in 1741. Within three years, his fortunes had completely reversed. In 1744, now thirty-one and facing bankruptcy, Chandler shot himself in the head – only then, in a further reversal, for his business partner Caesar Ward to retrieve the financial situation (going on to print, among other works, Sterne's *Political Romance* in 1759).[6] Such veering unpredictability persisted throughout the period, although attempts had already been made by early eighteenth-century booksellers to reduce their risk of failure by forming coalitions to expand both the number of works they could produce, and the places where these were sold. With this development, the fluid traditional pattern of book-trade relationships began to undergo radical change. These coalitions of trading booksellers, known as congers, banded together to buy the copyrights for new works, and indeed to buy up all the extant copies of works whose copyrights they held. Although in competition with one another, nonetheless they also collaborated, so that smaller booksellers were frequently put out of business. Moreover, the congers were able to expand their means of disseminating print, capitalizing on increasingly efficient networks of communication and distribution to offer their books not only across London, but all over rural England and Wales, Scotland, Ireland, and even in North America.

With the formation of congers, booksellers – traditionally rather lowly members of the book trade – achieved new prominence and influence. Previously, men and women who sold books from shops were merely retailers. Whereas printers produced fresh works, urban booksellers offered readers books from their ageing stock that were often already out of fashion, while travelling booksellers known as chapmen provided inexpensive, low-grade books (with ribbons, songs, and other ephemeral items) to country-bound consumers. Neither category of bookseller, however, had much influence on the kinds of book that he or she could offer for sale. The advent of congers meant that booksellers increasingly became producers of literature themselves. As an association of copyright-holding publishers who both ordered works to be printed and organized the selling of them, the conger became a kind of bookselling firm empowered to tell printers, and sometimes authors too, what to produce. By forming monopolies that fixed prices, they kept the cost of books artificially high, and by controlling the dissemination of literary works, they kept them in the category of precious and rare items. Congers thus helped to maintain the prestige of literature as a luxury item, even while profiteering from it. Moreover, they manoeuvred the courts into preserving the traditional common-law system of enduring copyright protection so that they, and they alone, had the power to issue fresh editions of old as well as new works. The bookseller became the most influential figure in publishing.

These congers had another profound effect on the literary culture of the eighteenth century. They made literature the pre-eminent subject of sophisticated conversation. This resulted partly from their skilful manipulation of the concept of a canon: a roster of renowned authors whose works exemplify the language and thought of the nation. The notion of a selective list of exemplary authors had existed from Elizabethan times, and although it stretched forward far enough to add Shakespeare, Jonson, and other Renaissance poets to the litany of medieval greats like Chaucer and Gower, it still remained by definition exclusive. Congers and enterprising booksellers, however, made literary exclusivity a matter of novelty rather than time-tested worth: their sales pitch was topicality, not timelessness. Since they could publish old as well as recent texts, however, they could also manipulate the audience to desire both. By repeatedly reissuing both renowned works by classical authors and English literature from recent decades (both 'ancients' and 'moderns', in the shorthand of the day), they identified a native, poetic tradition with the classics of the Graeco-Roman world. They kept topical literature like Pope's *The Rape of the Lock* in print, and made literature a fashionable commodity. High literary culture came to include ephemeral current works, delights to be savoured while fresh from the press, rather than only weighty and traditional matter, mulled over and meditated upon by clerics and historians. The literary canon became a question of contemporary debate.

Eighteenth-century publishing booksellers also used their copyright privileges to attract new audiences and to preserve the reputation and money-making power of the authors whose copyrights they owned. Through creative packaging, they broadened the appeal of rarified works, imitating the practice of the early innovator Jacob Tonson, who had issued his six volumes of *Miscellany Poems* (1684–1709) not as expensive folios but as unpretentious octavo volumes, adorned with stylish frontispieces, and later in miniature duodecimo, suitable for pocket or reticule. As congers controlled prices, copyrights, and even the distribution of copies of books, they also helped to establish niche markets: particular audiences attracted by specific kinds of literature. Booksellers began to work closely with writers to find, even invent, new tastes and desires in the reading audience. Some of this inventiveness appears in the presentation of books. Early eighteenth-century literature features elaborate printing devices, including fonts ranging from grim Gothic to spidery cursive; random italics; and startling capitals designed to attract even unskilled readers. Later books use crisp roman numerals on wide swathes of page to tout their classic simplicity. Early novels feature long, detail-dotted titles that provide a sample of the plenitude of narrative pleasures within, like Defoe's *Moll Flanders* (1722), which advertises on its title-page 'a Life of continu'd Variety' in which the heroine 'was Twelve Year a *Whore*, five times a *Wife* (whereof once to her own Brother) Twelve Year a *Thief*, Eight Year a Transported *Felon* in *Virginia*, at last grew *Rich*, liv'd *Honest*, and died a *Penitent*'. Subsequent fictions simplify their titles to signal familiar genres, as in Sterne's *The Life and Opinions of Tristram Shandy, Gentleman* (1759–67). Virtually no eighteenth-century book emerges from the printer without pages of advertisements, printed or pasted onto the back, for other books issued by the conger and sold at both local and far-flung shops. By diligent advertising in the newspapers, by soliciting critical reviews, and by printing catalogues of available stock in bookshops and libraries, publishing booksellers identified and differentiated genres for their readers. Through such delicate manipulations of the emerging distinctions between levels of literary culture, these new booksellers defined culture without actually writing or printing anything themselves. Rather, they facilitated the dissemination of literary works to the widest possible audience while preserving the aura of literature as a high-class commodity. Print promoted print.

By the middle of the eighteenth century, readers were growing more experienced and discriminating, while book sales temporarily stagnated. These were the second generation, at least, of novel-readers, accustomed to the titular lures of novels and their generic medley, and moreover they were surrounded by a competitive, sophisticated literary marketplace. In response, booksellers modified forms for selling poetry to assure readers not only of multiplicity and variety but also of quality. Since the Restoration, publishers had issued anthologies, miscellanies, and compendia of verse, ephemeral works, jokes, and literary fragments, but these had remained something of a second-class form, a patchwork creation slapped together from left-over poems and pamphlets. In the mid-eighteenth century, however, Robert Dodsley, an enterprising footman who had changed his livery for literature, issued a collection of verse that made contemporary poetry a matter of high moral seriousness. Entitled *A Collection of Poems by Several Hands*, the series appeared in six volumes from 1748 to 1758, and was revised, continued, and imitated throughout the century. Dodsley's *Collection* was a watershed in the transformation of eighteenth-century poetry from an ephemeral entertainment to a touchstone of refinement. Indeed, it continued to designate the elite, literary taste of the eighteenth century's 'Graveyard School' well into the next century, retaining a prestige registered by Jane Austen when, after selling her father's edition of Dodsley's *Poems* in 1801 for ten shillings, she naughtily confesses that the sale 'please[s] me to the quick, & I do not care how often I sell them for as much'.[7] Dodsley's feat was to commission fashionable poets such as Edward Young, Samuel Johnson, and Thomas Gray to compose fresh pieces specifically for his collection, to print these beside verse by Alexander Pope, Jonathan Swift, and other renowned names of the recent past, and to publicize the venture as the epitome of reading sophistication. This anthology created a taste for proto-Romantic poetry, and at the same time an audience for it composed of the culturally ambitious and fashionable gentry.

The evolution of the book trade into a profit-making machine – into big business – changed the way literature was quite literally produced: how it was conceived, written, printed, and sold. In order to publish their works, authors had long relied on the generosity of patrons whom they flattered in prefaces and dedications. An alternative, if they could afford it, was to publish by commission: authors would bring their manuscripts to printers and pay for the publication themselves, with the agreement that the printer would distribute copies and take a fee for each that was sold. However, once literature became a fashionable commodity, booksellers took a more direct part in actually creating literature. Now that publishing booksellers like Dodsley were willing to commission literary works themselves, poets and prose writers could turn to them for patronage, instead of relying on the whims of ambitious nobility as had generations before them, and the editors of critical journals also served as unofficial patrons to writers favoured for reasons that were often partisan. Pope prided himself on being the first poet to live purely on the public sale of his work, boasting that 'I live and thrive, / Indebted to no Prince or Peer alive',[8] while influential critics like Samuel Johnson came to act as patrons themselves for neglected talent. For writers, it may not have been any easier to please a publisher whose eyes were narrowly fixed on profit than an earl with a misty view of his own immortal fame; nor was writing to deadline necessarily congenial: Johnson would famously keep the printer's devil – the boy who delivered text to the press – knocking on his door as, paid by the word, he dashed off each last periodic sentence. Still, the real audience for literary authors was not the bookseller but a tolerant and varied readership: the shifting, increasingly opulent, urban classes, the colonials abroad, and the country gentry and professions in the rural British Isles.

Another way of producing books was by subscription: a contract between selected readers, and an author and a publisher. By this plan, interested readers, attracted by the description of a proposed new work, would provide the means to pay for its publication, and would eventually receive one of the limited number of copies themselves. This method was used throughout the century to promote elite works like expensive translations of the *Iliad* and *Odyssey*: indeed, in the passage quoted above, Pope's point is that his own freedom from patronage was in the first place 'thanks to *Homer*'. Henry Fielding noted Pope's success in *Joseph Andrews* (1742) and attempted to emulate it the following year with a three-volume subscription edition of his own *Miscellanies*. Authors and publishers also used subscription to raise money for poor or unknown authors, the conspicuous case being the Irish poet Mary Barber, whose London-published *Poems on Several Occasions* (1735) attracted 918 subscribers, a quarter of them of noble rank. Like many women who found it difficult to penetrate the literary market, Fielding's sister Sarah Fielding employed the same device for two of her works, and Johnson often turned to it for his charitable endeavours, attempting in the 1770s, for example, to help a poverty-stricken but ungrateful Charlotte Lennox by raising a subscription for 'A New and Elegant Edition, Enlarged and Corrected, of the Original Works of Mrs. Charlotte Lennox'.[9] As the failure of this venture shows, however, the days of subscription publication were numbered: the literary market was expanding, readers from the middling classes were multiplying, and speculative publication to readers at large was increasingly the better option. As the century drew to a close, the entire thrust of literary publishing moved away from limited, fine editions and towards the discovery or creation of works for a wide readership.

One form perfectly fulfilled the bookseller's need to keep readers buying fresh works that were inexpensive to produce: serial publication. Serial publication really began with daily journals of political news. Since London adopted the penny post in 1680, newspapers had sprung up everywhere: by 1710, London boasted twelve newspapers; by 1750, some twenty-four; and by 1790 there were thirteen morning, one evening, two bi-weekly, and seven tri-weekly newspapers.[10] In the process of this huge growth, the definition of news itself evolved to include gossip, announcements and discussions of cultural events, reviews of books, plays, and entertainments, and extracts from literary works. This mixture came to characterize a distinct form of serial publication and one of the quintessential eighteenth-century genres: the periodical. Topical, inclusive, shapeless, and collaborative, the periodical jumbles together snippets of different genres written by different people – from journalistic essays to poetry – and rushes them into print. Fact, fiction, literature, and gossip intermingle as authors, editors, and contributors from the readership together conjure an atmosphere of intimate, sophisticated, fashionable conversation. Indeed, since current information was blended with imaginative fiction, literature here became indistinguishable from news. Originating in the late seventeenth century with journals dedicated to answering readers' inquiries such as John Dunton's *Athenian Mercury* (1691–7), periodicals leapt into literary prominence with the huge success of Addison and Steele's *Spectator* (1711–12, 1714). Purportedly the observations of an urban *flaneur*, the *Spectator* interlarded reviews of London events with tales of a gaggle of characters, relayed in sentimental vignettes. Although no more than 3,000 copies of the original *Spectator* papers were published, and even the century's most influential journal, the *Gentleman's Magazine*, never topped 10,000, readers shared copies, coffee-houses provided them to clients, and circulating libraries stocked them. As a result, all London and much of provincial England knew what the latest issue had printed. The periodical was sociability in print.

Periodicals quickly grew into one of the century's most prolific and influential forms. By 1745, there were thirty periodical journals, and in the next fifteen years forty-five more would appear, but the one that most strongly shaped the literary culture of the second half of the eighteenth century was Edward Cave's *Gentleman's Magazine*. Founded in 1731, and continued in various forms until 1914, the *Gentleman's Magazine* propelled the profession of literary critic into public culture. Originally a miscellaneous digest of opinion, essays, poetry and political news that skirmished persistently with contemporary copyright and censorship laws, Cave's magazine included relatively little literary criticism in its early years, which are now best remembered for the audacious parliamentary reporting of Johnson (whose columns were dressed up as debates from the senate of Lilliput to evade an official ban). Cave later saw the opportunity for a separate reviewing magazine, and drew up plans with collaborators to issue a new periodical that would 'give an impartial account of *every* work publish'd' under the title 'the Monthly Review'.[11] But instead Cave's young rival, the dissenting Whig Ralph Griffiths, caught wind of his design, and two months later slipped into the press the first non-specialist periodical devoted exclusively to reviewing, insolently naming it the *Monthly Review* (1749–1844). In a quick countermove, the *Gentleman's* began including a substantial number of fresh compositions and serious essays of literary criticism, which evaluated recent poetry and fiction or (as in a celebrated later controversy of 1789–91) debated the relative ranking of such authors as Dryden and Pope. The *Gentleman's* not only made politics part of elite literary conversation, but also refigured literary criticism as a moral commentary on society; moreover, both politics and literary became consumer items whose value as 'news' lay in their freshness. Within a few years, Tobias Smollett's Tory venture the *Critical Review* (1756–91) and its short-lived but influential rival, Johnson's *Literary Magazine* (1756–8), sprang into print. The literary reviewer had become an ideological touchstone, and the reader became – if only by rhetorical conjuring – part of a public sphere of informed debate. The formal identification of politics with literary evaluation stamped literary critics and their readers as participants in national, public culture.

This pattern of duelling periodicals persists into the nineteenth century, but with changes of tenor. Immediately following the French Revolution, ideology became far more contentious than in the relatively consensual period that followed Walpole's fall and the defeat of Jacobitism in the 1740s. In 1796, the Jacobin Richard Phillips issued his first number of the radical *Monthly Magazine*, a wide-ranging periodical that ran until 1825. First edited by the physician John Aikin (brother of the poet and essayist Anna Laetitia Barbauld), it included essays on European and oriental literature, science, politics, and other topics by such writers as William Godwin, Thomas Malthus, and William Hazlitt, all men identified with revolutionary liberalism. In high-spirited defiance, the Tory George Canning founded the *Anti-Jacobin* (1797–8), which melded political and literary satire in crisp parodies of weighty German drama, Francophile morality, and Romantic verse. Subsequently, the more serious and literary *New Monthly Magazine* (1814–84) drifted away from condemning Jacobinism to concentrate on literary publishing, including works by respected poets such as Wordsworth and Keats.

This trend reflected the results of another duel that changed periodical culture itself, inaugurated by the Whiggish, confrontational *Edinburgh Review* (1802–1929). Instead of imitating the inclusive if disorderly format of the traditional journal, which welcomed a wide audience, it largely banished the old favourites of classical, popular, and antiquarian works, instead favouring academic writings, especially the Scottish specialities of science, philosophy, and political economy, along with political matters and scientifically documented travels. It was here (in the issue for August 1817) that the editor Francis Jeffrey immortally dismissed Wordsworth, Coleridge, and Southey as 'the Lake School'. Apart from writers such as these, who were admitted primarily as targets, there was little room for imaginative literature, the honourable exceptions being Scottish and/or utilitarian authors such as Walter Scott or Joanna Baillie. By its deliberately elite approach, 'the *Edinburgh* constructed an upmarket yet culturally receptive version of "the world," and helped train writers to address it'.[12] In response, the Tory bookseller John Murray, publisher of Byron and Austen, founded the *Quarterly Review* (1809–1967), a conservative organ that stood firm behind established hierarchies in church and state, sounded the defence of the Romantic poets, and served as the target of Thomas Love Peacock's radical prose satire of literary pretension, *Melincourt* (1817). Both journals became hugely popular during the Napoleonic wars, each selling over 12,000 copies monthly from 1812 to 1814, and they transformed the periodical into an organ of elite and contentious literacy.

The capacious melting-pot of periodicals had made them central to literary culture over the preceding century. In the format of the *Gentleman's Magazine*, readers encountered detailed political information alongside considered opinions on literary works, so that literary criticism appeared to occupy a level of cultural seriousness equivalent to that of national and international policy. In eulogizing Cave, indeed, Johnson claimed that the *Gentleman's* was 'one of the most successful and lucrative pamphlets which literary history has upon record'.[13] In their sheer versatility and opportunism, moreover, the magazines were perfectly placed to register and exploit ongoing developments in public taste. This capacity is most obviously seen in periodicals such as Smollett's *British Magazine* (1760–3) and the later *Sentimental Magazine* (1773–7), both of which made a feature, through serialization, of what was to become the premier form of popular literature of Romantic period, albeit one simultaneously disparaged in the periodical reviews: the novel.

The novel was initially just one among several ascendant genres. The fresh idea of literature as a national product that all readers could, indeed should, consume promoted the rich blossoming of a myriad of new printed forms that had begun in the early eighteenth century. There were still the traditional genres: plays, histories, sermons, and poetry. But forms that had become newly popular since the turn of the century grew into maturity by its end, including newspapers, almanacs, jest books, a host of ephemeral printed forms from broadside songs to recipe books, and, most significantly, long prose fictions and miscellanies of topical poems. Both these genres answered the needs of middle-class audiences without formal literary training but full of the desire to read; both welcomed topical matter like love stories and satires on recent events or political figures; both proved relatively easy to master for writers and poets jostling for space in a fickle market.

New genres, new writers, and new readers also opened up new topics. The burst of new literary forms resulted partly from new ways of selling old material, but it also reflected the new freedom in the marketplace of print. More people could write, print, sell, and read, and they could explore more topics. Released from the strict censorship of the Puritan regime at the Restoration of 1660, when press regulation became more erratic, writers and booksellers also exploited freshly licensed, or at least permissible, fields: erotica, politics, science, and scandal. In the seventeenth century, the Printing Act had limited the number of printers and of printed books. When it lapsed in 1695, however, it was not renewed, and, despite the restriction on parliamentary reporting and other spasms of government censorship such as the Stage Licensing Act of 1737, printers, writers, and booksellers enjoyed a freedom to say what they wanted in print that had never before been seen. Although prosecution for blasphemy, obscenity, or seditious libel remained a hazard, this freedom propelled a surge of new genres throughout the eighteenth century, from the publication of criminals' confessions and imitations of these such as *Moll Flanders*, to the high-class scandals of adulterous noblewomen in the poems and periodicals of the century's last decades, such as the notorious *Bon-Ton Magazine* (1791–6).

One central political event symbolizes the establishment of this remarkable eighteenth-century relaxation of official censorship: John Wilkes's publication of *An Essay on Woman* in 1763. Wilkes was a radical opponent of the government, and had just established a newspaper, the *North Briton*, to serve as the organ of his opposition. On 23 April 1763 he issued number 45, criticizing one of the King's speeches. Since this was not illegal, the ministry could do nothing to prevent him, but was able to discover, through spying and bribery, an efficient pretext for arresting him. Wilkes was publishing an obscene poem for his libertine companions, the Knights of Sir Francis, who met at the Hell-fire Club in the ancient ruins of Medmenham Abbey. The officers of the government broke into Wilkes's shop and seized his papers.

Sure enough, among them were three meticulous parodies of Alexander Pope's deistic works, *An Essay on Man*, the 'Universal Prayer', and 'The Dying Christian to his Soul'. Written in blunt, sexual slang, and dedicated mischievously to Bishop William Warburton (editor of Pope's posthumous *Works*), these were Wilkes's *An Essay on Woman* and two accompanying poems, 'The Universal Prayer' and 'The Dying Lover to His Prick'. Wilkes was arrested and charged first with blasphemy, and when that charge collapsed (since Pope, albeit canonical, was not biblical) with seditious libel. Despite his brief escape to Paris, Wilkes served twenty-two months in prison. When he emerged, however, he took his seat in Parliament, later serving as the Mayor of London, and sued the government for illegal entry. He was awarded £4,000. Although Wilkes was primarily hailed for establishing political liberty, his arrest and liberation dramatized the connection between English freedom and the freedom to publish.

Authorship itself was also undergoing significant change. In the early modern period, writers were typically amateurs, penning poems or satires for the gratification of themselves and their friends. Since such writers were predominantly men from the gentry, educated in the languages and literary traditions of the ancient world and the continent, they adapted or imitated classical genres like the epic and eclogue. In the seventeenth and especially eighteenth centuries, however, when the Bible appeared in the vernacular, and institutions of modern education taught dissenters different ways of thinking and writing, new kinds of people began to view themselves as authors, notably tradesmen such as Defoe and Richardson, and women of all ranks such as Eliza Haywood, Charlotte Lennox, Frances Burney, and many more. Indeed, research shows that the number of women authors was expanding by 'around 50 percent *every decade* starting in the 1760s'.[14] These new writers established new genres in poetry and prose, particularly the novel. As a chronicle of individual self-realization in the social world, the novel records the experience of new classes as they attained social power.

Changes in the social composition of authors paralleled changes in their legal powers. Throughout the eighteenth century, congers of publishing booksellers had kept firm their grip on copyright restrictions. Ironically, eighteenth-century authors had no authority over their own works after the ink was dry and the paper sold: authors received a set fee once they handed their work to the publisher, and any profits vanished into the publisher's coffers. Since publishing was where the money lay, however, pirates – publishers who printed copies of works whose copyrights they did not own and undercut the official price – multiplied. Copyright was, of course, the right to print copies of a work. In 1710, publishing booksellers had solidified their exclusive rights to sell English and foreign-language works in England by engineering the passage of the Act for the Encouragement of Learning. Popularly known as the Copyright Act, this bill in fact discouraged widespread learning by fixing the prices on imported editions of classics and works in the modern languages, and by extending extant copyright restrictions to twenty-one years. Thus, in the decades to follow, booksellers who owned the copyrights to popular works like *Gulliver's Travels* and school textbooks could continue to produce them without competition.

Given the appetite of readers for literature, and of pirates for profit, the matter of copyright remained fraught throughout the century. Although courts of law kept asserting that copyrights could extend for a period of time without limit, many copyrights had in practice already expired, since piracies littered the market. Even fiercely restricted works, particularly poetry by popular authors like Pope and Swift, seeped into the common market. Most violations were ignored, because booksellers could rarely prove who had issued the pirated edition and lacked the time or means to mount prosecutions. Authors never entered the debate, with the exception of a few savvy marketers like Pope himself; more often they were considered merely hacks who did literary piece-work. The price of their work did rise a little through the century, however, and if their works had proved popular, they could ask for fat fees. Fielding was reportedly prepared to accept £25 for *Joseph Andrews*, but then sold it for almost £200 (and his later novels, *Tom Jones* and *Amelia*, for £600 and £800 respectively) to Andrew Millar, the publishing bookseller whom Samuel Johnson approvingly called 'the Maecenas of the age' for having 'raised the price of literature'.[15] In 1803, by contrast, Jane Austen sold *Northanger Abbey* to Crosby and Co. for only £10, competing as she was with the hack writers of sentimental and gothic fiction, who were legion; years later she was compelled to repurchase the work when it had still failed to appear in print.

Copyright restrictions were repeatedly but unavailingly attacked throughout the eighteenth century, on a number of different grounds. While booksellers fought to preserve their monopolies, other public spokesmen saw the issue as one of national policy. Parliamentary and judicial debates raised questions about how this practice served the English principle of free trade and healthy competition, and whether it really promoted public access to new knowledge. These questions stirred the century's most significant legal test of copyright: the 1774 trial between Alexander Donaldson, a renowned Scottish bookseller operating in Edinburgh, and Andrew Millar's former apprentice Thomas Becket, now a London bookseller in his own right. In a separate case completed in 1769, Millar had successfully defended his exclusive rights to James Thomson's fashionable cycle of poems, *The Seasons* (1726–30), which Becket then bought up for £505. Deliberately challenging the Millar ruling, Donaldson opened a bookshop in London from which he flamboyantly sold his own unauthorized reprints, including *The Seasons*. Becket's proceedings ended on appeal in the House of Lords, which amidst intense public interest reversed the interpretation of copyright law apparently cemented in 1769, overthrowing indefinite copyright on the grounds, among others, that monopolist congers were robbing the public of their access to learning. In this celebrated case of *Donaldson v. Becket*, booksellers thus lost their entitlement to perpetual copyright, and the result was a rush of anthologies and series reprinting elite and fashionable literature from Shakespeare to Thomson.[16] Combined with the success of the anthology format, and the nationalistic fervour of the mid century symbolized by the cry of 'Wilkes and liberty', this freedom to publish historical and popular works from the previous hundred years transformed literary culture. A native literary tradition was born.

As literary culture became increasingly identified with an elite morality, authorship correspondingly became both a respectable profession and a sign of internal class. Very gradually, changes in copyright were beginning to recognize the rights of creation, not merely reproduction, in the selling of literature. In 1814, a new Copyright Act extended the term of copyright from a once-renewable fourteen-year limit to twenty-eight years or the life of the author, whichever was the longer. Although authors still did not immediately benefit from this legislation, the Act did show that the right to produce copies of a work could be connected to the act of authoring them, rather than to publishing alone. Moreover, a new conception of the author was rising: the concept of authorship, not as writing for pay, but as the creative shaping of social mores. This development is at its most conspicuous in Romantic verse that elevates the sensibility of the poet into what Keats called the 'egotistical sublime' (a strain of self-important magniloquence that was epitomized for Keats by Wordsworth),[17] and it underpins Shelley's famous identification of poets as unacknowledged legislators of the world. Nonetheless, even as such ideals were being promoted, nameless writers for publishing hack-houses like the Minerva Press were churning out three-decker (three-volume) novels every month, purveying stories of women's romantic fulfilment for cash. Whereas a mere sprinkling of new prose fictions was reaching the market in 1700, and never more than forty appeared annually before 1770, between 1800 and 1830 roughly eighty new novels were being published every year.[18] The novel too had its promoters, Austen's celebrated defence of the genre as one 'in which the most thorough knowledge of human nature' is 'conveyed to the world in the best chosen language' being only the best known example.[19] Both genres were designed to promote readerly identification, moral growth, and sensibility, and readers – often the same readers – consumed both. As the novel reached an apex of popularity, however, consciously anti-populist opinion was at pains to stress the superior credentials of highbrow verse, practised as it most conspicuously was by elite, male writers. While both Romantic poetry and courtship novels embody a new respect for feeling and emotional expressiveness, they operate in genres conventionally associated with gendered and class tastes. Novels in accessible prose, read once and forgotten, were fare for everyone; poetry, traditionally conceived as dense and referential despite the efforts of Wordsworth, Coleridge and others to write in common language, demanded to be re-read and meditated upon, and increasingly became matter for the leisured elite.

How did readers get access to this material? Since books remained expensive throughout the century, and literary fashion was shown by a work's topicality, only the wealthiest families – like Darcy's in *Pride and Prejudice* – could afford to keep their private libraries up to date. There were plenty of places for urban readers to catch up on the latest news and gossip, since coffee-houses habitually stocked several newspapers which customers could read on the premises; but books remained difficult to buy, and the new, profitable audience of women did not frequent coffee-houses. There was, however, the public library.

Several forms of public library existed in eighteenth-century England. The subscription library, by which members together decide what titles to buy, allowed like-minded people to share a slice of literary culture. In Austen's *Mansfield Park*, the heroine Fanny Price, exiled to Portsmouth, cannot survive without the solace of a subscription library to provide her with the delicious power of choosing her own reading matter and guiding that of her sister. This was also the form for various religious libraries, particularly in the provinces, that served to monitor the reading of a closed society. In contrast, the circulating library was run for profit by retailing booksellers who would buy up large libraries from auction houses, and lend them to members for a fee. These circulating libraries, although they also carried histories, sermons, travels, scientific reports, newspapers and periodicals, specialized in the latest novels, and possessed hundreds – in the case of James Lackington, thousands – of volumes. The earliest appeared in London and major provincial centres before mid-century. By 1739, when Francis and John Noble, publishing booksellers, established one in Holborn, specializing in second-hand books, there were already three others in London alone. Meanwhile, Richardson seized the chance in his 1738 revision of Defoe's *Tour* to promote the library that his bookseller brother-in-law, James Leake, had been operating in Bath since 1731, where subscription cost five shillings 'but Persons of Quality generally subscribe a Guinea'.[20] By the end of the century such institutions were plentiful and widespread.

By their terms of operation, circulating libraries influenced the development of the novel. They offered several levels of membership, asking clients to pay the highest dues for the right to borrow the most recent books (since topicality was a sign of fashion), and charging by the volume rather than by the entire work. Titles that encompassed several volumes thus proved more profitable to proprietors than single-volume works, especially if the multi-volume opus had features that lured readers to hunger for the next volume. This marketing motive prompted the development of one of the classic genres of the following century: the three-volume novel. Plot-driven, suspense-studded, and above all long, these weighty fictions supported not only booksellers like Lackington, John Bell, and the Nobles, but publishers like the Minerva Press and the anonymous authors who churned out formulaic novels by the volume. As one advertisement explains, circulating libraries ostentatiously refused to make elitist judgements, valuing fugitive fiction as much as classic literature, and respecting each individual's taste equally. Indeed, neatly dressed attendants were on hand at the larger libraries to assist customers by selecting for them the most recent texts of the same flavour as their last choices, like literary sommeliers. As the rhyming proprietor boasts,

> Printed Pamphlets, and Books, of all sorts and conditions,
> Well bound, in good order, the fairest editions;
> All tastes he can suit, be they ever so various,
> And please every fancy, however precarious;
> There are truths and grave maxims to please the discerning;
> There the wit may find jokes, and the scholar find learning;
> For the gay there is mirth, and sad tales for the grave,
> And sieges, and battles, and wars for the brave;
> For the curious inquisitive mind that loves facts,
> There are all kinds of histories, memoirs and tracts:
> For the poet there's rhyme, for the solid there's prose,
> And assistance for those who want help to compose;
> To pass the sad hours; there are novels in store,
> Fairy tales and romances, and fifty things more;
> COLLECTIONS of all the best SONGS that are sung;
> Devout books for the old, and love tales for the young . . .[21]

In this way, circulating libraries erased hierarchies between genres and genders. Moreover, since such libraries gave young men and women unmonitored access to a huge range of works, they not only provided opportunities for self-improvement but also served as places for flirtation and class mixing. This social freedom reflected the intellectual freedom from 'all controul' that was promised by the same library:

That all may enjoy the effect of this treasure,
And read, for a trifling expense, at their leisure,
Ten Shillings A Year gives command of the whole;
(You may read as you please, without any controul)
Or, if that seems too much and you chuse a time shorter,
The charge is Two Shillings and Sixpence a Quarter.

As these libraries grew in number and importance throughout the century, they became notorious as symbols of the early feminist revolution.
Their availability was blamed for the popularity of the transgressive novels
they featured, which contained stories of heroines falling in love, defying the
older generation, and following their feelings. 'The Circulating Library', a
print of 1804 (fig. 1), depicts a young woman selecting debased imitations
of Mackenzie's *The Man of Feeling* (1771), with other racy titles like *The
Unguarded Moment* (1771) and *Seduction* (1787), while rejecting austere-
sounding works like *The School of Virtue* (1787); all these novels actually
existed. And though the woman in question would have to read ceaselessly
and at breakneck speed to get through her selection in two days, indiscrim-
inate consumption as well as self-indulgence were among the delights these
libraries offered. Indeed, in the shadow and wake of the French Revolution,
and the accompanying domestic debate on gender hierarchies and roles, the
spread and popularity of circulating libraries ignited a reaction close to panic
about the intoxicating effects of novels on young women. 'Madam, a circulating library in a town is, as an evergreen tree, of diabolical knowledge!', as
Sir Anthony Absolute exclaims in Sheridan's *The Rivals* (1775). Even earlier,
David Garrick's epilogue to George Colman's *Polly Honeycombe* (1760)
parodies the sentimental heroine as really a headstrong adolescent, newly
justified by the female-flattering ideas in novels:

We Girls of Reading, and superior notions,
Who from the fountain-head drink love's sweet potions,
Pity our parents, when such passion blinds 'em,
One hears the good folks rave – One never minds 'em.[22]

As booksellers increased their production of novels, including sequels and
imitations, popular fiction propelled the erotic mode and female topics into
mainstream, middle-class literature.

Writers, readers, critics, booksellers, and publishers were all transformed
by the professionalization of the book trade in the period from 1740 to
1830. An entirely new way of conceiving of reading, writing, and bookselling
made literature the agent of culture in the English-speaking world. While the
period began by disseminating literature to a readership conjured as equal
members in a public sphere of cultural exchange, by the early nineteenth

Figure 1 *The Circulating Library*, satirical engraving published by the London printsellers Laurie and Whittle, 1804.

century literary culture had fractured, and two realms emerged: elite literature for the aspiring middle classes, and comforting novels for the general public. The remarkable burst of literary production throughout the period correspondingly made literary consumption central to national identity, and one of the prime sources for Britain's moral justification for imperial expansion and colonization. The professionalization of the book trade created not only professional booksellers and publishers, but also professional writers and critics. In the long eighteenth century, authorship was reinvented as anything from a pragmatic generation of copy for cash to a Romantic process of solitary conception; reading became a sign of middle-class self-improvement; and literature itself became a class commodity.

NOTES

1. Richard Steele, *The Tatler*, ed. Donald F. Bond, 3 vols. (Oxford: Clarendon Press, 1987), II: 331 (No. 147, 18 March 1710).
2. Jane Austen, *Pride and Prejudice*, ed. R. W. Chapman (Oxford: Oxford University Press, 1987), p. 87 (I.viii).

3. James Raven, 'The Book Trades', in Isabel Rivers (ed.), *Books and Their Readers in Eighteenth-Century England: New Essays* (London: Leicester University Press, 2001), pp. 1–34 (p. 2).
4. David Cressy, *Literacy and the Social Order: Reading and Writing in Tudor and Stuart England* (Cambridge: Cambridge University Press, 1980), p. 176; E. A. Wrigley and R. Schofield, *The Population History of England, 1541–1871: A Reconstruction* (London: Edward Arnold, 1981), pp. 208–9.
5. Patrick Curry, *Prophesy and Power: Astrology in Early Modern England* (Princeton: Princeton University Press, 1989), p. 101.
6. C. Y. Ferdinand, 'The Economics of the Eighteenth-Century Provincial Book Trade: The Case of Ward and Chandler', in Maureen Bell et al. (eds.), *Reconstructing the Book: Literary Texts in Transmission* (Aldershot: Ashgate, 2001), pp. 42–3, 53–4.
7. *Jane Austen's Letters to her Sister Cassandra and Others*, ed. R. W. Chapman, 2nd edn (Oxford: Oxford University Press, 1952), p. 133 (to Cassandra Austen, 21 May 1801).
8. Alexander Pope, *The Second Epistle of the Second Book of Horace, Imitated* (1737), lines 68–9.
9. Norma Clarke, *Dr Johnson's Women* (London: Hambledon and London, 2000), pp. 231–2; for Barber see Adam Budd, '"Merit in Distress": The Troubled Success of Mary Barber', *RES* 53 (2002), 204–27.
10. Jeremy Black, *The English Press in the Eighteenth Century* (Aldershot: Gregg Revivals, 1991), p. 14.
11. Undated letter from Thomas Marryat to Ralph Griffiths, quoted in Thomas Keymer (intr.), *The Gentleman's Magazine*, 16 vols. (London: Pickering and Chatto, 1998), I: xxxii.
12. Marilyn Butler, 'Culture's Medium: The Role of the Review', in Stuart Curran (ed.), *The Cambridge Companion to British Romanticism* (Cambridge: Cambridge University Press, 1993), p. 138.
13. *Gentleman's Magazine* 24 (February 1754), 57.
14. Judith Phillips Stanton, 'Profile of Women Writing in English from 1660 to 1800', in Frederick M. Keener and Susan E. Lorsch (eds.), *Eighteenth-Century Women and the Arts* (New York: Greenwood Press, 1988), p. 248.
15. *Boswell's Life of Johnson*, ed. George Birkbeck Hill, rev. L. F. Powell, 6 vols. (Oxford: Clarendon Press, 1934–64), I: 287–8 and n.
16. Thomas F. Bonnell, 'Bookselling and Canon-Making: The Trade Rivalry over the English Poets, 1776–1783', *Studies in Eighteenth-Century Culture* 19 (1989), 53–70.
17. John Keats, *Selected Letters*, ed. Robert Gittings, rev. and intr. Jon Mee (Oxford: Oxford University Press, 2002), p. 147 (to Richard Woodhouse, 27 October 1818).
18. See Peter Garside, James Raven, Rainer Schöwerling et al., *The English Novel 1770–1829: A Bibliographical Survey of Prose Fiction Published in the British Isles*, 2 vols. (Oxford: Oxford University Press, 2000), esp. II: 15–103.
19. Jane Austen, *Northanger Abbey*, ed. R. W. Chapman (Oxford: Oxford University Press, 1952), pp. 37–8 (I.v).
20. Daniel Defoe, *A Tour thro' the Whole Island of Great Britain*, 2nd edn, 4 vols. (1738), II: 241–2.

21. 1786 advertisement for 'Fowler's Circulating Library, in *Silver-Street*, Salisbury'; see also Barbara M. Benedict, 'Jane Austen and the Culture of the Circulating Library', in Paula Backscheider (ed.), *Revising Women: Eighteenth-Century 'Women's Fiction' and Social Engagement* (Baltimore: Johns Hopkins University Press, 2000), pp. 147–99.
22. *Sheridan's Plays*, ed. Cecil Price (London: Oxford University Press, 1975), p. 21 (*The Rivals*, 1.ii); George Colman, *Polly Honeycombe* (1760), p. 33 (Epilogue, lines 3–6).

FURTHER READING

Benedict, Barbara M., *Making the Modern Reader: Cultural Mediation in Early Modern Literary Anthologies*, Princeton: Princeton University Press, 1996.
'Publishing and Reading Poetry', in John Sitter (ed.), *The Cambridge Companion to Eighteenth-Century Poetry*, Cambridge: Cambridge University Press, 2001, pp. 63–82.
Brewer, John, *The Pleasures of the Imagination: English Culture in the Eighteenth Century*, London: HarperCollins, 1997.
DeMaria, Robert, Jr, *Samuel Johnson and the Life of Reading*, Baltimore: Johns Hopkins University Press, 1997.
Donoghue, Frank, *The Fame Machine: Book Reviewing and Eighteenth-Century Literary Careers*, Stanford: Stanford University Press, 1996.
Griffin, Dustin, *Literary Patronage in England, 1650–1800*, Cambridge: Cambridge University Press, 1996.
Hunter, J. Paul, *Before Novels: The Cultural Contexts of Eighteenth-Century English Fiction*, New York: Norton, 1990.
Johns, Adrian, *The Nature of the Book: Print and Knowledge in the Making*, Chicago: University of Chicago Press, 1998.
Kernan, Alvin, *Printing Technology, Letters, and Samuel Johnson*, Princeton: Princeton University Press, 1987.
Klancher, Jon P., *The Making of English Reading Audiences, 1790–1832*, Madison: University of Wisconsin Press, 1987.
Parker, Mark, *Literary Magazines and British Romanticism*, Cambridge: Cambridge University Press, 2001.
Price, Leah, *The Anthology and the Rise of the Novel: From Richardson to George Eliot*, Cambridge: Cambridge University Press, 2000.
Raven, James, *Judging New Wealth: Popular Publishing and Responses to Commerce in England, 1750–1800*, Oxford: Oxford University Press, 1992.
Rivers, Isabel (ed.), *Books and Their Readers in Eighteenth-Century England*, Leicester: Leicester University Press, 1982; *Books and Their Readers in Eighteenth-Century England: New Essays*, London: Leicester University Press, 2001.
Roper, Derek, *Reviewing before the 'Edinburgh', 1788–1802*, London: Methuen, 1978.
Rose, Mark, *Authors and Owners: The Invention of Copyright*, Cambridge, MA: Harvard University Press, 1993.

Shevelow, Kathryn, *Women and Print Culture: The Construction of Femininity in the Early Periodical*, London: Routledge, 1989.
Siskin, Clifford, *The Work of Writing: Literature and Social Change in Britain, 1700–1830*, Baltimore: Johns Hopkins University Press, 1998.
Terry, Richard, *Poetry and the Making of the English Literary Past, 1660–1781*, Oxford: Oxford University Press, 2001.

2

SIMON JARVIS

Criticism, taste, aesthetics

A serious thought standing single among many of a lighter nature, will sometimes strike the careless Wanderer after Amusement only, with useful Awe: As
monumental Marbles scattered in a wide Pleasure-Garden (and such there are)
will call to Recollection those who would never have sought it in a Churchyard-
walk of mournful Yews.[1]

When Edward Young compares his *Conjectures on Original Composition*
(1759) to a garden, he is also doing a number of other things. He is implying
that you will get pleasure, rather than only information about it, from his
writing. He is suggesting that you will want to wander, rather than march,
through his book. And he is reaffirming the flexibility of the kind of writing
he is undertaking. Its unity is not like that of the idea of a poem in one of
the neo-classical categories, given by prescribed manner or matter; nor is it
like that of a philosophical treatise, given by a deductive or inductive logic.
It is, instead, like that of a garden, a series of walks, prospects and emblems,
in which the designer hopes to make his caprice gratifying, and occasionally
instructive, to visitors.

What is *criticism*, in this period? Only at certain times and in certain
places has 'criticism', as it now does, primarily designated *literary* criticism.
Between 1740 and 1830 the term's meanings are complex, for a number
of reasons. Not only did *literature* only by the end of this period come to
refer chiefly to works of invention, rather than to a much wider range of the
products of the world of letters; but *criticism* bore a number of more specific
senses, all of which in various ways and to various extents interacted with and
informed the criticism of invented texts. At the start of our period *ars critica*
and 'critical' had long been used to indicate an emerging mode of textual
and historical enquiry in which evidence would be critically sifted rather
than copiously collected. Towards its middle the term took on a peculiar
meaning in a single philosophical authorship, the work of Immanuel Kant,
where it referred to Kant's own attempt to find a path for thinking which
would refuse the bad choice between dogmatic metaphysics and sceptical

relativism. Throughout the period it also retained its most straightforward sense: fault-finding, the detection of slips.

Criticism, then, is not a genre, nor even a name for a group of genres. It happens not only in essays, reviews, philosophical dialogues, lecture courses, treatises; but also in novels, epigrams, plays and theatrical prologues and epilogues, long poems, editions of texts, conversations, duels, gardens. This is why so much goes missing when the history of criticism in this period is written only as the history of changing opinion. At that level, many of the decisive critical exchanges take place not in any kind of text, but at the informal level of '"fair words" or smiles, handshakes or shrugs, compliments or attention, challenges or insults'.[2] Because criticism is an activity that can take place in almost any genre, written criticism is always giving out, alongside its judgements, a series of messages about the kind of writing to which it belongs, and the kind of authorial persona which goes along with this. For this reason it is hardly more adequate to treat the history of written criticism only as the history of its content than it would be to apply the same approach to poetry or the novel. This essay, therefore, will not be of the kind in which nothing is left out, but hopes to be one in which something is put in. In it, criticism is considered not as a subordinate or parasitic genre, interesting primarily for the light it can cast on 'literature proper', but as one of the central areas of achievement of the period's literary production. In this way, I hope to write the history of criticism in this period not as something dead and gone, but as something in which we are still caught.

Who is a critic?

Critical genres and critical personae in this period undergo a transformation. Yet the 'battle of the books' fought at the close of the seventeenth century continued powerfully to shape criticism. Sir William Temple had supported his claim that the most ancient writings were the best by appealing to the epistles of Phalaris. The classical philologist Richard Bentley, however, was able to show by minute attention to historically changing features of Greek that these texts could not possibly be amongst the most ancient examples of prose composition. Much more influential in the long run than the specific question at issue here were the antagonistic ideas of what criticism itself was. For the self-styled 'gentlemen of letters' who came to Temple's defence, Bentley was a 'professed pedant'.[3] The criticism was both epistemological and social. The pedant paid too much attention to minute details. This prevented him from seeing the whole as which a work could alone be properly appreciated. At the same time he 'professed' a special interest. His criticism was not the disinterested amusement of a gentleman but the career necessity of a low clown. This tension between the spheres of 'general' and 'minute' criticism, and between the personae of gentlemanly or witty critics and specialist or pedantic scholars, by no means disappears in our period (it still has not). It is still being worked through in Coleridge's awkward defence in 1817 of his coined word 'esemplastic': 'a well-conditioned mind would more easily, methinks, tolerate the *fox brush* of learned vanity, than the *sans culotterie* of a contemptuous ignorance, that assumes a merit from mutilation in the self-consoling sneer at the pompous incumbrance of tails.'[4]

But Coleridge's involved language here also indicates something of what has changed. The wits had cast the scholars as cultural poachers trespassing in the park of polite letters. Coleridge, by contrast, writes of the insistence that criticism should never involve specialized languages or knowledges as a resentful *sans culotterie*, a cultural levelling. To understand this gesture, we need to think about how the production, distribution and consumption of critical writing changes in our period. For much of the first half of it polite taste is importantly shaped by series of periodical essays. The personae of their titles are telling: *Rambler, Idler, Adventurer, Connoisseur*. These persons observe or move through a world in which they are not confined to any particular place. Conversely, and despite the factual restriction of their audience to quite a small social stratum, their appeal is not to any particular kind, type, profession or class of reader but to a Reader presumed free of such narrowing identifications. Around the turn of the century this situation begins to change. The critical journals are now no longer essays but reviews: the *Analytical*, the *Edinburgh*, the *Quarterly*, *Blackwood's*. Each will have a number of articles in which new writing is reviewed and often summarized in some detail. They thus serve as digests of intellectual production; but they are also at the same time carefully shaping distinct imagined readerships composed of quite particular social, political and cultural interest groups.

If we return to the argument over Phalaris, we can see that the particular conditions for its historical importance have disappeared. The wits responded allergically to Bentley because they still thought of classical learning not as a matter for specialists but as a central part of their territory. Bentley and the wits were competing for the same patch. But literary and intellectual production have grown and ramified over the period; new divisions among readerships have appeared, while old ones have intensified and become more open. The normative ideal of a world of letters has migrated into a number of spheres of interest, so that Coleridge can now experience the refusal of specialized language not as the defence of a world of polite letters, but as a curtailment of the just privilege of literary reflection. Meanwhile, conversely, a work like Isaac D'Israeli's *Curiosities of Literature* (1791–1834) was capable of making the realm of minute scholarship into a literary entertainment. D'Israeli's readers would not always be interested in just those particulars detailed by him, but would relish them vicariously, as *examples* of the romance of minute scholarship. What the *Spectator* could only treat parodically (as where it overwhelms a slight love lyric with an apparatus of manuscript variants in no. 470 of 29 August 1712) had become another pleasure of the imagination. Still more significantly, vernacular literary history can now become the object of a serious comprehensive scholarship of the kind exemplified in Thomas Warton's *History of English Poetry* (1774–81), or of nascent source criticism such as Charlotte Lennox's *Shakespear Illustrated* (1753); while Edward Capell could in 1760 publish an edition of various early modern English texts with the declared purpose, not of disseminating the works, but of illustrating editorial method.

'Minute' criticism thus develops an increasing autonomy from 'general' criticism. This can be seen by comparing Johnson's edition of Shakespeare (1765) with that of Edmond Malone (1790). Johnson is already much more reluctant than Pope had been to emend Shakespeare's text on aesthetic grounds alone. Nevertheless, he in practice still often treats the first Folio and the early Quartos as *ad hoc* sources of preferable variants. For Malone, by contrast, bibliographical assessment of the copies must take place before any such use is considered. Even Malone is not utterly consistent in this respect, but his edition as a whole testifies to the deepening separation between what would come to be called 'textual' and 'literary' criticism: a separation no longer thought to be an unmixed gain.

In practice, however, few critics understood their activity as purely general or purely minute. One of the most influential syntheses of the two kinds is provided by the career of Samuel Johnson, many of whose *Ramblers* are explicitly concerned with this question. Johnson is quite unembarrassed about writing criticism for money. Yet it is also essential to his critical authority that, while his writing can be bought, his good opinion cannot. To this persona of the incorruptible professional corresponds a career at once literary-critical and scholarly. The great *Dictionary* (1755) is at the centre of its paradoxes. Johnson thought that an important difference between English and French learning was that French critics relied on the power of their own minds alone, while English critics depended on each other, and thus produced more solid, if less glittering, results. Yet his *Dictionary* was celebrated precisely for performing solo what in France had been the work of forty. (In fact, of course, Johnson did have help.) Johnson felt perhaps more keenly than any other critic of his century the delicacy of the linked negotiations between solitariness and sociability, between minuteness and comprehensiveness, in criticism. The *Rambler* papers on Milton's versification show well how this sense helped him to become its most impressive critic. Johnson's acute awareness that excessive minuteness may disgust his public prompts him to apply a sharp razor to needless proliferations of classificatory terminology. Yet his equal and opposite determination not to fudge the details produces the deepest analysis of Milton's verse style to that date.

Within the sphere of general criticism itself, moreover, a polarity, less between wit and pedant than between man of the world and scholar or philosopher, is of fundamental importance. Even before 1740, there is already an important difference of emphasis between critical essays of the kind appearing in the *Spectator*, which tend to begin from 'pleasures of the imagination' and to work towards any larger principles from these, and the work of a figure like John Dennis, for whom the 'Grounds of Criticism' could lead to a series of specific prescriptive rules for writing. The difference is both one of persona, the difference between a spectator and a judge; and one of genre, between the essay and the treatise. That the *Spectator* itself aspires to bridge this gap, while Dennis lectures across it, is one reason for the former's superior influence in the period. Throughout it, critics keep trying to steer a path between polar risks: to avoid both aridity and vapidity, pedantry and smattering, venality and vanity; or, to possess both learning and wit, soundness and spirit, method and genius. As the antithetical rhetoric suggests, these oppositions are given their sharpest form before the beginning of our period. Yet they do not disappear in its course (nor have they since done so). Rather, they migrate into a number of more firmly differentiated circles, genres, and audiences.

As examples of the impure, rather than absolute, nature of some of these polarities, we may take Oliver Goldsmith's *Enquiry into the Present State of Polite Learning in Europe* (1759) and Hugh Blair's *Lectures on Rhetoric and Belles Lettres* (1783). Despite coming forward as a critic, Goldsmith at once declares it his aim 'to attempt the rescuing of genius from the shackles of pedantry and criticism'. Yet satire cannot accomplish this job alone. Goldsmith needs to show how those shackles were put on; and it turns out in the showing that they were closely connected to a more general emancipation, the defeat of superstition by philosophy. Before philosophy, 'learning was another name for magic'. Yet to this necessary correction succeeded a mob of 'critics, sophists, grammarians, rhetoricians, and commentators' who disastrously emended the works in their care and converted criticism into a business of 'dry rules'.[5] Goldsmith's wish to expel pedants finds itself obliged to show, then, that their rise is not plain benightedness but a consequence of more light. Blair's title already indicates the pedagogic origin of his work, and its content confirms its much more thoroughgoing procedure: his critical views on style and form are grounded in an account of 'The Rise and Progress of Language' that is steeped in the thought of the European enlightenment. Yet a century of attacks on rationalism and pedantry also leave their marks: 'Critics who judge by rule, not feeling . . . are pedants, not Critics.' Blair's lectures must insist on a philosophically grounded discrimination of terms in the lexicon of taste, and protest that 'Taste, Criticism, and Genius, are words currently employed, without distinct ideas annexed to them'; but this method must not usurp to the lecturer an authority that can belong only to the community of judges. 'That which men concur the most in admiring, must be held to be beautiful.'[6] In this respect Blair's lapidary style sends important reassurances to his audience.

Some of the same antagonisms, but in transformed shape, are still being negotiated in Samuel Taylor Coleridge's *Biographia Literaria* (1817). In terms of its genre, Coleridge's work is perhaps the strangest book of literary criticism ever written. Declared a literary (auto)biography by its title, it quickly turns into an attempt to provide a transcendental deduction of the imagination, an attempt broken off by a fictitious 'letter from a friend' advising against the deduction, and then moves forward to a close literary and cultural-political criticism of particular poems and passages of verse. The book's damaged shape probably cannot be attributed either to mere incapacity or to hermeneutic cunning. Instead, the book thus makes visible as an open wound the fact that no genre of criticism is any longer singly adequate. It recruits aspects of each of them. Hazlitt, however, had himself found a generic solution which (together with his aversion to Coleridge's politics) leads him to think of the *Biographia* as a failure. Reviewing the book in the *Edinburgh* for August 1817, Hazlitt argues that Coleridge's attempt to provide a metaphysically grounded theory of poetry has led to disastrous category-mistakes. It produces bad philosophy and bad criticism alike. Coleridge, who could have been a great poet, has become instead a bad philosopher. Hazlitt, by contrast, has committed himself firmly to the essay, which in his hands has also developed in a surprising way. By no means lacking in intellectual, even in philosophical, ambition, it makes no foundational or deductive claims. Its larger theoretical claims proceed instead by a kind of crescendo of speculative assertion. Poetry

> is not a branch of authorship: it is "the stuff of which our life is made". The rest is "mere oblivion", a dead letter: for all that is worth remembering in life, is the poetry of it. Fear is poetry, hope is poetry, love is poetry, hatred is poetry; contempt, jealousy, remorse, admiration, wonder, pity, despair, or madness, are all poetry.[7]

The form itself tends to excuse these assertions from detailed demonstration. Yet for Hazlitt this insusceptibility to demonstration is not an alibi but a consequence of the very nature of the arts criticized, which are of incomparable importance for human life, yet are not answerable to philosophical or political accounting. So the republican Hazlitt can regard poetry as 'right-royal'.[8] Hazlitt's essays do not usually exemplify general ideas by particular observations. They offer, instead, agile leaps from large assertion to local detail and back again. Both these critics have found different ways of solving, or openly failing to solve, the problem of the tension between principle and quiddity.

Taste or aesthetics?

These contests over how criticism should be written and what kind of person a critic should be have in their turn profound consequences for the substantive views of critics on matters of taste and aesthetics. The opposition between general and minute criticism connects with a thematic opposition between general and minute representations. Once again, the polarity can be socially, as well as epistemologically and aesthetically, loaded. For Sir Joshua Reynolds, 'The detail of particulars . . . presupposes *nicety* and *research*, which are only the business of the curious and attentive, and therefore does not speak to the general sense of the whole species; in which common, and, as I may so call it, mother tongue, everything grand and comprehensive must be uttered'. Excessive detail thus smacks of the pedant, but also of a social and historical particularity obnoxious to pleasure: 'the whole beauty of the art consists, in my opinion, in being able to get above all singular forms, local customs, particularities, and details of every kind.'[9] William Blake, on the other hand, responded to that thought thus in his copy of Reynolds's *Discourses*: 'A Folly! Singular & Particular Detail is the Foundation of the Sublime.'[10]

These contests need to be considered not merely as epiphenomena of supposedly more fundamental social and economic arrangements, but also as a series of cognitive responses to the real problem of how to understand the relation between two kinds of knowledge: on one hand, 'philosophical' knowledge, in the broadest sense of that term, covering not only theories of mind but also 'natural philosophy' and 'philosophical history'; on the other, something which Western philosophy has less readily thought of as a form of knowledge, but which, precisely, many of the most significant critics of this period come to defend as such – the practical, traditionary and experiential knowledge that is deployed in literary works. De Quincey's celebrated distinction between the literature of knowledge and the literature of power ('All that is literature seeks to communicate power; all that is not literature, to communicate knowledge'[11]) can thus be misleading when read retrospectively into earlier critical thought. In its way it prepares for Arnold's later judgement that 'the Romantic poets did not know enough'.[12] Certainly, Hazlitt thinks of the attempt to understand poetry as a form of knowledge as a disastrous category mistake. Poetry is, instead, a seductive deployment of superstition which is of incomparable importance to human life, yet which becomes toxic if deployed outside its proper sphere: no philosophical or political consequences may be drawn from it. For most important critics of the period, however – many of whom were also practitioners in other genres – the opposition to be negotiated was not primarily between knowledge and power, but between two different kinds of knowledge. For Wordsworth, in his preface to *Lyrical Ballads*, the knowledge of the 'Man of Science' and of 'the Poet' is qualitatively, but not absolutely, distinct. This means that a science of poetry is no more impossible in principle than it is that science may one day be a proper subject for poetry. Yet that day is not today, and so Wordsworth no more provides the former than he practises the latter. The kind of truth which is attributed to poetry – 'truth, not individual and local, but general, and operative; not standing upon external testimony, but carried alive into the heart by passion; truth which is its own testimony, which gives strength and divinity to the tribunal to which it appeals, and receives them from the same tribunal'[13] – is clearly non-propositional. Were criticism clearly to grant propositional truth priority over this other, more ambiguous kind, we should have a science of poetry. We might also, Wordsworth suspects, destroy the object that we claim to study.

The idea that poetry might be a form of knowledge by no means originates in our period. Gianvincenzo Gravina's *Della Ragion Poetica* (1708), borrowed from by Thomas Blackwell in his work on Homer, and cited with approval by such influential critics as Joseph Warton and Thomas Twining, had already developed a powerful account of poetry's decline from curriculum of civic and natural wisdom to a frivolous entertainment. But disagreement over the idea of poetry as knowledge was newly sharpened by arguments over the history of civilization in general and language in particular. This could be written so as to trace either an ascent from primitive simplicity and irrationality to abstract conceptuality or a descent from poetry to prose. Thomas Love Peacock's satirical essay 'The Four Ages of Poetry' (1820) combines elements of both kinds of account. For Peacock, science cannot flourish unless poetry surrender its improper claim to knowledge: 'Thus the empire of thought is withdrawn from poetry, as the empire of facts had been before.' Any attempt to reconquer these empires – such as Peacock spies in some contemporary poetry – will result not in a new age of gold, but only in brass, 'the second childhood of poetry'.[14] Percy Bysshe Shelley's answer to Peacock, *A Defence of Poetry* (written in 1821 but unpublished until 1840), also remains recognizably within a framework given by enlightenment historiography. Instead of suggesting, in Gravina's manner, that poetry should repossess a lost patrimony, Shelley suggests that it has never really lost it. Science – again including political and historical, as well as natural, knowledge – has never in fact managed to separate itself from poetry, mere fiction: 'The poetry in these systems of thought, is concealed by the accumulation of facts and calculating processes.'[15] Yet since even political economy consists of concepts that were once metaphors, the poetry is still there. Nothing can be more mistaken than to oppose a work like Shelley's *Defence* to an 'enlightenment' whose consequences it is, rather, developing and ramifying. If poets are the unacknowledged legislators of the world, this is only because legislators are its unacknowledged poets.

This is the problem for which 'aesthetics' offers one name. Of the three terms in my title, this is the one that would most have puzzled most of the writers named in the essay itself. Although the term is now ubiquitous as an instrument for interpreting the writing of this period (often followed in quick succession by 'ideology'), it was not used in English in anything like its current sense until the early nineteenth century. Originally signifying the science of sensuous perception in general, the term first took on its current sense in eighteenth-century Germany. Early aestheticians took themselves for, as it were, scientists of the beautiful. Judgements about the beauty of given objects could be deduced from general principles. This deductive tradition thus stood in strong contrast to the primarily inductive thinking assembled in Britain around 'taste'. When Kant writes, in his *Critique of the Power of Judgement*, of the 'pure aesthetic judgement of taste', he is thus attempting to think two very different traditions together. For Kant, there is no 'science of the beautiful'. Yet nor are such judgements merely subjective. They are 'subjectively universal'.[16] That is, we cannot prove them to anyone – and yet, conscious that we make them without any self-interest, we will try.

'Aesthetics' is for this reason a difficult term to apply strictly to British reflection on art and beauty in this period. 'Taste', a ubiquitous term, is only much more ambiguously susceptible to philosophical discipline. The word 'taste' at once suggests the possibility that there might not be any accounting for it. David Hume's essay 'Of the Standard of Taste' (1757), despite its opposition to absolute relativism in matters of taste, nevertheless lays bare many of the difficulties in arriving at such a standard. Hume faces the consequences of advanced epistemology. It is 'certain, that beauty and deformity, more than sweet and bitter, are not qualities in objects, but belong entirely to sentiment'. Yet Homer is still admired in both Paris and London, so that there must be some 'general principles of approbation and blame'. Nevertheless, few are qualified to give judgement, because palates are only variably sensitive, and differentially educated. Who shall judge the judges? 'These questions are embarrassing; and seem to throw us back into the same uncertainty, from which, during the course of this Essay, we have endeavoured to extricate ourselves.'[17] The questions are so embarrassing that no *epistemological* answer can in the end be given to them. Those who are universally agreed to judge well – by good and bad judges alike – must be allowed to determine the standard.

Yet if British writing on taste generally preferred to treat the beautiful inductively, the more general problem of how and whether the traditional domains of philosophical argument, logic, epistemology, and metaphysics may be applied to art and beauty is none the less central to it. A good deal of Locke's innovative epistemology had, with startling rapidity, already become common sense. This is one important impulse behind one of the most striking developments in taste and criticism: the declining prestige of rhetoric. A work such as George Campbell's *Philosophy of Rhetoric* (1776) already indicates the new terms on which rhetoric must develop: it can no longer be an abstract of traditional wisdom but must in its turn have a 'philosophy' grounding it. The course of one of our period's most important concepts in taste, that of the 'sublime', indicates this development. The opposition between the sublime and the beautiful is for most of the later part of the period taken for granted, but the *locus classicus* for the concept of the sublime, Longinus's treatise *Peri Hypsous* ('Of Loftiness'), does not require this opposition. Loftiness in style is one kind of beauty. The opposition between the sublime and the beautiful becomes as important as it does partly because a primarily rhetorical account is replaced by one which is, while not uninterested in rhetoric, conspicuously grounded in an account of the workings of the mind and emotions. In the most influential formulation of this opposition, Edmund Burke's *Philosophical Enquiry into the Origin of our Ideas of the Sublime and Beautiful* (1757), ideas of the sublime and the beautiful originate respectively in two fundamentally distinct orders of passions, those 'belonging to the preservation of the individual' which 'turn wholly on pain and danger', and 'those which belong to *generation*' and 'have their origin in gratifications and pleasures'. Of course, these passions only give rise to pleasures of taste when mediated in some way. A storm merely terrifies us if we think ourselves in danger; once safely inside we may experience 'a sort of delightful horror'.[18] But the distinction between the sublime and the beautiful is no longer primarily rhetorical. Instead it runs all the way down to a division supposed fundamental in a philosophical theory of human nature.

This holds true also for literary production. Central here is the transformed application of concepts such as 'genius' and 'originality'. For Alexander Gerard, genius is 'the power of invention, either in science or in the arts, either of truth or of beauty'.[19] Genius is not a simply aesthetic concept, then, but one that refers to intellectual labour in general. It is defined by its production of the new. It was possible to think of this production of the new, as William Duff did, as the infusion of life into what would otherwise be dead: 'Smooth versification and harmonious numbers will no more make genuine Poetry, than the atoms of a skeleton put together can make an animated and living figure. To produce either, a certain vital spirit must be infused; and in Poetry, this vital spirit is INVENTION.'[20] An influential treatment of this question was Young's, which mapped the distinction between originality and imitation on to that between the organic and the mechanical: 'An *Original* may be said to be of a *vegetable* nature; it rises spontaneously from the vital root of Genius; it *grows*, it is not *made*; *Imitations* are often a sort of *Manufacture* wrought up by those *Mechanics*, *Art*, and *Labour*, out of pre-existent materials not their own.'[21] The developing critical emphasis upon originality is clearly part of a wider context in which whatever is valuable is understood to have that value not as an inherent property but as conferred on it by human labour, whether physical or intellectual (what Marx saw as a 'labour theory of value' given expression in Adam Smith's political economy).[22] One particularly important context here was the struggle over literary copyright. Because, following Locke, property was understood as conferred by labour, the emerging idea of *intellectual* property demanded a notion of radically creative intellectual labour.

The disposition of genres

It would be mistaken, then, to understand philosophy of mind as the only or even as the primary agent of change in literary thinking. An important test case is provided by theory of genre. A contrast with Germany is useful here. There 'system' and 'fragment' were the key critical genres; in Britain, essay and review. System and fragment as differently practised by F. W. J. Schelling and Friedrich Schlegel allow both for all literary-historical concepts to be brought to the bar of philosophical reflection, and for philosophy to reflect upon its own literary form. There are few British equivalents to the directness with which Schlegel can write that 'All the classical poetical genres have now become ridiculous in their rigid purity'.[23] Nor does British criticism cease to use those categories. Yet their scope and authority are much altered by the close of our period. At least as important here as any psychologization of critical concepts is the broadening historical and geographical scope of comparative philology. Robert Lowth's course of *Lectures on the Sacred Poetry of the Hebrews* (translated in 1787 from the Latin original of 1753) is a crucial instance. Lowth's text owes part of its influence to the fact that its vigorous defence of the literary value of the Bible draws on the generic and rhetorical framework of classical literary criticism. Yet at the same time Lowth's own analysis indicates how approximate a guide to his material that framework offers. To later writers and critics his work suggested that the Bible offered models (of poetic prophecy, for example) unclassifiable in neo-classical terms. Blake's hostility to neo-classical genre theory is not primarily powered by philosophical scrutiny, but rather restates in his singular idiom a longstanding Christian suspicion of pagan letters, whose emblem is St Jerome's nightmare of his own condemnation by God himself: 'You are lying. You are not a Christian, but a Ciceronian.'[24] Much of this period's increasing distance from classical literary theory, indeed, takes place through a partial dissolution of the always unstable synthesis of Christianity and classical rhetoric represented by neo-classical criticism: a dissolution visible also in Wordsworth's preference for Hebrew prophecy over the 'anthropomorphitism' of classical literature.[25]

A case of particular importance is provided by critical responses to the transformation of the novel in this period. Despite the limited usefulness of classical genre categories for thinking about novels, they continued to shape much critical writing about fiction. Fielding's description of *Joseph Andrews* as 'a comic Epic-Poem in Prose'[26] is repeatedly quoted; as late as 1810 Anna Laetitia Barbauld can claim in her 'Origin and Progress of Novel-Writing' that 'a good novel is an epic in prose, with more of character and less (indeed in modern novels nothing) of the supernatural machinery'.[27] Richardson's postscript to *Clarissa*, meanwhile, describes the book as a 'history' or 'dramatic narrative', going on to deploy Aristotle's theory of tragedy, and rebukes those who might have thought it 'a mere *novel* or *romance*'.[28] These claims are more urgently concerned with securing for the novel the prestige which in this period attaches to the epic and to tragic drama than they are with detailed genre-theory. Barbauld's own later analysis, indeed, indicates the primarily evaluative rather than descriptive nature of her claim: having classified Fénelon's *Télémaque* as a '*Didactic Romance*', she goes on to qualify this by suggesting that it may, instead, be an 'Epic in prose' (p. 21). By this point in the analysis, the phrase 'epic in prose' has become a way, not of describing any good novel, but of describing an especially morally serious instance of that genre.

One important work to address the novel's relation to other genres in some depth is Clara Reeve's series of 'Evening Conversations', *The Progress of Romance* (1785). James Beattie's dissertation 'On Fable and Romance' (1783) had classified prose fiction into historical or moral allegory on one hand, and serious or comic poetical fable on the other, comprehending both the latter under the title of 'romance'. Within this category Beattie distinguished between 'old' and 'new' romance, subclasses whose watershed was marked for him, as for Barbauld, by Cervantes' elaborate games with the genre in *Don Quixote* (1605–15). To comprehend all fictional genres under the head of 'fable' was already a choice determined by the attempt to continue to fit new data into a neo-classical generic schema. It is the aim of Reeve's representative Euphrasia, by contrast, to detach the modern novel from the prose romance with which it has too often been confounded, and to affirm instead (to the shock of her male counterpart, Hortensius) that epic and romance are one and the same. Instead of attempting simply to secure the prestige of epic additionally for the novel, Euphrasia attempts a reorientation of the genre hierarchy, pointing out that while the improbabilities of romances are continually ridiculed, those of classical epic are more often hushed up: 'can you forbear smiling at the extravagant sallies of [Homer's] imagination, can you approve his violent machinery, in which he degrades his deities below his heroes, and makes deities of men.'[29] Here there is an important link between Reeve's recasting of the history of fiction and the new literary history which was replacing vernacular epic in the context of native ('Gothic') romance: Euphrasia's claim that Spenser and Milton owe part of their immortality to 'Gothick imagery' is closely related to Richard Hurd's insistence on the poetical value of popular superstition in his *Letters on Chivalry and Romance* (1762).

Questions of generic prestige are inevitably connected with two central (and linked) preoccupations of novel criticism: the question of probability, and the question of moral tendency. The novel's perceived assets in addressing the former made the latter more urgent. For Johnson in the *Rambler*, the modern romance or 'familiar history' was a form in which 'the power of example is so great, as to take possession of the memory by a kind of violence, and produce effects almost without the intervention of the will', just as for Aaron Hill what made *Pamela* exemplary of the sublime was Richardson's provision of 'a delightfully-adhering Idea, that clings fast to the Memory; and from which it is difficult for a Man to disengage his Attention'.[30] Later the pathological implications of this trope would be expanded through metaphors of sickness and addiction. The tension between the requirements of probability and decency led Johnson to insist in his *Rambler* paper that 'many characters ought never to be drawn'. A rather different solution emerges in Barbauld's essay. She thinks it 'sufficient therefore, as an end, that these writings add to the innocent pleasures of life; and if they do no harm, the entertainment they give is a sufficient good'. Yet this defence is also grounded in a confidence that the novel provides a means of moral education both quantitively and qualitatively more powerful than bare precept. Barbauld can thus close her essay with a thought stolen from (but more pointedly phrased than in) Blair's *Lectures*: 'It was said by Fletcher of Saltoun, "Let me make the ballads of a nation, and I care not who makes the laws." Might it not be said with as much propriety, Let me make the novels of a country, and let who will make the systems?'[31] Even where a defence of the novel appears to rest primarily on 'entertainment', then, it at the same time articulates a more powerful claim, that the novel is an autonomous form of knowledge with powers and resources unavailable to formal or explicit cognition. In the long run this aspect of the defence of fiction was to be more significant than the attempt to accommodate neo-classical genre theory.

One non-philosophical resource for rethinking literature as a non-philosophical form of knowledge was provided by the comparisons with other arts – especially with painting, but also with sculpture, architecture, music, dance, gardening and others – which this period's criticism developed in an unprecedentedly thoroughgoing way. To read through the whole of Joseph Warton's influential *Essay on the Genius and Writings of Pope* (1756–82) is to be struck by the all-pervasiveness of reading cast in painterly terms. One passage of Pope's 'Eloisa' provokes these instructions to an imaginary painter:

> He might place Eloisa in the long ile of a great Gothic church; a lamp should hang over her head, whose dim and dismal ray should afford only enough light to make darkness visible. She herself should be represented in the *instant*, when she first hears this aerial voice, and in the attitude of *starting round* with astonishment and fear. And this was the method a very great master took, to *paint a sound*, if I may be allowed the expression.[32]

Warton's reading implies that in a full response to literary texts the reader will supply details, attitudes, and contexts that may not be literally present in the text itself. Because painting is widely understood in this period to be a more fully mimetic medium than literature, painterly idioms offer a natural way of talking about what writing cannot exhaustively state and what the reader must bring. Equally characteristic, however, is the way in which this imaginary painting, imagined in order to help us read a poem, is itself evoked through a literary allusion, to the 'darkness visible' of Milton's Hell. There is a sleight of register here by which Warton is able to express an aspect of his response to the poem which he cannot demonstrate to be required by the text. Although the appeal to painting points to a fullness of mimesis which poetry lacks, the recourse to Milton redresses a balance by reminding us that our response to painting is in its turn shaped by our literary competence. An explicit argument that texts may leave room for such responses in a way that paintings do not is part of Burke's theory of the sublime: an 'amazingly sublime' passage in the book of Job is so just because it is, 'wrapt up in the shades of its own incomprehensible darkness, more aweful, more striking, more terrible, than the liveliest description, than the clearest painting could possibly represent it'.[33] This indicates why some later critics made less pervasive use of the analogy between writing and painting: not because mimesis ceased to be of importance (there is no critic in our period of whom this could be said) but because not all subjects appeared susceptible to painterly mimesis. When Wordsworth describes himself as having attempted to look steadily at his subject, that subject is often his own mind and its states, and that is one reason why critical responses to his work which continue to be organized in painterly terms – objections to his 'Dutch minuteness', for example – can seem to miss their target. For a critic such as Hazlitt, on the other hand, comparison with painting remained an essential resource, but one now cast less in terms of set-piece parallelisms than as a comparison of painterly idioms with poetical.

Equally important here is a qualitative shift in thinking about the history of literature. Johnson hailed Thomas Warton's work on Spenser as having shown the way forward for criticism: to read the works your author read. In the case of Spenser, this meant downgrading the reflex sense for Greek and Roman parallels, and admitting what Pope had thought of as 'all such reading as was never read' ('barbarous' romances and allegories, for example)[34] to a central place not merely in elucidating individual passages, but in illuminating broader questions of literary form and purpose. This accompanied a more strongly contested debate about literary taste. The increasingly settled centrality of Chaucer, Spenser, Milton, and Shakespeare as monuments of vernacular letters came to be turned in part by some critics against the perceived absence of some of their qualities from the poetry of Pope. Warton's *Essay* is central here. It does not attempt to deny Pope's greatness, only that he belongs among our sublime and pathetic poets: Spenser, Shakespeare, and Milton. Warton, though often (precisely) fulsome in his praise of Pope, stands at the head of one current in subsequent literary taste deploring excessive preoccupation with correctness and valuing sublimity and pathos more highly. Yet in the event many of Warton's criticisms of Pope are made from a perspective powerfully shaped by Pope himself: one of attention to propriety in sense, diction and decorum. One fact not always remembered about taste in this period is that the attention to prose sense which is so sharp in Pope and Johnson, and so underdeveloped in much of our own reading, remains an important part of most critics' equipment throughout. It is for this reason that the minutely hostile responses of critics such as Francis Jeffrey or John Wilson Croker to the poetry of Wordsworth or Keats so often give a much closer idea of what the poetry is actually like, and where the interesting problems in it lie, than does later more general adulation.

'A war embrace'

It is sometimes thought that it is easier to read an earlier period's criticism than its novels, its dramas or its poems; that a less radical leap of historical imagination is required. Because this period's criticism exists within a kind of force field of unreconciled model critical personae – wit and scholar, amateur and professional, philosopher and rhetorician, judge and practitioner, amongst many others – it can look steadily at complex subjects whose aspects our own era often splits up and distributes amongst the departments of a divided intellectual labour. What Coleridge says of Shakespeare's poems, that in them 'the creative power, and the intellectual energy wrestle as in a war embrace',[35] is emphatically true both of his own criticism and of the sources of strength of criticism in the whole of this period. It is possible, then, to overdraw the contrast between an earlier ideal of a world of letters and a later more sectarian collection of audiences. For Jon P. Klancher, this development is in the end a kind of fate, and any who persist in addressing a single public (as, in various ways, most of the period's major writers did) are attempting illusory cultural solutions to problems that are more fundamentally social and historical. Yet, as he concedes, the world of letters was always a hope rather than a fact. In the end, the history relevant to the tension between the idea of a single, and the fact of multiple, readerships goes back not merely a century but two millennia and a half. Even today just this problem persists for critics and for other writers too. Its survival is not merely an epiphenomenon of a particular economy of production, exchange and consumption, but closely connected to the long and continuing withdrawal of cognition from poetry whose inauguration was formulated by Plato.

Young's *Conjectures* walk us through a number of prospects of literary taste, closing, it seems, with a eulogy of Addison's writing. But before the reader is quite sensible of the fact, Young has turned to an encomium upon Addison's life; or, rather, upon his manner of holy dying: 'His compositions are but a preface; the grand work is his death: That is a work which is read in heaven.' The terms in which Young here describes his surprising turn remind us that he has throughout been concerned not only with literary, but with personal, originality: 'Born *Originals*, how comes it to pass that we die *Copies*?' It is only some pages later that Young, in a kind of echo of the first surprise, returns us to the analogy developed at the opening of his piece. 'For this is the *monumental marble* there mentioned, to which I promised to conduct you; this is the *sepulchral lamp*, the long-hidden lustre of our accomplished country-man, who now rises, as from his tomb, to receive the regard so greatly due to the dignity of his death.'[36] For Young, criticism must not merely be about, but must also bring about, experiences that we now, in so far as we have them, call 'aesthetic', but which this period tended to understand as a kind of shudder at once bodily and cognitive. So he both takes us around a garden and also brings us to a scene of 'useful Awe' or Christian *anagnorisis*. His 'marble' well memorializes a power in the criticism, taste, and aesthetics of this period of which we have still to become fully conscious.

NOTES

1. Edward Young, *Conjectures on Original Composition* (1759), p. 2.
2. Pierre Bourdieu, *Outline of a Theory of Practice*, trans. Richard Nice (Cambridge: Cambridge University Press, 1977), p. 177.
3. [Francis Atterbury], *A Short Review of the Controversy between Mr Boyle and Dr Bentley* (1701), p. 20.
4. Samuel Taylor Coleridge, *Biographia Literaria*, ed. Nigel Leask (London: Everyman, 1997), p. 98.
5. Oliver Goldsmith, *An Enquiry into the Present State of Polite Learning in Europe* (1759), pp. 4, 17, 20, 22.
6. Hugh Blair, *Lectures on Rhetoric and Belles Lettres*, 2 vols. (1783), I: 38; I: 36; I: 30.
7. William Hazlitt, 'Lectures on the English Poets. Lecture 1: Introductory – On Poetry in General', in Duncan Wu (ed.), *The Selected Writings of William Hazlitt*, 9 vols. (London: Pickering and Chatto, 1998), II: 165–80 (p. 165).
8. Hazlitt, 'Characters of Shakespeare's Plays – Coriolanus', in *Selected Writings*, I: 125–31 (p. 126).
9. Sir Joshua Reynolds, *Discourses on Art*, ed. Robert R. Wark (New Haven: Yale University Press, 1997), pp. 192, 45.
10. William Blake, *Complete Poetry and Prose*, ed. David V. Erdman (Berkeley: University of California Press, 1982), p. 647.
11. Thomas De Quincey, *Collected Writings*, ed. David Masson, 14 vols. (Edinburgh, 1890), X: 48.
12. Matthew Arnold, *Lectures and Essays in Criticism*, ed. R. H. Super (Ann Arbor: University of Michigan Press, 1962), p. 262.
13. William Wordsworth, *Lyrical Ballads and Other Poems, 1797–1800*, ed. James Butler and Karen Green (Ithaca: Cornell University Press, 1992), pp. 751–2.
14. Thomas Love Peacock, 'The Four Ages of Poetry', in David Bromwich (ed.), *Romantic Critical Essays* (Cambridge: Cambridge University Press, 1987), pp. 199–211 (p. 204).
15. Percy Bysshe Shelley, *Poetry and Prose*, ed. Donald Reiman and Sharon B. Powers (New York: Norton, 1977), p. 502.
16. Immanuel Kant, *Critique of the Power of Judgment*, ed. Paul Guyer, trans. Paul Guyer and Eric Matthews (Cambridge: Cambridge University Press, 2000), pp. 184, 100.
17. David Hume, *Essays Moral, Political, and Literary*, ed. Eugene F. Miller (Indianapolis: Liberty Fund, 1985), pp. 235, 233, 241.

18. Edmund Burke, *A Philosophical Enquiry into the Origin of our Ideas of the Sublime and Beautiful*, ed. Adam Phillips (Oxford: Oxford University Press, 1990), pp. 37, 123.

19. Alexander Gerard, *An Essay on Genius* (1774), p. 318.

20. William Duff, *An Essay on Original Genius* (1767), p. 125.

21. Young, *Conjectures*, p. 12.

22. Karl Marx, *Theories of Surplus Value*, trans. Emile Burns, 3 vols. (London: Lawrence and Wishart, 1969), I: 69–151.

23. Friedrich Schlegel, 'Critical Fragments', in *Philosophical Fragments*, trans. Peter Firchow (Minneapolis: University of Minnesota Press, 1991), no. 60.

24. Jerome, *Select Letters*, ed. and trans. F. A. Wright (Cambridge, Mass.: Harvard University Press, 1933), pp. 126–7.

25. William Wordsworth, 'Preface to *Poems, 1815*', in *Shorter Poems, 1807–1820*, ed. Carl H. Ketcham (Ithaca: Cornell University Press, 1989), p. 638.

26. Henry Fielding, *Joseph Andrews and Shamela*, ed. Douglas Brooks-Davies, rev. and intr. Thomas Keymer (Oxford: Oxford University Press, 1999), p. 3.

27. Anna Laetitia Barbauld, 'On the Origin and Progress of Novel-Writing', in *The British Novelists*, 50 vols. (1810; new edition, 1820), I: 3.

28. Samuel Richardson, *Clarissa*, ed. Angus Ross (Harmondsworth: Penguin, 1985), pp. 1495, 1498.

29. Clara Reeve, *The Progress of Romance* (1785), p. 20.

30. Samuel Johnson, *The Rambler*, ed. W. J. Bate and A. B. Strauss, The Yale Edition of the Works of Samuel Johnson, vols. III–V (New Haven: Yale University Press, 1969), III: 22 (No. 4, 31 March 1750); Samuel Richardson, *Pamela*, ed. Thomas Keymer and Alice Wakely (Oxford: Oxford University Press, 2001), p. 513 (quoting Hill).

31. Barbauld, 'Origin and Progress', pp. 45, 59; see also Blair, *Lectures*, I: 303.

32. Joseph Warton, *Essay on the Genius and Writings of Pope*, 2 vols. (1756–82), I: 328.

33. Burke, *Philosophical Enquiry*, p. 58.

34. Alexander Pope, *The Dunciad in Four Books*, ed. Valerie Rumbold (Harlow: Longman, 1999), iv.250.

35. Coleridge, *Biographia Literaria*, p. 191.

36. Young, *Conjectures*, pp. 104, 42, 109.

FURTHER READING

Ashfield, Andrew, and Peter De Bolla (eds.), *The Sublime: A Reader in British Eighteenth-Century Aesthetic Theory*, Cambridge: Cambridge University Press, 1996.

Bromwich, David (ed.), *Romantic Critical Essays*, Cambridge: Cambridge University Press, 1987.

Brown, Marshall (ed.), *The Cambridge History of Literary Criticism*, vol. V: *Romanticism*, Cambridge: Cambridge University Press, 2000.

Caygill, Howard, *Art of Judgement*, Oxford: Blackwell, 1989.

Elledge, Scott (ed.), *Eighteenth-Century Critical Essays*, 2 vols., Ithaca, New York: Cornell University Press, 1961.

Klancher, Jon P., *The Making of English Reading Audiences 1790–1832*, Madison: Wisconsin University Press, 1987.

Nisbet, H. B., and Claude Rawson (eds.), *The Cambridge History of Literary Criticism*, vol. IV: *The Eighteenth Century*, Cambridge: Cambridge University Press, 1997.

Rose, Mark, *Authors and Owners: The Invention of Copyright*, Cambridge, Mass.: Harvard University Press, 1993.

Williams, Ioan (ed.), *Novel and Romance 1700–1800: A Documentary Record*, London: Routledge, 1970.

3

MICHAEL SCRIVENER

Literature and politics

Neither of the key words in my title is unproblematic. 'Literature' signifies a tension between all kinds of writing and a special literary kind of writing: not until the 1830s is there a conception of literature as normatively belletristic, essentially different from other kinds of more public and instrumental writing. 'Politics' is even more problematic, as the word denotes not only the politics of the crown and parliament but also the politics of the extra-parliamentary opposition. Moreover, the Enlightenment public sphere that Jürgen Habermas describes as emerging in the eighteenth century generated a quasi-political republic of letters that invited all, regardless of social origins, to participate in the literary culture in a career open to all talents.[1] Finally, the sense we now have that everything cultural is also political originates in this period.

From the 1740s to the 1830s, the major political trends included the challenge to aristocratic power by an array of democratic forces; the strengthening of the British Empire; and, especially after the defeat of Jacobitism and the final consolidation of the Protestant claim to the throne, an increase of religious toleration, with anti-semitism and anti-Catholicism declining but hardly disappearing. Many other trends had political implications: agricultural capitalism flourished, with widespread enclosures of common land dispossessing the rural poor; the industrial revolution began in earnest, with the population roughly doubling in the period; literacy grew as the middle classes increased, so that by 1800 about half the women and two-thirds of the men could read. The questions of dynastic succession and the state religion had dominated politics from the time of Henry VIII, but after the Battle of Culloden (1746) the Stuart cause survived largely as a sentimental Jacobitism in writers like Samuel Johnson, Tobias Smollett, Robert Burns, and Walter Scott. Smollett's vivid description of the brutal suppression of the Jacobite highlands was available to Thomas Paine in his own criticism of the Hanoverian dynasty in *The American Crisis*, x (1782).[2] The religious toleration marked by the abolition of disabilities for Protestant Dissenters (1827) and by Catholic Emancipation (1828) assumed a constitutional rather than an ethnically homogenous state, an imperial state of different peoples, not only the English. As political contention shifted from Jacobites to Jacobins, so the terms of political controversy entailed a new rhetoric of representation. Pope's formal satire was adequate for opposing Walpole and the Whig hegemony, but other genres, not necessarily tied to classical models, were required to sustain an opposition powerful enough to challenge aristocratic power successfully in the period from the Wilkes controversy of the 1760s to the Reform Bill of 1832.

If the trajectory in politics was towards democracy, a market economy, and empire, the literary trajectory is more ambiguous, an ambiguity highlighted by the lack of critical consensus about the dates of the Romantic period. The category of 'Romantic' in Britain does not become wholly coherent until the 1830s, when John Stuart Mill's essays on poetry signal the triumph of an explicitly Romantic notion of the literary: the belief that the most subjectively inward is the most poetic subject matter.[3] In 1757 John Dyer wrote an ambitious georgic poem on the woollen industry, *The Fleece*, that could represent British society in a meaningful way, but a generation later an undertaking of this kind was not even conceivable to the Romantic poets, for whom such 'unpoetic' content required treatment in forms such as political economy and technical writing.[4] In poetry at least, Romanticism narrowed the range of subject matter even as it discredited the idea of a distinctive poetic diction. The Romantics nevertheless looked outward to society as much as they looked inward to the soul, and much of Romantic writing was public and actively engaged in political disputes. Paul Magnuson shows, for example, that Coleridge's conversation poems did not retreat from politics into a private realm, but strategically intervened in the public realm, as reformist poets defended their 'domestic virtue' against the slanders of the anti-Jacobins.[5] Coleridge was as publicly engaged in his world as Pope and Churchill had been in theirs. Byron's satires used to be viewed as the exceptions that proved the rule of the Romantic lyric, but politically inflected satire hardly perished with the death of Pope and Swift in the 1740s, or even with Churchill in 1764.

Literary history has now largely discredited any simple notion of an antagonism between public Augustanism and introspective Romanticism. Satire and drama are only the two most obvious spheres where aspects of the earlier period's literary practice survived into the later. An early poetic model for John Clare, for instance, was *The Seasons* (1726–30) by James Thomson, whose experience of land and labour could not have been more unlike Clare's. An influential example of emotionally heightened expression was the *Eloisa to Abelard* (1717) of Pope, who provided models for women writers despite the misogyny sometimes exhibited in his poetry. Dryden's and Pope's translations made Virgil, Ovid, and Homer available to those without a classical education; Keats could write a defiant sonnet of tribute to Chapman's Homer. An upholder of neo-classical norms like Samuel Johnson authorized the turn toward personality and individual uniqueness with his *Lives of the Poets* (1779–81), while Pope and Johnson provided proof that the literary market could emancipate writers from patronage.[6] The road to Romanticism then was neither straight nor without circuitous byways, the emergence of a culture of 'sensibility' providing one of the most obvious examples of the latter. The turn to sensibility and sentiment occurred not just in literature, but also as part of a deep cultural shift, especially in the reformation of manners.[7] Resting on the foundation of Locke's empiricist epistemology, Shaftesbury's sentimental aesthetics and ethics, and Rousseau's fiction and philosophy, sensibility established sensation, feeling, and individual experience as the measure by which meaning was constructed. Although sensibility was socially ambiguous – Hannah More's 'Sensibility' (1782) alludes to the 'low enjoyments' that exclude the 'vulgar' from the blessings of sensibility – and by the end of the century was criticized harshly by both conservatives and radicals for its excesses and complacencies, it nevertheless was the cultural opening through which the socially excluded could pass to participate as readers and writers.[8]

After the Seven Years War (1756–63) Britain had defeated its only real rival in the imperial competition, France, and could view confidently its holdings from India to Canada. The American War of Independence (1775–81) diminished but did not weaken the empire. Even so, various anxieties did haunt the imperial project. Edmund Burke's zealous prosecution of Warren Hastings, Governor General of the British East India Company, identified violations of morality, law, and native rights under British rule; so that, even though Hastings was acquitted, arbitrary treatment of imperial subjects was not upheld. After the loss of the American colonies, Britain's empire tried to rule with at least the appearance of justice. Both slavery and brutal treatment of the native population were embarrassments the empire sought to avoid through reform or control of information. Ending the slave trade became a major political issue in the 1780s, but even after the trade was abolished in 1807, slave-ownership was legal in the empire until the 1830s. Owning slaves on British soil itself had been ruled illegal by Lord Mansfield in 1772. Throughout this period, the abolitionist cause generated a large body of poetry and prose, but most writers fought shy of challenging the moral basis of empire itself.

On the home front, controlling the flow of information became one of the arts of governing in the eighteenth century because increased literacy created a public whose opinion had some consequence. The governing party and its opposition both used print culture to promote their interests. Because the 1695 Licensing Act ended pre-publication censorship, government had to use other means to control writing. The theatre from 1737 became subject to censorship in addition to its other restrictions: only two London theatres, Covent Garden and Drury Lane, were licensed to produce dramatic plays; the unlicensed theatres could produce operas, musicals, and pantomimes. The two patent theatres did not lose their monopolies until 1843. Repression in the theatre helped shift literary talent over to the novel, as in the example of Henry Fielding. Legal repression of unwanted publications, always an option, was exercised sparingly in ordinary circumstances; both because of the expense and because of popular libertarian traditions that were politically costly to violate, as George III's government learned when they tried to silence John Wilkes and his *North Briton* in 1762–3. Wilkes and his supporters, including the poet Charles Churchill, were hardly gagged and the repression ended up provoking the eloquent 'Junius' in the pages of the *Public Advertiser* (1769–72). Nor was the legal system, because of the relative independence of juries, always the most convenient vehicle for carrying out the government's will. The government, for example, could not impose their version of 'constructive treason' at the treason trials of 1794. Among the accused, the radical organizers Horne Tooke, Thomas Hardy and John Thelwall became heroes with the London public, just as Wilkes had become earlier, and just as other victims of repression would become later: the Hunt brothers (1813), William Hone (1817), Henry 'Orator' Hunt (1819–20), and William Cobbett (1831), among others. Bribing opposition journalists and publishers, secretly subsidizing party newspapers and journals, and taxing periodicals to make them too expensive to be popular were the ordinary means of exercising political will. In the thirty years between 1760 and 1790 there were only seventy seditious libel prosecutions, but there were 167 in the eight years of intensive reform activity between 1817 and 1824.[9] It was not until the early nineteenth century that the press – notably *The Times* – was strong enough to be truly independent of government coercion. Newspapers were taxed prohibitively until 1836, when the tax was reduced to a penny, but the other 'taxes on knowledge' were not abolished until 1855. The government resisted freedom of the press with such tenacity because it understood the connection between knowledge and power.

Journalistic reporting on parliamentary speeches was part of the battle between the government and the press. Although the government sometimes arranged for speeches to appear in newspapers, parliament could forbid publication of its activities (as it did in 1738). An unintended consequence of the struggle with Wilkes was that parliament lost its power to control publication of state proceedings: in 1771 an angry crowd forced the release of Wilkes's printers who had been jailed for publishing parliamentary speeches.[10] Nevertheless, parliament did not accommodate political reporters with a special press gallery until the 1830s. The claim that Britain's was a truly representative government was suspect when the representative body itself demanded autonomy from the public it supposedly represented. Here we have a crisis about legitimate representation that is played out in numerous ways. Wilkes never went as far as proposing universal suffrage, but many of his opponents at least believed it to be implicit in the notion of popular sovereignty. For literature the crisis of representation had numerous manifestations, including the practice of writers from excluded groups making their own representations that disrupted established stereotypes. The Wilkes controversy strengthened both the republic of letters and the idea of a public sphere as separate from the state. Charles Churchill's political satires in support of Wilkes built upon the models of Dryden, Pope, and Swift by reaffirming the normative autonomy of the satirist who ought to criticize social power fearlessly. In *The Author* (1763), Churchill typically contrasts his own integrity with the prostituted lies of writers bought by the wealthy and powerful: 'We scorn Preferment which is gain'd by Sin, / And will, tho' poor without, have peace within'.[11] The continuing power of such ideas can be seen six decades later in Lord Byron's *Vision of Judgment* (1822). At the moral centre of Byron's satire against Robert Southey and George III stands one of the figures from the Wilkes controversy, the prose writer 'Junius': 'My charges [against George III] upon record will outlast / The brass of both his epitaph and tomb'.[12]

The question of representation was tangled in issues of national identity. An earlier controversy, the 'Jew Bill' of 1753, was symptomatic of the anxieties surrounding the subject of Britishness. Putting aside partisan politics and ancient prejudice, the issue was how one *became* British if one were not born British. After Lord Pelham and his brother the Duke of Newcastle engineered a minor adjustment in the law of naturalization – Jews would be spared taking a Christian oath – the opposition to the 'Jew Bill' became so vehement that parliament was forced to repeal the legislation. The Tory squirearchy and supporters of the High Church exploited anti-semitism to bring into being a popular movement against the Jewish Naturalization Law by deploying pamphlets, speeches, and prints that represented Jews as deicides and active enemies of Christianity, and thereby instigated violence against Jewish peddlers who were 'molested, insulted, and abused'.[13] Although none of the 'Jew Bill' writings was anything but ephemeral, the controversy affected the London theatre. As the question of national identity was becoming more urgent, Britons championed Shakespeare as the national poet, whose most popular play on the London stage from the 1740s was *The Merchant of Venice*. During the 'Jew Bill' controversy *The Merchant* did not run in the London patent theatres until the legislation was repealed.[14] According to Linda Colley the construction of British identity was hegemonically Protestant,[15] but many outside this hegemony laid claim to Britishness, and used literature as a medium of doing so. The xenophobia of *The Merchant of Venice* is only part of the story here: one must add texts like Olaudah Equiano's *Interesting Narrative* (1789), Maria Edgeworth's *Castle Rackrent* (1800), and Scott's *Waverley* (1814) and *Ivanhoe* (1819), which in their various ways disrupt any inexorable connection between any single ethnicity or religion and Britishness. Equiano claims a British identity on terms that include an idealized African origin, an English language and literary tradition that are fully his own, and a Christian religion to suit his own needs. The comic ironies and the heteroglossic voice of Thady Quirk make Edgeworth's Anglo-Irish novel less a celebration of the Act of Union and more a reminder of imperial violence and coercion. *Waverley* affirms a British identity but insists that the Jacobite rebellion, remembered sympathetically and tragically, not just triumphantly from the victor's point of view, should become part of British history. Scott's *Ivanhoe* not only problematizes the Anglo-Saxon merger with the Norman French but records symbolically the violent expulsion of the Jews in 1290 and illustrates that nationality entails conquest and domination. Scott in *Ivanhoe* rewrites 'English history as Anglo-Jewish history', a history of exclusions, expulsions, and conversions, including the submerging of Scott's own ethnicity for the sake of a British identity.[16]

Questions of national identity also played their part in the French Revolution controversy of the 1790s, as they were to do in the struggles over the extension of the right to vote that dominated politics over the first half of the nineteenth century. During the 1790s Edmund Burke mobilized national identity against modernity in general, not just against democrats at home and abroad. His *Reflections on the Revolution in France* (1790) discovered in the aspirations of the Enlightenment, the culture of sensibility, and varieties of bourgeois individualism a chamber of Gothic horrors that ranged from sexual promiscuity to cannibalism. Burke's anti-Jacobinism was a hyperbolic rhetorical performance, theatrically compelling and stylistically extreme. He inverted and mirrored the declarations of the radicals to the point of parody, but in the process unintentionally authorized a revolutionary style, as several of his opponents pointed out. Indeed, in *Letter to a Noble Lord* (1796), his persuasive critique of the liberal Duke of Bedford, Burke even plays the Jacobin role in discrediting the duke by tracing the origin of his unearned wealth to violent confiscation of church lands during the reign of Henry VIII. Burke advanced the meritocratic argument that he had worked for the pension he received from the government.[17]

Charles James Fox and Richard Brinsley Sheridan, leaders of the parliamentary opposition against Pitt and Burke in the 1790s, only occasionally collaborated with the extra-parliamentary radicals, as during the agitation against the 'Gagging Acts' of 1795 – the repressive legislation that destroyed the political will of all but the most dedicated activists. The aristocratic, cosmopolitan style of political opposition, hearkening back to revolutionary Whigs of the late seventeenth century, maintained some currency until 1832, when its limitations became all too evident in the persons of Sir Francis Burdett and Lord Broughton (John C. Hobhouse), radical heroes in the pre-Reform era, reactionary dinosaurs in the post-Reform era. When the conflict could be framed as between a tyrannical sovereign and a champion of British liberty, then a Wilkes, a Junius, a Fox, a Burdett, a Hobhouse could use effectively the 'constitutionalist' rhetoric that was the political idiom. After 1832 the constitutionalist rhetoric moved into Chartism where neither Burdett nor Hobhouse could follow. The most innovative and influential arguments in the French Revolution debate opposed to Burke came from outside parliament.

Two kinds of extra-parliamentary opposition existed in the eighteenth century, the polite and the plebeian. In terms of the former, the Tory wits as well as the country Whigs like Thomson became a kind of extra-parliamentary opposition that formed a sphere of influence with its own sources of authority and legitimacy from which to criticize not just government but the entire culture. Extra-parliamentary associations emerged out of the Wilkes controversy and discontent with the American War and slavery: the Bill of Rights Society, the county association movement, the Society for Constitutional Information, the Society for the Abolition of the Slave Trade, and various anti-slavery societies. These genteel pressure groups sought limited reforms but the very existence of the associations themselves threatened to carry the politics in unforeseen directions. First, at a time of expanding literacy, the rhetoric of opposition resonated far beyond the original framework, as plebeian reformers deployed its polite libertarian language but turned it from 'moderate' to 'radical' goals. Secondly, the organizational example of propagandizing could not be restricted to gentlemen reformers alone. Artisans and abolitionist women also associated. Third, the extra-parliamentary associations challenged the adequacy of representation and sometimes rioted. The treason trials of 1794 pivoted around the question of whether the reform movements were merely petitioning parliament or organizing themselves as a revolutionary 'convention' to replace parliament. Writers had an important role to play in this extra-parliamentary politics. Thomas Paine, William Godwin, John Thelwall, Thomas Spence, and Mary Wollstonecraft were influential figures in the controversial debates surrounding the significance of the French Revolution for British politics. The spectacular popularity of Paine's *Rights of Man* (1791-2) – copies sold by the hundreds of thousands – proved that literacy was broader than had been believed, alarmed the government enough to launch a successful seditious libel prosecution, established a popular style of argumentative prose, and inspired several generations of artisan radicals with an anti-authoritarian, republican vision. Godwin's *Political Justice* (1793), more philosophically rigorous than Paine's treatise, was spared a government prosecution only because of its price, but the uncompromising critiques of aristocracy, the legal system, social inequality, and property distribution made their way to both polite intellectuals like Wordsworth and a popular audience; the latter had access to Godwin's treatise through excerpts in Daniel Eaton's *Politics for the People* (1793-5), reading clubs, and *Caleb Williams* (1794), a fictionalized treatment of its author's philosophical anarchism. Godwin's arguments were also woven into the writing and speeches of Thelwall, the most effective popular orator in London, who bridged the two worlds of genteel and artisan reformism. The most influential platform for popular reformism in the capital was the London Corresponding Society, set up early in 1792 by the shoemaker Thomas Hardy, among others. Compared with Thelwall, another member of the London Corresponding Society, Thomas Spence, looks unapologetically revolutionary in his advocacy for a reform of ownership of the land so radical that it would have abolished aristocracy and effected a massive redistribution of wealth. Although Mary Wollstonecraft's legacy was weakened by Godwin's indiscreet narrative of her life, her *Vindication of the Rights of Woman* (1792) established for many years the terms of argument for women's rights. Similarly, the political theory and ideological configuration of the radical labour movement for much of the nineteenth century were charted in the 1790s. *Caleb Williams* and Wollstonecraft's *The Wrongs of Woman* were not the only Jacobin novels published at the time. Robert Bage, Charlotte Smith, Mary Hays, John Thelwall, Elizabeth Inchbald, and Thomas Holcroft also published novels whose coherence was explicitly structured by democratic political intentions.

On the other side of the political question, Burke's was hardly the only voice directed against the democratic radicals. The government sponsored the *Anti-Jacobin* (1797-98) under the direction of William Gifford, George Canning, and John Hookham Frere. Among its most effective satires was 'The New Morality' (July 9, 1798), which made connections between the violence of the French Revolution, the Irish uprising of 1798, and prominent figures in the English democratic movement, linking them all together, as had Burke, with a common ideology of Enlightenment rationalism and sentimentalism. James Gillray's popular print *New Morality* (1798) caricatured Coleridge, Southey, Thelwall, and Godwin, as well as satirizing 'Sensibility' as one of the three modern Graces (Fig. 2). Also sponsored by the government, Hannah More produced *Cheap Repository Tracts* (1795–8) that were distributed to labourers to counter the influence of Thomas Paine. From the late 1790s reaction against the Revolution gained momentum. Anti-Jacobin novels such as Elizabeth Hamilton's *Memoirs of Modern Philosophers* (1800) and political satires such as Richard Polwhele's *The Unsex'd Females* (1798) attacked women writers as signs of the degeneracy of the times:

> See Wollstonecraft, whom no decorum checks,
> Arise, the intrepid champion of her sex;
> O'er humbled man assert the sovereign claim,
> And slight the timid blush of virgin fame.[18]

There were no writers unaffected by the reaction. Although Wordsworth's 1805 version of *The Prelude* has moving tributes to the French Revolution – 'France standing on the top of golden hours' (vi.353) and 'Bliss was it in that dawn to be alive, / But to be young was very heaven!' (x.692–3) – the very structure of the poem marks the transition from political hope to faith in childhood, memory, and the imagination:

> This love more intellectual cannot be
> Without Imagination, which in truth
> Is but another name for absolute strength
> And clearest insight, amplitude of mind,
> And reason in her most exalted mood.[19]

While by no means directly anti-Jacobin, it is impossible to ignore the poem's displacement of revolutionary idealism, especially because Wordsworth and Coleridge did become politically conservative and travelled far from the Nether Stowey visited by a beleaguered Thelwall in 1797, when he was hoping to settle his family with his fellow radical poets. As he wrote to Coleridge in 'Lines Written at Bridgewater':

> And 'twould be sweet, my Samuel (ah, most sweet!),
> To see our little infants stretch their limbs
> In gambols unrestrained, and early learn
> Practical love, and – wisdom's noblest lore –
> Fraternal kindliness, while rosiest health
> Bloomed on their sunburnt cheeks.[20]

Figure 2 James Gillray, *New Morality*, from the *Anti-Jacobin Review and Magazine*, 1798.

Even William Blake and Thelwall, who never became political conservatives, were affected by the reaction in various ways, especially in the generic move to allegory discussed below. For her part, Jane Austen's novels bear the traces of anti-Jacobinism in their criticism of sensibility and their plot structures that hinge on a fallible heroine learning from her errors; Austen, however, greatly complicates the schematic anti-Jacobin plot so that the heroine trusts blindly in social authority only at her peril. For all that the overall picture was complicated in these and other ways, it would not be an exaggeration to say that the French Revolution and the reaction against it dominated politics and literature for almost three decades.

The 1790s were repeated with a difference in 1816–24 when the reformist agitation was more extensive, with more plebeian periodicals, more demo-cratic lecturers who had mass followings, and widespread reformist support outside London, especially in the midlands and north of England. Again the influence of early eighteenth-century literary models on some of the reformist writers cannot be disputed: Percy Shelley and Lord Byron derived their satirist role in part from Pope and Swift, while Leigh and John Hunt named their weekly paper in 1808 after Swift's *Examiner* (1710–11), and Jonathan Wooler's more plebeian *Black Dwarf* (1817–24) printed in every issue a motto from Pope's imitation of Horace's 'First Satire of the Second Book':

> Satire's my weapon; but I'm too discreet
> To run a-muck and tilt at all I meet.
> I only wear it in a land of Hectors,
> Thieves, Super-cargoes, Sharpers, and Directors.[21]

From Pope and Swift later writers derived the concept of truthful writing waging battle against established power. The writer's legitimacy did not come from political connections but from a writerly guild with traditions and standards extending to classical antiquity. Maintaining such integrity was costly for the Hunt brothers who spent two years in jail (1812–14), and for Wooler who spent eighteen months there (1819–21). Even elite writers such as Shelley and Byron experienced the political repression in small and large ways: withdrawing material when publishers were afraid of prosecution and censoring themselves in anticipation of repression.

The most influential radical journalist of the period, William Cobbett, developed a populist satirical style in his *Political Register* (1805–35) that has hints of Burke at his most paranoid, and of Blake in his systematic rage against authoritarian system. Cobbett's wild rhetoric harnessed historical energies so effectively that in 1816 the two-penny version of his newspa-per reached an unprecedentedly large audience of plebeian readers, around

40,000. Like the Hunt brothers he spent two years in jail (1809–11), and his later defence of the rural 'Captain Swing' rioters earned him a seditious libel charge of which he was acquitted (1831). His vision of the political world that assumed a set of dichotomous antagonisms between oppressors and oppressed appealed to labourers victimized by unemployment, declining wages, and an incomprehensible economic system that replaced the older 'moral economy'.[22] Holding together the various parts of his vision is his systematic understanding of 'corruption' that prevents parliamentary reform and perpetuates social inequality. Bankers, Jews, Quakers, sinecurists, royal patronage, a standing army, government corruption, high taxes, the paper money system, the war debt, and financial speculators are the demonized powers and institutional structures of an avaricious modernity hostile to an agrarian tradition in danger of extinction. The rational and irrational, people as well as abstract systems, are mixed inextricably in his arguments. It is as though sensibility inspired politics that depends on poignant scenes of oppression is a zero-sum game: there is room in the culture for only so many politicized sentimental stories. Cobbett's racism and anti-semitism, nourished by his outrage at the injustice against English workers, are integral to the idiom of his version of Romantic anti-capitalism.

A norm for the writer, rarely if ever actualized, could be constructed from the print culture of the eighteenth century: he – or she – could participate in any aspect of the literary culture without regard to the writer's social origins, class, educational level, ethnicity, or regional location. In the republic of letters there was no arbitrary authority only the power of the stronger argument and the appeal of the most aesthetically compelling productions. Of course that was the most ideal construction of the theory, but however routinely the theory was contradicted by social prejudice and arbitrary power the very existence of the norm sanctioned the ambition of writers who were outside the centres of power. Two periodicals that embodied the Enlightenment ideals of the public sphere more rigorously than most of their rivals were the *Analytical Review* (1788–99) and the *Monthly Magazine* (1796–1826), owned respectively by Joseph Johnson – who was ultimately reduced to financial ruin by imprisonment – and Richard Phillips. Wollstonecraft wrote extensively for the *Analytical*. The *Monthly* was a remarkable product of middle-class, largely Dissenting reader-writers whose articles made up the periodical. This constituency provided the first discriminating readers of the experimental Romantic writers. Appropriately the final editor of the *Monthly Magazine* with its liberal identity was the aging John Thelwall.

Excluded from coffee houses, women formed their own salons and literary culture. Especially after Richardson's *Pamela* (1740) and *Clarissa* (1747–8) authorized the domestic novel, prose fiction became a genre that women shaped to suit their interests. The emergence of the Gothic novel allowed women to explore otherwise taboo subject matter in stylized and exotic ways, as in Charlotte Dacre's *Zofloya* (1806), which treats sexuality with a frankness not permitted in the domestic novel. If women were limited largely to literature as a medium of expression, middling- and labouring-class men cultivated various counter-public spheres in the face of the contradiction between the Enlightenment's theoretical universality and society's practical exclusions. John Thelwall provides a point of departure for an examination of these issues because his position as a lower-middle-class writer and political radical exemplifies many aspects of the Romantic public sphere. Son of a London tradesman, Thelwall becomes first a tailor's then a legal apprentice until he starts his literary career in 1787. Even though Thelwall seemed destined for a commercial or legal life, as a youth he imagined a role for himself in the arts. Enlightenment culture had made such imaginings plausible. A rapidly expanding literary market needed writers, many more writers – including women – than could have been supplied by the literati of the leisure class who had received an Oxbridge education. As a London editor and journalist he was able to make a modest living, study medical science at Guy's Hospital, publish his poetry and fiction, and participate in the debating clubs where he lost his stammer and his Toryism to become a proficient speaker and a radical. It was hardly an accident that several of the poets important to Thelwall were physicians, John Armstrong and especially Mark Akenside, whose odes and long poem *The Pleasures of Imagination* (1744) were of lasting influence. At Thelwall's treason trial all his character witnesses were physicians; he had delivered a lecture at Guy's Hospital expounding a materialist theory of life in 1793; his treatise on speech therapy (1810) was addressed to Henry Cline, friend, physician, medical professor and fellow radical. Thelwall's revolutionary idealism was compatible with the progressive attitudes of medical science as it was practised in the 1790s – up to a point, that is. Under political pressure, the Physical Society to which he belonged and had addressed his lecture at Guy's Hospital expelled him. About twenty years later when Keats was a medical student, he felt he had to choose between poetry and medicine, however interconnected they also were, whereas for Thelwall medicine and poetry were utterly compatible. In works like *The Peripatetic* (1793), *Poems Written in Close Confinement in the Tower and Newgate* (1795), and especially *Poems* (1801), Thelwall made ambitious claims for his writing, challenging the assumption that plebeian and women writers could succeed only in the least culturally valued genres, the most esteemed kinds of writing being reserved for gentlemen. In the pages of the *Edinburgh Review*, Francis Jeffrey ridiculed the account of Thelwall's literary ambition in the memoir that prefaced the 1801 *Poems*:

> In every page of this extraordinary memoir, we discover traces of that impatience of honest industry, that presumptuous vanity, and precarious principle, that have thrown so many adventurers upon the world, and drawn so many females from their plain work and embroidery, to delight the public by their beauty in the streets, and their novels in the circulating library.[23]

The writer as prostitute is a topos that Jeffrey applies equally to women and plebeian men who, in turn, can point to the legitimation of the professional writer established by Pope and Johnson. This contest between rival norms, one gentlemanly and the other egalitarian, has many twists and turns even after the apparent irrelevance of cultural snobbery like Jeffrey's – and later, Lockhart's attacks on the Cockney School.

The example of Thelwall, a secularist inspired by the radical Enlightenment, contrasts in obvious ways with Blake's achievement within a biblical and religious idiom, although both radical Londoners were sons of tradesmen apprenticed in their teenaged years. The politics of Blake's work, especially in the 1790s, overlap with Thelwall's, but at a certain point – perhaps *The Four Zoas* (1797) – the visionary mythmaking becomes the principal site for political imagining, culminating with his masterpiece, *Jerusalem* (1804–18), where allusions to ordinary politics are rare in the allegorical combination of psychological analysis and revisionary myth. As Coleridge, Wordsworth, and Southey became Burkean conservatives after the anti-Jacobin reaction, so Blake translated the radical politics of his illuminated books of the 1790s into an apocalyptic epic where Voltaire and Rousseau are the 'Covering Cherubs' of 'Natural Religion'.[24] Scornful of the literary market, Blake managed to finish his great deconstruction of Enlightenment metaphysics, but lack of encouragement meant that Thelwall's epic on the origins and prehistory of modern rationality, *The Hope of Albion* (1801–25), was never completed.

Like Blake, Shelley engaged politics at several levels, including the mythopoeic, apocalyptic, and deeply psychological, especially in *Prometheus Unbound* (1820), a poem he was 'vain enough to like' but thought was for the 'elect' only, not 'more than 5 or 6 persons'.[25] Shelley's quest for an audience, frustrated by the political repression and his own increasingly difficult, allusive style, was ironically successful with the pirated editions of *Queen Mab* (1813) that became popular in the nineteenth-century labour movement. Shelley's early poem became a vehicle for transmitting to the nineteenth-century labour movement some of the most radical ideas of the 1790s. Ambivalent about the literary market but also politically active,

Shelley envied the spectacular popularity of his friend, Lord Byron, whose masterpiece, the sprawling epic *Don Juan* (1820–24) with its Sternean digressions, did not find the same favour as his earlier *Childe Harold* (1812–18) and eastern tales. The complex politics of Byron and Shelley can be seen in the journal the *Liberal* (1822–3), a joint production of the Leigh Hunt and Byron-Shelley circles, aimed at undermining the reactionary politics of *Blackwood's*, the *Quarterly Review*, and the 'Lakers' – Wordsworth, Coleridge, and Southey.[26] Although Shelley's *Adonais* (1821) did not appear in the *Liberal*, the elegy on Keats coheres within the cultural politics of the day in its opposition to the *Quarterly Review* and the Lake School. The political vision of the Hunt and Shelley circles, however, had its blind spots. The *Examiner*, for instance, frequently regarded the mass-platform politics associated with Cobbett as a species of vulgarity and serious discussions of women's poetry are absent from the critical prose of Hazlitt, Hunt, Peacock, and Shelley, even though we know they had read a great deal of it.

One line of development from the Lockean foundations of empiricism and sensibility, reinforced by the logic of insurgent groups who represented their own interests and experience, is a decentred cultural authority. Laurence Sterne's *Tristram Shandy* (1759–67) is paradigmatic of the Lockean metaphysics. The flow of consciousness, the association of ideas, and the digressions of the writerly consciousness all retard and complicate the linear narration upon which the novel as a genre was supposedly based. If within empiricist assumptions the novel cannot represent *the* world, it can represent *a* world. Not that writers ceased trying to represent *the* world, even writers from non-elite groups; the metaphysics undergirding such representation had collapsed, but not the desire to represent 'truth' or to reconstitute metaphysics on a different basis – an ambition shared in different ways by Coleridge, Blake, and Shelley. Truly remarkable in this period is the huge increase in literacy and the influx of new writers from the ranks of those outside the social elites. Men and women from the middling and labouring classes assume influential roles as innovative writers. Democracy in the world of writing occurred earlier than in the world of parliamentary politics, but a perfect democracy it was not. Anna Barbauld's *Eighteen Hundred and Eleven* (1812), an ambitious and effective anti-war poem in pentameter couplets, united the male critics who pronounced the poem out of bounds; political satire by women attempting to represent *the* world and not just *a* world was not possible. One of the most distinguished female poets whose career had spanned many decades of successful writing was silenced; there were no voices speaking in her favour.[27] John Clare inserted himself into the pastoral tradition as a 'peasant poet' but the frustrating and humiliating negotiations between himself and his patrons over his poetry's spelling, grammar, and diction repeated the difficulties of other labouring-class poets from Stephen Duck to Ann Yearsley described by John Goodridge and Bridget Keegan later in this volume. Two ways to state the situation are that labourers could revise an ancient and politically contested genre, the pastoral, and that labourers were forced to accommodate their expression to the power of the cultural elite and the literary conventions. Both statements are true: there was agency and there was coercion.

NOTES

1. Jürgen Habermas, *The Structural Transformation of the Public Sphere*, trans. Thomas Berger and Frederick Lawrence (Cambridge, MA: MIT Press, 1989), pp. 1–88.
2. J. C. D. Clark, 'Religious Affiliation and Dynastic Allegiance in Eighteenth-Century England: Edmund Burke, Thomas Paine and Samuel Johnson', *ELH* 64 (1997), 1032–3.
3. 'What is Poetry?' *Monthly Repository*, new series 7 (January 1833), 60–70; 'The Two Kinds of Poetry', *Monthly Repository*, new series 7 (October 1833), 714–24; Marilyn Butler, *Romantics, Rebels, and Reactionaries: English Literature and Its Background, 1760–1830* (New York: Oxford University Press, 1981), p. 8.
4. John Barrell, *English Literature in History 1730–80: 'An Equal, Wide Survey'* (London: Hutchinson, 1983), p. 91.
5. Paul Magnuson, *Reading Public Romanticism* (Princeton: Princeton University Press, 1998), pp. 67–94.
6. On *Eloisa to Abelard*, see Robert Griffin, *Wordsworth's Pope: A Study in Literary Historiography* (Cambridge: Cambridge University Press, 1995), pp. 24–63; on Pope and women poets, see Donna Landry, *The Muses of Resistance: Labouring Class Women's Poetry, 1739–1796* (Cambridge: Cambridge University Press, 1990), pp. 47–51; on class and translation, see Marjorie Levinson, *Keats's Life of Allegory: The Origins of a Style* (Oxford: Blackwell, 1988), p. 7; on Johnson's biographies, see Annette Wheeler Cafarelli, *Prose and the Age of Poets: Romanticism and Biographical Narrative From Johnson to De Quincey* (Philadelphia: University of Pennsylvania Press, 1990), pp. 30–69.
7. G. J. Barker-Benfield, *The Culture of Sensibility: Sex and Society in Eighteenth-Century Britain* (Chicago: University of Chicago Press, 1992), p. xxv.
8. Hannah More, 'Sensibility', in Duncan Wu (ed.), *Romantic Women Poets: An Anthology* (Oxford: Blackwell, 1997), lines 151–4.
9. Michael Scrivener (ed.), *Poetry and Reform: Periodical Verse from the English Democratic Press 1792–1824* (Detroit: Wayne State University Press, 1992), p. 21.
10. George Rudé, *Wilkes and Liberty: A Social Study* (London: Lawrence and Wishart [1962] 1983), pp. 155–9.
11. *The Poetical Works of Charles Churchill*, ed. Douglas Grant (Oxford: Oxford University Press, 1956), p. 257 (lines 397–8).
12. Steven E. Jones, *Satire and Romanticism* (New York: St Martin's Press, 2000), pp. 1–3.

13. Roy S. Wolper (ed.), *Pieces on the "Jew Bill" (1753)* (Los Angeles: Augustan Reprint Society Publ. No. 217, 1983); Todd M. Endelman, *The Jews of Georgian England, 1714–1830: Tradition and Change in a Liberal Society* (Ann Arbor: University of Michigan Press, 1999), p. 91.

14. James Shapiro, *Shakespeare and the Jews* (New York: Columbia University Press, 1996), p. 215.

15. Linda Colley, *Britons: Forging the Nation, 1707–1837* (New Haven: Yale University Press, 1992), pp. 18–54.

16. Michael Ragussis, *Figures of Conversion: The Jewish Question and English National Identity* (Durham: Duke University Press, 1995), pp. 89–126.

17. Michael Scrivener, *Seditious Allegories: John Thelwall and Jacobin Writing* (University Park: Pennsylvania State University Press, 2001), pp. 43–50, 56–8.

18. Richard Polwhele, *The Unsex'd Females* (1798), p. 13.

19. William Wordsworth, *The Thirteen-Book Prelude*, ed. Mark Reed, 2 vols. (Ithaca: Cornell University Press, 1991), xiii.166–70.

20. John Thelwall, *Poems Written Chiefly in Retirement* (Hereford, 1801), lines 109–14.

21. Lines 69–72, see *The Poems of Alexander Pope*, ed. John Butt (London: Routledge, 1963).

22. E. P. Thompson, 'The Moral Economy', in *Customs in Common* (London: Merlin Press, 1991), pp. 185–258.

23. *Edinburgh Review* 2 (1803), 200.

24. *The Complete Poetry and Prose of William Blake*, ed. David V. Erdman, rev. edn (New York: Anchor Books, 1988), pl. 66: 8–12.

25. *The Letters of Percy Bysshe Shelley*, ed. Frederick L. Jones, 2 vols. (Oxford: Clarendon Press, 1964), II: 200 and 388. For Shelley's attempts to reach a popular audience, see *Reading Shelley's Interventionist Poetry, 1819–20*, ed. Michael Scrivener, *Romantic Circles Praxis Series* (May 2001): www.rc.umd.edu/praxis/interventionist.

26. Jeffrey Cox, *Poetry and Politics in the Cockney School: Keats, Shelley, Hunt and Their Circle* (Cambridge: Cambridge University Press, 1998), pp. 21–37.

27. William Keach, 'A Regency Prophecy and the End of Anna Barbauld's Career', *Studies in Romanticism* 33 (1994), 569–77.

FURTHER READING

Barrell, John, *Imagining the King's Death: Figurative Treason, Fantasies of Regicide, 1793–1796*, Oxford: Oxford University Press, 2000.

Basker, James G. (ed.), *Amazing Grace: An Anthology of Poems about Slavery, 1660–1810*, New Haven: Yale University Press, 2002.

Butler, Marilyn, *Romantics, Rebels, and Reactionaries: English Literature and Its Background, 1760–1830*, New York: Oxford University Press, 1981.

Caretta, Vincent (ed.), *Unchained Voices: An Anthology of Black Authors in the English-Speaking World of the Eighteenth Century*, Lexington: University Press of Kentucky, 1996.

Chandler, James, *England in 1819: The Politics of Literary Culture and the Case of Romantic Historicism*, Chicago: University of Chicago Press, 1998.

Felsenstein, Frank (ed.), *English Trader, Indian Maid: Representing Gender, Race, and Slavery in the New World, An Inkle and Yarico Reader*, Baltimore: Johns Hopkins University Press, 1999.

Hoagwood, Terence Alan, and Daniel P. Watkins (eds.), *British Romantic Drama: Historical and Critical Essays*, Madison: Fairleigh Dickinson University Press, 1998.

Kelly, Gary, *The English Jacobin Novel 1780–1805*, Oxford: Clarendon Press, 1976.

McCalman, Iain, *Radical Underworld: Prophets, Revolutionaries and Pornographers in London, 1795–1840*, Cambridge: Cambridge University Press, 1988.

McGann, Jerome J., *The Poetics of Sensibility: A Revolution in Literary Style*, Oxford: Clarendon Press, 1996.

Paley, Morton D., *Apocalypse and Millenium in English Romantic Poetry*, Oxford: Clarendon Press, 1999.

Richardson, Alan, *Literature, Education, and Romanticism: Reading as a Social Practice, 1780–1832*, Cambridge: Cambridge University Press, 1996.

Roe, Nicholas, *Wordsworth and Coleridge: The Radical Years*, Oxford: Clarendon Press, 1988.

Ruderman, David B., *Jewish Enlightenment in an English Key: Anglo-Jewry's Construction of Modern Jewish Thought*, Princeton: Princeton University Press, 2000.

Scrivener, Michael, *Seditious Allegories: John Thelwall and Jacobin Writing*, University Park: Pennsylvania State University Press, 2001.

Simpson, David, *Romanticism, Nationalism, and the Revolt against Theory*, Chicago: University of Chicago Press, 1993.

Thompson, E. P., *The Romantics: England in a Revolutionary Age*, New York: New Press, 1997.

Woodring, Carl, *Politics in English Romantic Poetry*, Cambridge: Harvard University Press, 1970.

4

SAREE MAKDISI

Literature, national identity, and empire

'I have no knowledge of either Sanscrit or Arabic', admitted Thomas Macaulay, in the middle of his 1835 *Minute on Indian Education*;

> But I have done what I could to form a correct estimate of their value. I have read translations of the most celebrated Arabic and Sanscrit works. I have conversed both here and at home with men distinguished by their proficiency in the Eastern tongues. I am quite ready to take the Oriental learning at the valuation of the Orientalists themselves. I have never found one among them who could deny that a single shelf of a good European library was worth the whole native literature of India and Arabia.[1]

With its profound faith in what Macaulay identified without hesitation as Britain's intrinsic cultural superiority – articulated through a sweeping contempt for other cultures that was in turn founded not on the profession of an immediate and detailed knowledge of the Other (the hallmark of Orientalist thought in the time of Sir William Jones, a mere thirty or forty years earlier) but rather on an exaggerated sense of mediation, generalization, distancing, almost ignorance – the *Minute on Indian Education* signalled the abrupt end of over a century of British indecisiveness about the East.

Over the previous decades, Britain's fascination with the East had mingled with a sense of dread and fear; myths and misconceptions had competed with forms of positive or at least quasi-scientific knowledge; genuine admiration had contended with rapacious and exploitative hostility. British Orientalists would of course continue to express a certain degree of ambivalence in the decades after Macaulay's intervention, but by the 1830s a fairly stable, albeit not quite homogeneous, consensus had developed in the prevailing British views of the East, a consensus founded on the kind of contemptuous and violent interventionism, as well as the easy faith in Britain's inherent cultural and moral superiority, characterizing Macaulay's text. This consensus, elaborated in literary as well as more explicitly political texts, formed a kind of backdrop against which the nineteenth century's various and sometimes dissenting expressions of unmediated experience – Lady Hester Stanhope's, for example, or Alexander Kinglake's, or Charles Doughty's, or Richard Burton's – would henceforth stand out. Indeed, the consensus that was consolidated by the 1830s proved so formidable that in broad terms it still defines the dominant Western approach to the Arab and Islamic world (the residual core of what had been a much larger geo-cultural conception of the Orient).

In the century before 1835, on the other hand, one prevailing British view of the East had quickly replaced another, and opposing conceptions of the Orient, none of which possessed the kind of self-satisfied durability that would be consolidated by Macaulay's time, had at times had to contend with each other in government circles, in the councils of the East India Company, in the public sphere, in historical and philosophical treatises, and in the pages of novels and volumes of poetry. What was at stake amid such a diversity of thought was not merely the struggle between competing attitudes or points of view, but the status of imperial policy, and the nature of Britain's changing understanding of itself and its relations with its others – or rather Britain's changing understanding of itself *in relation to* its others. If by the 1830s a new understanding of national identity had emerged in Britain, which Macaulay would be able to draw on in such a forthright and unambiguous way, that emergence, in all of its manifestations – in science and in the arts, in warfare and in politics, in economic policy and in consumerist self-fashioning, in poetry and the novel – was the product of the consolidation of a properly imperial culture. The latter did not involve simply an introspective affirmation of Britain's newly agreed-on sense of itself, but rather an articulation of Britain's supposed difference from and superiority to its cultural others, a project from which Britain's sense of itself cannot meaningfully be separated. For, however uneven and discontinuous it may have seemed at times, the developing sense of national identity underlying the work of writers from William Wordsworth to Jane Austen and Walter Scott was not – despite all appearances to the contrary – genuinely autonomous or home-grown, but was, rather, invariably articulated, whether explicitly or implicitly, in opposition to others. Even when it was expressed in the most passionately parochial forms of nativism, as for example in the celebration of 'rural virtue', 'humble happiness' and 'native charm' from Oliver Goldsmith's *Deserted Village* (1770) to Wordsworth and Coleridge's *Lyrical Ballads* (1798), Britain's national identity and national culture – Britain's sense of itself and of its very modernity – were by the end of the eighteenth century comprehensively shaped by the discourses of imperialism and by Britain's changing image of and relations with its cultural others.

At the beginning of the eighteenth century, indeed, Britain lacked such a systematic sense of itself as a 'self' as opposed to 'others', and hence it lacked both a modern sense of national identity and a modern form of imperial culture. The public issue of the day was instead internal, and it was only on the parliamentary union of England and Scotland in 1707 that Britain formally came into being as a political unit. Its knowledge of other cultures was limited to vague and much embellished leftover memories of the Crusades, tales of travellers, the accounts of the early transoceanic explorers, and travel compendia such as those of the fictitious fourteenth-century author John Mandeville – which freely combined fantastical and quasi-historical narratives – and those of collectors and editors such as Richard Hakluyt and Samuel Purchas, who published collections of voyages in the late sixteenth and early seventeenth centuries. Such accounts were regarded as curiosities or perhaps as repositories of useful information; it would be difficult to think of them as experiments in the formation of what we might identify as a national culture in the modern sense of that term, or for that matter as genuine accounts of other cultures. Indeed, many seventeenth-century travel writers – Henry Maundrell's *Journey from Aleppo to Jerusalem* (1697) is a good example – expressed a nearly total lack of interest in the different cultures they encountered and were far more engaged with such practical matters as industry and trade, and especially the prospect of further commercial opportunities.

All this began to change following two major events in the formation of modern British and indeed European culture; first, the 1697 publication of Barthélemy d'Herbelot's *Bibliothèque orientale,* a sort of encyclopedia of Oriental cultures in which some more or less accurate historical and bibliographical information was lavishly supplemented with extra material and an unhealthy dose of editorial intervention; and, second, the 1704 publication of *Les mille et une nuits,* a translation of one Arabic manuscript version of the *Thousand and One Nights,* by Antoine Galland. Galland had edited d'Herbelot's encyclopedia and had had it published after the latter's death, but from the beginning the difference between the two projects expressed the gap between knowledge and entertainment. Orientalist entertainment, in the form of Galland's *Thousand and One Nights,* easily outshone Orientalist 'knowledge'. In fact the Western world was not yet ready for or interested in Oriental knowledge, the market and uses for which would take almost a century to develop. The *Bibliothèque orientale* never was translated into English, but the first English edition of Galland's text appeared in just 1708. That the latter, the translation of a translation (and Galland's text itself had already been heavily modified from the original manuscript), was quite far removed from the Arabic original, and hence from any kind of claim to genuine 'authenticity', made no difference to its English readers. On the contrary, its appearance prompted a deluge of other 'translations', additions, 'discoveries' of new tales, and in general a boom in quasi-Oriental storytelling and essay writing in English, most of it invented from scratch or perhaps with some debt to a hasty reading of Galland, and hardly any of it having much to do with actual Arabic or Persian cultural or literary forms. (In fact the form of the frame-tale itself, as inherited by Chaucer from Boccaccio many centuries previously, was a much more genuine European derivation from Arabic literature, but by the early eighteenth century English readers had long since forgotten the original source of the frame-tale, which had been invisibly absorbed into their own literary tradition, and they were thus struck anew by the seeming novelty of its reappearance in Galland.)

As early as 1711, Addison and Steele were including quasi-Oriental material in the *Spectator* in the form of didactic tales and moralistic essays, making use of the sugar-pill of Orientalism in order to instruct and delight their highbrow audience. The publication of Montesquieu's *Persian Letters* in 1721 and its swift translation into English (1722) inspired a new wave of Orientalist writing, based now not on the alleged discovery of long-lost tales but rather on the equally fictional accounts of invented contemporary Eastern travellers modelled on Montesquieu's Usbek, the central narrator of *Persian Letters*. The popularity and guaranteed marketability of such texts inspired Samuel Johnson to hastily draft *Rasselas* (originally *The Prince of Abissinia: A Tale* (1759)), supposedly in order to clear debts. Written in less than a week, Johnson's tale consists of didactic narratives tied together through the voyage of Rasselas and his entourage, who travel to Egypt in search of happiness but never find it, though they pass on a good deal of moral instruction to the reader along the way. Oliver Goldsmith's series of 'Chinese Letters', which started to appear shortly after the publication of *Rasselas*, and were compiled into *The Citizen of the World* (1762), are more faithful to Montesquieu's precedent than to Johnson's, though they undoubtedly benefited from the latter's success. *The Citizen of the World* contains the letters of the fictional traveller Lien Chi Altangi written back to his friends and family in China from his residence in London. In fact, like *Persian Letters*, Goldsmith's text is far more concerned with Western and specifically English culture than with Eastern civilization; just as Montesquieu had done in his denunciation of the corruption of French aristocratic government, Goldsmith uses the distancing device of the foreign narrator in order to produce a satirical commentary on English tastes, politics and manners. Strangely enough, the fact that actual Persian, Indian, Turkish or Arabic material had little or no role to play in such narratives may be exactly what allowed Lady Mary Wortley Montagu's *Turkish Embassy Letters*, which were published posthumously in 1763, to be smoothly assimilated into the genre of the quasi-Oriental tale, even though they were (mostly) based on her actual experience as the wife of the ambassador to Istanbul, many of them having been written there during her stay in 1716 (though none of them were actually sent as letters in the proper sense). It would have been difficult for an English reader to judge the veracity of Montagu's text – although, inspired by actual Turkish medical practice, she was well known for having introduced inoculation against smallpox into England – as against such entirely fictional accounts as Johnson's and Goldsmith's, which had appeared in print slightly earlier.

Notwithstanding the appearance of Montagu's *Letters*, quasi-Oriental tales and poems such as *Rasselas* would continue to appear through the 1780s and 1790s and on into the nineteenth century. The genre would grow to include, for example, Elizabeth Hamilton's *Letters of a Hindoo Raja* (1795), Walter Savage Landor's *Gebir* (1798), Robert Southey's *Thalaba the Destroyer* (1801), Thomas Moore's *Lalla Rookh* (1817), and James Morier's *Adventures of Hajji Baba of Isfahan* (1824). But really the initial version of the genre may be said to have died with the publication of William Beckford's *Vathek, An Arabian Tale*, in 1786. Beckford had originally written *Vathek* in French, and when the novel was translated into English by Samuel Henley a set of notes on Oriental culture – largely derived from d'Herbelot – were added to the text, as well as a preface claiming the text's derivation from an Arabic source. Not all the later publications would follow *Vathek*'s example, of course, but Nigel Leask has pointed out that the most successful quasi-Orientalist works after the 1780s would be characterized by a deliberately manipulated contrast between the text's vaguely 'Oriental' style, images, allusions and themes on the one hand, and, on the other hand, a distancing device, such as notes or a preface. The latter served to undermine or at least to qualify the Oriental material and resituate the reader not simply as an avid consumer of the Orient in an unprotected and unmediated kind of way but rather as someone who also shares in a broader knowledge of and power over the Orient as well – someone whose Eastern pleasures are tempered, guided and protected by a sense of Western power and knowledge.[2]

In this sense, the publication of *Vathek* signalled a momentous shift in British attitudes towards non-European cultures. Whereas only a few years earlier Orientalist entertainment could easily outshine Orientalist knowledge, by the mid-1780s the knowledge of the Orient would assume a new importance and take on a new role. The Oriental tale would henceforth not be something merely to be enjoyed for the sake of it, not a form that one could innocently take advantage of in order to impart moral or intellectual precepts, as Addison and Steele had done decades earlier. Rather, the Oriental tale, and the Orient itself, would – wittingly or unwittingly – be drafted to the cause of British national and imperial self-definition, part of a process that had begun embryonically in the 1770s and would reach a kind of climax in the late 1790s. In his influential book *Orientalism*, Edward Said argues that all versions of this specifically modern form of a much older discourse share in common an underlying structural logic sharply distinguishing the same from the different, self from other, Occident from Orient.[3] Readers of Addison and Steele or of Montesquieu and Johnson would readily have recognized that the foreign scenes they encountered in those texts were decidedly not English, obviously; but in the early and even the mid-eighteenth century there was much less knowledge (genuine or otherwise) of the East; there was also much less of a political and cultural investment in the sharp differentiation between East and West observed by Said, so that the East could therefore be turned to as sugar-coating without too much qualification. That an early eighteenth-century English reader could unproblematically receive moral instruction from a supposedly Abyssinian or Persian or Chinese narrator ought to remind us that there was much less at stake in distinguishing between East and West in the 1710s or 1720s than there would be by the 1780s or 1790s – by which time it would be all but unthinkable for an Englishman to condescend to learning from an Oriental. This is because of a momentous shift in British imperial policy that began to be instituted in the 1770s by, among others, the East India Company's new governor of Bengal, Warren Hastings.

As more of India fell under British (and specifically East India Company) control in the second half of the eighteenth century, new techniques and strategies of imperial rule had to be invented. What Warren Hastings proposed was the extraction and circulation of knowledge concerning Oriental languages, literatures, religions and laws in order to rule the Company's Oriental possessions more effectively. He encouraged not only the translation of classic Sanskrit and Persian texts into English but also a process of acculturation whereby Englishmen could study these languages and literatures in order to master Indian culture – especially, but not only, jurisprudence – from *within*. Knowledge of the Oriental other here was no longer a matter of idle entertainment, as it had been earlier in the eighteenth century, but rather an essential component of imperial power. Or, rather, entertainment became a form of knowledge even as knowledge itself, including aesthetic and literary knowledge, became inseparable from power. The East India Company, for example, sponsored the first translation of the *Bhaghavad-Gita* into English in 1785. 'Every accumulation of knowledge, and especially such as is obtained by social communication with people over whom we exercise a dominion founded on the right of conquest, is useful to the state,' wrote Warren Hastings in the preface to that volume; but, he added, it is also 'the gain of humanity: in the specific instance which I have stated, it attracts and conciliates distant affections; it lessens the weight of the chain by which the natives are held in subjection; and it imprints on the heart of our own countrymen the sense and obligation of benevolence'.[4] This was, clearly, not merely a matter of taking advantage of information in a crude sense so as to more effectively bludgeon the other into submission: it was a matter of almost absorbing oneself into the other, of almost becoming other, in order to fuse power and knowledge together at the site of contact with subject peoples; it was, in effect, a way to selectively bridge the gap – even while otherwise maintaining it – between colonizer and colonized.

The best known of the work initially conducted under the influence of Hastings was done by Sir William Jones, who from 1783 until his death in 1794 served as an East India Company judge in Calcutta. However, Jones, who learned Arabic, Persian and Sanskrit, argued that although there was an immediately practical application of the knowledge obtained of the Oriental other, there was also a kind of excess of knowledge that had no immediate practical application but might serve somewhat more 'disinterested' cultural and aesthetic purposes. Europeans would gain from the Oriental knowledge they acquired not merely an expedient for imperial domination but an immense cultural resource that they might use for their own aesthetic purposes. The Orient, according to Jones, is 'the nurse of sciences, the inventress of delightful and useful arts, the scene of glorious actions, fertile in the productions of human genius, abounding in natural wonders, and infinitely diversified in the forms of religion and government, in the laws, manners, customs, and languages, as well as in the features and complexions of men'.[5] What Jones proposed to do, through the agency of the Asiatick Society of Calcutta, which he founded in 1784, and through the publication of the serial *Asiatick Researches* (beginning in 1788), was to establish an intellectual and cultural analogue to the extraction of material wealth from the Orient – which was of course the East India Company's main priority – in the discovery and then the translation and circulation of the indigenous cultural, literary, artistic, and scientific productions of the Orient.

Indeed, quite apart from the immediate usefulness of Orientalist knowledge to the imperial administration, Jones argued that knowledge of the Orient is valuable on its own terms. Thus 'An Essay on the poetry of the Eastern Nations' celebrates the virtues of Oriental literatures, not only comparing them to the works of Greece and Rome, but to a certain extent elevating them 'above' the European classics. In praising the writings of Asia he was not denying the merit of classical literature, he insists in the conclusion to this essay;

yet I cannot but think that our *European* poetry has subsisted too long on the perpetual repetition of the same images, and incessant allusions to the same fables: and it has been my endeavour for several years to inculcate this truth, that, if the principal writings of the *Asiaticks*, which are reposited in our public libraries, were printed with the usual advantage of notes and illustrations, and if the languages of the *Eastern* nations were studied in our great seminaries of learning, where every other branch of useful knowledge is taught to perfection, a new and ample field would be opened for speculation; we should have a more extensive insight into the history of the human mind; and we should be furnished with a new set of images and similitudes; and a number of excellent compositions would be brought to light, which future scholars might explain and future poets might imitate. (*Works*, v: 547–8)

Thus, just as Britain was benefiting from the discovery and extraction of new material commodities – cotton, silk, sugar, opium – it could, according to Jones, benefit from the discovery and circulation of such new sources of inspiration. The great value of such an intellectual resource, the potential it offered as a new field for 'speculation', lay not merely in its inherent beauty, its inspiration, its charm, but in its sheer difference from the standard European classics. Jones himself not only wrote essays, he also translated many works (notably *Sacontalá*) from Arabic, Persian and Sanskrit into English, and, moreover, composed poems of his own in imitation of Oriental sources. Intimately bound up with the knowledge of – and power over – the cultural other, this was quite unlike the superficial kind of imitation that passed as 'Oriental' earlier in the century, which was founded on ignorance rather than knowledge, and which had little or no investment in the larger imperial project that would be at stake for Jones or Hastings. If the earlier interest in Orientalism had been merely a passing fad, inspired perhaps by the commercial success of Galland, it now became a serious endeavour, part of a much broader cultural and political process of self-definition. 'Both geographically and historically', Raymond Schwab argues, 'what had been lacking through the centuries and what would come to dominate everything was cultural dissonance, a sense of *the dissident*. The known world had been wholly classical before 1800. Or, in a sense, it had been a classified world. Homer was simultaneously the essential beginning and the culmination.'[6] The world of difference whose exploration Jones and Hastings were promoting, however, enabled not merely the articulation of this dissidence, but also of the 'sameness' from which it marked a departure; in other words this process required not merely finding out what made 'them' different, but also what made 'us' who 'we' are. Schwab suggests that the very emergence of Romanticism as a cultural force field was inspired by the 'discovery' of the East in what he calls the Oriental Renaissance that took place at the end of the eighteenth century.

Thus the British 'discovery' of the East not only opened up whole new vistas of the imagination for British artists and writers as Jones had suggested, it also helped to define Britain's dramatically changing relationship with its newly invented others.[7] This relationship both determined and was determined by the political and cultural exigencies of European empire-building projects, of which, of course, the most extensive was the British: over one hundred and fifty million people would be brought under British imperial control between 1790 and 1830 (including the people of Ireland at the union of 1801). The imperial relationship between Britain and the peoples over whom it exercised imperial power inspired and compelled British writers to articulate what it was that made Britain different from its others. Indeed, when Edward Said argues that modern Orientalism posits a sharp distinction between West and East, self and other, 'us' and 'them', his point is that knowledge of the other is not only not a neutral process insofar as it contributes to imperial rule (Jones and Hastings were already claiming this themselves), but insofar as it necessitates the constitution both of the other *and* of the self. In defining the Orient as a field of study, then, Jones and Hastings were necessarily also defining an Occident against which the Orient's dissidence and difference could be measured; in bringing the Orient into existence, they were also bringing the Occident into existence at the same time, not just as what Said calls an imaginary geographical entity but even more specifically as a national and cultural container of moral, philosophical, aesthetic and political values. This prompted the emergence of an altogether new, and properly modern, sense of imperial British subjectivity, a sense of self that could be measured against the Afro-Asiatic objects of British rule. This process was at times exhilarating and at times threatening. However, though they are epistemologically inseparable from each other, the process of exploring the other, on the one hand, and that of defining the self, on the other, need not assume equal priority. For Jones and Hastings, clearly, the former was far more urgent and interesting than the latter. Their approach, however, was bound up with a very particular view of the nature and role of imperial government, and imperial policy began to change as the process of self-definition assumed greater priority than that of the exploration of difference, all but replacing it. Indeed, the transformation of the project of other-definition into one of self-definition was quite dramatic, and the centrepiece of the drama was the impeachment and trial in parliament of Warren Hastings himself on a charge of high crimes and misdemeanours.

The trial of Warren Hastings dragged on sporadically from 1788 to 1795 and ended with his acquittal. All along, however, what was really at stake was not so much the guilt or innocence of Hastings, but rather the nature of British imperial rule in India and above all Britain's understanding of itself as opposed to its others. Hastings was, in effect, accused of having 'gone native' by having allowed the supposedly unrestrained wealth, luxury and power of the East to corrupt him. Clearly, the project to govern India according to its own standards would not do, for it threatened to undermine the distinction between what was now regarded as the corrupt, degenerate, voluptuous, seductive East, and, on the other hand, what was now regarded as the honest, forthright, morally superior West, of which Britain was taken to be the exemplar. Clearly, the East could no longer be seen as 'the nurse of sciences, the inventress of delightful and useful arts'; as a gigantic source of wealth that the British could now tap with less and less restraint as their power over it grew, it was instead to be regarded as a source of contamination threatening to the very well-being of the Western and British self who sought to know and to rule it. Whereas for Jones and Hastings knowledge of the other – of the sheer difference of the other – was a source of self-enrichment, for those who overturned their approach what was different was merely a threat that had to be kept under strict control lest it overwhelm the precarious sense of self defined against it. More than ever before, the Orient assumed the role of an immense geo-cultural and geo-political abstraction; it still needed to be known and held in submission, but the knowledge and power used to control it now took an entirely different direction than that proposed by the (equally imperialist) agenda of Jones and Hastings.

This dramatic change in attitude was thus reflected in equally dramatic changes in imperial policy; modifications to the East India Company charter that were first instituted in 1793 were confirmed and strengthened in 1813. English, not Persian or Sanskrit, would henceforth take priority; India would be ruled according to English rules, not Indian ones; and with the changes mandated in 1813 missionaries were for the first time allowed into India – having been strictly excluded according to the affirmation of cultural difference that had dominated the Hastings approach to colonial rule. All these changes would ultimately lead to Macaulay's *Minute on Indian Education*. For by Macaulay's time it seemed obvious that although there was much that needed to be learned *about* the Orient in order to control it, there was nothing whatsoever worth learning *from* the Orient, least of all for the cultural improvement of the West. On the contrary, the imperialist project now involved teaching rather than that kind of learning which had been essential to Hastings' own imperial policies. Instead of an approach to colonial administration based on teaching Englishmen to assimilate themselves into Indian culture (which had led to the charges of corruption and degradation levelled against Hastings, a man allegedly properly British on the outside but monstrously Oriental on the inside), what was called for by the time of Macaulay's *Minute* was an approach that would allow the creation of

Indians who could be assimilated into *British* culture and thereby serve the empire. In view of the practical difficulty of ruling hundreds of millions of Indians with a relatively small number of colonial administrators, 'We must at present do our best', Macaulay himself would argue, 'to form a class who may be interpreters between us and the millions whom we govern; a class of persons, Indian in blood and colour, but English in taste, in opinions, in morals, and in intellect' (*Macaulay*, p. 249). This was, clearly, the complete inversion of the approach taken by Hastings and Jones just over a couple of decades earlier. Difference would henceforth be confronted and challenged, rewritten and obliterated wherever possible; sameness – or to be precise 'our' newly-discovered sameness – must rule the day.

In the colonial arena itself, this seems at first a fairly straightforward proposition. But ultimately what happened in the colonial realm, including the dramatic changes in colonial policy during and after the trial of Warren Hastings, cannot meaningfully be separated from the much broader cultural and political process of self-definition taking place, beginning long before Macaulay's *Minute*, in areas far removed from direct contact with colonial otherness. If the Orient became an obsession in late eighteenth-century British culture – which it did – it was in ways which, even with the work of Sir William Jones appearing in fresh editions, had increasingly little to do with the Orient itself (even the Orient as a cultural and political construction rather than an actual place).[8] Knowledge of the other, whose role was paramount in the imperial policies of Jones and Hastings, was by the 1790s increasingly regarded as at best useless and at worst positively dangerous. However, with this, the Orient would now serve not merely as a source of innocuously entertaining themes and images, as it had been earlier in the eighteenth century, but other, much more profound, purposes. The sense of danger, corruption, sensuality, eroticism, exoticism now associated with it – and these were all novel associations for a region that had once been thought of as dirty, austere, bestial, unrefined, even somewhat natural in the worst pre-Romantic sense of that term (for Henry Maundrell, for example, is was precisely the *lack* of 'art and design', the preponderance of 'Dirt and Nastiness', that defined Eastern culture) – made the Orient more than merely an imaginary zone reflecting back to Britain all that it was not; it also came to reflect back to Britain an image of all that it might be, all that it might have been, all that it might become – for better *and* for worse.

By the Romantic period, then, the Orient was an imaginary site grounding deeply ambivalent thoughts, feelings, fears and desires. Though they may have had in the Orient a kind of focal point, such feelings, fears, and desires in fact permeated Romanticism through and through, even those varieties of Romanticism that on the surface of it had nothing to do with the Orient at all. In fact, although they are most readily associated with the Lake District and nature poetry, it is no coincidence that each of the major poets of the Romantic period (with the notable exception of William Blake) had at least a passing flirtation with Orientalism, if not a full-blown Orientalist phase. For almost all the writers and artists of the period, the Orient provided an important point of reference for cultural or political difference, and for many it offered an essential component in the formation of a literary career ('stick to the East', Byron advised Thomas Moore). Following Sir William Jones's translations from and imitations of poetry in Arabic, Persian, and Sanskrit, a staggering variety of explicitly Orientalist works were published in the late eighteenth and early nineteenth centuries, including (other than texts that we have already mentioned, and many others besides) Robert Bage's *Fair Syrian* (1787), Cornelia Knight's *Dinarbas* (1790), Samuel Taylor Coleridge's *Kubla Khan* (written 1798, published 1816), Richard Johnson's *Oriental Moralist*, Charlotte Dacre's *Zofloya* (1806), Robert Southey's *Curse of Kehama* (1810), most of the best work of Lord Byron, Percy Shelley's *Alastor* (1815), 'Ozymandias' (1817), *The Revolt of Islam* (1818), and Thomas de Quincey's *Confessions of an English Opium-Eater* (1822).

In offering for sale his own 'samples of the finest Orientalism', however, Byron would scornfully distinguish his own interest in foreignness and exoticism from the nature poetry of Wordsworth, Southey, Coleridge and Keats. But it would be a mistake to accept the contrast posed by Byron without hesitation. For the Orient provided much more than merely an occasional thematic device for Romanticism. On the contrary, the persistent presence of Orientalist references, gestures and subtexts, even in forms of discourse that on the face of it have nothing to do with the East at all – for example, Nature poetry – suggests that Orientalism helped to define political, social and cultural practices in areas far removed from the East itself, and that it played an essential role in the consolidation of a British sense of self. For ultimately the new strand of Orientalism that began to emerge alongside Romanticism through the 1790s and on into the 1800s cannot meaningfully be separated from highly politically-charged discussions of the status and rights of the individual, and from a process of self-definition that extended far beyond the 'anxieties of empire' that have been most clearly elaborated specifically in terms of the Orient itself.[9] Given that the status, the rights and duties of the individual self provided the dominant political and cultural theme of the decade following the French Revolution, insofar as it became tied up with the question of self-definition, Orientalism was hardly just a thematic 'sideshow' for Romantic poetry. Implicitly if not explicitly, it saturated most forms of writing in the Romantic period – it became something of a structuring principle for cultural thought and political thought.

We can measure this significance in considering, for example, the role of Orientalist discourse in the explosion through the 1790s of writing on self-determination and the 'rights of man'. In the hands of writers like Tom Paine, Mary Wollstonecraft, and John Thelwall, the radical critique of the old regime and its culture of corruption and tradition helped to define an emergent culture of modernization based on a universalist discourse of individual rights and duties, rather than inherited privileges; a discourse of individual merit, rather than religious inspiration; and a discourse of sturdy frugality, control, virtue and linguistic as well as psychic self-regulation, rather than emotional and sensual excess. By the 1790s, the Orient would be recognized as the ultimate locus of the culture of excess – despotic, enthusiastic, sensual, exotic, erotic – that was the target of such radicalism. Hence it served as an ideal surrogate target for radical critique, an imaginary space on which to project all the supposed faults of the old regime and then subject them to attack. Indeed, the radicals sought to locate and articulate a middle-class sensibility as against the unruly excesses of both higher *and* lower orders. As Anna Clark argues, this tendency to articulate middle-class values would in fact eventually abandon radicalism as 'the "progressive and improving" middle class distanced itself even more from both the "effete aristocracy and the licentious rabble"'.[10] In the meantime, however, in warning of the dangers of excess, radical writers would repeatedly invoke the Orient as the clearest illustration of what they meant. For the supposed characteristics of Oriental society and culture were projected on to the aristocratic enemies of the radical cause ('the proud and polished, the debauched, effeminate, and luxurious'[11]) while at the same time the Oriental seraglio was seen as the dark cousin of the aristocratic palace, both oozing degeneration, corruption and filth into the society at large.

Thus, for example, in addressing itself 'to those in the middle class, because they appear to be in the most natural state', Mary Wollstonecraft's *Vindication of the Rights of Woman* opposes itself not only to an upper class made up of 'weak, artificial beings, raised above the common wants and affections of their race', who, 'in premature unnatural manner, undermine the very foundation of virtue, and spread corruption through the whole mass of society', but also, quite explicitly, to a discourse of the 'seraglio', and hence to all those Oriental despots supposedly indulging in the pleasures of their seraglios, to 'Mahometanism', to Eastern and Islamic culture in general – none of which, on the face of it, ought to have anything to do with the question of women's rights in England.[12] Such an attack on the East would seem entirely gratuitous were it not for the fact that the very same vocabulary (corruption, contagion, disease, debauchery, idleness, weakness, unnaturalness, degeneration, effeminacy) was being used throughout the period to denounce both aristocratic *and* Oriental degeneracy. In fact, though the *Vindication* is intended primarily as an attack on aristocratic corruption in Europe, an explicitly Orientist discourse provides the rhetorical and ideological foundation for Wollstonecraft's broader argument – so much so that the superstructural argument is inseparable from its Orientalist base. At the very beginning of the *Vindications*, for example, Wollstonecraft dismisses 'those pretty feminine phrases' and 'that weak elegancy of mind, exquisite sensibility, and sweet docility of manners, supposed to be the sexual characteristics of the weaker vessel'. Refusing to 'polish' her style, and hoping 'rather to persuade by the force of my arguments than to dazzle by the elegance of my language', she says that she will not waste her time 'in rounding periods, or in fabricating the turgid bombast of artificial feelings'. She declares that she will do her best 'to avoid that flowery diction which has slided from essays into novels, and from novels into familiar letters and conversations' (pp. 82–3). With all the references to the seraglio and the East in general, it is clear that for Wollstonecraft the most notorious source of that flowery diction, that dazzling elegance, that weak, effeminate language, those 'pretty superlatives, dropping glibly from the tongue', which 'vitiate the taste, and create a kind of sickly delicacy that turns away from simple unadorned truth', is the Orient. In seeking to articulate a contrasting, explicitly 'manly', discourse of sober, natural, unembellished individual rights and duties, then, Wollstonecraft uses the Orient as a foil.

Wollstonecraft was certainly not alone in her appropriation of the trope of Asiatic despotism in order to articulate an argument in favour of the manly Western subject, and the rights and duties of what must now be recognized as a specifically Western mode of citizenship, which was taken to be not only incompatible with the soft languid emotionalism and unproductive luxurious pleasures of the 'unmanly' East, but structurally at odds with it. Moreover, the vindication of a manly, honest, sober, virtuous aesthetic and the concomitant hostility towards the luxury, excess, effeminacy and weakness of which the Orient was taken to be the ultimate example, was not restricted to the explicitly political discourse of radical politics, and not even to the literary works of the famous radicals (for example, William Godwin's *Caleb Williams* (1794) or Wollstonecraft's *Maria* (1798)). Elsewhere in the literary realm, for example, we can trace in Wordsworthian Romanticism an attempt to rescue poetry from being merely 'a matter of amusement and idle pleasure' and a struggle, in the face of a supposedly Oriental 'idleness and unmanly despair', to create an explicitly 'manly' style, available only to the 'sound and vigorous mind' of the very same Western subject addressed in radical writing.[13] Indeed, following in the path of Paine and Wollstonecraft, the self-acknowledged task confronting Wordsworth is the creation of a new kind of taste for a new kind of reader.[14] For if the genius of the Poet represents 'an advance, or a conquest', Wordsworth asks in his 'Essay, Supplementary to the Preface' (1815), 'is it to be supposed that the reader can make progress of this kind, like an Indian prince or general – stretched on his palanquin, and borne by his slaves? No; he is invigorated and inspirited by his leader, in order that he may exert himself; for he cannot proceed in quiescence, he cannot be carried like a dead weight.' Therefore, Wordsworth concludes, 'to create taste is to call forth and bestow *power*, of which knowledge is the effect; and *there* lies the true difficulty'.[15] The difficulty, in other words, lies in creating not just a new kind of taste, but an altogether new kind of reader, an explicitly *Western* reader, who – unlike a lazy and luxuriating Oriental – is capable of the vigorous self-organization and self-discipline that Wordsworth says his poetry requires, and, indeed, calls forth as an expression of 'power, of which knowledge is the effect'.

In fact the first hints of this form of Orientalism, which permeates Romantic-period writing to such an extent that, paradoxically, it may have evaded scholarly recognition for so long precisely *because* it is such an essential feature of the writing, started to appear, though in a somewhat less coherent – and much less consistent – way, even earlier in the eighteenth century. Like Wordsworth's *Lyrical Ballads*, for example, Goldsmith's *The Deserted Village* has nothing obvious to do with the East. On the face of it, the poem is a Tory critique of the depredations and corruptions of the new Whig elite, and it is also sometimes read as articulating a specifically Irish nostalgia. And yet Goldsmith's elegiac narrative of the decline and fall of the village of Auburn is also characterized by what, at least in hindsight, seem remarkably Orientalist features.[16] The village's former 'health and plenty' (line 2) are at first threatened and then finally destroyed by the influx of 'rank luxuriance' (line 351) and 'tumultuous grandeur' (line 321), corrupting influences which would come to be seen as the hallmarks of Oriental despotism. In Auburn, these features are associated not simply with the unnamed 'tyrant's power' (line 76), and not simply with the spread of trade and commerce as opposed to humble peasant toil in the native soil, but specifically with foreign, and even more specifically Eastern, trade and commerce – the trade and commerce of excess and luxury *par excellence*:

> O luxury! thou curst by Heaven's decree,
> How ill exchanged are things like these for thee!
> How do thy potions with insidious joy
> Diffuse their pleasures only to destroy!
> Kingdoms, by thee to sickly greatness grown,

Boast of a florid vigour not their own.
At every draught more large and large they grow,
A bloated mass of rank unwieldy woe;
Till sapped their strength and every part unsound,
Down, down they sink and spread a ruin round.

(lines 385–94)

If 'Ill fares the land, to hastening ills a prey, / Where wealth accumulates and men decay' (lines 51–2), the accumulation of wealth, and the decay of the native British population, are due to the insidious contamination from the East. Thus the nostalgia for a native innocence lost is contrasted with Britain's experience in Oriental imperialism, a contrast that is read into the landscape itself, in the opposition between, on the one hand, the narrator's fading memories of 'The cooling brook, the grassy-vested green, / The breezy covert of the warbling grove, / That only sheltered thefts of harmless love' (lines 360–2), characteristic of the lost innocence of Auburn, and, on the other hand, the 'distant climes' (line 341) where the 'dark scorpion' (line 352) and 'crouching tigers' (line 355) blight a 'ravaged landscape' (line 358). In *The Deserted Village* we may recognize many of the features that would be more famously elaborated by Wordsworth two decades later; but already we may see the traces of Orientalism. Long before Romanticism itself, then, the desire for a sober, healthy, manly, productive, simple, virtuous, natural and above all autonomous Britain was already being contrasted with the threat of excessive, unhealthy, unmanly, unproductive, luxurious, degenerate, unnatural and foreign contamination coming from the East.

Britain's sense of itself as a bulwark of sober, natural, and regulated productivity (as against foreign and especially Oriental contamination and degradation) would develop as a thematic and even a structural concern of British literary and artistic production through the 1780s and 1790s and on well into the nineteenth century. The traces of this structure of feeling were registered in at times quite obvious and at times quite subtle ways. It is precisely such a claim to sobriety that would, for example, lead the narrator of Walter Scott's novel *Waverley* (1814) to warn his readers that he is not inviting them 'into a flying chariot drawn by hyppogriffs, or moved by enchantment'. Instead, Scott's narrator insists, 'Mine is a humble English post-chaise, drawn upon four wheels, and keeping his majesty's highway. Those who dislike the vehicle may leave it at the next halt, and wait for the conveyance of Prince Hussein's tapestry, or Malek the Weaver's flying sentry-box.'[17] We can detect similar claims in Jane Austen's novels as well:

the restoration of order that comes at the end of *Mansfield Park*, for example, involves the reassertion of a newly found set of moral virtues over and against the salacious anarchy and unproductive tumult of aristocratic degeneracy. In fact, it is perhaps most clearly in Austen – perhaps the novelist once least identifiable with the blood and sweat of empire-building – that we can detect the traces of the new-found moralism that would drive the British Empire through the nineteenth century.

For we have to remember that the earlier British empire was quite uninterested in moral matters, as we see not just in the work of the East India Company but also in the thriving plantations of the West Indies. Colonialism only became a major moral issue during the lifetime of Jane Austen. The transition towards a form of imperial domination in which moral questions, and specifically the imposition of 'our' glorious civilization, manners, morals, virtues, religion, way of life on other cultures took place all through the decades around 1800 (one of the key signs of this transition was the trial of Warren Hastings). Once it had successfully abandoned slavery (thanks not only to the domestic campaign but also to the ferocious resistance put up by the slaves themselves), the new British empire would use the moral virtues as the spearhead of new imperial adventures, which lends added force to William Blake's furious assertion that 'The Moral Virtues are continual Accusers of Sin & promote Eternal Wars & *Domineering over others*.'[18] For it was precisely in the name of moral virtues – the sweetness of temper, purity of mind, and excellence of principles – that *Mansfield Park* celebrates in Fanny, that the British empire itself would ransack the world, at home as well as overseas, looking for the sources of 'barbarism' in order to stamp and burn them out and replace them with sober, productive, efficient – and above all respectably proper – prosperity, precisely as we see when Sir Thomas goes through his estate after his return from Antigua, organizing, computing, calculating, and moralizing, burning every copy of *Lovers' Vows* that he could find and erasing every trace of the aborted performance that was put on in his absence from England.

There would, of course, be resistance to these tendencies, not only from across the empire but in Britain as well. Especially in the transitional moment of the 1790s, a burgeoning plebeian internationalism – in which the work of Blake must be situated alongside that of people like Robert Wedderburn, Daniel Isaac Eaton and others – posed a dire threat not only to the established order but also to the morally virtuous form of radicalism which opposed it. And even in the age of Austen and Scott, Lord Byron and others would mourn the withering away of an Oriental other, in whose sense of cultural difference they had felt a kind of welcome alienation from the much more severe estrangement they were already feeling in a United Kingdom basking securely in the warm glow of moral virtue.

NOTES

1. 'Minute on Indian Education', in *Thomas Babington Macaulay: Selected Writings*, ed. John Clive and Thomas Pinney (Chicago: Chicago University Press, 1972), p. 241.
2. See Nigel Leask, '"Wandering through Eblis": absorption and containment in Romantic exoticism', in Tim Fulford and Peter Kitson (eds.), *Romanticism and Colonialism: Writing and Empire, 1780–1830* (Cambridge: Cambridge University Press, 1998), pp. 164–88.
3. See Edward Said, *Orientalism* (London: Routledge, 1978).
4. Warren Hastings, 'Introductory Letter', in Charles Wilkins (trans.), *The Bhagvad-Geeta, or Dialogues of Kreeshna and Arjoon* (1785), pp. 12–13.
5. Sir William Jones, 'A Discourse on the Institution of a Society, for Enquiring into the History, Civil and Natural, the Antiquities, Arts, Sciences, Literature, of Asia', in *The Works of Sir William Jones*, 6 vols. (1799), 1: 2.
6. Raymond Schwab, *The Oriental Renaissance: Europe's Rediscovery of India and the East, 1680–1880*, trans. G. Patterson-Black and V. Reinking (New York: Columbia University Press, 1984), p. 23.
7. See, however, Martin Bernal, *Black Athena: The Afroasiatic Roots of Classical Civilization* (New Brunswick: Rutgers University Press, 1987).
8. See Said, *Orientalism*.
9. See Nigel Leask, *British Romantic Writers and the East: Anxieties of Empire* (Cambridge: Cambridge University Press, 1992).
10. Anna Clark, *The Struggle for the Breeches: Gender and the Making of the British Working Class* (Berkeley: University of California Press, 1995), p. 152.
11. John Thelwall, 'Rights of Britons', in Gregory Claeys (ed.), *The Politics of English Jacobinism: Writings of John Thelwall* (University Park: Pennsylvania State University Press, 1995), p. 473.
12. Mary Wollstonecraft, *A Vindication of the Rights of Woman*, ed. Miriam Brody (Harmondsworth: Penguin, 1992), p. 81.
13. William Wordsworth, 1800 *Preface* to *Lyrical Ballads* (see Wordsworth and Coleridge, *Lyrical Ballads* (London: Routledge, 1991)), pp. 257, 263, 266.
14. Wordsworth is of course fully aware of the extent to which, as he himself says, 'every author, as far as he is great and at the same time *original*, has had the task of *creating* the taste by which he is to be enjoyed'. See his 'Essay, Supplementary to the Preface', in *William Wordsworth: Selected Prose*, ed. John Hayden (Harmondsworth: Penguin, 1988), pp. 387–413 (p. 408).
15. Wordsworth, 'Essay', p. 410. Emphasis added.
16. *The Poems of Thomas Gray, William Collins, Oliver Goldsmith*, ed. Roger Lonsdale (London: Longman, 1976), pp. 669–94.
17. Sir Walter Scott, *Waverley*, ed. Claire Lamont (Oxford: Oxford University Press, 1986), p. 24.
18. William Blake, 'Annotations to Berkeley's *Siris*', in *Complete Poetry and Prose of William Blake*, ed. David Erdman (New York: Anchor Books, 1989), p. 664. Emphases added.

FURTHER READING

Colley, Linda, *Britons: Forging the Nation, 1707–1837*, New Haven: Yale University Press, 1992.

Captives: Britain, Empire, and the World, 1600–1850, London: Jonathan Cape, 2002.

Davis, Leith, *Acts of Union: Scotland and the Literary Negotiation of the British Nation, 1707–1830*, Stanford: Stanford University Press, 1998.

Drew, John, *India and the Romantic Imagination*, Oxford: Oxford University Press, 1987.

Fulford, Tim, and Peter Kitson (eds.), *Romanticism and Imperialism: Writing and Empire, 1780–1830*, Cambridge: Cambridge University Press, 1998.

Leask, Nigel, *British Romantic Writers and the East: Anxieties of Empire*, Cambridge: Cambridge University Press, 1992.

Majeed, Javed, *Ungoverned Imaginings: James Mill's The History of British India and Orientalism*, Oxford: Oxford University Press, 1992.

Makdisi, Saree, *Romantic Imperialism: Universal Empire and the Culture of Modernity*, Cambridge: Cambridge University Press, 1998.

Pratt, Mary Louise, *Imperial Eyes: Travel Writing and Transculturation*, London: Routledge, 1992.

Said, Edward, *Orientalism*, London: Routledge, 1978.

Schwab, Raymond, *The Oriental Renaissance: Europe's Rediscovery of India and the East, 1680–1880*, trans. Gene Patterson-Black and Victor Reinking, New York: Columbia University Press, 1984.

Teltscher, Kate, *India Inscribed: European and British Writing on India 1600–1800*, Oxford: Oxford University Press, 1995.

Trumpener, Katie, *Bardic Nationalism: The Romantic Novel and the British Empire*, Princeton: Princeton University Press, 1997.

Viswanathan, Gauri, *Masks of Conquest: Literary Study and British Rule in India*, London: Faber and Faber, 1989.

5

SUSAN MANNING

Sensibility

The reputation of the eighteenth-century literature of Sensibility[1] has never quite recovered from its embarrassing association with displays of unmeasured, extravagant emotion. It was 'excessive'. This was not simply distaste for a fading fashion; these are the terms in which it was criticized by some of its major practitioners, and they offer a key to this highly formulaic, but inherently unstable, kind of writing. Consider three scenes. In the first, a father enters with his dead daughter in his arms:

> Howl, howl, howl! O! you are men of stones:
> Had I your tongue and eyes, I'd use them so
> That heaven's vault should crack. She's gone for ever.
> I know when one is dead, and when one lives. . . .
> I might have sav'd her; now she's gone for ever!
> Cordelia, Cordelia! Stay a little. Ha!
> What is't thou say'st? Her voice was ever soft,
> Gentle and low, an excellent thing in woman.[2]

In the second, a father confronts his disowned daughter, who has fallen from virtue:

> His daughter was now prostrate at his feet. 'Strike,' said she, 'strike here a wretch, whose misery cannot end but with that death she deserves.' Her hair had fallen on her shoulders! her look had the horrid calmness of outbreathed despair! Her father would have spoken; his lip quivered, his cheek grew pale! his eyes lost the lightening of their fury! there was a reproach in them, but with a mingling of pity! He turned them up to heaven – then on his daughter. – He laid his left hand on his heart – the sword dropped from his right – he burst into tears.
> . . . 'Speak,' said he, addressing himself to his daughter; speak, I will hear thee.' – The desperation that supported her was lost; she fell to the ground, and bathed his feet with her tears![3]

The third evokes the death of another young girl through the responses of her closest companion:

> The old man held one languid arm in his, and had the small hand tight folded to his breast, for warmth. It was the hand she had stretched out to him with her last smile – the hand that had led him on, through all their wanderings. Ever and anon he pressed it to his lips; then hugged it to his breast again, murmuring that it was warmer now; and, as he said it, he looked, in agony, to those who stood around . . .
>
> 'It is not,' said the schoolmaster, as he . . . gave his tears free vent, 'it is not on earth that Heaven's justice ends. Think what earth is, compared, with the World to which her young spirit has winged its early flight . . .'4

In all three, maximum emotional capital is generated from extreme suffering. Spectators and readers are called to witness exclamation becoming declamation, grief modulating to self-pity, stoicism to emotional abandon. All are scenes in which the suffering dyad is observed by another who stands in the narrative for the audience, and through whose responses the unbearable expression of emotion is mediated. Only the second of these passages, from Henry Mackenzie's *The Man of Feeling* (1771), is usually associated with 'Sensibility', and it is so because feeling is represented as exceeding the capacity of language to express it, and is superseded by gesture. Lear's speech brings tragic recognition and unmitigated pathos into overwhelming dramatic immediacy; despite the presence of Kent on stage, a modern audience is not shielded from its impact in production (though, ironically, a bowdlerized ending prevented eighteenth-century theatre-goers from experiencing it). In the death-scene of Little Nell from Dickens's *The Old Curiosity Shop* (1841), Sensibility – to later readers at least – has unmistakably modulated into sentimental moralizing; Oscar Wilde famously quipped, 'One must have a heart of stone to read the death of Little Nell without laughing.'5

Literary history has placed Sensibility as a transitional phase of mid eighteenth-century writing, between the decline of neo-classical 'Reason' and the eruption of Romantic 'Imagination'. It identifies characteristic features including anti-rationalism, a focus on emotional response and somatized reactions (tears, swoons, deathly pallor), a prevailing mood of melancholy, fragmentation of form, and set-piece scenes of virtue in distress. But all these features, in isolation or in combination, occur not only in Shakespeare and Dickens, but also in works by representative neo-classical and Romantic writers. The heroine of Alexander Pope's Ovidian epistle 'Eloisa to Abelard' (1717), for example, whose fictional afterlife in the literature of Sensibility was substantial, was not being wholly satirized when she uttered her body's expressions of abandonment:

> Still rebel nature holds out half my heart
> Nor prayers nor fasts its stubborn pulse restrain,
> Nor tears for ages taught to flow in vain. . . .
> Oh name for ever sad, for ever dear,
> Still breathed in sighs, still ushered with a tear . . .
> Line after line my gushing eyes o-erflow,
> Led through a sad variety of woe.[6]

Similar embodied distress is evoked in Coleridge's 'Letter to Sara Hutchinson' (1802):

> Methinks to weep with you
> Were better far than to rejoice alone –
> But that my coarse domestic life has known
> No Habits of self-nursing Sympathy . . .[7]

Both of these employ the discursive counters that characterize the 'moment of Sensibility'; neither can be accommodated within its normal literary-historical parameters. Richardson was certainly employing many of its features in the 1740s; Dickens relied on their persistent emotional appeal to readers well into the 1840s. Any definition by itemized characteristics is a fiction of taxonomy, and the broader time-frame of this volume allows us to take a catholic view of Sensibility, as a system of relations and ruptures, part of a fluctuating but continuous repertoire in emotional representation.

As identity posited on itemized characteristics is a fiction, so (David Hume pointed out in 1740) is the notion of a continuum: both are ways of making sense of the otherwise fearfully random appearance of phenomena to perception. In the face of uncertainty, as Hume's own highly sceptical analysis made plain, attentive analysis succumbs to the desire for narrative, and the untidy or disturbing elements of literary texts tend to be subsumed within the neater explanations of History. Certainly, any story of Sensibility must start by recognizing its affinities with other contemporary impulses, literary, cultural, and ideological. Because Sensibility, as Julie Ellison has put it, was 'a transaction, not a character type' or a checklist of features, it could be enlisted to a range of eighteenth-century debates from (as I shall suggest) patriotism to personal conduct, slave ownership to sexual morality.[8]

The eighteenth-century study of sensibility was part of what Mackenzie described as 'the science of manners'.[9] As a literary mode it embodied an experimental approach to character based on Hume's acceptance of the ubiquity of the passions as motivators to action: 'Morality . . . is more properly felt than judg'd of'; sympathy is 'the chief source of moral distinctions'.[10] Where Descartes had reasoned on the basis of analytic separation of mind and body, Scottish Enlightenment writers attempting to realize a comprehensive 'Science of Man' realigned the moral and physical selves. Drawing on a well-established eighteenth-century tradition of psycho-physiological thinking in Anglo-Scottish thought, Alexander Munro located sensibility in the physiological organization of the nervous system; his *Structure and Function of the Nervous System* (1783) analysed the position and function of the 'great sympathetic nerve' running through the spinal column, connecting and transmitting messages from all over the body. The embodiment of sensibility in masculine or feminine persons, its precise somatic location and expression, and the possibility that class and ethical distinction were physically manifest (in for, example, a highly 'refined' nervous organization), were all matters of inquiry that connect Freud's nineteenth-century re-conceptualizing of hysteria with Lear's '*hysterica passio*' (II.iv.55), the smothering, choking sensation occasioned by rising of the womb into the throat. Nerves were compared to musical strings vibrating in company, an analogy elaborated by James Beattie in *An Essay on Poetry and Music* (1776). In 1759, Alexander Gerard articulated an orthodox, and powerful, compound of ethical and aesthetic value: 'In order to form a fine taste, the mental powers which compose it must possess exquisite *sensibility* and delicacy.'[11] Wordsworth's 'sensations sweet, / Felt in the blood, and felt along the heart', and Keats's 'true voice of feeling', the only proof of 'axioms in philosophy' being registered 'upon our pulses', are closely aligned with this psycho-physiological theory.[12]

Sensibility also functioned as a kind of social cement that holds individuals together in a moralized and emotionalized public sphere, through a 'language [of] the heart' that 'strengthens the bond of society, and attracts individuals from their private system to exert themselves in acts of generosity and benevolence'.[13] Both the ethical theory of sympathy and the literature which tested, elaborated and complicated it depended on propriety. Adam Smith's *Theory of Moral Sentiments* (1759) described it as the regulatory impulse that underpinned personal security, protection of property, and pleasure in self-reflection and sympathetic relationships. If the passions motivated human behaviour, propriety directed otherwise wayward and subjective impulses into social channels and protected the stability of societies through time. The assumption that humanity was naturally social, and could best be studied through observation of relationships, was fundamental to the 'Science of Man'. The study of sociability was therefore the basis of Sensibility. The Man of Feeling was a product and an index of 'Civil Society'. He belonged, according to Scottish theory, to a particular phase within a universal model of societal progression, a 'moment' in which a society's economic surplus over subsistence need enabled humanity to cultivate the luxury of emotional expression in relationships. The principle of 'conjectural history', as it came to be called, was that all societies pass through similar stages from barbarism to the civil polity, and that the study of societies of other places and other times provided access to understanding of the history and current state of the British present.

Another Scottish Enlightenment writer, the historian William Robertson, experimented with character-depiction as the agent and focal point of historical change, and by the turn of the nineteenth century novelists were writing the *éducation sentimentale* of their eponymous heroes as 'personified history'. In his Preface to *Fleetwood; or, the New Man of Feeling* (1805), William Godwin insisted that the protagonist's reactions were to be understood in relation to 'such adventures as for the most part have occurred to at least one half of the Englishmen now existing, who are of the same rank of life'.[14] Of overwhelming importance for the subsequent history of the novel was Scott's *Waverley, or 'Tis Sixty Years Since*, also begun in 1805 and published in 1814. These were exemplary 'natural histories' of sentiment, stories of the formation of individual belief systems, on an analogy with the study of the history of 'Civil Society' which was one of the great achievements of the Scottish Enlightenment. Waverley embarks on a sentimental journey from his English home to Lowland Scotland and thence to the furthest fastnesses of the Highlands; his geographical progress corresponds to a journey back in time, in which he encounters pastoral, and then martial, hunter-gathering societies at earlier stages of development than those he has left behind at Waverley-Honour. He also confronts political realities and the real personal consequences of emotional indulgence. In the course of this journey, Waverley is educated out of his naive understanding (the product of a diet of chivalric romances and sentimental novels) of Sensibility as free expression of the feelings into a mature ethical understanding that the emotional basis of action must include prudential reflection on the passionate impulses of the moment. Sympathies initiate moral response; judgement directs it. His progress from passions to prudence stands both as an embodiment of Smithian theory and as an accelerated synecdoche of the history of Britain since the Union of Parliaments in 1707. Scott's later novel *Rob Roy* traced its hero's sentimental education in relation to the world of commercial exchange, as Frank Osbaldistone's trajectory from resistance to participation is interleaved with his physical journey northwards from the Civil Society of London to the feudal barbarity of the Highlands. In both cases, individual progress towards integration takes place against a backdrop of public rebellion (the Jacobite risings of 1745 and 1715); the price of compliance in the public sphere is unrecuperable loss of intense emotional ties.

Sense and Sensibility (1811) is strikingly similar in its pedagogical assumptions. Austen's Elinor Dashwood is a better Smithian than many professional philosophers or economists, and certainly than most exponents of sensibility in fiction. She understands that truly *moral* sentiments involve strenuous stoicism as much as a spontaneous expression of feelings. The novel plays out the implications of the *Theory of Moral Sentiments*: as a condition where emotions exceed words, Sensibility does not belong only to Marianne's sobs, screams and precipitate exits from the drawing room; the inarticulate Edward Ferrars is as much a victim of his feelings as the irrepressibly vocal heroine. In both cases, somatized spectacle supplants language: Marianne's eyes 'expressed the astonishment, which her lips could not utter'; Edward, with a 'complexion white with agitation . . . stammered out an unintelligible reply', the violence of his feelings conveyed by his absent-mindedly spoiling both a pair of scissors and their sheath 'by cutting the latter to pieces' with the former.[15] *She* is disabled as a moral agent by her feelings – 'without any power, because she was without any desire of command over herself' (p. 71); *he* causes confusion and pain through his inability to be sufficiently aware of his own feelings and their effects on Elinor. Smith's *Theory* contained insecurities that were exactly suited to the kinds of inquiry explored in Austen's fiction: the enabler of sociability, sensibility often seemed to lead instead to incapacity to participate effectively in society. Strong private emotions did not readily accommodate to what Hannah More described in *Sensibility: A Poetical Epistle* (1782) as 'the social sympathy, the sense humane'.[16]

The 'history of ideas' approach to understanding the novel of Sensibility works best in relation to fictional 'histories of sentiment' like Scott's or Austen's. Its implicit ranking of forms of knowledge (philosophy placed 'above' and anterior to fiction) is problematic, however, as are its inherent gendering and power relations ('ideas' are public, masculine, inaugural; novels are private, feminine, responsive and secondary). There is, too, a more general question about the transferability of knowledge from one genre to another: a moral sentiment as described in a philosophical treatise becomes something quite different when embodied in character, plot and transmitted through the commercial transactions of publication. Having registered this, it seems important not simply to substitute another master-narrative – of cultural politics, gender definition or emancipation – for that of intellectual history. Here again it may be helpful to think of Sensibility as transactional rather than elemental in character, belonging to many stories. But common to them all is a formal investigation into the viability of narrative itself, in relation to the expression of emotion.

The represented 'scene' of sympathetic engagement is characteristically followed either by the protagonist's recollection in tranquillity or by a narrator's or observer's connected account: the 'history', in other words, of the moment. Both Waverley and Elinor Dashwood are represented as experiencing moments of overwhelming feeling, which can nonetheless be subsumed in the narrative of sociability. But the immediacy of emotional connection (it was typically described in a lexicon of 'wounds', piercings, and transfixings) troubled connected exposition. Sensibility was experienced, observed, and lost again in the moment of contact; in this sense it had and could have no 'history'. If Sensibility as a narrative mode was a product of the evolutionary and progressive assumptions of the eighteenth-century 'Science of Man', it also challenged them. Typically invested in 'scenes' rather than continuous stories, its narrative signature was (both structurally and syntactically) disjunctive, fragmentary.[17] The fictional experience was simultaneously a connecting and a disconnected one. It brought readers (or spectators) and protagonists together in a community of feeling, but in separated episodes authenticated, as the contemporary commentator Vicesimus Knox noted, by that which 'cannot be pointed out by verbal description, and which can only be perceived by the vibrations it produces on the nervous system'.[18] Its symptomatic physical experience also tended, as Ann Yearsley's 'To Indifference' intoned, to be opposed to abstract thought:

> IDEA, smother'd, leaves my mind a waste,
> Where SENSIBILITY must lose her prey.[19]

In Henry Mackenzie's *Julia de Roubigné* (1777), the heroine's 'very thoughts are not accurate representations of what [she] feel[s]'; she senses 'something busy about my heart which I cannot reduce into thinking'.[20] Her epistolary description of this failure is subsequently enacted in the text, as the conventions of correspondence give way to the broken exclamations of melodrama which link it with the 'unspeakable' horror at the heart of Romantic dramas such as Shelley's *The Cenci* (1819) or Byron's *Manfred* (1817).

The pervasive success of the literature of Sensibility can only be understood through its slippery relation to the declared pedagogical function of literature in the eighteenth century. Fiction's capacity to deliver instructive visions of virtue rewarded and vice confounded was repeatedly adduced to justify its questionable tendency to represent (in the language of Swift's rational animals the Houyhnhnms) *the thing which was not*.[21] Educating the passions rather than inflaming them, displaying the 'proper' degree of sensibility, in conjunction with virtue, was the function of the fictional 'impartial spectator' in Smith's *Moral Sentiments*, who sympathized with passionate encounters without succumbing to them.[22] But expressed intention is not the same thing as effect; readerly satisfaction related treacherously to didactic fables, and only tangentially to aesthetic quality. It was evident to commentators, practitioners and consumers alike, that while the theory of the literature of Sensibility was about instruction, the practice – what kept people actually *reading* it – had more to do with pleasure. As Mackenzie himself pointed out, 'it cannot always be said that [such novels] are equally calculated to improve as to delight' (*Works*, v: 179). The non-improving pleasures of sympathy, those aspects of response that could not be described as edifying, were sanitized in proportion as they were perceived to be dangerous.

Hume's *Treatise* had re-expressed sympathy and sensibility as principles of connection (p. 228). A character in *Fleetwood* accounts for his patriotism on the grounds that 'the human mind irresistibly wishes to connect itself with something' (p. 197); Sensibility was enlisted in historiography in interesting, and conflicting, ways, as historians reconstructed affecting national stories of heroines like Mary Queen of Scots (the subject of a series of passionate Romantic dramas of Sensibility), and encouraged affective investment in relics from the past. The pleasures of Sensibility were linked to perception intensified in momentary sensation: iterative and indefinitely renewable, but not able to be subsumed within larger explanatory paradigms of connected narrative. Sensibility simultaneously subscribed to and resisted philosophical history, embodying in its characteristic forms loss and melancholy as the inevitable price of progress in the world of Civil Society. It exulted in the particularity of sympathy in local and particular relations, extolling connection, and embodying its rupture. Antiquarian collections, like fictions of Sensibility, were committed to a public narrative of connection, but their actual attraction lay more in sequence without development, private pleasures rather than public utility. The objects of family history promised connection with the past, but their contemplation invoked a sense of loss rather than progress; the activity was denigrated by its association with excess and solipsistic or miserly pleasures, and the figure of the antiquary gloating over his collection was familiar in caricature. Sensibility featured heroes who had been rendered morbidly misanthropic through excessive emotional investment, and who drew generic characteristics from the 'humourists' of Renaissance writing: Smollett's Matthew Bramble in *Humphry Clinker* (1771), for example, or – more analytically – Godwin's Fleetwood. The virtue of such figures was measured by their abhorrence of 'the society of man in general' (*Fleetwood*, p. 59); they were impotent benevolists. *Fleetwood* makes clear that a career in business offers unique opportunity for 'extensive . . . power of relieving distress, of exciting industry, of developing talents' and 'supplying means of improvement' – all of which are denied to men in retirement (p. 194). From the 1770s the hero or heroine of Sensibility delighted in 'Nature' rather than in cities or in company. Apart, that is, from the yearning desire for perfect, untroubled sympathetic communication with a single soul-mate. In ironic acknowledgement of the vicissitudes of human interaction, the 'affectionate friend' (*Fleetwood*, p. 68) in the literature and art of Sensibility was commonly a dog.

An inherently theatrical literary mode, Sensibility was rhapsodic both in its tendency to disconnect utterance from logical sequence, and in its essentially ecstatic organization. Feeling is in excess of the needs of narrative in representation, and therefore tends to subvert its explicatory power. Even Richardson's story of Clarissa, as Samuel Johnson put it, was 'only giving occasion to the sentiment'.[23] The literature of Sensibility was characteristically self-referential; its fictional plots embroiled in meta-fictional discussions about both the conditions of virtue and of storytelling. The fragments of *The Man of Feeling* presuppose a once-connected, now ruined narrative savaged by the violent shredding which transforms it to fodder for a curate's gun. It is an image of the untranslatability of emotion from the language of the heart to the language of the page. Fragments are survivors of a failed story: 'turbulent passions,' wrote Lord Kames, 'require an expression both rough and broken' (*Elements*, I: 211). This mutilation is a feature of utterance imagined as solitary and dissociated, which at first sight sits oddly with Sensibility's standing as a social connective. The emotional authenticity so crucial to the ethos was most effectively demonstrated by corruption of narrative, and of expression. If the politics of style invoked the socially coercive ethic of Sensibility, it also indexed 'true' self-expression. In form and structure, then, the *literature* of Sensibility tended to challenge measure and propriety, and (at least implicitly) teleological narratives of progress. The fragmentary form of novels like *The Man of Feeling* and 'epic' like the rediscovered 'Ossianic' verse emphasized the failure (or perhaps refusal) of sympathy to connect, develop, or progress; its basic organizational mode was taxonomic rather than analytic. Representing the insufficiencies of language in words, the fiction of sensibility supplemented storytelling by graphic elements such as Sterne's celebrated black and blank pages, and Mackenzie's asterisks, dashes, liberal use of exclamation marks, signs of mutilation and fragmentation which drew attention to the illusory nature of connected narration. This is, in Jerome McGann's words, performative rather than constative writing.[24] *A Sentimental Journey* (1768) breaks off with a bookish joke that creates a classic double-entendre: 'So that when I stretch'd out my hand, I caught hold of the Fille de Chambre's / END OF VOL. II.'[25]

Genre always exerts pressure on theory; 'Moral Sense' was distorted into excess by its embodiment in character and scene. The appropriateness of a theatrical vocabulary of 'scene' and 'representation' highlights an affinity that would hasten Sensibility's subsequent devaluation in the hierarchy of literary-historical modes. Its readily parodied rhapsodic style adheres to an expressionist aesthetic which defies measure (whether in the shape of stoic restraint, or of poetic metre) and explanation. Where History's generic affiliations were with tragedy, the disjointed 'frame by frame' representation in performance and substitution of bodily gesture and expression for verbal articulacy that guaranteed the authenticity of 'true feeling' associated Sensibility with melodrama, which specializes (as Peter Brooks has put it) in 'visual summary of the emotional situation'.[26] It is helpful, in fact, to regard Sensibility as the repressed face of melodrama; where the latter unbridles expression, the former strangulates it to intensify emotional effect. While the ethical standing of Sensibility might be defended by emphasizing its didactic and pedagogical orientation – the education of the passions was its 'business' – its actual impact inclined towards emotion that exceeded utility. The heroine of melodrama is a victim who must suffer but cannot learn. Her pain is expression without sublimation for either character or audience; emotional analysis is performed as gestural sequence. Nor is it contained – as Pope's Eloisa's self-dramatizing outbursts assuredly are – in the wit of form, where the conventions of the Ovidian epistle allowed latitude for direct expression of a heroine's most abandoned feelings in tightly controlled heroic couplets. Mackenzie's *Julia de Roubigné* was, according to Walter Scott, moved by 'the excess and over-indulgence of passions and feelings, in themselves blameless, nay praiseworthy, but which, indulged to morbid excess, and coming into fatal though fortuitous concourse with each other, lead to a most disastrous consequence'.[27] Scott aligned Mackenzie's intentions with 'actual life'; but the resulting fiction transformed the psychological revelations of its epistolary conventions to melodrama: hero and heroine were represented in increasingly stagey terms which referred itself to readers' familiarity with extremes of Shakespearian tragic expression and put the scene of suffering at the centre of the novel. The extravagant jealousy of Othello, interpreted as the overwhelming of social sympathies by immoderate passion, was reworked in a number of fictions of Sensibility, including *Julia* and *Fleetwood*.

In American writing of the post-Revolutionary period Sensibility metamorphosed perhaps even more readily into melodrama, as established ethical and narrative models were exposed to new social conditions. At the first test of her virtue – a test she is destined to fail without effective struggle – the heroine of Susanna Rowson's *Charlotte Temple* (1791; 1794) seals her own fate by the excess of her response: 'it is not too late to recede from the brink of a precipice, from which I can only behold the dark abyss of ruin, shame, and remorse!'[28] Simply to articulate her dilemma in this way is to slide into the rhetorical world of excess in which her ruin is guaranteed. So the 'unguarded step' of Rousseau's Julie spells – in her eyes – irrevocable ruin:

'I have fallen into the abyss of shame from which a girl never returns.'[29] Similarly, in the ambivalent first-person narrative of Charles Brockden Brown's *Wieland* (1798), Clara comes within one step of the 'abyss', 'hurrying to the verge of the same gulf', drawn into a nightmare world of murderous excess by the misleading evidence of her senses.[30] This 'single step' – elsewhere, in this highly formulaic mode, a 'precipice' (*Fleetwood*, p. 61) – is interesting. It is the step that must (the ethical imperative) be resisted, but cannot be. The narrative imperative is that it be taken: without Charlotte's 'fall', there will be no exemplary tale for the reader to sympathize with and the narrator to moralize over. It is also the fulcrum on which sensibility tips irrevocably over into excess and melodrama. The didactic (narrative, third person) and the expressive (emotive, first person) impulses of sensibility are fundamentally at odds.

The potentially voyeuristic and self-gratifying implications of the literature of Sensibility posed a particular problem for critics. It was perceived to inflame conflicting passions in a way that had led Plato famously to banish poets from his ideal *Republic*; on these grounds Wollstonecraft castigated its pernicious effect on women's education in Civil Society:

> Novels . . . tend to make women the creatures of sensation, and their character is thus formed in the mould of folly. . . . This overstretched sensibility naturally relaxes the other powers of the mind, and prevents intellect from attaining that sovereignty which it ought to attain to render a rational creature useful to others.[31]

Sensibility's tendency to play with excess and arousal (with all the connotations of uncontrollable sexual excitation implied) was especially troublesome to moralists: feelings are *excited* and *stimulated* by the spectacle of suffering. Stylistically, Sensibility depended on intensification: heightened emotions, a language of superlatives, in the cause of rendering the actuality of feeling on the page, to induce 'real' response in a reader to a fictional, manufactured scene of pain, distress, overwhelming emotion. It was an ethic founded on material or psychological suffering induced by difference in status: the workings of sensibility in the opulent were aroused by observing a suffering subject, often a social or economic inferior (Sterne's Maria), or (as in the substantial Anglo-American body of sentimental literature addressing itself to slavery or the extirpation of native Americans) a racial 'other'. In *Julia de Roubigné*, Mackenzie's philanthropic character Savillon ameliorates the conditions of the slaves under his control, and is rewarded by their self-abasing gratitude; more emphatically, and even more ambiguously, Sarah Scott's *Sir George Ellison* (1766) evokes the complex emotional economics of the hero's 'extacy' at the response of 'a numerous race of slaves' whom he acquires on his marriage to a Jamaican wife, and treats humanely.[32] Godwin's narrative insists on the egotism of Fleetwood's benevolence, its capacity to satisfy some highly questionable impulses to emotional gratification.

An even more troubling possibility was that the integrity of individual identity might be threatened by sympathetic identification: in Mackenzie's periodical *The Mirror* the letter of Leontius tells how his ward becomes so closely identified with the sufferings of her friend, that she gives up her own life to take the friend's place after death. *The Man of Feeling* demonstrates repeatedly how intense sensibility and sympathetic identification, no matter how lovely to contemplate, in practice *unfits* its possessor for prudential, useful living. The book comes to an end when Harley dies, literally, of too much feeling. The sensible heart may be 'wounded', 'pierced' or 'stabbed' by the bolt of emotional contact through sight or touch. In a quasi-religious masochistic twist, pain itself became an index of virtue: Frances Greville's 'Prayer for Indifference' begged for release from the acute pain of sensitivity, thereby affirming the poet's (and reader's) superior sensibility. This is the poem Helen Maria Williams answered in 'To Sensibility' (1786), and Hannah More in her *Sensibility: A Poetical Epistle*:

> . . . where bright imagination reigns,
> The fine-wrought spirit feels acuter pains:
> Where glow exalted sense, and sense refined,
> There keener anguish rankles in the mind;
> There feeling is diffused through every part,
> Thrills in each nerve, and lives in all the heart . . .
>
> (lines 67–72)

Again the spiritual and the bodily are mingled, with a strong leaven of moral superiority.

The literature of Sensibility disturbed its reader's quiescent state with seductive demands for emotional engagement. Repeated arousal might inflame the passions to 'the allurements of guilty pleasures' (*Charlotte Temple*, p. 101), but deaden the sensibilities. As a letter to the Editor of *The Bee* put it, 'let us beware of becoming spectators in scenes of cruelty, lest, by repeated and horrid spectacles of this kind, we lose the sympathetic sense which vibrates at the pain of another'.[33] Anna Barbauld offered a version of the same argument bolstered by physiological reference: 'Sensibility does not increase with exercise. By the constitution of our frame our habits increase, our emotions decrease, by repeated acts.'[34] As late as 1825 she wrote this 'Inquiry into Those Kinds of Distress Which Excite Agreeable Sensations', to address the uncomfortable, and sinister, possibility that suffering and sensibility could become a spectator sport, in which a reader's private and perhaps guilty sympathies might be aroused without being educated. There was a kind of sublimated aggression in this vicarious suffering female body, that the Marquis de Sade would be quick to spot and exploit: the association of pain with pleasure raised questionable connotations of passivity implied by the spectatorial aspect of sympathy. Observation of another's pain is the highly questionable pleasure offered within an aesthetics of sensibility – 'exquisite' torture though it may be to overlook a fellow being in torment. Structurally, too, repetition without progression is a fundamental feature of pornography, which operates by a duplicitous principle of intensification.

Melodrama and Sensibility also focused unease about the relationship between critical value and popularity in the first era of mass publishing and widening literacy. Sensibility coincided with an explosion in the habit of reading, the proliferation of circulating libraries, reading societies, periodicals and journals. To contemporary commentators there were inescapable parallels between the burgeoning national wealth of commercial society, the cultural capital of an emergent bourgeois class with leisure and affluence, and what we might call the 'emotional capital' of sensibility. Smith's two great published works, the *Theory of Moral Sentiments* and *The Wealth of Nations* (1776) were both founded on a principle of *exchange* – of sympathetic emotion, in the first case, of capital and goods in the second. Parallel in some sense, the precise equivalence between them was actively contested, and the source of inquiries carried on in literary genres from political economy to ethics, from historiography to domestic drama. Sentiment and sympathy, however 'heartfelt' the emotion, however 'private' the occasion or scene, are always issues of social and cultural politics in the literature that embodied and investigated them. If the moral sense was universal, and innate, in all undamaged individuals, its currency as a measure of value could only be quantitative – that is, a quasi-utilitarian measure derived from Hume, and based in the greatest pleasure to the greatest number of people. The economics of Sensibility (its 'use-value') existed in tension with its spontaneous, wayward and unpredictable nature; it was a real question as to whether the second could be harnessed to the first by instruction, whether physiology and imagination could be taught universally to respond responsibly, sociably, predictably.

The public discourse of Sensibility was in fact shaped by the concerns and interests of a select group of individuals. The universal claims made on its behalf by Smith rest in practice on a reading public with leisure to observe, to reflect on and to understand the mechanics of sympathetic response. In socio-political terms, Sensibility articulated the values of an emergent middle class; it reflected anxiety about virtue in a newly privatized social context, no longer (like the 'Roman Virtue' of the Augustan public sphere) available to view in action, but in the domestic sphere, where women and men were defined in terms of the quality of their internal responses, their emotional natures. Writing on sensibility was always concerned to discover, and to represent, the 'bounds beyond which virtuous feelings cease to be virtue', to convey the imperative need for 'the decisions of sentiment [to be] subject to the controul of prudence' (Mackenzie, *Works*, v: 17). Mackenzie's lightly moralized fables about young ladies who fly into conniptions about the drowning of flies in cream-pots (v: 303) but neglect their families and servants are as much about how to balance, control and regulate sensibility as how to encourage or nourish it.

Smith had expanded Hutcheson's alignment of ethics with aesthetics to define the *quality* of response: 'The amiable virtues consist in that degree of sensibility which surprises by its exquisite and unexpected delicacy and tenderness' (*Theory of Moral Sentiments*, p. 25). As a crucial determinant of taste, sensibility was a yardstick of value whose *exclusivity* was underlined by the literature. The episode where estranged father and fallen daughter are reunited in *The Man of Feeling* is orchestrated by Harley, the eponym of Sensibility; recovered from their transports of emotion, father and daughter run to embrace him,

> and made the warmest protestations of gratitude for his favours. We would attempt to describe the joy which Harley felt on this occasion, did it not occur to us, that one half of the world could not understand it though we did; and the other half will, by this time, have understood it without any description at all.
>
> (p. 52)

The coerciveness is clear: a reader of Sensibility will share these emotions without instruction; without it, no amount of description will suffice. The more tears you can shed, the finer a sensibility you exhibit, the better person you are. The value of the reader's taste was computed according to the intensity of her response. 'No species of composition,' wrote Mackenzie's Lounger in 1785, 'is more generally read by one class of readers, or more undervalued by another, than that of the novel' (*Works*, v: 176).

As a working generalization, we might say that since Wordsworth and Coleridge's controversial experiments on the public taste, the *Lyrical Ballads* of 1798, poets and critics have had an interest in theorizing a split between popular pleasure (the maligned felicific calculus developed by Jeremy Bentham from Hume), and aesthetic value. Sensibility as a mode was enmired in its own popularity and consequently suffered the subsequent embarrassment of the popular, both in the sense of unease, and of entanglement or encumbrance. The aesthetics of Sensibility as a mode of ethical representation became, incipiently, implicated with the politics of democratic representation. Wordsworth and Coleridge were agreed that the purpose of poetry is pleasure, and both felt that their battle against the depraved taste created by eighteenth-century poetic artifice had to be won by appealing to the responses and the pleasures of Samuel Johnson's notional figure, the 'common reader' or (in their terms) 'real men'. But what gave most pleasure to most people, apparently, was the literature of Sensibility, denigrated by Wordsworth as a 'degrading thirst after outrageous stimulation'. He proposed pleasure 'of a kind very different from that which is supposed by many persons to be the proper object of poetry' ('Preface' (1800) to *Lyrical Ballads*, pp. 249, 251). This 'grand elementary principle of pleasure' constituted 'the native and naked dignity of man', by which he 'knows, and *feels*, and lives, and moves'. Developing the idea of 'taste' as the product of acute sensitivity, at once 'natural' and highly cultivated, Wordsworth's 'Poet' is 'a man . . . endued with *more* lively sensibility, *more* enthusiasm and tenderness, who has a *greater* knowledge of human nature, and a *more* comprehensive soul, than are supposed to be common among mankind'; he is the 'Man of Feeling' redeemed from the prison of inarticulacy to 'a *greater* readiness and power in expressing what he thinks and feels', and his universality is confirmed by his uniqueness ('Preface' (1802), pp. 255–8, italics added). Wordsworth's debt to eighteenth-century Sensibility and his crucial departures from it are clear. The poet produces pleasure by his ability to provoke a reader's natural, sympathetic responses to shared human experience. But though he is a 'man speaking to men', this passage stresses throughout not so much their common humanity, as the quantitative *difference* (which becomes in effect a qualitative one) of the poet's sensibilities from those of his audience. His special ability rests on a quite exceptional degree of human sensibility. And, when he does not 'find' the necessary sympathetic emotions in the world beyond himself, he is 'habitually impelled to *create*' them within the magic circle of his own self. When sympathy turns to find its responses within, aesthetics can become an entirely singular affair.

Because of the uncertain status of 'sympathy' (located as it was variously between the somatic, the figurative, and the ethical imperative) Sensibility was by its nature an 'impure' and unstable literary mode, readily combining with and leaking into other forms of literary representation: we can trace literary continuities through streams as diverse as the Gothic novel and the cult of the occult, nineteenth-century social realism (in particular the sentimental emotionalism of Dickens's novels), Wordsworth's celebration of the primitive virtues of Cumberland peasant life in touch with the 'beautiful and permanent forms of nature' ('Preface' (1800), p. 245), operatic melodrama, and Victorian religious and temperance tracts. There are suggestive points

of intersection between Sensibility and the picturesque mode in which observation of ruins in the outdoors leads to withdrawal into 'private space' of
contemplation. Both, also, respond to the pathos of the present, the way
it constantly evanesces into pastness, and the difficulty of grasping it as it
withdraws. Behind all lay implicit acknowledgement that the imagination
was as powerful as reason in ruling not only human behaviour but perception itself. 'This,' as the most uncompromising theorist of human nature on
empirical principles put it in 1739, 'is the universe of the imagination, nor
have we any idea but what is there produc'd' (Hume, *Treatise*, p. 49). In
this framework, the passions control the production of knowledge across all
domains, and Sensibility is the shared, transferable, instrument of knowledge
and understanding, the one factor that neutralizes or overwhelms intellectual scepticism. From the *Treatise* onwards, Sensibility was, implicitly or
overtly, concerned as much with self-writing as with the nature of social
relationships.

Rousseau was the first master and theorist of modern autobiography's
foundation in imaginative sensibility:

> Assume that someone is in a painful situation which you know perfectly well:
> you will not easily be moved to cry in seeing the afflicted person, but give him
> time to tell you everything he feels, and soon you will burst into tears.[35]

This is exactly the scene of perfect sympathetic communication imagined at
the beginning of Mary Shelley's *Frankenstein* (1818), when Walton finds 'the
brother of my heart' in the suffering Victor Frankenstein; identifying with the
inventor's 'elevated' emotions Walton is almost overwhelmed: 'My thoughts,
and every feeling of my soul, have been drunk up by the interest for my guest,
which this tale, and his own elevated and gentle manners, have created.'[36]
But the body of Frankenstein's tale is a fable of the *failure* of sympathy
between the creator and his creature. When the monster seeks to awaken
Frankenstein's sympathy, the latter cannot accept his bonds of connection
with the storyteller. The monster, like another Rousseauvian figure, the 'solitary walker' of the later (posthumously published) *Reveries*, is a man 'made'
for sympathy, but cast out into solitude. Rousseau's solitary takes refuge
not (like Frankenstein's monster or Fleetwood) in misanthropy, but in self-
reflection, turning inward to his own responses and thereby becoming a kind
of literary progenitor of the solitary pleasures of Wordsworth's persona in
The Prelude. Emotional extravagance here is linked to its etymological roots
with vagary, wandering, as Rousseau's *promeneur solitaire* is represented
as an outcast of a sociable world.[37] Solitary walking or communion in the
outdoors replaces the hothouse interiors of the eighteenth-century novel as
the characteristic 'site' of Sensibility in the Romantic period. Its alienated

aspect is embodied in Coleridge's Ancient Mariner, cast out of relationship with nature and super-nature into the abyss of nightmare and monstrosity:

> Alone, alone, all, all alone,
> Alone on a wide wide sea;
> And Christ would take no pity on
> My soul in agony.
>
> (*Lyrical Ballads*, p. 19)

In different ways from Scott or Austen, Coleridge and Mary Shelley recovered narrative from sensibility. Telling one's own story to elicit sympathetic response in a reader relocated literary pleasures in the revival of fable, beyond vicarious enjoyment of the protagonist's pain to a positive celebration of the 'shaping power' of imagination.

Like another unstable mode, pastoral, Sensibility always includes or implies its shadow-self:

> . . . exclamations, tender tones, fond tears,
> and all the graceful drapery Pity wears;
> these are not Pity's self, they but express
> her inward sufferings by their pictured dress;
> and these fair marks, reluctant I relate,
> these lovely symbols may be counterfeit.
>
> (More, 'Sensibility', lines 271–6)

The Man of Feeling was specifically parodied by Robert Fergusson's 'Sow'; contemporary magazines and journals supplied a run of burlesques. An 'Ode to Sensibility' published in the *Scots Magazine* in 1772 is prefaced by a headnote that draws attention to the composite aesthetic of the 'Age of Sensibility':

> I have often thought, that future ages will be strangely puzzled about the true characteristics of this age . . . with respect to literature. There is no such thing among us as original prose. . . . And as to our poetry, the little, the very little we have of it is so trimmed, and so refined, and so full of zigzag sentiments and disjointed expressions, that it is impossible for common understandings to conceive it.[38]

The revival of interest in Sensibility as a literary mode coincides with post-modern recognition of the artifice in all aesthetic and ethical systems. Raising the issue of inauthenticity as an inseparable aspect of the 'authentic' voice of personal feeling underlines the staged – and therefore potentially stagey – nature of all representation. After Freud, representations of repression and excess seem inescapably symptomatic, but re-historicized into the cultural, political and philosophical contexts of the 'long eighteenth century', the generically unstable modes of Sensibility can be viewed as opening discussions about the consensual prospects of normative response in a cultural climate in which the relativity of value had become a present spectre. Sensibility's capacity to voice the aesthetic possibility of the excess of pleasure over use value – an emotional economy of expression surviving in an ethical and commercial climate of prudent exchange – remains equally challenging.

NOTES

1. Throughout this chapter, 'sensibility' refers to emotional, physical or ethical qualities; 'Sensibility' to the literary modes that embody and interrogate these characteristics.
2. Shakespeare, *King Lear*, v.iii.256–60; 269–72.
3. Henry Mackenzie, *The Man of Feeling*, ed. Brian Vickers, rev. and intr. Stephen Bending and Stephen Bygrave (Oxford: Oxford University Press, 2001), pp. 50–1.
4. Charles Dickens, *The Old Curiosity Shop*, ed. Paul Schlicke (London: Everyman, 1995), pp. 555–6.
5. Cited in Richard Ellmann, *Oscar Wilde* (Harmondsworth: Penguin, 1997), p. 441.
6. *The Poems of Alexander Pope*, ed. John Butt (London: Methuen, 1963), p. 253.
7. Samuel Taylor Coleridge, *Poems*, ed. John Beer (London: Everyman, 1993), p. 360.
8. Julie Ellison, *Cato's Tears and the Making of Anglo-American Emotion* (Chicago: University of Chicago Press, 1999), p. 98.
9. Susan Manning (ed.), *The Works of Henry Mackenzie*, 8 vols. (London: Routledge / Thoemmes Press, 1996), v: 18.
10. David Hume, *A Treatise of Human Nature*, ed. David Fate Norton and Mary J. Norton (Oxford: Oxford University Press, 2000), pp. 302, 394.
11. Alexander Gerard, *An Essay on Taste* (1759), p. 106.
12. William Wordsworth, 'Lines Composed a Few Miles Above Tintern Abbey', in *Lyrical Ballads*, ed. R. L. Brett and A. R. Jones, 2nd edn (London: Methuen, 1991), p. 114 (lines 27–8); Keats to J. H. Reynolds, 21 September 1819 and 3 May 1818, in John Keats, *Selected Letters*, ed. Robert Gittings, rev. and intr. Jon Mee (Oxford: Oxford University Press, 2002), pp. 272, 88.
13. Henry Home, Lord Kames, *Elements of Criticism*, 3 vols. (1762), i: 121.
14. William Godwin, *Fleetwood: or, The New Man of Feeling*, ed. Gary Handwerk and A. A. Markley (Peterborough, Ontario: Broadview, 2001), pp. 47–8.
15. Jane Austen, *Sense and Sensibility*, ed. Claire Lamont (London: Oxford University Press, 1970), pp. 228, 314–15.
16. Hannah More, *Sensibility: A Poetical Epistle*, in Duncan Wu (ed.), *Romantic Women Poets: An Anthology* (Oxford: Blackwell, 1997), pp. 24–34 (line 164).
17. See Susan Manning, *Fragments of Union: Making Connections in Scottish and American Writing* (Basingstoke: Palgrave, 2002), ch. 4.
18. Vicesimus Knox, 'On Modern Criticism', in *Essays, Moral and Literary*, 15th edn, 3 vols. (1803), i: 164.

19. Ann Yearsley, *Poems on Various Subjects, 1787*, intr. Jonathan Wordsworth (Oxford: Woodstock, 1994), p. 53 (lines 55–6).

20. Henry Mackenzie *Julia de Roubigné*, ed. Susan Manning (East Linton: Tuckwell, 1999), p. 68.

21. Jonathan Swift, *Gulliver's Travels* (1726), ed. Robert de Maria, Jr. (London: Penguin, 2001), p. 217.

22. Adam Smith, *The Theory of Moral Sentiments*, ed. D. D. Raphael and A. L. MacFie (Oxford: Clarendon Press, 1976), p. 26.

23. *Boswell's Life of Johnson*, ed. George Birkbeck Hill, rev. L. F. Powell, 6 vols. (Oxford: Clarendon Press, 1934–64), II: 175.

24. Jerome McGann, *The Poetics of Sensibility: A Revolution in Literary Style* (Oxford: Clarendon Press, 1996), p. 49.

25. Laurence Sterne, *A Sentimental Journey and Continuation of the Bramine's Journal*, ed. Melvyn New and W. G. Day (Gainesville: University Press of Florida, 2002), p. 165.

26. Peter Brooks, *The Melodramatic Imagination: Balzac, Henry James, Melodrama and the Mode of Excess* , 2nd edn (New Haven: Yale University Press, 1995), p. 48; see also pp. viii, 15.

27. Ioan Williams (ed.), *Sir Walter Scott on Novelists and Fiction* (London: Routledge, 1968), p. 81.

28. Susanna Rowson, *Charlotte Temple*, ed. Ann Douglas (Harmondsworth: Penguin, 1991), p. 46. Douglas's introduction makes a case for the particular association of American Sensibility with melodrama.

29. Jean-Jacques Rousseau, *Julie, or the New Eloise*, trans. and ed. Judith H. McDowell (University Park: University of Pennsylvania Press, 1968), p. 78.

30. Charles Brockden Brown, *Wieland; or, The Transformation: An American Tale*, ed. Jay Fliegelman (Harmondsworth: Penguin, 1991), pp. 71, 169.

31. Mary Wollstonecraft, *A Vindication of the Rights of Woman*, ed. Charles W. Hagelman (New York: W.W. Norton, 1967), p. 105.

32. Sarah Scott, *The History of Sir George Ellison*, ed. Betty Rizzo (Lexington: University Press of Kentucky, 1996), p. 11.

33. *The Bee, or Literary Weekly Intelligencer* 1 (9 February 1791), 213.

34. *Works of A. L. Barbauld*, 2 vols. (1825), II: 227.

35. Jean-Jacques Rousseau, *Essay on the Origin of Languages and Writings Related to Music*, trans. John Scott (Hanover: University Press of New England, 1998), p. 291.

36. Mary Shelley, *Frankenstein; or, The Modern Prometheus*, ed. M. K. Joseph (Oxford: Oxford World's Classics, 1980), p. 210.

37. See Jean-Jacques Rousseau, *Reveries of the Solitary Walker*, trans. Peter France (Harmondsworth: Penguin, 1979).

38. 'Character of Modern Poetry, with a specimen', *Scots Magazine* 34 (November 1772), 619.

FURTHER READING

Bannet, Eve Tavor, *The Domestic Revolution: Enlightenment Feminisms and the Novel*, Baltimore: Johns Hopkins University Press, 2000.

Barker-Benfield, G. J., *The Culture of Sensibility: Sex and Society in Eighteenth-Century Britain*, Chicago: University of Chicago Press, 1992.

Benedict, Barbara M., *Framing Feeling: Sentiment and Style in English Prose Fiction, 1745–1800*, New York: AMS Press, 1994.

Brissenden, R. F., *Virtue in Distress: Studies in the Novel of Sentiment from Richardson to Sade*, London: Macmillan, 1974.

Brown, Marshall, *Preromanticism*, Stanford: Stanford University Press, 1991.

Conger, Sydney McMillen, ed., *Sensibility in Transformation: Creative Resistance to Sentiment from the Augustans to the Romantics*, Rutherford: Fairleigh Dickinson University Press, 1990.

Ellis, Markman, *The Politics of Sensibility: Race, Gender and Commerce in the Sentimental Novel*, Cambridge: Cambridge University Press, 1996.

Ellison, Julie, *Cato's Tears and the Making of Anglo-American Emotion*, Chicago: University of Chicago Press, 1999.

Empson, William, 'Sense and Sensibility', in *The Structure of Complex Words*, intr. Jonathan Culler, Cambridge, Mass.: Harvard University Press, 1989.

Jones, Chris, *Radical Sensibility: Literature and Ideas in the 1790s*, London: Routledge, 1993.

Keymer, Thomas, 'Sentimental Fiction: Ethics, Philanthropy, and Social Critique', in John Richetti (ed.), *The Cambridge History of English Literature 1660–1780*, Cambridge: Cambridge University Press, in press.

Langford, Paul, *A Polite and Commercial People: England 1727–1783*, Oxford: Oxford University Press, 1989.

McGann, Jerome, *The Poetics of Sensibility: A Revolution in Literary Style*, Oxford: Clarendon Press, 1996.

Mullan, John, *Sentiment and Sociability: The Language of Feeling in the Eighteenth-Century Novel*, Oxford: Clarendon Press, 1988.

'Sentimental Novels', in John Richetti (ed.), *The Cambridge Companion to the Eighteenth-Century Novel*, Cambridge: Cambridge University Press, 1996, pp. 236–54.

Novak, Maximillian E., and Anne Mellor (eds.), *Passionate Encounters in a Time of Sensibility*, Newark: University of Delaware Press, 2000.

Rivers, Isabel, *Reason, Grace, and Sentiment: A Study of the Language of Religion and Ethics in England, 1660–1780*, 2 vols., Cambridge: Cambridge University Press, 1991–2000.

Todd, Janet, *Sensibility: An Introduction*, London: Methuen, 1986.

Van Sant, Ann Jessie, *Eighteenth-Century Sensibility and the Novel: The Senses in Social Context*, Cambridge: Cambridge University Press, 1993.

6

GILLIAN RUSSELL

Theatrical culture

It is only comparatively recently, as a result of realignments in the disciplines of literary studies and history, that the centrality of the theatre in Georgian culture and society has been properly recognized. As the pre-eminent forum of entertainment, art and instruction, the status of which was affirmed by royal authority in the form of patents or licences to perform, and by parliamentary scrutiny in the form of censorship, the stage loomed large in the Georgian cultural landscape, often literally so. The imposing neo-classical edifices of Covent Garden and Drury Lane theatres, employing thousands of people, were unmistakable landmarks in Regency London, as indeed were the so-called 'minor' theatres across the Thames such as the Royal Coburg which competed with Covent Garden and Drury Lane in scale and opulence.[1] As the memoirs, fiction, and visual art of the period suggest, the experience of theatre meant much more than what was happening on the stage, striking though that was with its spectacular scenery and effects, and the towering presence of star actors. It also entailed the drama of the audience's self-representation, ranging from the crush of bodies outside the pit door, the display of dandies and prostitutes in the lobbies, to the monarch's appearances in the royal box. The role of Covent Garden and Drury Lane in metropolitan life was emulated, with varying degrees of success, by many smaller theatres throughout the British isles. The Georgian period is remarkable for the growth of the theatre in the provinces and in the empire as a whole. There were over three hundred playhouses in Great Britain and Ireland by the early nineteenth century, a development which reflected the crucial role played by the theatre in the commercialization of culture in the eighteenth century. As businesses, theatres participated in the development of local and regional economies, as well as serving as forums in which commercial self-confidence could be articulated as claims to civility and politeness, entitling such communities to a 'place' in the political nation as a whole. In the context of empire, the networks of exchange in personnel, repertoire, and finances between the theatres of North America, the West Indies, the Cape Colony,

India, and Australia, paralleled the networks of colonial trade, producing a recognizable and transportable category of British cultural identity that was crucial in binding Cork to Calcutta or Port Jackson to Portsmouth. However, the binding force of theatre could also enhance local self-consciousness and alternative versions of patriotism, particularly during periods of national crisis such as the 1790s when many provincial theatres became forums for disputes over the singing of 'God save the King'.

The gulf in cultural prestige which seemed to separate Covent Garden and Drury Lane from the barns and fairground booths frequented by itinerant actors or strolling players was in practice not so absolute. The metropolitan and provincial theatres shared repertoire and often actors: star performers such as Sarah Siddons made much of their income from touring, and provincial companies were the seedbed for later star careers such as that of Edmund Kean, or the child prodigy Master Betty, who began his career in Belfast in 1803. Moreover, the improvised 'theatres royal' of the military, such as the mud-walled convict hut in which Farquhar's *The Recruiting Officer* was staged at Port Jackson in Australia in 1789, highlighted the fact that while Covent Garden and Drury Lane may have had a legal monopoly over the performance of the spoken drama, they did not have a monopoly over theatre as an adaptable vehicle of British identity.[2] The permeability of bodies, spaces and ideologies that characterized theatrical culture is illustrated by a night out spent by John Keats in January 1818. With his friend the poet Charles Jeremiah Wells, he went to a private theatre in London, an establishment of the 'lowest order', 'all greasy & oily'. To relieve the prospective tedium of an entire evening in this 'dirty hole', Keats decided to go to Drury Lane theatre nearby, where he caught Edmund Kean performing as Shakespeare's Richard III, before returning to the private theatre. Wells introduced him to the company behind the scenes where 'there was not a yard around for actors, scene shifters & interlopers to move in'. Private theatres, also known as spouting clubs, were active from the mid eighteenth century. They were places where aspiring actors paid for the chance to strut their stuff in imitation of stars such as Kean. Keats was amused to see one such performer 'in the very sweat of anxiety to shew himself' as the King in the burlesque tragic opera *Bombastes Furioso*: 'but Alas the thing was not played'.[3] Keats's bracketing of Kean as Richard III by this attendance at a private theatre illustrates how the respectable face of the late Georgian theatre, its status as the home of national icons such as Shakespeare, existed in close proximity to its identification with the disreputable and culturally inferior and, in some cases, the politically suspect. Kean himself embodied the fluidity of these distinctions because of his own social and professional origins in the milieu of the private theatres – he received his initial training in circuses and fairgrounds – and his maintenance of links with that world even when he became famous. He had himself experienced the 'sweat of anxiety' as a poor player and his success in roles such as Richard III and Shylock was in part shaped by his capacity to articulate the threat to the established order of little men who wanted to be kings. It is therefore important to acknowledge the full spectrum of the Georgian theatre, ranging from the palaces of the patent houses to the 'dirty holes' of the spouting clubs, because it is only by linking these spaces, as Keats did both literally and textually, that we can begin to understand the impact of the theatre upon the culture as a whole.

The experience of the theatre in the Georgian period was therefore manifold, encompassing the sociable, the aesthetic, the political and also the erotic, insofar as the playhouse was a recognized place of assignation, both licit and illicit. It was also, surprisingly perhaps, a site for reading. It was customary, at least until the later part of the eighteenth century, for playgoers to buy the text of the play either at the theatre or elsewhere and sometimes read it while viewing the performance. One such playgoer was the diarist Sylas Neville who in 1767 saw John Gay's *Beggar's Opera*: he describes how he had 'read some parts' of the text, which he had borrowed from Thomas Davies's bookshop, 'before it began & between the acts'.[4] The theatre's pre-eminent role in Georgian cultural life was closely linked with the development of print culture in this period. The rise of the newspaper and periodical press, the increasing identification of the public sphere with the reading public, changes to the copyright law and the redefinition of authorship, all had profound consequences for the theatre. Not the least significant of these was the view that the drama of the period was lacking in literary merit: the values associated with Shakespeare and the Restoration drama were regarded as being debased by crude spectacularism and the major writers increasingly defined themselves by rejecting writing for the stage as a lost cause. Reinforced by the antitheatricalism of Romantic literary studies in the twentieth century, such attitudes have dominated perspectives on the theatre and drama of the period and are only beginning to be seriously challenged. They produced, for example, a bifurcated model of analysis whereby the Georgian theatre was either discussed in literary terms as drama, i.e. as a history of the work of a limited number of canonical authors and the development of the privileged genres of tragedy and comedy, or from a theatre history perspective which focuses on institutions, performances, and staging practices. The first approach is problematic because the period after 1770 is remarkable for the proliferation of dramatic genres, the fluidity in distinctions between them – Matthew 'Monk' Lewis's *The Castle Spectre* was described in 1797 as 'a drama of a mingled nature, Operatic, Comical and Tragical' – and by experimentation within established generic modes.[5] Examples of the latter include Elizabeth Inchbald's and Hannah Cowley's reworkings of the genre of sentimental comedy after 1780, in plays such as *Such Things Are* and *A Day in Turkey*, to produce subtle analyses of patriarchal and imperial power. The most notable generic innovation of the period, insofar that it endures in twenty-first-century television and cinema, was melodrama, which was inaugurated at Covent Garden in 1802 by Thomas Holcroft's *The Tale of Mystery*, an adaptation of a *mélo-drame* by the French dramatist Pixérécourt. As it developed in the nineteenth century, melodrama's most notable aspect was its confounding of orthodox distinctions – between the genres of tragedy and comedy, between literary and non-literary performance styles (particularly the relationship between the spoken word and the expressiveness of the body) and between culture hierarchies and media, melding as it did elements of the novel, visual art, popular song and folk tale. The hybridity of theatrical culture, highlighted by Keats's experience in January 1818, is therefore bound up with a hybridity of dramatic forms which renders a history of the theatre in terms of the traditional literary genres not only inappropriate but also impossible. This essay seeks to re-define the category of dramatic literature by interpreting the meaning of the dramatic text in its broadest sense. It explores the relationship between print culture and theatre in terms of how the published text entered the theatre, sometimes literally so, as in the case of Sylas Neville, and vice versa – how the theatre manifests its presence in the reading of dramatic literature.

An important element of Georgian dramatic literature was the playbill, the single-sheet advertisement for a performance which was circulated at theatres, pasted up on walls and buildings, declaimed by strolling players on their arrival in towns and villages, or published in newspapers. Circulating between many hands and spaces, the playbill had an enunciative power that went beyond its function as advertisement. It signified a kind of contract between theatres and their patrons that managers ignored at their peril but also the importance of the specific performance event and the wider cultural and social significance of the theatre itself. Writing in the 1820s when, as a result of cheap printing the playbill had become an extravagant artefact of the Regency commercialism, Charles Lamb nostalgically recalled the more austere playbill of the Garrick era: how he would spell out 'every name, down to the very mutes and servants of the scene . . . "Orsino, by Mr Barrymore." – What a full Shakespearian sound it carries!'[6] Such was the importance of the playbill as a performance text in its own right that it is the main body of evidence relating to theatre in the empire during this period. The early convict theatres of Australia were commemorated in the form of playbills published in newspapers and journals in London, thereby marking not only the performance event but also its implicit 'place' within the British theatre as a whole. The textual and typographic conventions and cultural politics of the playbill were so recognizable to all classes of society that burlesque versions served as a mode of political satire throughout the eighteenth century, but particularly in the 1790s. Representing the Prime Minister William Pitt as the puppet-master 'Gulielmo Pittachio' (fig. 3), or proclaiming 'sublime and animating' spectacles such as the 'Storming of the Cabinet' (fig. 4), these texts exploited the mutual reflexivity of theatre and politics.[7] But their meaning also relied on the particular status of the playbill within theatrical culture as a public commitment of management to their audiences and as texts which in effect made performances happen: as the authors of the mock playbill knew, nothing could occur within the Georgian 'theatre of the world' without a playbill to announce it.

Closely related to the playbill as a theatrical paratext, that is, a text which marks boundaries between genres, events and spaces and facilitates crossings between these boundaries, are prologues and epilogues. These were short performance pieces, most often but not invariably verse monologues, that framed the performance of the five-act drama forming the centre or mainpiece of an evening's programme of entertainment. The most celebrated example is the prologue written by Samuel Johnson in 1747 to inaugurate the first season at Drury Lane theatre under the management of David Garrick. As spoken by Garrick, the prologue was a manifesto for his new regime: it asserted his capacity to restore the 'scenic virtue' of the stage, rescuing it from the contaminating effects of spectacular genres such as pantomime and the influence of popular and foreign or infidel forms of entertainment, represented in the prologue by Edward Hunt, a pugilist, and 'Mahomet', a Turkish rope-dancer. The latter usurp the proper place of the tragic heroes of Shakespeare:

> Perhaps, where *Lear* has rav'd, and *Hamlet* dy'd,
> On flying Cars new Sorcerers may ride.
> Perhaps, for who can guess th'Effects of Chance?
> Here *Hunt* may box, or *Mahomet* may dance.[8]

As such, Johnson's prologue was a paradigmatic example of the cultural politics shaping discourse on the theatre throughout the period, particularly in its invocation of Shakespeare as the embodiment of an indigenous British dramatic tradition and its characterization of the patent theatres as vulnerable to the threat of both popular and foreign cultural influences. As Johnson makes clear, however, the integrity of the theatre had been compromised by the rise of pantomime earlier in the century. While the prologue pleads Garrick's case it also suggests that the theatre is already a lost cause. The most famous couplet of the prologue – 'The Drama's Laws the Drama's

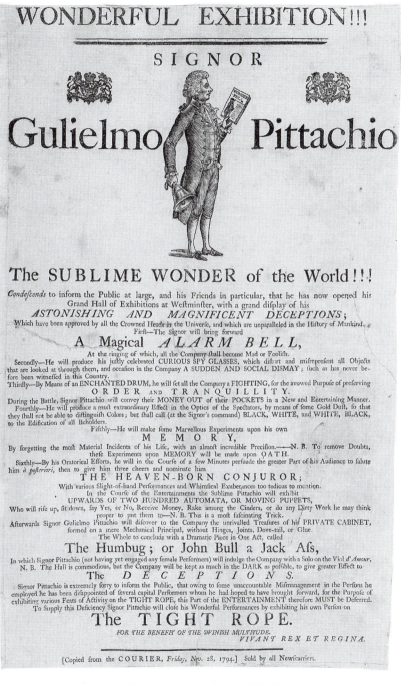

Figure 3 *Wonderful Exhibition!!!*, mock playbill by Robert Merry, 1794.

Figure 4 *Harlequin Impeacher*, mock playbill of *c*. 1794–5.

Patrons give, / For we that live to please, must please to live' (lines 53–4) – argues that the public gets the drama it deserves, implicitly identifying the theatre as an intrinsically commercial institution, catering to pleasure rather than virtue.

Johnson's prologue illustrates the importance of the genre as a forum for cultural politics in general but prologues and epilogues were also crucial to the successful day-to-day running of the Georgian theatre. They were important vehicles for communication between management and audience (and sometimes vice versa in terms of playgoers' occasionally violent responses). They could serve as a means of introducing new actors and writers, signalling innovation or change in the mainpiece or apologizing for deficiencies such as the non-appearance of a favourite performer. Insofar as the prologue was customarily delivered by an actor and the epilogue by an actress, they were also articulated issues relating to gender politics. Garrick's epilogues for actresses such as Frances Abington in the 1770s are complex negotiations of the relationship between feminine character as defined by the main play, the celebrity identity of the actress herself and the performative behaviour of women of fashion in the audience. Like his fellow playwright-managers George Colman the Elder and Richard Brinsley Sheridan, Garrick used the epilogue to assert the capacity of the theatre to regulate the excesses of feminized fashionable culture, at the same time implicitly defending himself and his institution against the charge that the theatre dangerously destabilized normative categories of masculinity. As performance pieces these epilogues therefore supplement and amplify the meanings of the plays they frame, such as Sheridan's *The School for Scandal*, in ways that the canonizing processes of literary history, privileging the mainpiece play, have tended to obscure. For in many respects these paratexts, rather than being marginal, were in fact central to defining what was distinctive about Georgian theatrical culture – a highly self-conscious mediation of its conventions and practices, a capacity to theatricalize itself in other words. The prologue and epilogue explored the artificiality of the genres they framed, pointing out the audience's own performative behaviour and ultimately the theatricality of British society in general. They did this not simply in the universalizing terms of 'all the world's a stage' but in very specific topical analyses of cultural and social change that located the theatre both in the midst of such change and above it, as its natural arbiter. Published widely in newspapers and journals, often as a means of advertising plays, and anthologized in collections, prologues and epilogues were a significant aspect of Georgian dramatic literature, another example of the permeability of print and theatrical cultures. They rank among the most significant achievements of Georgian culture as a whole. Their decline reflected theatre's increasing emphasis on visual effects, but, more significantly, also signalled the loss of its status as the defining site for Georgian ideas of 'the public'. Print culture with its appeal to a more diffuse public of readers rather than a body of theatre-goers increasingly claimed that role.

Prologues and epilogues, like mainpiece dramas and revisions to old plays, were subject to the censoring eyes of the Lord Chamberlain, the government official given the task of scrutinizing all pieces prior to performance by the Licensing Act of 1737. The immediate purpose of this measure was to suppress the anti-ministerial satires of Henry Fielding and John Gay emanating from unlicensed theatres then proliferating in London. This latter circumstance accounts for the other significant dimension of the Licensing Act, namely its restriction of the spoken drama to those theatres holding patents granted by the monarch, thereby instituting control not only over the dramatic text but also the spaces in which it could be performed. This measure increased the value, in both a political and a commercial sense, of the patents or licences to perform that had been granted by Charles II to the courtiers Davenant and Killigrew in 1660 and used by successive owners of Covent Garden and Drury Lane to claim privileged royal status. The rights of the patent theatres as *de facto* national theatres, linked with monarchical authority, British prestige, and the high cultural values associated with writers such as Shakespeare, became inextricably bound up with the rights of the patent holders to protect and improve their property in the theatres. The 1737 Licensing Act was therefore crucial in determining the ideological, legal and economic frameworks conditioning the development of theatre in the metropolis, and indirectly the empire as a whole, for over a century. It was first challenged in the 1740s by the actor-entrepreneurs Charles Macklin and Samuel Foote who in order to evade the terms of the Act devised subscription entertainments such as tea parties, musical concerts and auctions, during which the actor would entertain his audience with a dramatic performance.[9]

The growth in non-theatrical entertainment venues such as taverns and tea-gardens and the success of theatres outside Westminster such as Sadler's Wells led parliament to pass an act in 1752 (made permanent in 1755) which allowed for the licensing of such entertainments by local magistrates. This measure was designed to create a mechanism for regulating such venues which were identified by government as sources of disorder and crime. In 1787 the actor John Palmer used this act to mount the first major challenge to the patent theatres by opening the Royalty Theatre in Wellclose Square in the East End of London. Proclaiming the rights of the people of this area to experience the plays of Shakespeare and other dramatists such as Thomas Otway and Nicholas Rowe, Palmer threw down the gauntlet to Covent Garden and Drury Lane by performing *As You Like It*. The owners of the patent theatres retaliated by mobilizing the resources of both the press and the law, including statutes dating from the Elizabethan period allowing actors to be imprisoned as rogues and vagabonds. Some of Palmer's rebel company spent time in jail. Although on this occasion the threat of a winter theatre to challenge the hegemony of Covent Garden and Drury Lane was beaten off, a succession of actor-managers and entrepreneurs followed Palmer's example by using the 1752 Act for regulating places of entertainment to establish theatres across the metropolis, particularly to the south of the Thames. These developments reflected the rapid expansion of London from a population of about 675,000 in 1750 to around a million in 1800. The owners of the patent houses responded by increasing the capacity of their theatres, a significant factor in the shift from the more intimate performance styles of the Garrick theatre to the increased reliance on scenic effects in the late Georgian period, but the controversy over the Royalty had not only highlighted the inability of the West End theatres to meet the needs of an expanding metropolis, but also the complex cultural politics of the issue. As Foote and Macklin had done before, the minor theatres cleverly worked around the Licensing Act by adapting forms such as the burletta. Originating in the patent theatres, the burletta was a short musical drama, often burlesquing serious opera, but was gradually adapted by the minor theatres to enable them to stage versions of the plays of Shakespeare and other canonical authors as musicals. The prohibition on the spoken word could be circumvented by the parading of banners displaying text from the plays concerned, a performance practice linking Shakespeare with the increasing presence on the streets of billboards, posters and other forms of commercial signage, as well as anticipating the intertitles of silent cinema.

The struggle for the regulation and development of the theatre throughout the eighteenth century was profoundly political in a number of ways. The treatment of John Palmer by the tyrannical patent houses resonated with issues in contemporary party politics, particularly Wilkite radicalism, while the language of legitimacy and illegitimacy was readily adaptable to the crisis period after the Napoleonic wars when, for writers such as William Hazlitt, the persistence of Covent Garden and Drury Lane as bastions of legitimacy paralleled the restoration of 'legitimate' royal houses across Europe. More generally, the debate surrounding the regulation of the theatre articulated important issues relating to the definition of the public and the kind of entertainment to which it was entitled, issues inflected by considerations of commerce, class and morality. How could the increasingly commercial identity of the theatre (and both the major and minor theatres did defend themselves in terms of their rights to make money) be accommodated to theatre's traditional role in public culture as a mirror of society, a school of morality and one of the highest of the liberal arts? The intractability of this issue partly accounts for the failure of a number of attempts to establish a third winter theatre and the fact that it took over ten years for government to act on the recommendations of a parliamentary inquiry in 1832 into the state of the drama. The Theatres Regulation Act of 1843 abolished the distinction between the major and the minor theatres and therefore between the legitimate and illegitimate drama. Often represented as the culmination of the long struggle to 'free' the stage, this measure, as Tracy C. Davis has shown, was a long overdue legal recognition that the distinction between the major and minor theatres was not only unenforceable but also meaningless. Nor, as Davis emphasizes, was the stage necessarily 'free': central authority over the content of plays was actually extended insofar as the Lord Chamberlain was able to censor plays produced throughout the country whereas previously his jurisdiction had been limited to the patent theatres of Westminster.[10]

One of the effects of this censorship had been to reduce the number of new plays produced after 1737 as managers and writers rejected risky ventures (both commercially and politically) in favour of the safer commodity of the established repertory. This strategy partly accounts for the increased popularity of the plays of Shakespeare and his consolidation as the pre-eminent figure in the dramatic canon. Censorship made explicit political comment impossible but this does not mean that the drama was lacking in political bite – far from it in fact. This was partly due to the fact that the theatre existed in close proximity, literally, ideologically and in terms of textual production, with other spheres of Georgian public life in which politics dominated, particularly the newspaper and periodical press and print culture in general. The metropolitan theatres formed a kind of Grand Central Station of eighteenth-century cultural and social networks, a place of meeting for individuals but also of ranks, circles and genders, where one might cross over from one defining category to another. One such nexus was between the theatre and the world of Grub Street. The press and the stage were mutually implicated as forums for publicity: Garrick held shares in some newspapers and had writers in his pay.[11] The press in turn thrived on theatrical 'intelligence', gossip and scandal to attract readers, a context which inevitably permeated its reporting of high politics. As a meeting place and site of sociability and an arena in which an aspiring writer could attract attention with a new play or pointed prologue or epilogue, the theatre could serve as a springboard to a political career. One of the most celebrated examples of this was the career of Richard Brinsley Sheridan. A son of the Irish theatre manager, grammarian and rhetorician Thomas Sheridan, he made his name in the early 1770s as a writer of comedies that dramatized his celebrity as a young man of fashion, graduating to ownership of Drury Lane in 1776 and eventually becoming a leading figure in the Whig faction associated with the Prince of Wales. Lacking in inherited wealth and property, Sheridan used Drury Lane as a source of funds and as an informal political headquarters. His highly dramatic mode of oratory, like that of his fellow Irishman Edmund Burke, also continually reminded his audience of Sheridan's origins in the theatre and of the reflexivity of politics and the stage.

The enmeshing of the spheres of politics, journalism and the theatre was therefore one way in which the Georgian stage was politicized. Another was the nature of the performance event itself which brought people together in a space that symbolized hierarchies of rank and permitted the audience to respond and sometimes determine its own meanings of censored texts. The government could control the explicit political content of plays but it could not predict the ways in which audiences could freely adapt passages of old plays to contemporary circumstances. Other ritualistic aspects of the performance event such as the singing of anthems occasionally galvanized the theatre with political emotion and tension. The activism of theatre audiences reached its apogee in the Old Price disturbances of 1809, when rioters, objecting to the increase of prices at the rebuilt Covent Garden, caused performances to be suspended for sixty-seven nights. They installed their own show of fighting, destruction of benches and fittings, displays of placards and even singing and dancing. The rioters' opposition to the increase in prices was the pretext for a larger symbolic struggle for the meaning of theatre in the early nineteenth century which pitted the rights of a socially heterogeneous public to be entertained at a price it could afford against the rights of management led by John Philip Kemble to make money from their property in the theatre. The fact that the struggle resonated with contemporary politics, with Kemble being represented as a tyrannical and corrupt monarch of the stage abusing the rights of freeborn Englishmen only intensified the drama of the riots, but theatre politics was never subsumed by the more orthodox politics of the wider world. Indeed, for the sixty-seven nights that the riots lasted it seemed the opposite was the case, such was the crucial significance of theatre to late Georgian public culture.

More often than not, however, the potency of the theatre as a political institution was directed in the service of the crown and the established order. Throughout the period the patent theatres in particular were important as venues in which the monarch could display himself before the public and loyalty could be demonstrated in the form of afterpieces, interludes and pageants and the singing of anthems. Such conventions supplemented the endorsements of the British monarchy and empire in the plots of mainpiece plays. During the crisis years of the 1790s, for example, John Philip Kemble reinforced the patent theatres' identification with the crown by producing pro-monarchical and anti-Jacobin adaptations of the plays of Shakespeare. The importance of the theatre as a forum to which people came to see representations of contemporary society was enhanced during wartime when the stage assumed the role of a newscaster, publicizing and commemorating events such as the naval victories of Admiral Vernon in the 1740s and later the battles of Trafalgar and Waterloo.[12] The trend towards more spectacular modes of production, facilitated by the larger stages of the patent theatres, enabled the theatre to declare its loyalty to the crown in ever more complex ways, culminating in the competition between the two patent houses to stage re-enactments of the coronation of George IV in 1821. Drury Lane's 'Coronation' deployed four hundred performers and the construction of a platform over the pit for the 'King' to parade on horseback. These productions demonstrated the affiliations between the theatre and the monarchy, not simply in terms of ideology, but also on account of a shared investment in theatricality and spectacle.

The multi-faceted politics of the Georgian stage exerted a profound influence on the production and reception of the mainpiece dramas of the period. I have already noted the effect of the Licensing Act on the production of new drama and in amplifying the status of Shakespeare. Another important dimension of the Act was the way in which it implicitly recruited the genres of tragedy and comedy to the cause of the patent theatres and legitimacy. This message was reinforced by publishing projects such as *Bell's British Theatre*, a collection of mainpiece dramas first published by John Bell in 1776 (revised in the 1790s).[13] Following his collection of the plays of Shakespeare published two years before, *Bell's British Theatre* included a range of both contemporary and old plays, popular pieces of the repertory, by dramatists such as Addison, Otway, Rowe and Colman. The texts were derived from the promptbooks, that is, the acting text of a play, thereby encouraging the reader to view the collection as being authorized by the theatre, specifically Drury Lane. However, aspects of the original text which had been omitted in the performance, usually for reasons of length, were indicated by inverted commas, allowing the reader to relate the performance text of the play to an alternative version (which may have derived from previous performance text editions or from a dramatic author's works).

Bell's British Theatre was therefore an advertisement for the ideologies underpinning the institution of the patent theatres. It successfully mediated between the 'stage and the closet', the formulation that emerged in this period as a means of negotiating three closely related phenomena: firstly, the permeable boundary between theatrical culture and print culture; secondly the way in which the theatrical public was increasingly superseded by a public defined primarily as a reading public, and thirdly, the construction of literary value as distinct from, rather than embedded in, theatrical culture. Bell's collection was dedicated to David Garrick. Its publication in 1776 not only coincided with the American War of Independence, thereby enhancing the patriotic meanings of the title, but also marked Garrick's retirement from the stage in the same year. This collection of canonical dramas, prefaced by Bell's *Shakespeare*, was therefore a monument to the great actor-manager and his theatre. But as such it misrepresented the totality of Garrick's achievement. As Johnson's 1747 prologue had insinuated, the claims of the patent theatres had been compromised by their engagement with 'low' dramatic forms such as pantomime, which Garrick himself had promoted. Constantly striving to maintain the position of his theatre, Garrick's career combined high-cultural pretension (as book-collector, patron and European man of letters) with the crowd-pulling instincts of the showman. He was an innovator, not only in acting styles but also technically, improving lighting and scenic design. As a dramatist his most significant achievement was in non-canonical forms, particularly farce (*Miss in her Teens, The Lying Valet* and *Bon Ton* remained in the repertory well into the nineteenth century) and in prologues and epilogues. Equally, if not more important was his role in developing new writing for the stage. In the 1760s and 1770s he particularly encouraged women writers such as Hannah Cowley, Hannah More and Elizabeth Griffith, though as Ellen Donkin has shown, his relationship with them was sometimes fraught.[14]

Garrick's career was therefore characterized by a largely successful project of defending and extending the privileged status of the patent theatres by assimilating and adapting the genres, practices and ideologies against which that very privilege was defined, i.e. illegitimate forms such as spectacle and pantomime and 'foreign' art forms such as ballet. After 1750 this project was complicated by the emergence of a range of commercialized forms of fashionable public entertainment such as masquerades, music concerts, auctions, art exhibitions, and lecturing which, while not conventionally theatrical, were developing innovative styles of social performance and use of material space that implicitly challenged the theatre's hegemony in British cultural life. In conjunction with the proliferating tea-gardens and taverns of the metropolis, venues such as Teresa Cornelys's Carlisle House in Soho, and the Pantheon in Oxford Street, threatened the theatre's pre-eminent role from both 'high' and 'low'. Garrick's response was to develop the theatre's critique of the fashionable world both in the mainpiece play and in the prologue and epilogue, thereby bolstering the theatre's claims to be a bastion of 'manly' British values against the contaminating influences of fashionable, Frenchified effeminacy. He also attempted to beat the fashionable world at its own game by emulating its practices in his Shakespeare Jubilee staged at Stratford-upon-Avon in September 1769. Often described as a key event in the canonization of Shakespeare, the Jubilee was also important for Georgian cultural politics in general. It was experimental theatre on a grand scale involving performance events such as processioning and a masquerade that combined elements of elite entertaining with popular outdoor festival. All this was conducted with an eye to the publicity machine of the London media, establishing Shakespeare as the paradigmatic modern literary celebrity, and inaugurating cultural tourism. Most importantly, in relocating Drury Lane to Stratford, the Jubilee suggested that the status of the patent theatres was not defined by the four walls of a particular playhouse but was a transportable cultural category which, with Shakespeare as its figurehead, could both mobilize and contain the diverse energies and meanings of the 'British theatre'.

If *Bell's British Theatre* was a monument to the Garrick stage, then the collection of plays with the same title published by Longmans in 1808 commemorated the theatre of John Philip Kemble and his sister Sarah Siddons.[15] By the early nineteenth century the need to make the link between canonical mainpiece drama and the patent theatres was more pressing than ever, as Covent Garden and Drury Lane faced increasing competition from the minor theatres and from 'illegitimate' forms such as melodrama which, in some cases, the majors themselves had spawned. A critique of the patent houses in a caricature of 1807 depicted managers such as Sheridan sucking from the teats of a many-headed monster labelled 'Melo-drama', signifying the hybrid drama which the patents had created and indeed needed in order to survive. The Longmans' *British Theatre* differs from its precedent in Bell's insofar as it omits prologues and epilogues and includes illustrations (by notable artists such as Fuseli) that were not explicitly linked with a theatrical production or actor. The texts were, however, derived from the Covent Garden promptbooks and performance remained the defining context for the collection. The contemporary theatre informed the 1808 *British Theatre* as much as it did Bell's collection of 1776. This is especially apparent in the prefaces to the plays by the former actress, playwright and novelist Elizabeth Inchbald, which continually return to the question of the relationship between seeing and reading a play. Responding to the increasing importance of literary value in shaping perceptions of the theatre, Inchbald does not come down conclusively on the side of either the stage or the closet, arguing instead for a plurality of ways of reading a dramatic text that implicitly allows for the validity of her own perspective as a woman writer.[16] The prefaces to *The British Theatre* amount to an exercise in dramatic theory, as does the work of Inchbald's contemporary, Joanna Baillie. Her *Series of*

Plays in which it is attempted to delineate the Stronger Passions of the Mind (1798–1812) was explicitly aimed at an audience of readers, though she also appeals to knowledge of theatre practice, in particular the acting of Sarah Siddons and Kemble's experiments in Gothic scene design. The character of Jane de Monfort in Baillie's *De Monfort* was not only influenced by Siddons's acting but is an exploration of the type of the Siddonian tragic heroine, therefore invoking both the mainpiece plays in which the actress starred and the history of other female performers in these roles.

In its attempt to dramatize interiority, Baillie's *Series of Plays* exemplifies what Judith Pascoe has defined as 'Romantic theatricality', 'an attraction to and appropriation of performative modes of self-representation' that reorients and expands traditional models of Romantic literary culture by foregrounding the presence of theatre, both in a material sense and in its wider cultural and ideological ramifications.[17] Such a conceptualization of late Georgian culture has the effect, as Pascoe shows, of breaking down distinctions between 'theatre' and 'literature', and between hierarchies of genre that have shaped perspectives on the period for decades. It generates relationships between genres such as lyric poetry and journalism, and between the spheres of literature, politics and painting, much in the same way as the theatre itself was a place of exchange between cultural, social and political networks. To acknowledge 'Romantic theatricality' also entails a recognition of the role of women as playwrights, performers, dramatic critics and theorists, and as public figures in general. Throughout the eighteenth century the theatre was an important entry point for women into the public sphere but the complicated status of the theatre, particularly in relation to sexual morality, left a question mark over women who had 'gone public' in such a way. Conversely, the success of women such as Inchbald and Mary Robinson, actress, courtesan and later writer, and most powerfully, Sarah Siddons, also reflected on the status and meaning of theatre. The anti-theatrical prejudice of the period, a complex phenomenon derived from long-standing antipathy to the theatre as idolatrous, licentious and a site for the promotion of social disorder, was inflected by issues of gender. What troubled commentators about the theatre – its emphasis on the superficiality of display, the dubious attractions of the body, the trading in inauthentic selves, and most crucially the capacity to generate desire and fantasy – was also what disturbed them about women. Garrick carefully negotiated these attitudes by defending his art against charges of suspicious effeminacy and by constructing the theatre as a bastion of 'manly' patriotic values. His project to legitimate the theatre therefore also entailed an attempt to legitimate it in gender terms. After 1782, however, Garrick's iconic role in the theatre and

British culture in general was assumed by a woman, Sarah Siddons. Her success, as manifested in many portraits of her, most famously Reynolds's 1784 study of her as the Tragic Muse, and the extensive press commentary on her both on and off the stage, built on Garrick's fashioning of the actor as the embodiment of the virtue and energy of the commercialized public sphere. Because of her gender, however, Siddons was never able to exert the kind of influence over the development of the theatre as an institution in the way that Garrick had. While it was not unusual for women to manage provincial theatres, the idea of a woman having a controlling interest in one of the London patent theatres was unthinkable. Siddons sought to define and enhance her status as an artist by forging links with circles of female literati, the bluestockings, who revered her as an icon of female creativity. But it was on the stage that she concentrated most fully her power as both a performer and a public figure, in the terms defined by Garrick. While many of the roles she played represented women as victims, her performances were such that she often transformed this victimhood into an assertion of strength. Many commentators noted the physicality of her acting – her leaps, the triumphal deliberation of her walk, the power of her stare, the expressiveness of her arms and above all, the searching penetration of her voice. Her speaking of a particular line from *Venice Preserv'd*, for example, was said to 'breathe indeed unutterable things'.[18]

As Julie Carlson has shown, the rejection of the stage by Romantic writers such as Coleridge was in part a rejection of Siddons: 'they cannot face theatre when it feminizes Shakespeare and thus England's native genius. Female power presses too closely in theatre; attempts to distance themselves from it only intensify the pressure.'[19] Carlson's work, like Pascoe's, demonstrates what is at stake when the presence of Siddons in late Georgian culture begins to be properly acknowledged. She troubles definitions of Romanticism and gender, by surpassing Garrick's success in harnessing Shakespeare as a force of legitimation and challenging male artists to see themselves in her. But the lessons regarding Siddons go further than this. By seeing her properly, in the sense of acknowledging the media in which she was represented – newspapers, journals, letters, biography, playbills, prologues, epilogues, portraiture, caricature, not to mention plays such as Baillie's *Series of Plays*, and Inchbald's *British Theatre* – dramatic literature itself can be reconfigured as a more inclusive category that integrates the cultures of print and the stage rather than identifying them as antithetical. Such an approach also compels a reconsideration of literary culture as a whole in that it highlights literature's embeddedness in the performative and sociable contexts of its production – the 'theatres' of the coffeehouse, the club, the lecture room, and the domestic fireside with which the actual stage was always in lively traffic.

NOTES

1. See Jane Moody, *Illegitimate Theatre in London, 1770–1840* (Cambridge: Cambridge University Press, 2000), p. 151.
2. See Robert Jordan, *The Convict Theatres of Early Australia 1788–1840* (Strawberry Hills: Currency House, 2002).
3. John Keats, *Letters*, ed. H. E. Rollins, 2 vols. (Cambridge: Cambridge University Press, 1958), II: 215–16.
4. *The Diary of Sylas Neville*, ed. Basil Cozens-Hardy (Oxford: Oxford University Press, 1950), p. 22.
5. *St James's Chronicle*, 16–19 December 1797.
6. Charles Lamb, *Works*, ed. E. V. Lucas, 7 vols. (London: Methuen, 1903), II: 132.
7. See John Barrell, *'Exhibition Extraordinary!!': Radical Broadsides of the mid 1790s* (Nottingham: Trent Editions, 2001).
8. *The Poems of Samuel Johnson*, ed. David Nicol Smith and Edward L. McAdam, 2nd edn (Oxford: Clarendon Press, 1974), p. 109 (lines 43–6).
9. For Foote and Macklin, see Matthew Kinservik, *Disciplining Satire: the Censoring of English Comedy on the Eighteenth-Century London Stage* (Lewisburg, PA: Bucknell University Press, 2002).
10. Tracy C. Davis, *The Economics of the British Stage 1800–1914* (Cambridge: Cambridge University Press, 2000), p. 37.
11. See Robert R. Bataille, *The Writing Life of Hugh Kelly: Politics, Journalism, and Theater in Late-Eighteenth-Century London* (Carbondale: Southern Illinois University Press, 2000).
12. See Gillian Russell, *The Theatres of War: Performance, Politics and Society 1793–1815* (Oxford: Oxford University Press, 1995).
13. *Bell's British Theatre*, 20 vols. (1776–78).
14. Ellen Donkin, *Getting into the Act: Women Playwrights in London 1776–1829* (New York: Routledge, 1995).
15. *The British Theatre: A Collection of Plays with Remarks, Biographical and Critical by Mrs Inchbald*, 25 vols. (1808).
16. *The British Theatre* included Inchbald's correspondence with the dramatist George Colman the Younger, who had insisted that her gender disqualified her as a critic.
17. Judith Pascoe, *Romantic Theatricality: Gender, Poetry, and Spectatorship* (Ithaca: Cornell University Press, 1997), p. 3.
18. *Belfast News Letter*, 14–17 June 1785.
19. Julie Carlson, *In the Theatre of Romanticism: Coleridge, Nationalism, Women* (Cambridge: Cambridge University Press, 1994), p. 173.

FURTHER READING

Baer, Marc, *Theatre and Disorder in Late Georgian London*, Oxford: Oxford University Press, 1992.
Bate, Jonathan, *Shakespearean Constitutions: Politics, Theatre, Criticism, 1730–1830*, Oxford: Oxford University Press, 1992.
Burroughs, Catherine B., *Closet Stages: Joanna Baillie and the Theater Theory of British Romantic Writers*, Philadelphia: Pennsylvania State University Press, 1997.

Carlson, Julie, *In the Theatre of Romanticism: Coleridge, Nationalism, Women*, Cambridge: Cambridge University Press, 1994.

Conolly, L. W., *The Censorship of English Drama, 1737–1824*, San Marino: Huntington Library Press, 1976.

Donkin, Ellen, *Getting into the Act: Women Playwrights in London 1776–1829*, New York: Routledge, 1995.

Moody, Jane, *Illegitimate Theatre in London, 1770–1840*, Cambridge: Cambridge University Press, 2000.

Nicoll, Allardyce, *The Garrick Stage: Theatres and Audience in the Eighteenth Century*, Manchester: Manchester University Press, 1980.

Pascoe, Judith, *Romantic Theatricality: Gender, Poetry, and Spectatorship*, Ithaca: Cornell University Press, 1997.

Russell, Gillian, 'Theatre' in *An Oxford Companion to the Romantic Age: British Culture 1776–1832*, ed. Iain McCalman et al., Oxford: Oxford University Press, 1999, pp. 223–31.

Stephen, John Russell, *The Censorship of English Drama 1824–1901*, Cambridge: Cambridge University Press, 1980.

Straub, Kristina, *Sexual Suspects: Eighteenth-Century Players and Sexual Ideology*, Princeton: Princeton University Press, 1992.

Thomas, David (ed.), *Restoration and Georgian England, 1660–1768*, Cambridge: Cambridge University Press, 1989.

7

JAMES WATT

Gothic

In Richard Hurd's 'Dialogue on the Age of Queen Elizabeth', the third of his *Moral and Political Dialogues* (1760), the figure of Mr Addison states that the Gothic ruins of Kenilworth Castle at once awaken 'an indignation against . . . the tyranny of those wretched times', and foster 'a generous pleasure in . . . the happiness we enjoy under a juster and more equal government'. For Addison's antagonist Dr Arbuthnot, by contrast, Kenilworth offers the aura of a heroic past, and a 'memorial of the virtue, industry [and] ingenuity of our ancestors'.[1] The Gothic in Hurd's dialogue provides a differential by which the consequences of economic, political, and social change might be assessed. Adapting the long-standing view of the Goths as destroyers of classical Rome, innumerable eighteenth-century writers – in a similar way to Hurd's Addison – represented the Gothic past as a distant epoch, on which the enlightened present could look back in complacent triumph. The Gothic past also retained a potential critical function in the period, however, standing – in Arbuthnot's terms – for what had been lost, or what was seen to be lacking, in the present. Given that the Gothic peoples who had repelled Roman invasion went on to settle in Britain, the Gothic could also be resorted to, in a wide variety of ways, as the fount of a native spirit of liberty, or even of an incipient democratic tradition. Hurd's dialogue by no means exhausts the possible meanings and uses of this elusive term, but it helpfully points to the way in which the category of Gothic was invoked in different contexts, in order to serve different agendas. While sometimes referring specifically to the Goths themselves, constructions of the Gothic as a pseudo-historical period almost always offered in more general terms a reading of the past and its legacy.

Even if they rarely describe themselves as such, many of the late eighteenth- and early nineteenth-century literary works now classified as Gothic can also be seen to offer ways of understanding the past, and the relations between past and present. In broad terms, the Gothic as a new literary form emerged out of the revaluation of an indigenous aesthetic, defined in opposition to a rule-based neo-classicism. The eighteenth-century rediscovery of medieval cultural artefacts to a large extent circumvented the schematism of the debate between Hurd's Addison and Arbuthnot, but nonetheless served to focus attention on different aspects of a pre-modern heritage that was both strange and native, distant and familiar. In his *Letters on Chivalry and Romance* (1762), Hurd asserted 'the pre-eminence of the Gothic manners and fictions, as adapted to the ends of poetry', and helped to define and contextualize a distinctive literary tradition comprising, in addition to Ariosto and Tasso, English writers such as Chaucer, Spenser, and Shakespeare.[2] Like many of his contemporaries, Hurd claimed that the modern reader was able to indulge in the pleasures of romance by projecting belief in its improbabilities onto the past societies in which such works were written or set. The literary supernatural acquired further legitimacy at around the same time, as a result of the growing interest in the transporting power of 'sublime' experience and the recognition of what the young Anna Laetitia Barbauld referred to, after Edmund Burke, as 'the Pleasure Derived from Objects of Terror'.[3] Put simply, the mid-eighteenth century revival of romance allied to this partial rehabilitation of fictional marvel and miracle helped to prepare the way for the hybrid literary form of Gothic. Identifying itself as 'romance', and therefore relatively uninhibited by formal constraints, Gothic fiction – the main focus of this chapter – offered an alternative to the novel of modern life that could be adapted and refigured in many different ways.

In the preface to the second edition of *The Castle of Otranto* (1764), Horace Walpole delivered what has often been regarded as a manifesto for the modern Gothic romance, stating that his work, now subtitled 'A Gothic Story', sought to restore the qualities of imagination and invention to contemporary fiction. Walpole first presented *Otranto* anonymously (the original title-page calls it a translation 'from the Original Italian of Onuphrio Muralto'), perhaps because of its potentially ambiguous critical status as a modern work representing supernatural effects. Walpole's self-representation as a cautious innovator working in a native aesthetic tradition is nonetheless complicated by the obvious playfulness of the two prefaces and the narrative itself. The tone of the work is set by the bizarre opening episode – described as 'unprecedented' – in which Conrad, the son and heir of Manfred Prince of Otranto, is crushed to death on his wedding day by a gigantic helmet belonging to the statue of a previous Lord, Alfonso the Good; not only is the helmet said to be 'an hundred times more large than any casque ever made for human being', but it is also 'shaded with a proportionable quantity of black feathers'.[4] *Otranto*'s position within any larger cultural movement needs to be qualified, since it seems to construct the Gothic as a source of the ridiculous as much as the sublime, and to have represented a form of attention-seeking continuous with many of Walpole's other works and projects, such as his villa Strawberry Hill. Walpole's narrative of 'improbable and absurd adventures'[5] in effect divided its initial readership, packaging diverting eccentricity for a leisured audience, while confounding those readers who were unable to assimilate such novelty.

If Walpole's claim to have followed the example of Shakespeare seems comically extravagant, however, *Otranto* does offer echoes of Shakespearean tragedy – and especially *Hamlet* – in the basic outline of its plot. *Otranto*'s pantomime-style fragments of arms and armour initially appear bathetic, but they nonetheless finally reassemble so as to present a vision of the usurped Alfonso, who proclaims the legitimate nobility of the virtuous peasant, Theodore, and prompts Manfred to confess the extent of his complicity in his grandfather's crimes. For all the levity of *Otranto*, Walpole helped to establish a vocabulary of themes and tropes that was later resorted to across the genres; perhaps above all, he provided a resonant and potentially adaptable account of the past returning to destabilize the present.

Though John Aikin's fragment 'Sir Bertrand' (1773) employs various effects partly derived from *Otranto*, the first full-length work to engage with Walpole's example was Clara Reeve's *The Old English Baron* (1778), originally published as *The Champion of Virtue* in 1777. While Reeve similarly presented her work as 'A Gothic Story' based on a recovered manuscript, she saw *The Old English Baron* as a corrective to the tonal instability of *Otranto*, and accentuated the didactic and exemplary potential of romance as an antidote to the 'melancholy retrospect' of history.[6] Readers from Walpole onwards have dismissed Reeve's work as a feeble imitation of *Otranto*, since it makes only minimal use of supernatural effects, and devotes far more space to the detail of the final property settlement than to its account of the original act of usurpation. More recently, Reeve's work has also been seen as a distinctly bourgeois revision of *Otranto* that looks ahead of its medieval setting, so as to enact the defeat of feudal despotism by the middle-class values of its hero, Edmund. Importantly, however, Reeve's hero represents the principle of legitimacy as well as merit, and the aura of his nobility is widely recognized, especially by servants and retainers, before it is officially acknowledged. Whereas the Castle of Otranto self-destructs at the end of Walpole's work, Lovel Castle spontaneously opens its gates to receive its rightful occupant, and becomes again the focus of a harmonious, and pre-modern, moral economy.

The Old English Baron is the prototype of what I elsewhere term the 'loyalist Gothic' romance.[7] Although only a handful of later works such as Richard Warner's *Netley Abbey* (1795) or the anonymous *Mort Castle* (1798) describe themselves as 'Gothic', others besides these similarly set tales of usurpation, and its reversal, in the English medieval past. These works generally depict a conflict between patriotic heroes, aligned with historical figures from the pantheon of Edwards and Henries, and ambitious, scheming villains, representing an alien – usually French – presence. Rather than stage the uncanny eruption of the past in the manner of *Otranto*, loyalist Gothic romances invoke the agency of the supernatural in more straightforwardly benign terms, as a means of exorcizing past corruption or criminality, and restoring the status quo. Such works were especially prominent in the 1790s, and need to be read in the context of the counter-revolutionary construction of the Gothic as an exemplary pseudo-historical period, characterized by hierarchy and stability, as well as a heritage of military victory. Clara Reeve's historical romance *Memoirs of Sir Roger De Clarendon* (1793), for example, set during the reign of Edward III, explicitly praises 'our Gothic ancestors', and the 'good government' they provided, as an antidote to the threat posed by 'the new philosophy of the present day'.[8] Gothic architecture as well as ancestry was widely accorded a heightened symbolic value in the 1790s, as the embodiment of an immemorial authority and a proud national history. If British patriotism often took a markedly Protestant and Whiggish form in the eighteenth century, in the 1790s at least atheistic innovators were seen to pose more of a threat than the vestiges of Catholicism or feudalism described by Hurd's Addison. In 'this age of threatened invasion', 'An Architect' wrote in the *Gentleman's Magazine* in 1799, 'our antient remains of art, that every where meet our eyes . . . remind us of the sublime genius of their authors; remind us of the heroic acts of those defenders of their country who brought perfidious France beneath their triumphant swords; remind us of our long race of sovereigns, the admiration and dread of surrounding nations, and remind us of our duty to our Creator, to ourselves, and to mankind'.[9]

While counter-revolutionary constructions of the Gothic appealed to the stable hierarchy of the Middle Ages, 'Gothic feminists' in the late eighteenth and early nineteenth centuries seized upon the high status accorded to women in ancient Germanic or Anglo-Saxon societies: writers such as the Whig patriots Lucy Aikin and Elizabeth Hamilton traced the connections between this Gothic inheritance and a distinctively modern and British notion of polite femininity.[10] Despite such assertions of continuity with the Gothic past, however, the understanding of 'Gothic' now most often attributed to the fiction known by that name is the sense that was popularized especially by radicals and reformers in the 1790s. Responding to Edmund Burke's *Reflections on the Revolution in France* (1790), Mary Wollstonecraft questioned why it should be necessary to repair rather than pull down 'an ancient castle, built in barbarous ages, of Gothic materials'.[11] Writers such as Wollstonecraft and Tom Paine sought to conceive of the future without reference to custom or precedent, and characterized Burke as an author of sentimental fictions that glossed over the injustice and oppression of Gothic feudalism. Instead of offering 'a faithful picture of a well-governed kingdom' in the manner of Reeve's *Sir Roger De Clarendon* (*Clarendon*, 1: xvi), the best-known works of Gothic fiction in the late eighteenth century depict the effects of arbitrary or despotic power on the liberty of the individual. Probably the majority of Gothic works in this period were by female authors and about female protagonists; if it was widely accepted that the condition of women in any society was the best gauge of its level of civilization, many Gothic fictions counter myths of past or present felicity by focusing on the persecution of women. The first heroine-centred work to employ a historical setting was probably Sophia Lee's *The Recess* (1785), a self-described 'tale of other times' claiming origins, like *Otranto* and *The Old English Baron*, in a found manuscript. Lee's work provides a supplement to the official historical record by blending history with romance, via the estranged perspective of its narrators, Ellinor and Matilda, daughters of Mary, Queen of Scots by a secret marriage to the Duke of Norfolk. For their own safety, Ellinor and Matilda have to be raised in a subterranean apartment – at once sanctuary and prison – in the Gothic ruins of St Vincent's Abbey. Depicting the Elizabethan era as an age of almost anarchic strife, Lee's work demythologizes the Gothic castle, and presents it as the embodiment of an oppressive restraint rather than a stable hierarchy.

Like *The Recess*, the works of Ann Radcliffe from *A Sicilian Romance* (1790) to *The Italian* (1797) similarly depict the confinement and persecution of their heroines in alien and oppressive, geographically as well as historically distant, environments. Radcliffe's fiction differs from Lee's example, however, in the detail and intensity of its focus on the heroine's consciousness. In *The Mysteries of Udolpho* (1794), the death of Emily St Aubert's father forces her to go and live with her aunt, whose marriage to the Italian Signor Montoni places Emily under his control in the Castle of Udolpho. While Emily is introduced as a heroine possessed of a potentially excessive sensibility, the terrors she experiences during her captivity in Udolpho are shown to be more than simply a function of an over-active imagination, since they are clearly grounded in the real threats she faces to her person and property. Most vividly in *A Sicilian Romance* (1790), where the twin heroines discover their imprisoned mother within the apparently haunted Castle of Mazzini, the uncanny and seemingly supernatural phenomena of Radcliffean romance signify the actuality of patriarchal coercion. In contrast to Sophia Lee's Ellinor and Matilda, though, Radcliffe's heroines always triumph in their struggle against arbitrary power, and their virtue receives its due reward. Emily St Aubert eventually escapes the custody of Montoni, and she is apprised of her full family history (and disabused of any suspicions about her father), before being reunited with the feminized hero Valancourt. *Udolpho* ultimately stages the defeat of the patriarchal tyranny represented by Montoni, and, in contrast to *The Old English Baron*, abandons rather than redeems the Gothic castle. The transition from the feudal to the modern apparently enacted by *Udolpho* is complicated by the fact that the work finally returns to the idyllic romance retreat of La Vallée. Radcliffe's work clearly locates Montoni and the Castle of Udolpho in a past stage of society, however, and contrasts this with the more progressive order heralded by the mutual esteem and domestic happiness of Emily and Valancourt.

Even if *Udolpho* seems to stage the transcendence of the past in Whiggish terms, Radcliffean romance has nonetheless been distinguished above all for its style and trademark effects. Radcliffe is especially renowned for the way that her work builds suspense, conjuring up, only finally to explain away, the 'nameless terrors' experienced by her heroines and her readers: [12] the famous black veil in Udolpho conceals a waxwork rather than a corpse. This signature technique, while it exasperated some critics and readers, was consistent with Radcliffe's progressive agenda, since it serves to underline the defeat of superstition by the forces of enlightenment. Alongside the 'official' warnings against first impressions that *Udolpho* in particular provides, however, Radcliffe's works credit not only the intuitive imagining but also the creative enthusiasm of their heroines. As well as exhibiting the rhetoric of bodily feeling familiar from earlier sentimental fiction, Radcliffe's heroines demonstrate an affinity for poetic composition and an elevated responsiveness to the natural world. Such solitary pleasures represent an empowering release rather than an immature absorption in Radcliffe's terms, and this heightened individual experience remains uncontained by the relatively brief tableaux of domestic harmony and marital happiness with which these works conclude. Radcliffe certainly helped to bring a new rhetorical complexity to the Gothic, and – in recent years especially – many readers have claimed that her heroines' flights of imagination constitute the real truth, or core, of Radcliffean romance. The initial critical acclaim garnered by these long and digressive works perhaps owed most, though, to the cultural capital of their 'surplus' material. Radcliffe's works repeatedly allude to the conventions of picturesque tourism or the terminology of the sublime and the beautiful, and make extensive reference to British writers such as Shakespeare, Milton, Thomson, and Gray. Celebrated by Nathan Drake as the 'Shakespeare of romance writers', Radcliffe was the star of 1790s Gothic, widely credited with raising the standards of prose fiction in general.[13]

Radcliffe's success coincided with a significant rise in the prominence and status of the Gothic, and her work lent itself to imitation, as well as abridgement and dramatic adaptation, inspiring a host of other professional writers, such as Isabella Kelly, Mary Meeke, Eliza Parsons, and Regina Maria Roche. If they differed over what to call it, critics from around the mid-1790s began to register the emergence of a new style of romance with distinct and recognizable characteristics. So-called 'recipe satires' seized upon the widespread repetition of certain generic givens, and reduced 'Terrorist Novel Writing' or 'Modern Romance' to a series of ingredients or effects in a fairly genial manner.[14] Just as Matthew Lewis's *The Monk* (1796) was followed by Richard Sicklemore's *The New Monk* (1798), so many Gothic works were trailed by parodies. Critics and commentators also engaged more seriously with the popularity of this new kind of writing, and especially with the circumstances of its production and reception. While there is no reliable evidence that women read significantly more fiction than men, responsibility for the consumption of Gothic novels or romances was often projected onto women, partly at least because these works were commonly identified as fashionable or luxury commodities. Numerous writers claimed that Gothic fiction posed a specific threat to women, often making a connection between romance-reading and quixotic delusion – an association at once upheld and complicated by Jane Austen's *Northanger Abbey* (1818), a work originally drafted in the late 1790s. Other critics in this period who addressed the Gothic as a cultural phenomenon took it to be symptomatic of even wider, and more general, social upheaval. The vast number of novels and romances produced by commercial publishers such as William Lane's Minerva Press, often characterized in terms of overwhelming swarms and deluges, offered a new focus for long-standing concerns about the responsiveness of literature to popular demand, the impact of circulating libraries, and the consequent bypassing of critical regulation and authority. In the 1790s, anxieties about who read what – and where and when they read it – were especially fraught, and Gothic fiction, taken en bloc, was often seen to be complicit with the growth of an undisciplined, and therefore dangerously susceptible, reading public.

By the late 1790s, commentators began to offer wholesale denunciations of the literature of terror, while writers such as Wordsworth famously sought to distance their work from the contamination of 'frantic novels' that pandered to a debased popular demand.[15] At the same time, however, many critics and reviewers were much more discriminating when discussing the functioning of individual novels or romances. Some works were seen to be simply dull rather than in any way subversive, while the fiction of a writer such as Ann Radcliffe was widely seen to offer a healthy escapism: even for prominent anti-Jacobins such as Richard Polwhele, author of the censorious satire *The Unsex'd Females* (1798), Radcliffe still retained the 'power to please'.[16] Other women writers, by contrast, were attacked for betraying their femininity and polluting the pure realm of romance enchantment. Numerous works of fiction by women in this period engage with things as they are, crediting female sexual desire, and provocatively describing the confinement of their heroines in contemporary Britain, while offering no consolatory romantic closure; in works such as these the kinds of terrors described by Radcliffe's *Udolpho* are not consigned to the distant or Gothic past. Eliza Fenwick's epistolary novel *Secresy; or, The Ruin on the Rock* (1795), for example, describes a heroine, Sibella Valmont, who is confined by her uncle within Valmont Castle to ensure her submission to his will; Sibella dies at the close of the work, following the death of her child. Mary Wollstonecraft's unfinished *The Wrongs of Woman, or Maria* (1798) explicitly contrasts the artificial 'abodes of horror . . . conjured up by the magic spell of genius' with 'the real mansion of despair' occupied by the title character – 'bastilled for life' in an asylum on the orders of her husband. *The Wrongs of Woman* offers a universalizing gloss on the experience of its heroine, emphasizing that it is not just the story of an individual but stands for the 'history . . . of woman' in general.[17]

The more detailed critical focus on the Gothic in the last twenty years or so has enriched our understanding of the way that writers in this period responded to each other's work and refigured the possibilities of the form. Whereas Wollstonecraft, for example, located the terrors of Radcliffean romance in the present, and in Britain rather than Mediterranean Europe, other writers in the 1790s defined their work against the feminization of prose fiction to which the rise of the Gothic romance was often seen to have contributed. Presenting itself as a 'Rhapsodical Romance' by one Lady Harriet Marlow, William Beckford's *Modern Novel Writing* (1796) heavy-handedly satirizes some of Radcliffe's stylistic trademarks such as the explained supernatural or extended picturesque description. Matthew Lewis's *The Monk* (1796), in turn, blends Radcliffean romance with a primarily French tradition of libertine or 'philosophical' pornography and the *Sturm und Drang* sensation of contemporary German fiction. Set in Spain in an unspecified period, *The Monk* accentuates the Whiggish coordinates of Radcliffe's work by offering a much more direct focus on the corruption of the Catholic Church. The devout public persona of the Monk Ambrosio, like all other performances of religious piety in the novel, is shown to be a façade: Ambrosio is seduced by the charms of the Satanic temptress Matilda, initially disguised as the male novice Rosario, who spurs him on to find further ways of satisfying his newly awakened, and insatiable, desire. Clearly presented as a product of 'monastic fetters', Ambrosio's sexual awakening is described as an assertion of freedom from restraint, just as the allegorically resonant storming of the Convent of St Clare is contextualized, and to a large extent justified, as a mass revolt against Catholic hypocrisy and repression.[18] While the reader is intermittently invited to identify with Ambrosio, however, the main object of his lust, Antonia, is cynically and voyeuristically presented throughout, and her exhibition of virtue in distress – in Sadean terms – only serves further to excite the desire of her persecutor. Lewis scandalously rewrote Radcliffe by demonstrating the powerlessness of innocence, and by offering a far more literal take on the 'family secrets' plot of *Udolpho*: *The Monk* finally reveals not only that Ambrosio has raped and murdered, but that his victims are members of his own family. Whereas Radcliffean romance offers a Burkean formulation of terror dependent on obscurity, Lewis's work leaves little to the imagination and assaults the reader with luridly-detailed scenes of horror, describing the rape and murder of Antonia amid the 'rotting bones' and 'putrid, half-corrupted Bodies' of the Abbey of St Clare's dungeons (*Monk*, p. 379). Lewis exceeded Radcliffe, too, by employing supernatural effects without rationalizing explanation, a strategy that culminates in the final episode where, following his fatal pact, Ambrosio is hurled into an abyss by Satan, tortured, and finally torn to pieces. The appearance of *The Monk* perhaps prompted Radcliffe to write *The Italian* (1797) in a bid to re-establish some distance between Lewis's work and her own. Virtue and innocence offer sufficient protection for the heroine Ellena di Rosalba, and she is finally reunited with her suitor Vivaldi, while her main persecutor, the monk Schedoni, is tried and condemned by the Inquisition – now more of a legitimate legal tribunal than a limb of the old regime.

For the Marquis de Sade, there was a certain inevitability about the appearance of works such as *The Monk*, since it seemed to be necessary 'to call upon the aid of hell itself' simply to attract the attention of readers, at a time when everyday reality was already so shocking. Sade classed Lewis's work as 'superior in all respects' to Radcliffean romance,[19] and some contemporary critics similarly praised *The Monk* by appealing to the masculine rhetoric of daring, energy, or genius; some reviewers even defended Ambrosio in Enlightenment materialist terms as a figure whose response to sexual temptation was natural and instinctive. Although a scandal followed the revelation of his authorship, Lewis continued in his attempts to shock readers, and bait critics, with works such as the bizarre comic melodrama *The Castle Spectre* (1798), probably the first Gothic play to exhibit a ghost on stage. The example set by Lewis seems to have provoked others to try and outdo him in the quest for reputation, and certain prominent male writers in this period likewise presented themselves as risk-takers or innovators, striving like Charles Robert Maturin to 'out-Herod all the Herods of the German school & get possession of the Magic Lamp from the Conjuror Lewis himself'.[20]

Referring to the figure of Barkiarokh in his unpublished *Episodes of Vathek*, William Beckford claimed that his character made Lord Byron's 'Corsairs & Don Juans' seem like 'milk and water Puritans'.[21] The tonal and thematic similarities between a range of works such as *Otranto*, *Vathek*, and *The Monk*, allied to the class position and sexual orientation of their writers, might encourage readers to classify the 'male Gothic' as a distinct subgenre, providing an arena for transgressive fantasy and the performance of homosexual identities. While there are suggestive parallels between all of these writers, though, the work of Charlotte Dacre serves to qualify the explanatory force of any essential distinction between Gothic fictions written by men and by women, about overreaching 'villain-heroes' and persecuted heroines respectively. Dacre's *The Confessions of The Nun of St Omer* (1805) was dedicated to Lewis, and her subsequent novel, *Zofloya; or, the Moor* (1806), set in fifteenth-century Venice, can be read as a revision – perhaps even a trumping – of *The Monk* that replaces Ambrosio with a female protagonist. *Zofloya* prompted the *Literary Journal* to describe its author as one 'afflicted with the dismal malady of maggots in the brain'.[22] Dacre's anti-heroine, Victoria di Loredani, is a desiring woman driven by her passions, who is spurred on to greater heights of criminality and sexual obsession by the noble and majestic Moorish servant Zofloya. Even more depraved than Ambrosio, Victoria at one point instigates the torture of the innocent Lilla, the fiancée of a man who has resisted her advances, and stabs her to death, before dashing her into an abyss; at the end of the work, Victoria too (like Ambrosio) meets a similar fate, at the hands of the demon to whom she has resigned herself.

Just as Lewis influenced Dacre, so Dacre inspired the teenaged Percy Bysshe Shelley: Shelley's *Zastrozzi* (1810) and *St Irvyne* (1811), written by way of adolescent homage to Dacre, similarly exhibit the destructive consequences of passion and revenge. Works in this tradition are clearly preoccupied with sensation and affect ahead of any concern with the legacy of the past or the connections between past and present. In relation to Lewis, Dacre, or Shelley, the influential 'tales of terror' published by *Blackwood's Edinburgh Magazine* in this period, such as William Maginn's 'The Man in the Bell' or John Galt's 'The Buried Alive' (both 1821), focus even more intensely on an individual event or episode. As well as describing physical sensation in clinically precise detail, the tales published by *Blackwood's* also commonly explore the psychological dimensions of extreme experience. From about the end of the eighteenth century onwards, indeed, many works can be seen to concentrate in materialist terms on the workings of the mind, evoking their protagonists' states of claustrophobia, dread, and paranoia in contemporary settings, or unspecified historical locations, rather than the distant past. Although already implicit in the fiction of Ann Radcliffe, this new psychological focus was given both definition and intellectual justification in Joanna Baillie's 'Introductory Discourse' to the first volume of *A Series of Plays: In Which It Is Attempted to Delineate the Stronger Passions of the Mind* (1798). As in her acclaimed tragedy *De Monfort* (1798), a study of a protagonist driven to commit murder by an irrational and uncontrollable hatred, Baillie sought to provide access to what she represented as hitherto neglected subject-matter: 'the progress of the higher passions in the human breast'.[23] While *Frankenstein* (1818) famously originated in a ghost-story contest, and has been adapted with a sensational slant by numerous films and dramas, Mary Shelley similarly saw her work in philosophical terms. Echoing Joanna Baillie, Percy Shelley wrote in his preface to the novel that Frankenstein's reanimation of the creature provided scope for a 'more comprehensive and commanding' delineation of the 'human passions', via the often unreliable first-person narration of Walton, Frankenstein, and the creature.[24] Whereas the works of the German writer Ernest William Hoffmann gave 'wild and unbounded license . . . to an irregular fancy', according to Sir Walter Scott in his 1827 essay 'On the Supernatural in Fictitious Composition', *Frankenstein* at once resorted to and transcended the fantastic in the service of a larger, intellectual purpose.[25] *Frankenstein* has probably attracted more critical commentary than any other Gothic work from the Romantic period, and its highly resonant myth of creation has been seen to allegorize, among other things, the French Revolution, relations between Capital and Labour, slave rebellions in the Caribbean, scientific irresponsibility, and the author's experience of childbirth.

A writer such as Joanna Baillie addressed the passions of her protagonists in terms of an abstract and timeless human nature, making little reference to the impact of social or cultural determinants. In the different varieties of 'national Gothic' that emerged in the same period, however, such a focus on psychological interiority was also marked by specific political concerns. Charles Brockden Brown's most famous novel *Wieland* (1798), for example, declares its interest in 'the latent springs and occasional perversions of the human mind', but also draws attention to an immediate, local resonance with the subtitle 'An American Tale'. *Wieland* helped to establish a distinctive American Gothic tradition, preoccupied with examining the origins and destiny of the United States. Set in rural Pennsylvania just before the American Revolution, *Wieland* describes the impact of the outsider Francis Carwin on the apparently utopian community of Clara and Theodore Wieland, orphaned after the mysterious death of their father. Believing that he has heard the voice of God, Theodore Wieland murders his wife and children, then kills himself on realizing what he has done. Despite what the novel goes on to reveal about Carwin's powers of ventriloquy, Brown does not conclusively resolve the issue of whether Carwin is responsible for conjuring up the voices that Wieland hears, or whether the voices are generated by Wieland's own religious enthusiasm. The precise cause of Wieland's downfall remains a mystery in the novel's terms, and the reader is left to consider 'the evils that may flow from the consequent deductions of the understanding' when the senses themselves are deceived.[26] Read allegorically, in the context of the factional disputes between Federalists and Republicans in the 1790s, Brown's work dramatizes the threats posed to the young republic by foreign subversives such as Carwin. Since Wieland is so easily deluded, though, the novel can also be seen to issue a sceptical challenge to the republican faith in the voice of the people, and to the representative claims of democracy itself.

Whereas Brown revised the narrative technique of the explained supernatural familiar from Gothic works of the 1790s, other 'national' varieties of Gothic fiction in the nineteenth century continued to address the relations between the past and the present in a manner similar to Walpole's *Otranto*. What is distinctive about Scottish Gothic, for example, is the way it depicts the resurgence of the past in the form of a pre-modern ancestral or native culture, delineated in different ways in the eighteenth century by writers such as James Macpherson and Robert Burns.[27] Sir Walter Scott's first novel *Waverley* (1814) presents the Jacobite rebellion of 1745 as an eruption of primitive energies from the Gothic past that engulfs the title character and endangers the order of modernity established by the Revolution of 1688–9 and the Union of 1707. *Waverley* also depicts the defeat of this rebellion, though, and reconfirms the temporal sequence of the stages of society while according the vestiges of clan culture aesthetic value as the embodiment of 'evanescent manners': following the execution of Fergus Mac-Ivor, Scott's work describes the 'large and spirited painting' that is exhibited at Tully-Veolan, showing Edward Waverley and Fergus 'in their Highland dress, the scene a wild, rocky, and mountainous pass, down which the clan were descending in the background'.[28]

Not all of Scott's novels absorb the effects of the past in the same way as *Waverley*. *The Bride of Lammermoor* (1819), set around the time of the Act of Union, dramatizes the continuing hold of the past, and offers no resolution to the conflict between the dispossessed Edgar Ravenswood and the new proprietor of his ancestral home, Sir William Ashton; unable to transcend the legacy of revenge he has inherited, Ravenswood meets his death in accordance with the terms of a prophecy transmitted by a pre-modern oral tradition. In an English setting, meanwhile, *Ivanhoe* (1820) complicates its apparently Whiggish account of a reconciliation between Saxon and Norman, offering no illusions about the rest of King Richard's reign, and no security for the Jews Isaac and Rebecca, who opt for exile in Muslim Spain. While it is true that Scott's fiction does not always straightforwardly underwrite a narrative of modernization, however, the Waverley novels – whatever their settings – insistently return to the subject of societal transition, and offer ideologically powerful accounts of national tradition within a larger British or Unionist framework. In *Redgauntlet* (1824), another novel that deals with a failed Jacobite rising, Scott contextualizes the Gothic past as the embodiment of glamorous and heroic but nonetheless archaic identities, ultimately contained within modern civil society and its attendant commercial prosperity.

In direct contrast with the novels of Scott, the fiction of James Hogg eschews the rhetoric of national union, and offers a far less contained or distanced account of an enduringly vital pre-modern popular culture. Hogg's best-known work *The Private Memoirs and Confessions of a Justified Sinner* (1824) is built around the ultimately fatal conflict between the brothers George Colwan and Robert Wringhim, who schematically represent the religious and political faultlines of Scottish society at the beginning of the eighteenth century. In a similar fashion to Brown's *Wieland*, Hogg's novel deals with the psychology of fanaticism, offering external (editorial) and internal (autobiographical) perspectives on the life and crimes of Robert Wringhim, an antinomian who believes himself to be one of the Elect. According to his confessional narrative, Wringhim loses control over his life under the influence of a mysterious double, and becomes a social pariah, before apparently committing suicide. Like *Wieland*, Hogg's work offers no conclusive account of Wringhim's psychological state, leaving it unclear whether his second self is the devil or a product of his unconscious. Hogg's editor-figure is bewildered by the manuscript of the sinner's confessions, and receives no assistance from the shepherd called James Hogg he encounters near the grave of the suicide during his quest for further information. In the absence of an authoritative framing of the novel's events, truth and wisdom rest, if anywhere, with a common people whose Scots dialect evades or resists absorption by any enlightened intellectual framework.

Hogg's work needs to be read as a response to the way in which Scott sought to harmonize class and regional divisions in the name of a new sense of Romantic nationhood. Works within the tradition known as Irish Gothic, meanwhile, address the model of reconciliation between Gaelic Irish and English offered by 'national tales' such as Sydney Owenson's *The Wild Irish Girl* (1806), written in the aftermath of a still more recent Act of Union. The Protestant Church of Ireland curate Charles Robert Maturin is known as an author of national tales that imitated Owenson, but also as the most prominent exponent of Irish Gothic. Maturin's remarkable *Melmoth the Wanderer*

(1820) displays obvious affinities with previous works such as *The Monk* in its sensationalism and overt anti-Catholicism, most vividly exemplified by an episode describing the live burial of two lovers in a Spanish convent. Alongside such sectarian propaganda, though, *Melmoth* also offers an angle on the precarious position of the Protestant elite – seeking to safeguard its privilege and status in the face of an increasingly organized Catholic majority. Via a structurally complex series of interlinked first-person narratives and embedded tales, Maturin's work describes the process whereby the cursed title character searches for someone to release him from his bargain with the devil. For all the global sweep of the novel, encompassing Spain, England, and an Indian island as well as Ireland itself, Maturin's work continually refers back to its native political context, and dramatizes the legacy of past conflicts in the present. Melmoth is introduced as the brother of an officer in Cromwell's army who obtained his lands in Ireland by expropriating a royalist family, and Melmoth's pact with the devil is often read as a metaphor of this primal violence. Victim as well as victimizer, Melmoth betrays in his efforts to relinquish his burden not only a sense of guilt but also an underlying fear of vengeance.

If the works we classify as Gothic very often explore the relations between past and present, as suggested at the outset, the relation to the past offered by Maturin's *Melmoth* might be seen as a distinctly anxious or troubled one. Many of the novels and romances discussed above stage in different ways either the defeat of feudal tyranny – most clearly in the case of Radcliffe's fiction – or the potentially disturbing recurrence of what was thought to have been defeated, forgotten, or superseded – as in the numerous works that adapt the plot outline of *Otranto*. Any larger characterization of the Gothic as a literary tradition in this period, however, needs to take account of the fact that the possibilities of the form were refigured under diverse conditions, and in diverse ways. Certain works prioritized sensation and affect or developed a psychological focus in a near-contemporary setting; the romances that resorted to the Gothic past, from *The Old English Baron* onwards, meanwhile, did not always simply represent the Gothic as a source of barbarism, menace, or terror. Later in the nineteenth century, many constructions of the medieval era displayed continuities with the counter-revolutionary loyalist Gothic of the 1790s, and writers such as John Ruskin asserted a connection with Gothic ancestry and culture in unambiguously positive terms. Later versions of Gothic fiction, though, moved away from the territory disputed by Hurd's Addison and Arbuthnot, and from the depiction of the distant past in general. Whereas eighteenth-century works tended to announce themselves as romances, subsequent works that adapted similar patterns and tropes – notably the eruption of the past in the present – employed modern and realistic settings that acknowledged changing historical circumstances, such as the expansion of the British Empire. A range of Victorian writers continued to appeal to the Gothic as a pseudo-historical period in native or familiar terms, and claimed that an Anglo-Saxon or Germanic racial fitness helped to explain British imperial pre-eminence. Many of the works of fiction now classified as Victorian Gothic, by contrast, are renowned primarily for staging the instability of that pre-eminence, and for addressing new and specific concerns about imperial guilt, racial degeneration, and societal regression.

NOTES

1. Richard Hurd, 'On the Age of Queen Elizabeth', in *Moral and Political Dialogues; With Letters on Chivalry and Romance*, 3 vols. (Farnborough: Gregg International, 1972), I: 153; I: 159.
2. Hurd, *Moral and Political Dialogues*, III: 265.
3. 'On the Pleasure Derived from Objects of Terror; with Sir Bertrand, A Fragment', in John Aikin and Anna Laetitia Aikin, *Miscellaneous Pieces in Prose* (1773), pp. 119–37.
4. Horace Walpole, *The Castle of Otranto*, ed. E. J. Clery (Oxford: Oxford University Press, 1996), pp. 20, 19.
5. *The Yale Edition of the Correspondence of Horace Walpole*, ed. W. S. Lewis, 48 vols. (New Haven: Yale University Press, 1937–83), XL: 379 (Walpole to Elie de Beaumont, 18 March 1765).
6. Clara Reeve, *The Old English Baron*, ed. James Trainer (Oxford: Oxford University Press, 1977), p. 3.
7. James Watt, *Contesting the Gothic: Fiction, Genre, and Cultural Conflict 1764–1832* (Cambridge: Cambridge University Press, 1999), pp. 42–69.
8. Clara Reeve, *Memoirs of Sir Roger De Clarendon*, 3 vols. (1793), I: 67; I: xvi–xvii.
9. *Gentleman's Magazine* 69 (1799), 190.
10. See, for example, Jane Rendall, 'Tacitus engendered: "Gothic Feminism" and British histories, *c.* 1750–1850', in Geoffrey Cubitt (ed.), *Imagining Nations* (Manchester: Manchester University Press, 1998), pp. 57–74.
11. Mary Wollstonecraft, *A Vindication of the Rights of Men*, in *The Works of Mary Wollstonecraft*, ed. Janet Todd and Marilyn Butler, 7 vols. (London: Pickering and Chatto, 1989), V: 41.
12. Ann Radcliffe, *The Mysteries of Udolpho: A Romance*, ed. Bonamy Dobree (Oxford: Oxford University Press, 1966), p. 240.
13. Nathan Drake, *Literary Hours, or Sketches Critical and Narrative*, 2nd edn, 2 vols. (1800), I: 359.
14. See, for example, 'Terrorist Novel Writing', *Spirit of the Public Journals for 1797* I (1798), reprinted in E. J. Clery and Robert Miles (eds), *Gothic Documents: A Sourcebook 1700–1820* (Manchester: Manchester University Press, 2000), pp. 183–4.
15. William Wordsworth, 'Preface' (1800), in *Lyrical Ballads*, ed. R. L. Brett and A. R. Jones, 2nd edn (London: Routledge, 1991), p. 249.
16. Richard Polwhele, *Poems* (1810), p. 39.

17. Mary Wollstonecraft, *Mary and The Wrongs of Woman*, ed. Gary Kelly (Oxford: Oxford University Press, 1976), pp. 154–5, 73.
18. Matthew Lewis, *The Monk: A Romance*, ed. Howard Anderson (Oxford: Oxford University Press, 1973), p. 90.
19. Sade, 'Reflections on the Novel', in *The 120 Days of Sodom and Other Writings*, trans. Austyn Wainhouse and Richard Seaver (London: Arrow Books, 1989), pp. 114, 109.
20. *Correspondence of Sir Walter Scott and Charles Robert Maturin*, ed. Fanny E. Ratchford and W. H. McCarthy (Austin, TX: Austin Texas Library Publications, 1937), p. 14.
21. MS note in Beckford's copy of Thomas Moore's *Letters and Journals of Lord Byron*, cited in Louis Crompton, *Byron and Greek Love: Homophobia in Nineteenth-Century England* (London: Faber, 1985), p. 142.
22. Review of *Zofloya*, *New Literary Journal*, 2nd series 1 (June 1806), 634.
23. Joanna Baillie, 'Introductory Discourse', in Paul Baines and Edward Burns (eds.), *Five Romantic Plays* (Oxford: Oxford University Press, 2000), p. 104.
24. Mary Shelley, *Frankenstein* (1818 text), ed. Marilyn Butler (Oxford: Oxford University Press, 1994), p. 3.
25. Sir Walter Scott, 'On the Supernatural in Fictitious Composition', *Foreign Quarterly Review* 1 (1827), extract reprinted in Clery and Miles (eds), *Gothic Documents*, pp. 285–6.
26. Charles Brockden Brown, *Wieland; and Memoirs of Carwin the Biloquist*, ed. Jay Fliegelman (Harmondsworth: Penguin, 1991), p. 39.
27. Ian Duncan, 'Walter Scott, James Hogg and Scottish Gothic', in David Punter (ed.), *A Companion to Gothic* (Oxford: Blackwell, 2000), pp. 70–80.
28. Sir Walter Scott, *Waverley; or, 'Tis Sixty Years Since*, ed. Claire Lamont (Oxford: Oxford University Press, 1986), pp. 341, 338.

FURTHER READING

Botting, Fred, *Gothic*, London: Routledge, 1996.
Clery, E. J., *The Rise of Supernatural Fiction 1762–1800*, Cambridge: Cambridge University Press, 1995.
    Women's Gothic: From Clara Reeve to Mary Shelley, Tavistock: Northcote House, 2000.
Duncan, Ian, *Modern Romance and Transformations of the Novel: The Gothic, Scott, Dickens*, Cambridge: Cambridge University Press, 1992.
Ellis, Markman, *The History of Gothic Fiction*, Edinburgh: Edinburgh University Press, 2000.
Gamer, Michael, *Romanticism and the Gothic*, Cambridge: Cambridge University Press, 2000.
Hogle, Jerrold E., *The Cambridge Companion to Gothic Fiction*, Cambridge: Cambridge University Press, 2002.
Howard, Jacqueline, *Reading Gothic Fiction: A Bakhtinian Approach*, Oxford: Clarendon Press, 1994.
Kilgour, Maggie, *The Rise of the Gothic Novel*, London: Routledge, 1995.
Mighall, Robert, *A Geography of Victorian Gothic Fiction: Mapping History's Nightmares*, Oxford: Oxford University Press, 1999.

Miles, Robert, *Ann Radcliffe: The Great Enchantress*, Manchester: Manchester University Press, 1995.

Punter, David, *The Literature of Terror: A History of Gothic Fictions from 1765 to the Present*, London: Longman, 1980.

Punter, David (ed.), *A Companion to the Gothic*, Oxford: Blackwell, 2000.

Robertson, Fiona, *Legitimate Histories: Scott, Gothic, and the Authorities of Fiction*, Oxford: Clarendon Press, 1994.

Watt, James, *Contesting the Gothic: Fiction, Genre, and Cultural Conflict 1764–1832*, Cambridge: Cambridge University Press, 1999.

2

WRITERS, CIRCLES, TRADITIONS

8

PETER SABOR

Richardson, Henry Fielding, and Sarah Fielding

Between 1740 and 1760, Samuel Richardson (1689–1761), Henry Fielding (1707–54), and his sister Sarah Fielding (1710–68) published a total of some eighteen novels – from Richardson's astonishingly successful and influential *Pamela* and its continuation (1740–1) to Sarah Fielding's *The History of Ophelia* (1760). During the 1740s, the three authors published their finest works: Richardson's *Clarissa* (1747–8), Fielding's *Tom Jones* (1749), and Sarah Fielding's *The Adventures of David Simple* (1744, with a continuation in 1753). Thereafter Fielding and Richardson brought out ambitious and innovative last novels, *Amelia* (1751) and *Sir Charles Grandison* (1753–4), neither as well received as their predecessors, while Sarah Fielding published three of her most significant works: *The Cry* (1754), in collaboration with Jane Collier, *The Lives of Cleopatra and Octavia* (1757), and *The History of the Countess of Dellwyn* (1759). The relationships among these writers, and among their novels, are intricate and shifting, and shed valuable light on the larger phenomenon associated with their influence throughout the century to follow: the bifurcation of the novel genre into competing, though of course regularly intersecting, traditions, one building on the techniques of psychological representation pioneered by Richardson, the other on the social panoramas and self-conscious artifice of Fielding.

Here the mediating role of Sarah Fielding is a crucially complicating factor. She collaborated with Henry on several occasions, but also received advice from Richardson and published an important critical treatise, *Remarks on Clarissa* (1749). Nor is any picture of unwavering polarization between Henry Fielding and Richardson entirely accurate. Their rivalry has been notorious since the publication of *Shamela* (1741) and *Joseph Andrews* (1742) – Fielding's dual assault on *Pamela* – but Richardson was not always hostile to Fielding's novels, and Fielding was as capable as his sister of recognizing the greatness of *Clarissa*. This chapter will look at the conflict between Richardson and Fielding, with their respective claims to have created a 'new species' or 'new Province' of writing,[1] by examining some of the points of contact among the three authors during their novel-writing careers.

Richardson and Henry Fielding

Henry Fielding's last work, *The Journal of a Voyage to Lisbon*, was published posthumously in 1755. He completed it in Lisbon in the final weeks of his life, equipping it with a preface in which, for the last time, he brooded over the techniques and function of historical writing and prose fiction – as he had in his more famous prefaces to his own novels and to Sarah Fielding's *The Adventures of David Simple* and *Familiar Letters between the Principal Characters in David Simple* (1747). In the penultimate paragraph, Fielding assures his readers that he will not imitate

> the conduct of authors, who often fill a whole sheet with their own praises, to which they sometimes set their own real names, and sometimes a fictitious one. One hint, however, I must give the kind reader; which is, that if he should be able to find no sort of amusement in the book, he will be pleased to remember the public utility which will arise from it. If entertainment, as Mr Richardson observes, be but a secondary consideration in a romance . . . sure it may well be so considered in a work founded, like this, on truth.[2]

In mocking authors given to fulsome self-praise, Fielding has an old adversary squarely in his sights: Samuel Richardson. *Pamela* contains a preface 'by the Editor', commending the work with pseudo-objectivity 'because an *Editor* may reasonably be supposed to judge with an Impartiality which is rarely to be met with in an *Author* towards his own Works'.[3] This preface is followed by two exclamatory letters to the Editor – 'Little Book, charming PAMELA! face the World' (p. 6) – and, in the second edition, by a further series of extravagant encomia, primarily by Aaron Hill but unsigned. In *Shamela*, Fielding had satirized this ill-judged material brilliantly through his own, much terser mock-prefatory matter: letters from 'the Editor to *Himself*' and 'John Puff, *Esq*; *to the* Editor', and a wonderfully deadpan editorial note, 'Reader, several other Commendatory Letters and Copies of Verses will be prepared against the Next Edition'.[4] Now, fourteen years later, Fielding was still on the attack. In addition to *Pamela*, he is also taking aim here at *Clarissa*: the final sentence quoted above alludes both to the preface to *Clarissa*, in which Richardson declares that 'Story, or Amusement, should be considered as little more than the *Vehicle* to the more necessary Instruction',[5] and to the title-page of *Pamela*, proclaiming that the novel is a 'Narrative which has its Foundation in Truth and Nature'. Fielding concludes his preface to the *Journal* with a final fling: his own undertaking is 'surely more feasible, than that of reforming a whole people, by making use of a vehicular story, to wheel in among them worse manners than their own'. In his postscript to the third edition of *Clarissa*, Richardson complains of a 'general depravity, when even the Pulpit has lost great part of its weight'; his novel was a contribution 'towards introducing a Reformation so much wanted'.[6] Ingeniously distorting Richardson's words by linking 'vehicular' to 'wheel in' (Richardson's image is from the primary sense of 'vehicle' as a medium in which medicine is diluted), Fielding once again mocks his rival's pomposity and didactic pretensions; the deflationary technique he had used to brilliant effect in *Shamela* and *Joseph Andrews* is still at work.

The trajectory of Fielding's response to Richardson between the early 1740s and the mid 1750s, however, is more complex than these links between *Shamela* and the *Journal* suggest. In a letter to his favourite correspondent, Lady Bradshaigh, of late 1749, Richardson complained about his treatment by 'this fashionable author': 'The Pamela, which he abused in his Shamela, taught him how to write to please, tho' his manners are so different. Before his Joseph Andrews (hints and names taken from that story, with a lewd and ungenerous engraftment) the poor man wrote without being read.'[7] Like most of Richardson's comments on Fielding, this is both malicious and wide of the mark. Before turning to prose fiction, Fielding had been a spectacularly successful dramatist, writing over twenty comedies and burlesques between 1728 and 1737, when the Stage Licensing Act put an end to his work for the theatre. And *Joseph Andrews* is far more than a mere 'engraftment' on *Pamela*. The use of Pamela and Booby, Fielding's comic version of *Pamela*'s Mr B., as minor characters in *Joseph Andrews*, the parallels between the virtuous Joseph and Richardson's heroine, and the frequent allusions to *Pamela* do not constitute imitation: *Joseph Andrews* is *Pamela*'s comic antithesis.

The contrast between the two novels is manifested by their strikingly different narrative techniques and structures. Where *Pamela* is narrated in the heroine's epistolary voice, the letters implying direct access to her consciousness as the action unfolds, *Joseph Andrews* is narrated from a wittily detached position, that of a self-conscious practitioner of the 'Trade . . . of *Authoring*' (p. 76). The first hundred pages of *Pamela* consist of numbered letters, but the remainder is a series of journal entries that concludes abruptly when Pamela's parents visit the household of their newly married daughter and the need for her journal supposedly ends. In his continuation of *Pamela*, which appeared ten weeks before *Joseph Andrews* and which Fielding may have seen earlier in proof, the letters are numbered throughout, but the use of journal form within the letters causes huge variations in their lengths. Richardson himself laments, in a concluding note to his *Pamela* sequel, 'how difficult it was to reduce Materials so ample within the compass which the

Editor had assigned them'.[8] Fielding, in contrast, delights in the pleasures of symmetry, as his chapter 'Of Divisions in Authors', with its remarks on the 'Art of dividing', reveals (p. 76).

Even on their title-pages, the novels are worlds apart. While *Pamela* 'has its Foundation in Truth and Nature', with all the untidiness that following 'Nature' implies, *Joseph Andrews* is 'Written in Imitation of the *Manner* of Cervantes, Author of *Don Quixote*'. The distance between the unilingual Richardson and the multilingual Fielding is measured by their contrasting sources of inspiration. Richardson resembles the 'mere *English* Reader' whom Fielding addresses in his preface to *Joseph Andrews* (p. 3). Richardson's preface to *Pamela* contains no reference to other works of fiction, but the introductory letters, one by Jean Baptiste de Freval and the other probably by William Webster, single out French 'Dross', 'Froth', and 'Whip-syllabub' (pp. 6, 9) for special disapproval. In explaining the nature of his fiction, Fielding refers to works by Homer, Aristotle, Fénelon, d'Urfé, La Calprenède, Scudéry, Shaftesbury, Hogarth, Bellegarde, Jonson and Congreve: it is a dazzling display of erudition, establishing his cosmopolitanism against Richardson's provincialism. Fielding also establishes the difference between his technique and that of Richardson in his preface to *Familiar Letters between the Principal Characters in David Simple*. Rather disconcertingly, in introducing an epistolary novel, he declares that 'no one will contend, that the epistolary Style is in general the most proper to a Novelist, or that it hath been used by the best Writers of this Kind' (I: ix).

The publication of the first two volumes of Richardson's seven-volume *Clarissa* in December 1747 seems to have made Fielding change his mind about both the merits of epistolary fiction and the significance of his rival. A huge advance technically on *Pamela*, *Clarissa* combines multiple finely distinguished narrative viewpoints, each advancing its own account of the action, the overall effect being to complicate and intensify the novel's meaning and impact. In a remarkable passage in the *Jacobite's Journal*, Fielding welcomes 'a new Production in the Region of Fancy, capable of giving me the same Delight which I have received from my most favourite Authors at my first Acquaintance with them'. *Clarissa*, he declares, is written with 'such Simplicity, such Manners, such deep Penetration into Nature; such Power to raise and alarm the Passions', that 'few Writers, either ancient or modern, have been possessed of'. Fielding goes on to deplore the mutually contradictory cavils of *Clarissa*'s critics: the heroine is at once 'too cold; she is too fond. She uses her Father, Mother, Uncles, Brother, Sister, Lover, Friend, too ill, too well.' In March 1748, a month before volumes three and four of *Clarissa* were published, Fielding again used the pages of the *Jacobite's Journal* to commend the novel.[9]

Richardson appears to have been sufficiently impressed by this support to send Fielding, in October 1748, an advance copy of volume five of the novel, which would be published, together with the last two volumes, only in December. The presentation copy elicited from Fielding a letter described by Richardson's biographers as 'one of the warmest letters of praise ever written by an author to a rival', and by Fielding's as 'among the finest tributes ever paid by one great writer to another, his rival, whose sense of his craft was antithetical to his own'.[10] But the effect of the letter on Richardson himself was more problematic. The opening paragraph strikes a discordant note, with its punning deformation of the name of the libertine Lovelace and an unexpected emphasis on comic elements in Richardson's tragic novel: 'In all the Accounts which Lovelass gives of the Transactions at Hampstead, you preserve the same vein of Humour which hath run through the preceding Volumes', Fielding writes, adding that 'there is much of the true Comic Force in the Widow Bevis'.[11] Although Fielding goes on to declare that Lovelace's 'former Admirers must lose all Regard for him on his Perseverance', the initial stress on Lovelace's 'vein of Humour' resembles the admiration held by many readers for his rake that always vexed Richardson. The central part of the letter, in which Fielding commends Richardson's ability to arouse compassion and admiration for his heroine, comes closer to Richardson's own view of the novel. Fielding records his reactions to the major events of the volume – Clarissa's imprisonment and rape by Lovelace, followed by her adamant refusal of his proposal of marriage – in cardiographic style, tracing his alternately tremulous and exclamatory responses: 'Here my Terror ends and my Grief begins which the Cause of all my Tumultuous Passion soon changes into Raptures of Admiration and Astonishment by a Behaviour the most elevated I can possibly conceive, and what is at the same time most gentle and natural'.

Fielding's conclusion, however, is more likely to have offended Richardson than flattered him. After reminding Richardson needlessly that they are 'Rivals for that coy Mrs. Fame', Fielding declares: 'as to this Mrs. I have ravished her long ago, and live in a settled cohabitation with her, in defiance of that Public Voice which is supposed to be her Guardian, and to have alone the Power of giving her away'. Here Fielding shifts from praising *Clarissa* to praising his own indifference to fame, and with an elaborately risqué metaphor of ravishment that comes dangerously close to mocking Richardson's own tragic treatment of seduction and rape. As the metaphor develops, Fielding comes to resemble Lovelace in one of his wish-fulfilling fantasies, dreaming of his assured possession of Clarissa and his successful defiance of her family. It is an intriguing question why Fielding was impelled to undermine the effect of his panegyric with this disquieting passage, and why he concluded the letter with the cryptic observation that if Richardson should not achieve success with *Clarissa*, 'it would be in me unpardonable Presumption to hope for Success, and at the same time almost contemptible Humility to desire it'. Fielding's admiration for *Clarissa* has thus been replaced by the suggestion that it might not achieve popular esteem: an irritating prophecy that would soon be fulfilled when the novel was outsold by the hugely popular *Tom Jones*, published only two months after the final instalment of *Clarissa*, in February 1749.[12]

Although this is the only surviving letter between Fielding and Richardson, we know from a letter from Richardson to Johannes Stinstra that Fielding, like several of Richardson's other correspondents, 'had been a zealous Contender for the Piece [*Clarissa*] ending, as it is called, happily',[13] in keeping with his emphasis on comic elements in the novel. With this letter Richardson sent a substantial excerpt from Fielding's commentary, omitting, significantly, the unpalatable concluding remarks. That Fielding signed his letter 'yrs. most Affectionately', and that he asked Richardson 'to send me immediately the two remaining Vols:', are further signs of a surprising degree of friendship between the two writers in 1748. Another such sign is a remark by Richardson, in a letter to his friend Edward Moore, that *Clarissa* was designed only to 'fill a gap in the Reading World' while Moore himself and Fielding were 'reposing their Understandings'.[14] Since Moore, a minor comic dramatist, was no threat to Richardson, the comment is clearly tongue in cheek, but even in bracketing Fielding and Moore together Richardson is taking an exceptionally relaxed attitude towards his adversary.

After the publication of *Tom Jones* in February 1749, Richardson began a steady stream of invective against Fielding in his correspondence that he maintained beyond Fielding's death. This striking change of attitude is puzzling, and no satisfactory explanation has ever been furnished. Since Richardson first attributes *Shamela* to Fielding in 1749 (in the letter to Lady Bradshaigh quoted above), it has been suggested that he discovered Fielding's authorship only in that year, and responded with wounded indignation. Other conjectures are that Richardson might have heard some particularly unfavourable reports about Fielding's private life in 1749, or that the exceptional popularity of *Tom Jones*, and its warm reception by many of Richardson's own friends and admirers, did the damage. Another explanation is that the novel itself, as well as its success, elicited Richardson's fury.

Richardson claimed, on several occasions, not to have read *Tom Jones*, which given normal human curiosity seems improbable. Had he read even part of the novel, he would have seen that the author of *Joseph Andrews* remained intent on creating a work that in many ways was the antithesis of a Richardsonian novel. Now Fielding pursues his self-conscious technique with a sophistication that heralds Sterne's *Tristram Shandy*, signalling his lack of interest in the psychological claims of Richardson's fiction by jesting about one of his own characters that 'it would be an ill Office in us to pay a Visit to the inmost Recesses of his Mind' (p. 159). In his heroine Sophia, Fielding created his comic version of Clarissa, and in Tom Jones his comic counterpart to the libertine Lovelace. Like *Clarissa*, *Tom Jones* tells the story of a young woman compelled by a tyrannical father to marry a man she abhors – Solmes in the case of *Clarissa*, Blifil in the case of *Tom Jones* – but, as Ronald Paulson remarks, 'instead of placing all virtue in a passive/aggressive heroine, and in the sin of sex, Fielding sends her out to pursue Tom and renders his infidelities relatively unimportant to her'.[15] Insistent virtue, of the kind displayed by Pamela, is again a subject of satire. Sophia's maid is named Mrs Honour, a word frequently in Pamela's mouth, and like Shamela she is made to trumpet virtue's rewards: 'To be sure, Ma'am . . . one's Virtue is a dear Thing, especially to us poor Servants; for it is our Livelihood, as a Body may say' (p. 352). Another challenge to Richardson's depiction of female virtue is posed by Sophia, who declares to Lady Bellaston: 'I will never run away with any Man; nor will I ever marry contrary to my Father's Inclinations' (p. 793). Clarissa does not marry contrary to her father's inclinations, but she does 'run away' from Harlowe Place with Lovelace, the man her father most abhors. As Martin C. Battestin rightly suggests at this point in his edition, Fielding 'seems to have designed certain passages in *Tom Jones* to invite comparisons between his own heroine and Richardson's, who are caught in similar circumstances but comport themselves according to quite different standards of conduct'.

In the latter part of *Tom Jones*, written in late 1748, after he had read at least the first five volumes of *Clarissa*, Richardson's novel is repeatedly in Fielding's sights. In a comic counterpart to Richardson's grim depiction of the Harlowe family joining forces against Clarissa as they strive to force her into Solmes's arms, Fielding has Squire Western, aided by his sister and Lady Bellaston, pleading 'Come, *Sophy*, be a good Girl, and be dutiful, and make your Father happy'. His heroine's response, 'If my Death will make you happy, Sir . . . you will shortly be so' (p. 800), is risible, given her vigorous good health, and an obvious thrust at the protracted scene of holy dying played out by Richardson's heroine. A little later Fielding circles back to *Pamela*, and its unfortunate subtitle, as he writes of a Mrs Hunt, who 'had been married young' to a wealthy husband and whose 'Virtue was rewarded by his dying, and leaving her very rich' (p. 826).

These and other such passages in *Tom Jones* would account for Richardson's intense hostility towards Fielding from 1749 onwards, and for his sense of betrayal whenever the novel was praised by members of his own circle, such as the daughters of his old friend Aaron Hill, Astraea and Minerva. In a notorious letter to the Hill daughters, berating them for expressing favourable remarks on *Tom Jones*, Richardson describes Fielding's hero as 'a Kept Fellow, the lowest of all Fellows, yet in Love with a Young Creature who was trapsing after him, a Fugitive from her Father's House'.[16] Ostensibly, Richardson is merely reporting 'the Opinions of Several judicious Friends', but here and elsewhere his hostile responses to Fielding's novel have the immediacy of a fully engaged reader. A few months later, in a letter to Frances Grainger, he contrasts the 'Character of the weak, the insipid, the Runaway, the Inn-frequenting Sophia' with that of Clarissa, which to Fielding's ill-guided admirers 'might be supposed Prudish, too delicate, and a silent Reproach to themselves'.[17]

Far from avoiding *Tom Jones*, as he liked to claim, Richardson saw it as a challenge to his own concept of novel-writing, but his answers to the challenge were made in manuscript, rather than in print. In his 'Hints of Prefaces for *Clarissa*', shards of a treatise that Richardson was drafting in 1749 while preparing the second edition of *Clarissa*, at least two passages are directed at *Joseph Andrews* and *Tom Jones*. In the first, Richardson questions whether '*Ridicule* is a proper Basis (without the help of more solid Buttresses) whereon to build Instruction, whatever Delight it may administer to the Reader': an allusion to Fielding's theories on the ridiculous as a source of comedy in his prefaces to both *Joseph Andrews* and his sister's *David Simple*. In the second, Richardson mounts a powerful defence of epistolary fiction, contrasting it with

> the dry Narrative; where the *Novelist* moves on, his own dull Pace, to the End of his Chapter and Book, interweaving impertinent Digressions, for fear the Reader's Patience should be exhausted by his tedious Dwelling on one Subject, in the same Style: Which may not unfitly be compared to the dead Tolling of a single Bell, in Opposition to the wonderful Variety of Sounds, which constitute the Harmony of a Handel.[18]

Here Richardson challenges both Fielding's attack on 'epistolary Style' in his preface to *Familiar Letters between the Principal Characters in David Simple* and the whole body of Fielding's fiction, memorably written off as 'the dead Tolling of a single Bell'. 'Hints of Prefaces' makes claims that Richardson was too cautious to print, and neither of these thrusts at Fielding appears in any published edition of *Clarissa*. The preface to the third edition, however, does contain a quotation, from one of Belford's letters, in which epistolary fiction is contrasted with 'the dry, narrative, unanimated Style of a Person relating difficulties and dangers surmounted . . . the relater perfectly at ease;

and if himself unmoved by his own Story, not likely greatly to affect the Heart of the Reader'.[19] And in the postscript to the third edition, harking back to the wish expressed by Fielding and others for *Clarissa* to end happily, Richardson reiterates his opposition to '*sudden Conversions*'. It would be unthinkable, he insisted, 'to have a Lovelace for a series of years glory in his wickedness, and think that he had nothing to do, but as an act of grace and favour to hold out his hand to receive that of the best of women, whenever he pleased'.[20]

Richardson's private responses to Fielding's final novel, *Amelia*, were equally passionate. Well before its first publication in January 1751 he was already taking notice of the work in progress, telling Lady Bradshaigh late in 1749 that some of its scenes would be set in Newgate, 'removed from inns and alehouses . . . and perhaps not unusefully; I hope not'.[21] When the novel appeared he at once reviled it, 'the characters and situations so wretchedly low and dirty', while claiming that he had been unable to read beyond the first volume.[22] Many of Richardson's correspondents responded with equally disparaging remarks while encouraging him to complete his own new novel, *Sir Charles Grandison*, the seven volumes of which were published in three instalments between November 1753 and March 1754.

It is unfortunate that *Amelia* has been habitually judged as an unsuccessful *Tom Jones* and *Grandison* as an inferior *Clarissa* when both are experimental works, attempting to achieve effects very different from those of the two acknowledged masterpieces. *Amelia*, in particular, has suffered from comparisons with its predecessor and was severely criticized by early reviewers, causing Fielding to declare in the *Covent-Garden Journal*, within weeks of its publication, that he would 'trouble the World no more with any Children of mine by the same Muse'.[23] Admirers of Richardson have felt uncomfortable with *Grandison* because in some respects it reads like a Fielding novel, while advocates of Fielding have been disturbed by the Richardsonian elements of *Amelia*. The title of *Amelia* at once recalls those of both *Pamela* and *Shamela*, ameliorated – a play on words noted by Bonnell Thornton, who printed a mock-advertisement for a spurious novel entitled 'Shamelia', which had been swollen to four volumes with the help of 'Dedication, Introductory Chapters, long Digressions, short Repetitions, polite Expletives of Conversation, genteel Dialogues, a wide Margin, and large Letter'.[24] Fielding's heroine can be seen as an attempt to eclipse the merits of Pamela and Clarissa, while Richardson's hero is designed to overshadow the seductive vices of Lovelace and the alarming popularity of Tom Jones. There is also a much greater emphasis on domestic scenes in *Amelia* than in Fielding's previous novels. Like Pamela and Clarissa, Fielding's hero, Captain Booth, is imprisoned for large parts of the work, and is also a captive in his own house because of the threats of his creditors. *Grandison*, conversely, is the least domestic of Richardson's three novels: Sir Charles's appetite for arduous journeys across England and Europe is inexhaustible. The London settings of *Amelia*, in comparison, seem claustrophobically confined.

The convergence of the two novels goes beyond these questions of the name and sex of the eponyms, or of interior and exterior settings. A more fundamental point of contact is the interest of both writers in complex moral dilemmas and in the psychology of the characters, interests hitherto associated primarily with Richardson. Fielding had, of course, been concerned with difficult moral choices in his previous novels: Blifil's freeing Sophia's canary, an ostensibly humanitarian action undertaken for a culpable motive, is a celebrated case in *Tom Jones*.[25] But in *Amelia*, for the first time, intricate questions of proper conduct become a major part of the novel. To what extent should Amelia obey Booth, when his financial recklessness is ruining their family, and how far should she scheme behind his back? Is Amelia justified in asking the unreliable Mrs Atkinson to impersonate her at a masquerade? Is Dr Harrison justified in committing Booth to prison when Booth appears to be squandering money on extravagant purchases? Such teasing ethical problems are the essence of Richardsonian fiction – vigorously debated, in his case, by an enthusiastic group of correspondents. In a remarkable variety of situations, Sir Charles must make moral judgements, including whether to dock horses' tails (he does not), whether to imitate his father's taste for expensive apparel as a way of justifying his father's extravagance (he does), and how to provide for his deceased father's mistress (with generous discretion). These delicate issues provide Sir Charles with an excellent schooling for the most difficult choice of all – that between Harriet and Clementina, two worthy and beautiful young women, both equally in love with him but one a Catholic and an Italian (he discourages the foreigner by insisting that their sons be raised as Protestants).

The exploration of psychology that takes place in both novels is closely related to their concern with proper conduct. In *Amelia*, Fielding adopts the characteristically Richardsonian device of using the limited perspective of one of the characters to supply the reader with false information. This technique forces the reader to scrutinize situations and characters intensely, and gives Richardson's novels the psychological richness for which they are celebrated. In letters on *Grandison* to Lady Bradshaigh, Richardson wrote that he had designedly 'play'd the Rogue with my Readers; intending to make them think now one way, now another, of the very same Characters', and that a principal aim had been to 'occasion many Debates upon different Parts of my Management'.[26] Fielding, as narrator of *Joseph Andrews* and *Tom Jones*, had given much firmer guidance to his readers, and his derision of

Richardson's technique of 'writing, to the moment',[27] memorably satirized in *Shamela*, stems not only from its improbability but also from the loss of authorial control that such a method entails. That Fielding relinquished much of this control in *Amelia* suggests that *Clarissa* had made him reconsider the validity of Richardson's technique. But this change did not prevent Richardson from making a rare public attack on Fielding in his 'Concluding Note' to *Grandison*. With novels such as *Tom Jones* and *Amelia* clearly in view, Richardson writes:

> It has been said, in behalf of many modern fictitious pieces, in which authors have given success (and *happiness*, as it is called) to their heroes of vicious, if not of profligate characters, that they have exhibited Human Nature as it *is*. Its corruption may, indeed, be exhibited in the faulty character; but need pictures of this be held out in books? Is not vice crowned with success, triumphant, and rewarded, and perhaps set off with wit and spirit, a dangerous representation?[28]

These remarks were published in March 1754, three months before Fielding set sail for Lisbon. It is not known whether he read *Grandison*, but his final attack on Richardson in the preface to the *Journal of a Voyage to Lisbon*, quoted above, could have been prompted in part by these hostile reflections on 'vice crowned with success, triumphant, and rewarded'.

Sarah Fielding

A further complication in the rivalry between Richardson and Henry Fielding remains to be considered: the part played by Sarah Fielding. In the 1740s, Sarah's literary career was enmeshed with that of her famous brother. Her first appearance in print was probably as the author of Leonora's letter to Horatio in *Joseph Andrews*; the second as the author of the concluding chapter of Henry's *A Journey from This World to the Next* (1743). Her first novel, *David Simple*, was published anonymously and widely attributed to Henry, who for the second edition added a preface denying his authorship and made extensive revisions to the text. These revisions, ostensibly designed to expunge stylistic errors, in practice shape his sister's novel into one more closely reflecting his own concept of fiction. He also supplied a preface and five letters to *Familiar Letters between the Principal Characters in David Simple*. Sarah's brief 'advertisement' to the first edition of *David Simple* is strikingly defensive, making excuses for the novel's 'many Inaccuracies . . . in the Style, and other Faults of the Composition', but in terming the work a 'Moral Romance' she finds a useful way of defining her own approach to writing fiction.[29] Henry's preface, which replaced it in the second edition, is far more ambitious, but also rebarbative in many ways. Seeming to take his cue from his sister, he draws attention to the novel's 'Grammatical and other Errors in Style', which, however, 'no Man of Learning would think worth his Censure in a Romance; nor any Gentleman, in the Writings of a young Woman'. Wishing to reinforce and supplement the account of comic fiction he had given in the preface to *Joseph Andrews*, he terms it a 'comic Epic Poem' in prose, thus linking it to his own first novel at the expense of the term 'Moral Romance' that Sarah herself had chosen. Henry does, though, go on to point to the novel's 'vast Penetration into human Nature, a deep and profound Discernment of all the Mazes, Windings and Labyrinths, which perplex the Heart of Man' – and continues with an analysis of Sarah's strengths that goes far beyond the apologetics and special pleading of her own preface (pp. 345–6).

That Sarah Fielding replaced her advertisement to *David Simple* with Henry's much more complex preface indicates her lack of faith in her critical skills at this early stage in her authorial career. Both here and in his preface to Sarah's *Familiar Letters*, however, Henry was more concerned with advertising his own fiction and with disparaging Richardson than with promoting his sister's work. And in stating, in the preface to *Familiar Letters*, that the work is designed specifically for a female readership – 'no Book extant is so well calculated for their Instruction and Improvement' (I: xiii) – Henry is paying his sister a distinctly double-edged compliment.

In the late 1740s, Richardson succeeded Henry Fielding as Sarah's principal literary advisor, and also provided practical assistance in his professional capacity as a printer. Anna Laetitia Barbauld, Richardson's early nineteenth-century editor and biographer, claimed that he was already 'very intimate' with Sarah Fielding before *Joseph Andrews* appeared in 1742, but there is no evidence for this statement.[30] By 1748, though, the situation is clear: Richardson was printing Sarah's novel for children, *The Governess*, and giving her advice, via their mutual friend Jane Collier, about its contents.[31] *The Governess* was published in January 1749, almost simultaneously with Sarah's anonymous pamphlet, *Remarks on Clarissa*. In this astute and wideranging treatise, a group of fictional disputants discuss what they consider the strengths and weaknesses of Richardson's novel. Sarah sent Richardson a copy of the newly published work on 8 January 1749, seeking approval for her 'daring attempt' while acknowledging her 'vanity in daring but to touch the hem of [Clarissa's] garment'.[32] Its influence on Richardson's revisions of *Clarissa* was substantial; many of the footnotes that Richardson added to the second and third editions of his novel, as well as the much-expanded preface and postscript, answer criticisms first raised and dealt with in the *Remarks*.

Richardson printed two of Sarah Fielding's works in the 1750s, *The Lives of Cleopatra and Octavia* and *The History of the Countess of Dellwyn*. He also printed Jane Collier's *Essay on the Art of Ingeniously Tormenting* (1753), written while Collier and Fielding were sharing lodgings. Surviving letters record Richardson's assistance with a play that Fielding wished to have produced during the 1754–5 London theatre season; with *The Cry* (1754), which she had co-authored with Jane Collier and which in 1757 he urged her to revise for a second edition; and with the *Countess of Dellwyn*, which Fielding hoped either Richardson or his nephew William Richardson would correct for her in proof.[33]

Since Sarah and Henry Fielding are not known to have collaborated after 1747, while there is ample evidence of her dealings with Richardson from 1748 to 1759, it is tempting to envisage her moving from one camp to the other: beginning her authorial career under Fielding's tutelage and ending it as a loyal Richardsonian. Hester Lynch Thrale claimed, in a diary entry for June 1777, that Henry had grown jealous of Sarah – whose last publication was a translation of Xenophon's *Memoirs of Socrates* (1762) – because of her superior classical learning. He had encouraged her

while She only read English Books, and made English Verses . . . but as soon [as] he perceived She once read Virgil, Farewell to Fondness, the Author's Jealousy was become stronger than the Brother's Affection, and he saw her future progress in literature not without pleasure only – but with Pain.[34]

As Thrale's informant (Arthur Collier) had quarrelled with Henry, however, the report might be unfounded. And the suggestion that Sarah and Henry grew apart does not withstand much inspection. Sarah might have contributed an essay by 'Honoria Hunter' to Henry's periodical, the *Jacobite's Journal*, in June 1748. She certainly supplied James Harris with manuscript notes for his 'Essay on the Life and Genius of Henry Fielding', written in 1758 and designed to be prefixed to a new edition of Henry's works, but never published. Most of Sarah's novels, in the 1750s as well as in the 1740s, contain quotations from Henry's writings, and *Tom Jones*, in turn, contains a panegyric by Sophia on a novel, unnamed but probably *David Simple*, written by 'a young Lady of Fashion, whose good Understanding, I think, doth Honour to her Sex' (p. 286).[35]

In 1750, the anonymous author of the novel *The History of Charlotte Summers* referred to Richardson and Henry Fielding as 'two brother Biographers', and to *Clarissa* and *Tom Jones* as 'two wonderful Performances' by 'two inimitable Moderns'. Richardson, not surprisingly, resented the comparison.[36] This anonymous writer was only one of many in the 1740s and

1750s who, instead of declaring in favour of either novelist, expressed admiration for both. Elizabeth Carter, in a letter of 1749, reproached Catherine Talbot for being 'so outrageous about poor Tom Jones' and urged her friend to acknowledge Fielding's strengths in depicting 'the mixture of good and bad' as well as Richardson's skill in 'painting excellence'.[37] In the same year the *Gentleman's Magazine*, as Allen Michie observes, contains repeated comparisons between Richardson and Fielding, including 'a frontispiece drawing of a pile of books with *Tom Jones* underneath *Clarissa*',[38] leaving it to readers to determine whether Fielding's novel is supporting or being crushed by Richardson's. In her *Art of Tormenting*, Jane Collier refers to 'all that a Swift, an Addison, a Richardson, a Fielding, or any other good ethical writer intended to teach', linking Richardson not only to Fielding but also to another author for whom he felt especial antipathy, Jonathan Swift.[39] And Sarah Fielding too was not averse to yoking her brother and Richardson together. In her introduction to *The Lives of Cleopatra and Octavia*, for example, she writes of 'our insatiable Curiosity for Novels or Romances', which provide us with the 'rural Innocence of a *Joseph Andrews*, or the inimitable Virtues of Sir *Charles Grandison*'.[40]

Richardson's aim, in contrast, was to distance himself as far from Henry Fielding as possible. And to help establish a *cordon sanitaire*, he had to distinguish Sarah's writings clearly from those of her brother. This compulsion helps explain the offensive remarks to Sarah on Henry's 'continued lowness' that he quotes with embarrassing relish to Lady Bradshaigh:

> Had your brother, said I, been born in a stable, or been a runner at a sponging-house, we should have thought him a genius, and wished he had had the advantage of a liberal education, and of being admitted into good company; but it is beyond my conception, that a man of family, and who had some learning, and who really is a writer, should descend so excessively low, in all his pieces. Who can care for any of his people?[41]

Some years later, Richardson wrote to Sarah Fielding after rereading her *Familiar Letters between the Principal Characters in David Simple*, in which he had found 'many new beauties'. To show his admiration for Sarah's 'knowledge of the human heart', Richardson cites an unnamed 'critical judge of writing', who had told him 'that your late brother's knowledge of it was not (fine writer as he was) comparable to your's. His was but as the knowledge of a clock-work machine, while your's was that of all the finer springs and movements of the inside.'[42] This anonymous authority who preferred Sarah's psychological insights to what he regarded as Henry's more superficial grasp of human nature was probably Samuel Johnson, a close friend of Richardson. In Boswell's *Life of Johnson*, Johnson is said to have made a similar remark in spring 1768, at about the time of Sarah's death, contrasting Richardson and Henry Fielding as respectively 'a man who knew how a watch was made, and a man who could tell the hour by looking on the dial-plate'.[43] The transition from contrasting Henry and Sarah to contrasting Fielding and Richardson is significant. Far from acting as a bridge between the rival novelists, as has often been suggested, Sarah Fielding served, unwittingly, to drive them ever further apart. As Jane Spencer remarks, 'where Henry Fielding claimed his sister for the comic epic poem, Richardson claims her for the Richardsonian novel. Each found it important to have this female novelist on his side.'[44] And the more that Richardson and Henry Fielding strove to claim Sarah for their own, the less able they were to make accommodations with each other. In telling Sarah Fielding why she was a finer novelist than her brother, Richardson was also rehearsing, yet again, the reasons why his own 'new species of writing' was superior to that of Henry Fielding, and why *Clarissa*, not *Tom Jones*, was the masterpiece of eighteenth-century English fiction.

NOTES

1. For these phrases see *Selected Letters of Samuel Richardson*, ed. John Carroll (Oxford: Clarendon Press, 1964), p. 41 (to Aaron Hill, *c.* 1 February 1741); Henry Fielding, *Tom Jones*, ed. Martin C. Battestin and Fredson Bowers (Oxford: Clarendon Press, 1974), p. 77.

2. *The Journal of a Voyage to Lisbon*, ed. Tom Keymer (London: Penguin, 1996), p. 11.

3. *Pamela*, ed. Thomas Keymer and Alice Wakely (Oxford: Oxford University Press, 2001), p. 4.

4. *Joseph Andrews and Shamela*, ed. Douglas Brooks-Davies, rev. and intr. Thomas Keymer (Oxford: Oxford University Press, 1999), p. 309.

5. *Richardson's Published Commentary on Clarissa 1747–65*, 3 vols. (London: Pickering and Chatto, 1998), Volume I, *Prefaces, Postscripts and Related Writings*, ed. Thomas Keymer, p. 16. In the *Covent-Garden Journal* for 4 February 1752, Fielding had quoted, with no apparent satirical intent, the same sentence by 'the ingenious Author of Clarissa' (*Covent-Garden Journal*, ed. Bertrand A. Goldgar (Oxford: Clarendon Press, 1988), p. 73).

6. *Richardson's Published Commentary*, I: 255.

7. *Selected Letters of Samuel Richardson*, p. 133.

8. *Pamela*, 4 vols. (1740–1), IV: 469. There is as yet no reliable modern edition of Richardson's continuation of *Pamela*.

9. *The Jacobite's Journal and Related Writings*, ed. W. B. Coley (Oxford: Clarendon Press, 1975), pp. 119–20 (2 January 1748), 187–8 (3 March 1748).

10. T. C. Duncan Eaves and Ben D. Kimpel, *Samuel Richardson: A Biography* (Oxford: Clarendon Press, 1971), p. 294; Martin C. Battestin with Ruthe R. Battestin, *Henry Fielding: A Life* (London: Routledge, 1989), p. 432.

11. *The Correspondence of Henry and Sarah Fielding*, ed. Martin C. Battestin and Clive T. Probyn (Oxford: Clarendon Press, 1993), p. 70 (to Richardson,

15 October 1748); the quotations to follow are from pp. 70–2. When transcribing this passage for another correspondent, Richardson removed the pun on Lovelace's name: see *The Richardson-Stinstra Correspondence*, ed. William C. Slattery (Carbondale: Southern Illinois University Press, 1969), p. 33.

12. 3,000 copies of *Clarissa* were sold by 21 January 1751; *Tom Jones*, however, went through 10,000 copies by February 1750, a year after publication: see *Selected Letters*, ed. Carroll, p. 86 n.

13. *Richardson-Stinstra Correspondence*, p. 33 (5 June 1753).

14. Eaves and Kimpel, *Samuel Richardson*, p. 294 (quoting Richardson's letter to Moore of 3 October 1748).

15. Ronald Paulson, *The Life of Henry Fielding* (Oxford: Blackwell, 2000), p. 201.

16. *Selected Letters*, p. 127 (4 August 1749).

17. *Selected Letters*, p. 143 (22 January 1750).

18. *Richardson's Published Commentary on Clarissa*, I: 332; I: 334.

19. *Richardson's Published Commentary on Clarissa*, Volume II, *Letters and Passages Restored*, ed. Peter Sabor, p. iv.

20. *Richardson's Published Commentary on Clarissa*, I: 254.

21. *Selected Letters*, p. 134.

22. *Selected Letters*, pp. 196 (to Anne Donnellan, 22 February 1752), 198 (to Lady Bradshaigh, 23 February 1752).

23. *Covent-Garden Journal*, p. 66 (28 January 1752).

24. *Drury-Lane Journal*, 16 January 1752. On 13 February, Thornton also printed a witty parody entitled 'A New Chapter in Amelia'; see Ronald Paulson and Thomas Lockwood (eds.), *Henry Fielding: The Critical Heritage* (London: Routledge, 1969), pp. 321–4.

25. See Coleridge's brilliant analysis of this passage in his marginalia to *Tom Jones*, in Claude Rawson (ed.), *Henry Fielding: A Critical Anthology* (Harmondsworth: Penguin, 1973), pp. 205–6.

26. *Selected Letters*, pp. 248 (12 November 1753), 257 (8 December 1753).

27. Richardson coined this useful term in a letter to Lady Bradshaigh of 14 February 1754 (*Selected Letters*, p. 289).

28. *Sir Charles Grandison*, ed. Jocelyn Harris, 3 vols. (London: Oxford University Press, 1972), III: 466.

29. *The Adventures of David Simple and Volume the Last*, ed. Peter Sabor (Lexington: University Press of Kentucky, 1998), p. [3].

30. Barbauld, Introduction to *The Correspondence of Samuel Richardson*, 6 vols. (1804), I: lxxix. Barbauld also claims, without providing evidence, that Richardson and Henry Fielding were on good terms at this time.

31. *Correspondence of Samuel Richardson*, II: 61–5 (Collier to Richardson, 4 October 1748).

32. *Correspondence of Henry and Sarah Fielding*, p. 123.

33. *Correspondence of Henry and Sarah Fielding*, pp. 127–8 (Sarah Fielding to Richardson, May–June 1754), 134–6 (Richardson to Sarah Fielding, 17 January 1757), 144–50 (Sarah Fielding to Richardson, 14 December 1758).

34. *Thraliana: The Diary of Mrs. Hester Lynch Thrale*, ed. Katharine C. Balderston, 2nd edn, 2 vols. (Oxford: Clarendon Press, 1951), I: 79. Later, in a letter of 15 March 1795, Thrale claimed that once Sarah could construe Virgil, her brother 'began to teize and *taunt* her with being a literary Lady': *The Piozzi Letters*,

ed. Edward A. Bloom and Lillian D. Bloom, 6 vols. (Newark: University of Delaware Press, 1989–), II: 249.

35. For Henry's debt to *David Simple* in both *Tom Jones* and *Amelia*, see Linda Bree, 'Henry Fielding, Sarah Fielding, and Stories of Sibling Rivalry', in Walter Göbel et al. (ed.), *Engendering Images of Man in the Long Eighteenth Century* (Trier: Wissenschaftlicher Verlag Trier, 2001), pp. 163–75.

36. See Eaves and Kimpel, *Samuel Richardson*, p. 300; *Charlotte Summers*, 2 vols. (1750), I: 220.

37. *Henry Fielding: The Critical Heritage*, p. 169 (Carter to Talbot, 20 June 1749).

38. Allen Michie, *Richardson and Fielding: The Dynamics of a Critical Rivalry* (Lewisburg: Bucknell University Press, 1999), p. 59; *Gentleman's Magazine* 19 (1749), frontispiece to general title-page.

39. Jane Collier, *An Essay on the Art of Ingeniously Tormenting*, intr. Judith Hawley (Bristol: Thoemmes, 1994), p. 229.

40. *The Lives of Cleopatra and Octavia*, ed. Christopher D. Johnson (Lewisburg: Bucknell University Press, 1994), p. 54.

41. *Selected Letters*, pp. 198–9 (23 February 1752).

42. *Correspondence of Henry and Sarah Fielding*, p. 132 (7 December 1756).

43. *Boswell's Life of Johnson*, ed. George Birkbeck Hill, rev. L. F. Powell, 6 vols. (Oxford: Clarendon Press, 1934–64), II: 49.

44. Jane Spencer, *Literary Relations: Kinship and the Creation of the Canon, Dryden to Austen* (forthcoming), ch. 3.

FURTHER READING

Bell, Ian A., *Henry Fielding: Authorship and Authority*, London: Longman, 1994.

Blewett, David (ed.), *Passion and Virtue: Essays on the Novels of Samuel Richardson*, Toronto: University of Toronto Press, 2001.

Bree, Linda, *Sarah Fielding*, Boston: Twayne, 1996.

Campbell, Jill, *Natural Masques: Gender and Identity in Fielding's Plays and Novels*, Stanford: Stanford University Press, 1995.

Castle, Terry, *Clarissa's Ciphers: Meaning and Disruption in Richardson's Clarissa*, Ithaca, NY: Cornell University Press, 1982.

Doody, Margaret Anne, *A Natural Passion: A Study of the Novels of Samuel Richardson*, Oxford: Clarendon Press, 1974.

Doody, Margaret Anne, and Peter Sabor (eds.), *Samuel Richardson: Tercentenary Essays*, Cambridge: Cambridge University Press, 1989.

Eagleton, Terry, *The Rape of Clarissa: Writing, Sexuality and Class Struggle in Samuel Richardson*, Oxford: Blackwell, 1982.

Flynn, Carol Houlihan, *Samuel Richardson: A Man of Letters*, Princeton: Princeton University Press, 1982.

Gwilliam, Tassie, *Samuel Richardson's Fictions of Gender*, Stanford: Stanford University Press, 1993.

Harris, Jocelyn, *Samuel Richardson*, Cambridge: Cambridge University Press, 1987.

Hunter, J. Paul, *Occasional Form: Henry Fielding and the Chains of Circumstance*, Baltimore: Johns Hopkins University Press, 1975.

Keymer, Tom, *Richardson's Clarissa and the Eighteenth-Century Reader*, Cambridge: Cambridge University Press, 1992.

Kinkead-Weekes, Mark, *Samuel Richardson: Dramatic Novelist*, London: Methuen, 1973.

Rawson, Claude, *Henry Fielding and the Augustan Ideal Under Stress*, 2nd edn, New Jersey: Humanities Press International, 1991.

Richetti, John, *The English Novel in History 1700–1780*, London: Routledge, 1999.

Rivero, Albert J. (ed.), *Critical Essays on Henry Fielding*, New York: G. K. Hall, 1998.

New Essays on Samuel Richardson, New York: St Martin's Press, 1996.

Schellenberg, Betty A., *The Conversational Circle: Rereading the English Novel, 1740–1775*, Lexington: University Press of Kentucky, 1996.

Smallwood, Angela J., *Fielding and the Woman Question: The Novels of Henry Fielding and Feminist Debate, 1700–1750*, New York: St Martin's Press, 1989.

Varey, Simon, *Henry Fielding*, Cambridge: Cambridge University Press, 1986.

9

MURRAY PITTOCK

Johnson, Boswell, and their circle

Samuel Johnson's status as an author is very much bound up with his circle. If it is true that sociability and the study of man as a social animal were key features of the Scottish Enlightenment, it is equally the case that Johnson's reputation depends in significant part on his close friendships with a group almost as famous as himself, and on his depiction as a sociable being in the memoirs of his friends, notably in James Boswell's *Life of Johnson* (1791). In the seven years after Johnson's death, eleven biographies were published. The struggle over his reputation among his own circle began at once, and the importance of the possession of Johnson's memory seemed at times almost as much part of his value as anything he wrote and spoke in life.[1]

In recent years, some Johnson scholars have questioned whether Boswell's account is to be trusted, or whether his picture of Johnson as the 'Hercules of toryism' is not angled by the perspective of Boswell's own views.[2] This revisionism no doubt bears a symbiotic relationship to the revaluation of Boswell since 1940: a re-evaluation that has begun to recognize him as an artist rather than an amanuensis, the shaper of a great *Life* rather than a man who – as Macaulay saw him in the Victorian period – wrote a great book by accident. It is worth noting in respect of Johnson's politics at least – at present a matter of some controversy in the context of the *Life* – that Hannah More, Sir John Hawkins, and Mrs Thrale all substantively agree with Boswell regarding his sympathies. Perhaps more important, as Pat Rogers has argued, is Johnson's status as a man who set much of the tone of modern literary scholarship while being intimately concerned with the circumstances of academic book production. Johnson was a man, moreover, who did this *after* he had acquired extensive experience of Grub Street, as a contributor to virtually the full range of journalist productions that characterized the burgeoning print culture of the day (a culture of 'Journals, Medleys, Merc'ries, Magazines', as Pope put it in the expanded *Dunciad* of 1743).[3] Johnson the journalist and Johnson the artist are one and the same. In that sense, Johnson still challenges what we identify as the frontier of 'literature', for even as a high cultural lion he kept, in Edward A. Bloom's words, a 'permanent sympathy' bred of association with such men as Moses Browne, John Duick, Richard Savage, William Collins, and Samuel Boyse: sometimes gifted, more often workaday figures struggling at the margins 'in the wretched environment of Grub Street'.[4]

Johnson transformed these limiting circumstances by taking advantage of the intellectual potential of the genres from which he was obliged to earn, and in which he chose to excel. Indeed, it is arguable that the disciplinary narrowness of 'English' in the twentieth century, as opposed to 'Literature' in the nineteenth, has led to Johnson's being generally valued by his Boswellized conversation and a handful of critical and creative texts, rather than by the breadth of his transformations within prefatory, periodical, and essay genres. In Johnson's hands, journalism becomes an expression not just of a transient sentiment or judgement, but of the transience of human existence itself: a genre of sympathetic form. Similarly, his prefaces and conclusions (modes in which Johnson believed himself particularly gifted), together with his interest in biography, are fitting forms in which to represent the expression of a moral life and death, the unachievable hopes of youth and age's dutiful performance of life's last resistance to its end.

Johnson's impoverished youth and emergence into hackwork in London are part of the legend of the *Life*, first presented in Boswell's pages, though the two did not meet until 1763, when Johnson was fifty-four. After leaving Lichfield with his former pupil David Garrick in 1737, Johnson made a living in London through translation hackwork (a kind of work he had already begun in the Midlands) and by contributing extensively to the pioneering *Gentleman's Magazine*, in which a publishing form we now take for granted was in effect invented. The *Gentleman's* had been founded in 1731 by Edward Cave, a self-made and notoriously hard-nosed entrepreneur to whose rigorous control of costs and schedules Johnson once famously responded by signing a letter 'Yours, impransus' (i.e. without dinner).[5] Cave had begun his journalistic career as a writer for the crypto-Jacobite organ *Mist's Weekly Journal*, and from 1738 Johnson supervised William Guthrie, the Scottish son of an Episcopalian priest and another man of Jacobite connections, in composing a version of Parliamentary debates that evaded an official ban by using the Swiftian guise of debates in the senate of Lilliput (with the names of politicians derisively scrambled: Walpole became Walelop; Pitt became Ptit). In about 1740 Johnson began to write these largely fictionalized reports himself. His regular editorial stint for the magazine, which included essays, biographies, and poems in English and Latin, came to an end in about 1744, although ten years later he returned to contribute a substantial obituary of Cave.

Johnson also entered the political lists, defending liberty of expression in *A Compleat Vindication of the Licensers of the Stage* (1739) and publishing other ironic attacks on the administration of Sir Robert Walpole in its dying years. In 1737 he completed a tragedy, *Irene*, which was belatedly produced and published in 1749, enjoying a run at Drury Lane Theatre and earning him nearly £300 (about £25 000 in modern terms). Garrick, who managed and appeared in the production, had achieved success much earlier, and after his triumph in the title role of *Richard III* in 1741 was soon reaping unprecedented accolades and riches at Drury Lane. This was success in which, for the time being, Johnson could not share, and his low-life experience remained extensive and close. In the late 1730s, he became friends in London with the erstwhile Jacobite poet Richard Savage, whose status as a convicted murderer he guardedly excused in the *Life of Savage* (1744), a forerunner to his *Lives of the English Poets* (1779–81), in which he creates a myth of the poet as vagabond and outcast, 'a creative personality in torment'.[6] The character of Savage has been identified by some with that of the self-exiled Thales in Johnson's first important poem, *London* (1738): as though emulating Thales, Savage left London for Wales in 1739, though he returned to England the next year.

Johnson's early poetry, particularly *London* and *The Vanity of Human Wishes* (1749), owed a considerable debt to Latin verse, being constructed as formal imitations ('a method of translating looser than paraphrase, in which modern examples and illustrations are used for ancient', as Johnson was to define the term in his *Dictionary*) of Juvenal's third and tenth *Satires* respectively. *London* was printed with the original Latin alongside, with Thales as a replacement for the Latin poet's Umbritius. If Johnson's London was loved, it was also the place of corruption and disappointment depicted by the Roman satirist: a place 'devote to Vice and Gain', and one in which (the laboured line enacting the struggle) 'SLOW RISES WORTH, BY POVERTY DEPREST'.[7] Johnson was at times so poor he shrank from appearing in public, and he not only consorted but closely identified with professional writers on the breadline like Christopher Smart, in whose decline into penury and the madhouse he seems to have seen a fearful glimpse of his own potential condition. As late as 1756, Johnson himself was arrested for debt, and twice in the *Rambler* essays he feelingly explores the image of the author's garret, where the writer lives 'in the solitude of a hermit, with the anxiety of a miser, and the caution of an outlaw'.[8]

Johnson's disappointment may also have been political, and this has been a matter of recent controversy, with some scholars continuing to claim the presence of Jacobite language in Johnson's early poetry. Undoubtedly such language is there. In *Marmor Norfolciense* (1739) a critique of Prime

Minister Walpole is conjoined to a more general 'warm Anti-Hanoverian zeal' (*Life*, 1: 141), and the pattern persists beyond the failure of the 1745 rebellion. For example, *The Vanity of Human Wishes* contains at line 48 an echo of Dryden's translation of Juvenal's Satire III ('I neither will, nor can Prognosticate / To the young, gaping Heir, his Father's Fate'), which in its turn had echoed the first two lines of the famous Jacobite broadside, *The King Shall Enjoy His Own Again* ('What Booker doth Prognosticate / Concerning Kings or Kingdoms' Fate'). Johnson's 'gaping heir' is thus itself a reference marking the culmination of a theme of contested succession that begins with the allusion to 'rival Kings . . . And dubious Title' (lines 28–9) in a passage clearly alluding to the Jacobite rising of 1745 – most markedly so in the original version of 1749, with its reference to the 'bonny Traytor in the *Tow'r*' (line 34). Confiscation of Jacobite estates was more effective after 1745 than after the previous rising of 1715: Johnson refers to 'Confiscation's Vulturs' (line 36), and the association of confiscation with the thief and his 'Plunder' (line 44) suggests the arbitrary nature of justice in a world of 'dubious Title'. The most controversial reference in the poem is arguably to Charles XII of Sweden, on whom Johnson had considered writing a tragedy in 1742. Whether or not '*Swedish Charles*' (line 192) is himself a Jacobite surrogate is a cause of lasting controversy: 'The King of Sweedland' was a Jacobite air, and as Niall Mackenzie has noted, contemporary sources contain many comparisons of Prince Charles and Charles XII, including one in the *Gentleman's Magazine* for December 1748, whose proprietor, Cave, printed *Vanity* only a few weeks later. Whatever politics are being implied, the evocation of Charles XII's failure and folly bears eloquent witness to Johnson's depth and sophistication as a poet.[9]

Underpinning the political Johnson was the Christian pessimist, the author of forty sermons, of which twenty-eight survive. Johnson was greatly affected by the Nonjuror William Law's *Serious Call to a Devout and Holy Life* (1728), and by disheartening experiences of early poverty, which had a profound, if largely irrecoverable, influence on his writing. It is noteworthy how he often returned to his work of the 1730s, particularly travel literature, for later source material. Johnson was also to return to the themes of *Vanity* again and again, not least in *Rasselas*, a novella of 1759 (originally to be titled *The Choice of Life*) which drew in part on his 1733 translation of Lobo's *Voyage to Abyssinia*, and was published after the death of his mother. In *Rasselas*, human wishes are equally vain whether or not they are protected from the consequences of desire. The iron gates of the womb-like Happy Valley – perhaps related to the sexual imagery of 'the iron gates of life' in Marvell's 'To his Coy Mistress' (a poem that had become well known as early as 1711, when Addison ran a sustained implicit allusion to it in *Spectator* 89) – cannot guarantee human happiness, even by excluding every evil, for enjoyment lies in desire, and in desire, whether fulfilled or unfulfilled, lies only ultimate disappointment. Johnson's prolonged allusion to Marvell's Christian critique of Cavalier *carpe diem* poetry shows not only that sexual, but all other forms of desire, serve only to make the 'sun . . . run' (in Marvell's words), and waste what little life we only have in wanting.

By the time *Rasselas* appeared, Johnson's position as an influential literary figure was much more secure, thanks in no small part to the labour he expended over almost a decade on his *Dictionary* (1755), a monument of linguistic scholarship that surpassed earlier efforts and made an instant cultural impact. Disappointed in the level of support he had hoped for from Lord Chesterfield (revenge is taken in the *Dictionary*'s celebrated definition of 'Patron' as 'a wretch who supports with insolence, and is paid with flattery'), Johnson and his assistants persevered in the task, their method heralding the one employed by James Murray and his fellow editors of the *Oxford English Dictionary*: primarily empirical (the emphasis falling on authors writing between 1550 and 1750), but also using reference works and encyclopaedias. The *Dictionary* combines a moral rigidity (and in the examples chosen, ample evidence of Johnson's theological and political prejudices) with an acknowledgement of the inevitability of linguistic change. 'Sounds are too volatile and subtle for legal restraints; to enchain syllables, and to lash the wind, are equally the undertakings of pride, unwilling to measure its desires by its strength', as Johnson puts it in the Preface; and here again the vanity theme is resumed, his words recalling the condition of the frustrated conqueror of *Vanity*: 'The Waves he lashes, and enchains the Wind' (line 232). In his extensive revisions of the *Dictionary* for the fourth edition of 1773, Johnson incorporated a sweeping influx of Stuart sympathizers, mainly from the seventeenth century, as exemplars of his high Anglican Christian outlook, thereby reinforcing the identity that made one early critic call it 'a vehicle for Jacobite and High-flying tenets'.[10] The *Dictionary* was, and would remain, theologically oriented to God and Providence, and politically tendentious.

Among other accolades the *Dictionary* earned Johnson, through the efforts of Thomas Warton and others, the Oxford degree that he had failed to gain earlier in life, and in 1762 he was granted a government pension of £300 by the incoming administration of the Earl of Bute (on the initial suggestion of Alexander Wedderburn, MP for Inveraray burghs and later Earl of Rosslyn). The irony of Johnson's pension being proposed by one Scot to another is worth remarking on in the context of his reputation for Scotophobia,[11] and there was concern at the time given Johnson's reputed jacobitical politics. His public attitudes and pronouncements, however, were becoming more mainstream, though he had not yet reached the position that made him, in his late *Lives of the Poets*, seem almost to disown the stridently oppositional *London* of his youth, looking back on the political moment of the poem as one in which 'a long course of opposition to Sir Robert Walpole had filled the nation with clamours for liberty, of which no man felt the want, and with care for liberty, which was not in danger'.[12] In these mid-career years, Johnson surrounded himself with a literary circle that included not only old friends such as Garrick but also figures as diverse as the Whig politician Edmund Burke, the painter and academician Joshua Reynolds, James Boswell, and Oliver Goldsmith, the Irish writer whom Johnson famously rescued from arrest for debt in 1762 by selling his manuscript of *The Vicar of Wakefield* (a novel eventually published, with great commercial success, four years later). In the diversity of their national origins, the members of this group, formally constituted as the 'Club' in 1764, vividly display the cultural heterogeneity of the metropolitan centre to which all were drawn. Though less rigorously organized, the Club had some resemblance to the societies of the Edinburgh enlightenment, and provided a forum for Johnson to shine in a distinguished circle as his reputation increased. The politician Charles James Fox, the political economist Adam Smith, and the historian Edward Gibbon were all eventually members, as was Sir John Hawkins, who in 1787 brought out a life of Johnson that did much to provoke Boswell's rival work, and was permanently eclipsed by it.

Johnson had begun to be known in London through his association with Cave, and in 1750 John Payne, another future member of the Club, joined Cave in publishing a periodical that was to become Johnson's most famous forum: the *Rambler*, of which he wrote all but four of those issued. In this journal, published twice weekly for two years (the last number came out on the day his wife died), Johnson developed a successful persona, based in its pilgrim high seriousness in part on Francis Bacon's *Essays*, teeming 'with classical allusion and poetical imagery' (*Life*, I: 217), yet nonetheless characteristically his own voice, stoical and opposed to 'the fruitless anguish of impatience' (No. 32, 7 July 1750; *Rambler*, III: 179). Johnson's *Rambler* essays have indeed been called 'a form of wisdom literature, like the *Vanity* and like *Rasselas*'.[13] With his former *Gentleman's Magazine* associate John Hawkesworth, Johnson later helped set up a successor periodical called the *Adventurer* (1752–4), for which he persuaded Joseph Warton (later elected a member of the Club, as was his brother Thomas) to write. In both the *Adventurer* and, later, his *Idler* papers for the *Universal Chronicle* (1758–60), Johnson appears as a simpler and plainer vernacular figure, well balanced and opposed to party and partisanship, as in the essay on Tom Tempest and Jack Sneaker, Jacobite and Hanoverian respectively, in his issue for

17 June 1758. Even after the appearance of the *Dictionary*, Johnson still needed to write to make money: he contributed to the *Literary Magazine* (1756–8) and was associated (though largely as an act of charity to the editor) with Christopher Smart's ill-fated *Universal Visiter* of 1756.

Johnson's opposition to empire and imperialism was manifest as early as his leader in the *Gentleman's Magazine* for June 1738 (in the series of 'Debates in the Senate of Magna Lilliputia', and possibly co-authored with Guthrie). According to Jeremy Black, his 'longstanding hostility to colonialism and oppressive war . . . owed much to his Nonjuring Christian beliefs',[14] and certainly Johnson showed a lifelong distaste for imperialism and gratuitous bloodshed. In 'Observations on the Present State of Affairs' in the *Literary Magazine* for 1756, Johnson condemns the purposes of the deadly war for empire between Britain and France. Just after Quebec had fallen, he published an arresting *Idler* essay, viewing the victory through the persona of a native American who comments that 'their treaties are only to deceive, and their traffick only to defraud us', and that 'the death of every European delivers the country from a tyrant and a robber'[15] – remarkable words to write in the context of General Wolfe's heroic death on the Heights of Abraham. The same ethos is visible in Johnson's later work, such as *Thoughts on the late Transactions respecting Falkland's Islands* (1771), a commentary that briefly returned to prominence during the Falklands War of 1982. In *Thoughts*, as Jeremy Black has argued, Johnson's attack on the corrupting effects of financial activity and speculation looks back to Swift's *The Conduct of the Allies* (1711). On the other hand, unlike many others among those with reservations concerning empire, Johnson had no time for American independence. In *Taxation No Tyranny* (1775), Johnson responded to American claims, arguing with some justice that the leaders of American society wanted to consolidate their own slave-owning ascendancy ('how is it that we hear the loudest yelps for liberty among the drivers of negroes?'),[16] and providing a thoughtful disquisition on the nature of nations and nationalism by comparing the American colonies with Cornwall and contemplating (jestingly) the case for Cornish independence.

If Johnson's central place in the academy owes much to his great biographer, it also owes something to his contribution to what was to become (indeed, by the appointment of Hugh Blair to the Regius Chair of Rhetoric and Belles Lettres at Edinburgh in 1762, was already becoming) the discipline of English. Johnson's eight-volume *The Plays of William Shakespeare* (1765) extended his domain to literary scholarship, and in its Preface rescues Shakespeare from neo-classical critique while avoiding the bardolatry of Victorian and later times. His Shakespeare edition can indeed be seen as standing at the heart of an impressive attempt to establish the canon and text,

one innovation taken up by his successors being the provision of a vario-
rum commentary embodying the readings and conjectures of earlier editors.
Although no scholar of the Jacobethan stage, as Pat Rogers has argued,
Johnson's robust good sense as an editor and his unwillingness to over-read
'allegedly corrupt lines' or 'enter into competition to produce new readings'
were indicative of the importance he placed on critical judgement.[17]

In *Lives of the English Poets* (a series of prefaces, commissioned for 200
guineas, to a multi-volume anthology over which he had no editorial control),
Johnson arguably laid the ground for a morally based and intellectually rigorous literary criticism still evident in F. R. Leavis's *Nor Shall My Sword* (1976)
almost two hundred years later. As a critic, Johnson favoured, in Rogers's
words, 'freshness, truth to nature, vigour, clarity, energy, sharpness of focus,
and wit'. He was moral and biographical (his positive view of biography can
be found in *Rambler* 60): not for him the abolition of the author, whether via
New Criticism or later substitutions of aesthetics or metaphor for the boundaries of experience and the circumstances of production. Rather, Johnson,
conscious of his own Grub Street beginnings, exemplified like Burke the correct if complex predominance of circumstance, and as a result 'in most of
the key lives . . . there is an intricate mental commerce between the inner
being of the poet and the external realities of his career in the world'.[18]

The 1760s saw two of the most important personal encounters of
Johnson's career. In 1763 he met James Boswell, whose profane, anxious and
obsessional mind would provide a counterweight to his own; two years later
he was introduced into the family of Henry Thrale, MP for Southwark and a
wealthy brewer. Thrale liked sparring conversations, and admired Johnson
enough to allow him to edit or compose his election addresses. Johnson was,
however, closer to Thrale's Welsh wife Hester, who had married Thrale two
years earlier, and became almost domesticated at their house in Streatham
Park, where he was surrounded by a coterie of 'Streathamites' including
the actor-dramatists David Garrick and Arthur Murphy, the painter Joshua
Reynolds, the scholar William Seward, and Boswell himself, who migrated
thither to be in Johnson's circle. From 1776 Dr Charles Burney, the father of
Frances (whose *Evelina* was published soon afterwards), joined this group
as music master to the Thrales' eldest child. Johnson became estranged
from Mrs Thrale in her last years following her second marriage to Gabriel
Piozzi, the Italian singer, but it was she who left the first published record of
Johnson's life in *Anecdotes of the Late Samuel Johnson* (1786) – a work
she defined as 'a mere *candle-light* picture of his latter days, where every
thing falls in dark shadow except the face, the index of the mind'.[19] In its
disenchanted tone, it constitutes her side of a farewell for which Johnson,
in his plangent last letter about her remarriage, had found a resonant

historical analogy: 'When Queen Mary took the resolution of sheltering herself in England, the Archbishop of St Andrew's attempting to dissuade her, attended on her journey and when they came to the irremeable Stream that separated the two kingdoms, walked by her side into the water, in the middle of which he seized her bridle, and with earnestness proportioned to her danger and his own affection, pressed her to return. The Queen went forward' (*Letters*, IV: 343–4).

As well as the wider world of the Club, Johnson was thus in the 1760s developing a circle of elite friends containing both a younger man (Boswell) and a younger woman (Thrale) on whom he could depend. Neither was English, and Johnson visited the homelands of both. Although his 1774 tour of Wales with the Thrales was a disappointment, Wales being 'so little different from England, that it offers nothing to the speculation of the traveller' (*Letters*, II: 149), the celebrated 1773 visit of Johnson and Boswell to Scotland, documented in Johnson's *Journey to the Western Islands of Scotland* (1775) and Boswell's *Tour to the Hebrides* (1785), was a key moment in defining not only the relationship of the two men, but also elements of many of the major social, political, literary, and theological debates within Johnson's own work.

The key to understanding the relationship between Johnson and Boswell is threefold: father and son; Englishman and Scot who both disliked modern Scotland, sometimes in surprisingly similar ways; and closeness of spirit in religion and politics. Both writers disliked Presbyterianism and the Scottish narrowness they believed it both cultivated and represented; both had high church leanings, in Boswell's case quasi- or crypto-Catholic; both were ready to give vent to Jacobite sentiments, and at times to regret the fall of the Stuart dynasty, although to both it was perhaps what I elsewhere term a *felix culpa* or fortunate fall.[20] Boswell's fidelity to the truth as far as he could recover it is a noteworthy feature of his writing, so despite the defensiveness of some critics towards anything that might associate Johnson with Boswell's sentiments in these matters, the *Life of Johnson* continues to enjoy its status as a substantially accurate record, especially where supported by parallel statements in Boswell's journals, in both Johnson and Boswell's versions of their 1773 Scottish tour, and in Johnson's letters on tour to Hester Thrale.

Expert manipulator as he was of everything liminal, both physical and material, Boswell himself was by the time of the tour an established author who had already made use of the Scottish patriot historiographical tradition in new and unexpected contexts. The roots of this tradition were known by many non-Scots, due to its foundation in Sallust and Tacitus and its alignment with the traditions of classical republicanism: it stressed the themes of primitive patriot valour and history as a struggle for liberty. Indeed, Sallust had provided part of the text for the Declaration of Arbroath (1320), one of the earliest texts in a tradition that stressed the defensive qualities of a patriotism distrustful of empire – a congenial position for Johnson. During his historic journey in Corsica in autumn 1765, as Philip Martin puts it, 'one of Boswell's themes . . . was the happiness of . . . "primitive" or "savage" peoples whose lives combined the innocence and purity of nature, with a revival, under Pasquale Paoli's enlightened leadership, of the classical republicanism of the ancients'.[21] Paoli himself expressed sentiments strongly aligned with the anti-empire school of Scottish defensive patriotism, when he said to Boswell that 'Corsica aspired only for independence and had no hope and no chance of empire'.[22] On his return, his title page of *An Account of Corsica* (1768) quoted the Declaration of Arbroath (1320): 'Non enim propter gloriam, divitias aut honores pugnamus, sed propter libertate solummodo, quam homo bonus nisi simul vita amittit' ('We fight not for glory, riches or honours, but for liberty alone, which no good man quits but with life'). Boswell lightly disguised this sentiment by leaving it in the Latin; he also calls it a letter from the barons of Scotland, a category under which he included himself. Habitually (and in strict terms legitimately), Boswell had given himself the title of 'Baron' on his European tour, on which he had spoken of the Declaration of Arbroath to the exiled Jacobite Earl Marischal, had received a copy of Barbour's *Bruce* (1375) inscribed to him as 'Scotus Scoto' (a Scot of Scots), and had acted as go-between for the Earl Marischal and Rousseau, to supply the latter with the details for a biography of Andrew Fletcher of Saltoun (1653–1716), another Scottish patriot in this tradition.

Boswell talked this same language with his English friends, notably General James Francis Edward Oglethorpe (who contributed three essays to Boswell's *British Essays in Favour of the Brave Corsicans* (1768)) and Johnson. Oglethorpe summed it up in a letter to Boswell on 1 March 1776: 'But the Caledonian Picts & Scots defended their Libertys against the Romans in their full blown Power, & Beat them. The Stamina of these Scotts, and their Education kept up their Glory even to the time of Buccannon, & down to our Times.'[23] In 1772 Johnson and Boswell talked of Tacitus in relation to Scotland. Most significantly, in the *Journey* itself, Johnson makes a direct allusion to Tacitus' place in the Scottish patriot tradition, when he writes of the beginning of the clearing of the Highlands that 'where there was formerly an insurrection, there is now a wilderness', a clear paraphrase of the words of the Caledonian leader Calgacus' defiance of the Romans in Tacitus' *Agricola*: 'they make a desolation, and call it peace'.[24]

Such a tradition was thus not as alien to Johnson as might be supposed, not only given the importance of classical republicanism in general political debate, but especially given the adoption of the patriot tradition in the earlier eighteenth century by the Jacobite language of resistance: Lord Lovat's last words from the scaffold, *'Dulce et decorum est pro patria mori'* ('How sweet and fitting it is to die for one's country'), are quoted by Boswell in the *Life of Johnson* (1: 181 n.), while the importance of the Latin tradition to Jacobite patriotism has recently been stressed by Jonathan Clark. Both men had close connections with Jacobites, and were familiar with the Jacobite world-view, even if they did not subscribe to its practical agenda.

In Edinburgh in 1773, Boswell and Johnson both breakfasted with William Drummond, the Episcopalian bookseller who had been in arms in 1745, and who published the *Scottish Communion Office* of 1764, one of the main liturgical documents of Jacobite Episcopalianism. Drummond had first met Johnson while a fugitive in London after the rising, and in 1766–7 received Johnson's warm support in his efforts to achieve the publication of the first New Testament in Gaelic (*Life*, II: 26–30). Boswell and Johnson also shared an admiration for Thomas Ruddiman, one of the exponents of this outlook, while Johnson was also partial to George Buchanan as a representative of heights of classical scholarship to which a Scotland he saw as declining could seldom now aspire: 'Johnson, like Ruddiman, believed that the decline of learning went together with the advance of Presbyterianism.'[25] At Laurencekirk, Johnson 'respectfully remembered' Ruddiman, who had been schoolmaster there (*Tour*, p. 206).

On tour in Scotland, Johnson sees the country as having betrayed its past, a view to which Boswell was no stranger, arguing both in *Reflections on the Bankruptcies in Scotland* (1772) and *Letter to the People of Scotland* (1785) that many undesirable innovations had grown up in response to indifference to breaches of the Union. Johnson's comment 'if we allow the Scotch to be a nation' (*Life*, III: 387) represented a judgement on the country's own conduct, and the view he expressed of it on tour is consonant with this. When Boswell tried Johnson with the claim that 'our [Scotland's] independent kingdom was lost', Johnson countered with a comment on how Scotland sold Mary Queen of Scots, and later greeted criticism of the Union by suggesting that the Scots can go home to enjoy their Presbyterianism there. 'Never talk of your independency', he reproves Boswell as representing a people who would not fight for their queen (*Tour*, p. 184), and this sentiment is repeated elsewhere in Johnson's regard for William Tytler's defence of Mary from the attacks of other Enlightenment historians.[26] Johnson is on the other hand clearly touched by Scotland's non-Presbyterian past, calling Holyrood 'that deserted mansion of royalty', and quoting the Jacobite poet Hamilton of Bangour on the occasion (*Tour*, p. 186). In fact, he treats Scotland as a country in decline rather than innately inferior, suffering from the effects of a Reformation to which 'the blackest midnight of Popery is meridian sunshine' and where 'the malignant influence of *Calvinism* has blasted ceremony and decency together' (*Letters*, I: 270; *Journey*, p. 58). Although Johnson thought that Scotland 'had hardly any trade, any money, or any elegance, before the Union', it is also clear that his view of the country in earlier times was somewhat different. If Scotland is now a 'barbarous nation', it is because it has declined into Presbyterianism; in the sixteenth century and among the Scoto-Latin Episcopalian writers and thinkers of the seventeenth the case was different. He believed that 'the episcopal cities of Scotland . . . fell with their churches', and that learning vanished in the seventeenth century (*Journey*, p. 21). Most tellingly, Johnson remarks that although Scotland at the Union was 'unformed', 'coarse' and 'filthy', this was implicitly a result of what Scotland had become: 'they must be for ever content to owe to the English that elegance and culture, which, if they had been vigilant and active, perhaps the English might have owed to them' (*Journey*, p. 24). As Thomas Curley remarks, Johnson's *Journey* 'chronicles a cumulative *memento mori* of a culture's demise and a people's degradation'.[27] On visiting Lord Monboddo, whose father had fought for the Jacobites, Johnson remarked to his son on the quality of his Latin, with the sly comment that 'When King James comes back, you shall be in the "Muses' Welcome!"': the title of a book composed in 1617 for the return of James VI and I to Scotland, though clearly Johnson's remark was capable of a different interpretation (*Tour*, p. 210).

In the *Journey*, Johnson lays particular stress on a subject that much affected him in an English context, and with which he connected cultural decadence: the destruction and spoliation of churches in general and cathedrals in particular. He and Boswell both lamented 'the number of ruined religious buildings' (*Tour*, p. 405), of which St Andrews, 'once the See of the Primate of Scotland', now with only 'the poor remains of a stately Cathedral', offered the prime case (*Letters*, II: 55). The 'silence and solitude of inactive indolence and gloomy depopulation' Johnson finds there is not just the way in which Scotland differs from England: it is the divergence of voluntary decline, in a city with a ruined cathedral, whose last Cardinal had been 'murdered by the ruffians of reformation' in 1546 and whose archbishop had been killed in front of his daughter by Presbyterian extremists in the lifetime of Johnson's own father. St Andrews, whose low numbers of students Johnson attributes to there being 'no episcopal chapel in the place', now shows 'an university declining, a college alienated, and a church profaned and hastening to the ground'. For good measure, Johnson compares John Knox, father of the Reformation, with Alaric, the Vandal who sacked Rome – a city laden with symbolic meaning in a church context – in 410 (*Journey*, pp. 6–8). Similarly, the High Kirk of St Giles in Edinburgh is 'what was once a church!'; 'the ruins of the cathedral of Elgin afforded us another proof of the waste of reformation'; while the lead stolen from cathedral roofs is a 'cargo of sacrilege' (*Tour*, p. 185; *Journey*, pp. 20, 21). Johnson's view was that 'of the destruction of churches, the decay of religion must in time be the consequence' (*Journey*, p. 58): this dreadful process was well under way in Scotland, which thus served as a monitory example to its southern neighbour. Johnson had viewed the scars of the civil wars on the cathedrals of Winchester, Exeter, Ely, and Norwich, which he visited before going to Scotland, and his childhood memories of accounts of the spoliation of Lichfield Cathedral also reminded him how close England had been to going the same way in the middle of the seventeenth century. There was still a risk – Johnson had remarked in 1749 on the number of churches sinking into ruin in England (*Political Writings*, pp. 114–15) – but on the whole England had avoided the abyss, and Scotland had not. Johnson, unlike some of his contemporaries, saw nothing stylish in decayed buildings. Rather, places such as Iona bore witness to the connection between the ruins and the intellectual and religious decay of society. At Inch Kenneth, Johnson found a church with an 'altar . . . not yet quite demolished' with 'a Bas relief of the Virgin with her Child' and 'a hand bell, which though it has no clapper neither presbyterian bigotry, nor barbarian wantonness has yet taken away' (*Letters*, II: 105). The tongue of the bell would have rung for the exaltation of the Host; and Johnson's Latin poem on the occasion makes clear his High Church views of a place once full of 'the offices of holy religion . . . the true faith'.[28] Johnson pointedly refused to enter a Presbyterian church throughout the duration of his stay in Scotland.

Both Johnson and Boswell, in the *Journey to the Western Islands of Scotland* and *An Account of a Tour to Corsica*, are seeking to do much the same thing: to hold up the past as an example to the present, except that in Boswell's case the past is alive in the present and holds out the possibility of national liberation for Corsica, and for Johnson in Scotland the death of the past is a national death. Boswell tries to realize the Scottish patriot tradition through Corsica; Johnson offers Scotland as a dreadful example of what a country that despises and neglects its history, religion and traditions may become: a simoniac nation, which sells Mary, Charles I, and itself, then hastens south for more money to feed its avarice. Both he and Boswell are (as Pat Rogers observes in *Johnson and Boswell: The Transit of Caledonia*) conscious of the dialogue with nationality and history being played out in their travel writing in Scotland. Their other dialogues, whether publicly on Catholicism or hidden in their own work (such as Boswell's plan to produce a 'Scots dictionary' to save 'the Scottish language from someday becoming unintelligible and thereby rescuing Scottish literature from oblivion') remain the richest in Johnson's circle.[29] They combine nationality, religion and the quest of life: an intense interest in physical experience, the passing of time and the spiritual dimension in human being: some of the deepest motivating forces of the human personality in any and every age. Truly, Boswell had only two subjects, as Johnson observed: yourself and myself. But he was not so dissimilar from his English father-figure, who wrote his own preoccupations into almost every genre of journalism and literature in a different kind of critical autobiography from that of Boswell's journals.

Samuel Johnson died in 1784. Just as he is a figure who cannot be understood without his relationships to others, so he remains one whose identity compels relationship: whose personality is part of his value. One of the reasons for this is in the record of him left (and indeed contested among) those who knew him; another is his expression through art of humanity, in terms of the contest between experience and time which underpins creative and critical judgement, which hope despite themselves, and perhaps more wisely than Rasselas, to escape it.

NOTES

1. Robert E. Kelley and O. M. Brack, Jr, *Samuel Johnson's Early Biographers* (Iowa City: University of Iowa Press, 1971), p. xiii.
2. *Boswell's Life of Johnson*, ed. George Birkbeck Hill, rev. L. F. Powell, 6 vols. (Oxford: Clarendon Press, 1934–64), I: 38.
3. Pat Rogers, *Samuel Johnson* (Oxford: Oxford University Press, 1993), p. 19; Alexander Pope, *The Dunciad: In Four Books*, ed. Valerie Rumbold (London: Longman, 1999), p. 104 (i.34).
4. Edward A. Bloom, *Samuel Johnson in Grub Street* (Providence, RI: Brown University Press, 1957), pp. vii, 69.
5. *The Letters of Samuel Johnson*, ed. Bruce Redford, 5 vols. (Oxford: Clarendon Press, 1992), I: 21 (November 1738).
6. Rogers, *Samuel Johnson*, p. 15.
7. *The Poems of Samuel Johnson*, ed. David Nicol Smith and Edward L. McAdam, 2nd edn (Oxford: Clarendon Press, 1974), pp. 69, 76 (lines 37, 177).
8. *The Rambler*, ed. W. J. Bate and Albrecht B. Strauss, The Yale Edition of the Works of Samuel Johnson, vols. III–V (New Haven: Yale University Press, 1969), III: 91 (No. 16, 12 May 1750).
9. Niall Mackenzie, '"A Great Affinity in Many Things": Further Evidence for the Jacobite Gloss on "Swedish Charles"', *Age of Johnson* 12 (2001), 255–72 (p. 261).
10. Thomas Edwards, quoted from a letter of 1755 by Robert DeMaria, *The Life of Samuel Johnson* (Oxford: Blackwell, 1993), p. 123.
11. Murray G. H. Pittock, 'Johnson and Scotland', in Jonathan Clark and Howard Erskine-Hill (eds), *Samuel Johnson in Historical Context* (Basingstoke: Palgrave, 2002), pp. 184–96.
12. *Lives of the English Poets*, ed. George Birkbeck Hill, 3 vols. (Oxford: Clarendon Press, 1905), III: 289. Johnson may be recalling the wording of one of his early parliamentary reports, in which 'Walelop' mocks his opponents for 'complaining

of grievances which they do not suffer' (*Samuel Johnson: The Major Works*, ed. Donald L. Greene (Oxford: Oxford University Press, 1984), p. 111).

13. DeMaria, *Life of Samuel Johnson*, p. 159.
14. Jeremy Black, 'Samuel Johnson and the Tory Tradition in Foreign Policy', in Clark and Erskine-Hill (eds.), *Samuel Johnson in Historical Context*, pp. 169–83 (p. 177).
15. *The Idler and the Adventurer*, ed. W. J. Bate, John M. Bullitt, and L. F. Powell (New Haven: Yale University Press, 1963), pp. 253–4 (No. 81, 3 November 1759).
16. Johnson, *Political Writings*, ed. Donald Greene (New Haven: Yale University Press, 1977), p. 454.
17. Rogers, *Samuel Johnson*, pp. 83–4.
18. Rogers, *Samuel Johnson*, pp. 93, 18.
19. Piozzi, *Anecdotes of Samuel Johnson* (Gloucester: Alan Sutton, 1984), p. 109.
20. Murray G. H. Pittock, *Poetry and Jacobite Politics in Eighteenth-Century Britain and Ireland* (Cambridge: Cambridge University Press, 1994), pp. 128–32.
21. Philip Martin, *James Boswell: A Life* (London: Pimlico, 2000), p. 205.
22. Frederick Pottle, *James Boswell: The Earlier Years* (New York: McGraw-Hill, 1966), p. 255.
23. James Boswell, *The Political Correspondence*, ed. Murray G. H. Pittock (New Haven: Yale University Press, forthcoming). Oglethorpe means the humanist George Buchanan (1506–82).
24. Samuel Johnson and James Boswell, *A Journey to the Western Islands of Scotland; The Journal of a Tour to the Hebrides*, ed. R. W. Chapman (London: Oxford University Press, 1924), p. 88. Further references to both the *Journey* and the *Tour* are to this edition.
25. J. C. D. Clark, *Samuel Johnson: Literature, Religion, and English Cultural Politics from the Restoration to Romanticism* (Cambridge: Cambridge University Press, 1994), p. 36; see also pp. 32–43 passim.
26. See Pat Rogers, *Johnson and Boswell: The Transit of Caledonia* (Oxford: Clarendon Press, 1995), p. 167; also Johnson's review of Tytler in *Major Works*, pp. 551, 557.
27. Cited in John A. Vance, *Samuel Johnson and the Sense of History* (Athens: University of Georgia Press, 1984), p. 80.
28. *The Latin and Greek Poems of Samuel Johnson*, ed. Barry Baldwin (London: Duckworth, 1995), pp. 106–7.
29. Frederick Pottle, *Boswell in Holland* (New York: McGraw-Hill, 1952), pp. 160–1.

FURTHER READING

Bronson, Bertrand H., *Johnson Agonistes and Other Essays*, Berkeley: University of California Press, 1965.
Cannon, John, *Samuel Johnson and the Politics of Hanoverian England*, Oxford: Clarendon Press, 1994.
Clark, J. C. D., *Samuel Johnson: Literature, Religion and English Cultural Politics from the Restoration to Romanticism*, Cambridge: Cambridge University Press, 1994.

Clark, Jonathan and Howard Erskine-Hill (eds.), *Samuel Johnson in Historical Context*, Basingstoke: Palgrave, 2002.

Clingham, Greg (ed.), *The Cambridge Companion to Samuel Johnson*, Cambridge: Cambridge University Press, 1997.

  New Light on Boswell: Critical and Historical Essays on the Occasion of the Bicentenary of the Life of Johnson, Cambridge: Cambridge University Press, 1991.

De Maria, Robert, Jr, *The Life of Samuel Johnson*, Oxford: Blackwell, 1993.

Hudson, Nicholas, *Samuel Johnson and Eighteenth-Century Thought*, Oxford: Clarendon Press, 1988.

Kernan, Alvin, *Samuel Johnson and the Impact of Print*, Princeton: Princeton University Press, 1987.

Lipking, Lawrence, *Samuel Johnson: The Life of an Author*, Cambridge: Harvard University Press, 1998.

Lynn, Steven, *Samuel Johnson after Deconstruction: Rhetoric and the Rambler*, Carbondale: Southern Illinois University Press, 1992.

Redford, Bruce, *Designing the Life of Johnson*, Oxford: Oxford University Press, 2002.

Rogers, Pat, *Samuel Johnson*, Oxford: Oxford University Press, 1993.

  Johnson and Boswell: The Transit of Caledonia, Oxford: Clarendon Press, 1995.

Vance, John A. (ed.), *Boswell's 'Life of Johnson': New Questions, New Answers*, Athens: University of Georgia Press, 1985.

Wimsatt, W. K., *The Prose Style of Samuel Johnson*, New Haven: Yale University Press, 1941.

10

THOMAS KEYMER

Sterne and Romantic autobiography

Recoiling from the term 'self-biography' as coined in Isaac D'Israeli's *Miscellanies* (1796), William Taylor of the *Monthly Review* was at a loss for more felicitous options: 'it is not very usual in English to employ hybrid words partly Saxon and partly Greek: yet *autobiography* would have seemed pedantic.' Given the rash of autobiographical writing in various modes that had begun to appear by 1800, however (and more, from William Wordsworth's *Prelude* to his sister Dorothy's journals, was being privately produced), the need for some such term was becoming pressing. 'Autobiography' and its cognates quickly gained currency in the years that followed, notably in the hands of reviewers who otherwise lacked a taxonomy answerable to what Thomas Carlyle was to call, in 1831, 'these Autobiographical times of ours'.[1]

In early usage the connotation of 'autobiography' was often pejorative, as though the genre, though newly named, was not at all new in substance, and simply perpetuated a tradition of more or less mercenary, self-promotional, often ghostwritten 'memoirs' and 'apologies' that included such notorious works as *An Apology for the Conduct of Mrs. Teresia Constantia Phillips* (1748–9) and *The Memoirs of Mrs. Laetitia Pilkington* (1748–54). This was the implication when Robert Montgomery inveighed against 'the memoir-scribblers, reminiscent-furbishers, &c. – The impudence of these auto-biographists', or again when Robert Southey deplored (with a witty sting in the tail of his list) a culture in which 'booksellers, public lecturers, pickpockets, and poets, become autobiographers'.[2]

Yet there was also a sense that works in this mode could now amount to more than mere brazen posturing or catchpenny scandal. Autobiography remained a suspect undertaking in those deemed socially or morally low, inconsequential in the scope of their lives and incapable of self-conscious reflection, but looked a different prospect in the hands of public figures or established authors. Where lives of historical importance were at stake, or where lives were artfully shaped in developmental narratives of organic selfhood, the new autobiography could seem radically distinct from the prurient gossip and discontinuous accumulations that typified earlier memoirs. Translated into English in 1783–90, Jean-Jacques Rousseau's two-part *Confessions* was a heady instance of the power of autobiography to trace personal identity in all its intricacies and involutions, and embodied bold new claims for the significance and uniqueness of the essential self. Subjectivity was now fit material for literary expression of the highest kind, even to the point of elevation, as in Wordsworth's audacious practice, in an epic mode hitherto reserved for large public subjects like the loss of Eden or the fall of Troy. It was with a sense of high potential – above all the potential to transcribe and interpret human consciousness with previously unachieved precision – that Taylor returned to his neologism in 1807, declaring that Benjamin Franklin's 'autobiography, if published without mutilation, would no doubt illuminate many recesses of the human heart'.[3]

If autobiography was a powerful expressive resource, however, it was also problematic. The very quality that allowed it to distinguish itself from memoir – its characteristic effort to order and narrate the raw material of experience in terms of a unified, autonomous, knowable self – also lays it open to question. 'Autobiography represents an effort made by those who write it at the integration of their past lives and present selves', as John Sturrock writes: 'the autobiographer wishes to stand forth in print in the form of a *whole*.'[4] Yet is the self necessarily coherent, or amenable to such integration, as opposed to being indescribably complex, fluid, or unstable? Is it in place when writing begins, inertly awaiting the work of description, or is it creatively constituted in the process of composition? Does the autobiographer's characteristic effort to fashion a unity stop at neutral documentation and dispassionate analysis, or is to be self-conscious necessarily to be self-serving, to engage in the rhetorical construction of an identity that is not only integrated but also flatteringly defined? Are the conventional resources of discursive language and linear narrative in any case up to the job, able to fix in print the dynamics of subjectivity over time without blurring, distortion, or loss?

The famous opening of Rousseau's *Confessions* does little to register such problems. Confident in the penetrating rigour of his self-knowledge, the truthful impartiality of his memory, and the comprehensive transparency of his revelations, Rousseau promises to lay bare a self that is like no other in the world – not least so, now, in being so profoundly and publicly known. These confident assertions come under repeated strain, however, as Rousseau's text unfolds. Though facts, deeds, and words can be adequately recorded, feelings prove resistant to description; heart and mind pull contrary ways, as though not the property of a single individual; the complexities of emotion and memory jeopardize order and sequence, throwing up data 'too numerous, too confused, too unpleasant to be capable of straightforward narration'.[5] At best the narrative of subjectivity becomes interminable, always in need of supplementation by further experiential evidence, or by fresh tokens of the textual presence of the writer's authentic self. These were tokens that Rousseau eventually felt compelled to provide in the flesh, as though in acknowledgement of the insufficiency of his text, by giving emotive public recitations from the *Confessions* – recitations that could last, it was reported, for marathon stretches of up to seventeen hours.

Fictions of identity in the eighteenth century

For the spiritual autobiographers of earlier generations, as opposed to the new breed of secular autobiographer who sprang up in Rousseau's wake, anxieties of this kind seem not to have bulked very large. With its plangent figures of a soul in turmoil – mired packhorses and subsiding houses; birds clogged, limed, or shot from trees – John Bunyan's *Grace Abounding to the Chief of Sinners* (1666) is nothing if not an anxious text. In this most influential of spiritual autobiographies, religious dread is everywhere, above all in Bunyan's fear that the moment of conversion is never secure, jeopardized as it is by endless backsliding, and demanding endless struggle. Anxiety about literary misrepresentation, however, is ruled out from the start. Bunyan's preface stridently renounces high style and literary adornment, claiming for his text a quality of transparency and authenticity that flows from its rigorous eschewal of play, its determination to 'be plain and simple, and lay down the thing as it was'. As *Grace Abounding* proceeds, this capacity to reproduce the simple truth of lived experience is reaffirmed by Bunyan's insistence that he merely transcribes, without significant shaping of his own, a narrative that is divinely authored. The story he tells of sin and redemption, of struggle between the inward life of grace and the outward life of temptation, is organized by providence throughout, and marked by recurrent implications that 'in this my relation of the merciful working of God upon my Soul' the true protagonist is the Deity himself. Bunyan is simply the witness of patterns that are objectively given and transcendently true, with God as guarantor of their meanings. These patterns, moreover, repeat a hallowed model, so that when Bunyan chances on a work by Martin Luther the certainties of his self-analysis are bolstered again: 'I found my condition in his experience, so largely and profoundly handled, as if his Book had been written out of my heart.'[6]

Similar appeals to transcendent authority – though rarely distinguished by the tortured vigilance of Bunyan's prose – were to typify the genre of spiritual autobiography as it persisted in the eighteenth century. Sometimes these were little more than screens to hide behind, as when the flamboyant Methodist leader George Whitefield sought to validate a self-serving account of his own rather worldly wheelings and dealings under the title *A Short Account of God's Dealings with the Reverend Mr George Whitefield*. Published in 1740, when its author – a transatlantic celebrity whose open-air meetings drew crowds as far apart as London and Charleston – was only twenty-five, *God's Dealings* systematically disavows any agency of Whitefield's own as either actor in, or author of, his precociously stellar life. This life is shaped instead by the operations of grace, as is its memorial reconstruction in the form of a text now dictated, or at least greatly determined, by 'the Assistance I have had from the Holy Spirit, in bringing many Things to my Remembrance'. Unmediated by any human will, the unified spiritual subject to which Whitefield resolves his richly conflicted personality would be recognized by all readers as divinely produced. Only the reprobate, 'when they read this, will contradict and blaspheme'.[7]

It is instead to the emerging novel that we must look for sceptical self-consciousness about the capacity of narrative to render subjectivity on the page. Defoe and Richardson both drew on the techniques of spiritual autobiography to structure fictional lives, and at first sight their representations of the narrating self seem confident enough. Couched in the middle-class 'Trading Stile' that was Defoe's counterpart to Bunyanesque plainness, works such as *Robinson Crusoe* (1719) or *Moll Flanders* (1722) fused the spiritual autobiographer's focus on inward conscience with a journalistic concern for outward circumstance, and seemed able to portray consciousness in its social operation with new specificity. The fictionality of these narratives is strategically denied, and many readers approached them as genuine memoirs. In the 1740s, Richardson too presented himself (though more equivocally) as an editor of found documents, exploiting traditional views of the familiar letter as a uniquely capacious and authentic medium for transcribing consciousness over time. In his first and most popular novel, however, the narrating heroine's dominant assumptions remain those of spiritual autobiography, and these suffuse her experience and identity with the gratifying clarity of puritan myth. Pamela's story is moulded at the time, and endowed with retrospective meaning, by 'the Goodness of that Providence, which has, thro' so many intricate Mazes, made me tread the Paths of Innocence, and so amply rewarded me'. With claims of this kind, *Pamela* seems to confer on its heroine a pure and simple identity in which inward self and outward expression are luminously at one. In the unctuous prefatory matter supplied by Richardson's friends, the novel professes an utter transparency of representation. Pamela's narrative becomes, like Pamela herself, 'a pure clear

Fountain of Truth and Innocence'; it brings to view 'the inmost Recesses of her Mind'.[8]

On closer inspection, however, one sees that novels like these were opening up questions that would be fundamental to autobiography as it developed. Identity is never more than provisional for Defoe's mobile protagonists, a matter not of organic growth but of constant improvisation in a struggle to survive that recurrently unfixes personal and social definitions. Rather than veiling an essentially stable identity, Defoe's narrators have more in common with the enigmatic 'domino' in masquerades of the day – a blank or neutral costume that suggests no inherent identity at all, but instead an ongoing capacity for the adoption, erasure, and reinscription of successive new meanings. Roxana is so accomplished in this mode that when she chooses to disguise herself as (or, as she puts it, 'be') a quaker for the day, her plausibility seems to subvert the real thing, 'and there was not a QUAKER in the Town look'd less like a Counterfeit than I did'. Moll remains obstinately pseudonymous, and her teasing early acknowledgement of fissured identity – of the space between 'who I have been, as well as who I am' – is never resolved by a narrative in which she oscillates, sometimes within a single sentence, between multiple roles as scheming predator and innocent prey, abject penitent and gleeful thief.[9]

As for Richardson, the ironies and innuendoes that lurk beneath Pamela's providentialism were wittily exposed by Fielding, whose *Shamela* (1741) re-reads her epistolary narrative as the fraudulent crowning act of a fraudulent career. Like the most spurious of autobiographers, Pamela now seems to fashion a fake identity for the sake of worldly self-advancement, and then passes it off on the reader in literary form. With the extended title *An Apology for the Life of Mrs Shamela Andrews . . . by Mr Conny Keyber*, Fielding's title-page deftly links 'the many notorious FALSHOODS and MISREPRESENTATIONS of a Book called PAMELA' with patterns he also found in *An Apology for the Life of Colley Cibber* (1740), a bumptious secular autobiography in which the talentless Cibber (Walpole's poet laureate and a leading actor–dramatist) attributes to his natural genius, charm, and luck the fruits of a lifetime's professional scheming and political ingratiation. With wonderful inevitability, Shamela is then shown reading *God's Dealings with the Reverend Mr George Whitefield*, as though her ability to fabricate an innocently spiritual self flows straight from this model. All three works had appeared within a year, and by yoking them together Fielding quietly alleges that the genres of novel and autobiography, in their parallel constructions of identity, deal alike in fiction.

It might be objected that *Shamela* implies nothing more serious here than that autobiographical narrators sometimes lie. Certainly, no fundamental critique of the genre's inherent capacity to abstract from subjectivity a genuine essence, and render it in textual form, falls within Fielding's scope. The novel Richardson produced in light of *Shamela*, however, is among much else a massive meditation on just this issue. The heroine of *Clarissa* (1747–8) begins her narrative confident of its capacity to detect and describe the secret springs of her inward life, but later recognizes the defectiveness of her own self-knowledge and the structurally inevitable distortions of 'self-partiality, that strange misleader'. Now the vaunted inmost recesses of novelistic subjectivity begin to look stubbornly unfathomable, enigmatic, opaque. The crisis of the novel is one in which Clarissa's narrative literally fragments, falling first into syntactical incoherence under pressure of an experience too disruptive to be rendered in conventionally ordered prose, and then torn to pieces by Clarissa herself, in a gesture that eloquently rejects her own first person as a valid principle of representation. Urged thereafter to resume her narrative in the 'connected and particular manner' of retrospective memoir, Clarissa insists instead on the need to 'shake . . . off' the self, or again 'to go out of ourselves'.[10] No first-person mode will now do, and in structuring the novel Richardson pursues the consequences of this apprehension by dispersing his narrative among competing unreliable narrators. Each of *Clarissa*'s voices is activated by a recognition that 'it is much better . . . to tell your own story, when it *must* be known, than to have an adversary tell it for you' (p. 1038), and each is duly compromised. Only through multiple perspectives – if then – can character be fully known.

No work before *Tristram Shandy* comes close to the sophistication with which *Clarissa* problematizes the enterprise of stabilizing and communicating a self in literary form, but something of the same self-consciousness colours many novels of the day. In the extreme case of Thomas Amory's *The Life of John Buncle, Esq.* (1756–66), the narrator's efforts 'to write a true history of my life and notions' are overtly influenced by the associationist psychology of John Locke, the result being a chaotic swirl of narrative fragments that mimics the wayward impulses of consciousness in process.[11] Meanwhile, just as spiritual autobiography and other forms of life-writing had helped to shape the novel, so novels came in turn to exert a pull on autobiographical practice. The seamless integration in Tobias Smollett's *Peregrine Pickle* (1751) of a real-life memoir by Lady Vane, a Roxana-like adventuress, is only the most extreme instance of this ongoing generic convergence. Of course, many published memoirs betray little anxiety about the privileged nature of first-person insight, enlisting a rhetoric of explanation that tended to preclude the sceptical reflexivity of novels. As Felicity Nussbaum has argued, however, much of the most vigilant autobiographical writing of the period took shape – or, rather, resisted shape – in the incremental form of journals and diaries, and these are works that characteristically fail or refuse to settle on a finished, integrated self. With their structural resemblance to Richardsonian fiction, and their corresponding ability to articulate shifting identities without facile reconciliation, or to document selfhood in flux, such works 'are testimonies to the uncertainties and incoherences of eighteenth-century "selves" as experienced through time'.[12]

In marked contrast to the assertions of Whitefield here are the journal extracts that his fellow Methodist John Wesley issued in twenty-one instalments between 1739 and 1791. Here the patterned certainties of spiritual autobiography give way to a more tentative mode of self-examination, where stability and conclusiveness are never on offer, and only authorial death brings closure to the work. Even autobiographies that have been celebrated for their achieved presentation of unitary selfhood turn out to derive their illusions of coherence from posthumous editorial intervention. In the six autobiographical sketches left by Edward Gibbon at his death in 1794, alternative models of the self are tested and discarded in turn, as though no one version could satisfy Gibbon's desire to lay down a definitive 'image of [his] mind'.[13] Benjamin Franklin's autobiography gets no closer to resolution. A discontinuous patchwork composed in four distinct stages between 1771 and 1790, it fails to progress its narrative beyond Franklin's middle age in 1758, and is now usually published (like *Ulysses*) without a terminal full stop. Both these works reached print in the 1790s, within a few years of their authors' deaths, but in versions that smoothed over their painful, piecemeal origins. When William Taylor later appealed for publication of Franklin's unedited papers, in which the 'recesses of the human heart would be displayed', his Richardsonian formulation expresses a truly Richardsonian assumption: that the flux of identity resists neat shaping, and best expresses its complexities through writing and rewriting as an ongoing process, a messy continuum of subjectivity in motion.

Biography too was affected, with James Boswell's monumental *Life of Johnson* (1791) the conspicuous case. A world away from the terse synopses and lofty overviews of Johnson's own biographical writings, the *Life* immerses itself in a Richardsonian world of minute particulars, multiple perspectives, and incremental diurnal narration, with heavy reliance on inserted letters and transcribed conversation. In its relentless accumulations, Boswell's book becomes a campaign to convert the absence it laments – Johnson's death seven years beforehand – into an unprecedented textual presence, through which its subject 'will be seen in this work more completely than any man who has ever yet lived'.[14] Yet the *Life* is also in practice a tendentious work, doggedly effacing awkward features of Johnson's identity that rival biographers had played up: seditious politics in Hawkins's *Life* of 1787, psychological turmoil in Piozzi's *Anecdotes* of 1786. It is to Boswell's own journals that we must turn for a more unblinking encounter with human personality in all its contradictions and aberrations. 'Nothing is more disagreeable than for a man to find himself unstable and changeful', Boswell laments under his magazine pseudonym 'the Hypochondriack', adding that in his own case 'sometimes there remains only a mere consciousness of identity' as opposed to the substance he sought.[15] In the protected arena of private journals, these disagreeable instabilities could be articulated as they emerged, and directly encountered, perhaps as a prelude to corrective self-fashioning in life itself.

Hume and Sterne

In all these respects, eighteenth-century fiction and autobiography confronted and explored problems to which the sceptical philosophy of the period gave systematic expression. Central here is David Hume, who inherited and complicated a tradition of enquiry, inaugurated in Locke's *Essay Concerning Human Understanding* (1690), into the individual's consciousness of selfhood, its origins in memory, and its stability over time. Conceptualizing identity is central to Hume's project in *A Treatise of Human Nature* (1739–40), and he continues to worry in his appendix to the work that questions remain unresolved. The opening book culminates in his bravura chapter 'Of personal identity', and here Hume studiously dismantles commonsense assumptions that 'we are every moment intimately conscious of what we call our SELF; that we feel its existence and its continuance in existence; and are certain . . . of its perfect identity and simplicity'. Unable to detect a continuous or unitary self in his own case, Hume represents subjectivity instead as instability, as a teeming chaos of fugitive perceptions, from which coherent identity is only an enabling fiction constructed by memory. Men are 'nothing but a bundle or collection of different perceptions, which succeed each other with an inconceivable rapidity, and are in a perpetual flux and movement', he affirms. Then his metaphor shifts to performance, the mind becoming 'a kind of theatre, where several perceptions successively make their appearance; pass, re-pass, glide away, and mingle in an infinite variety of postures and situations'.[16]

Hume adds that in daily practice he resists the debilitating consequences of his thinking, being 'determin'd to live, and talk, and act like other people in the common affairs of life' (p. 259). It was perhaps in this spirit that he was able to produce a coherent (though, at eleven pages, strikingly minimalist) autobiography of his own. Declaring an identity grounded in temper, and asserting the consistency of this temper, Hume poses yet another paradox, in which, as Patricia Meyer Spacks writes, 'the great questioner of personal continuity vividly asserts his own'.[17] Setting aside the pragmatism of Hume's autobiography, however, we can see that the consequences of his thought for the genre – the consequences for the endeavour to construct an image of continuous selfhood and transmit it in continuous prose – are severe indeed. Nor was this scepticism confined to philosophers. Just how widespread was the loss of faith in stable and describable identity to which Hume gives voice is shown by a set of sermons originally preached to a mid-century Yorkshire congregation. We are 'strange compounds of contradictory qualities', these rural parishioners were told, and the contradictions resist our knowledge. For our inner lives are labyrinthine, vexed by 'irregularities and unsuspected passions . . . secret turns and windings . . . hidden springs and motives', and the individual is often 'a much greater stranger to his own disposition and true character than all the world besides'.[18] A further sermon insists that 'the bulk of mankind live in such a contradiction to themselves, that there is no character . . . altogether uniform, and in every point consistent with itself'. Time exacerbates the problem, wholly remaking each individual 'in the very cast and turn of his mind'; but the instability is not merely diachronic, and 'the observation is to be made of men . . . that in the same day, sometimes in the very same action, they are utterly inconsistent and irreconcileable with themselves' (pp. 103–4).

These sermons draw on work by Joseph Butler, a philosopher–theologian who wrote in Locke's wake, and nothing they express is exceptional for the day. The one remarkable thing about them is that their author was Laurence Sterne, a frustrated cleric who shot from provincial obscurity to cosmopolitan fame with *The Life and Opinions of Tristram Shandy, Gentleman* (1759–67). Like Hume, Sterne was the author of a brief effort at autobiography, sketched out in 1758 and posthumously published in 1775. But it is in *Tristram Shandy* that the consequences of his scepticism about identity take on imaginative life. As his narrator puts it, 'our minds shine not through the body, but are wrapt up here in a dark covering of uncrystalized flesh and blood; so that if we would come to the specifick characters of them, we must go some other way to work'.[19]

A work notoriously resistant to categorization, *Tristram Shandy* draws on a tradition of learned-wit satire that runs back through Swift to Montaigne, while also engaging parodically with the formal and rhetorical conventions of the emergent novel. However, Sterne's celebrated invocation of Cibber – 'I wrote not [to] be *fed*, but to be *famous*', he declares, pointedly reworking Cibber's 'I wrote more to be Fed, than to be Famous'[20] – is a good reminder that the generic conditions played on in *Tristram Shandy* are also those of autobiography. As well as being a tragicomic exploration, on the page, of the impossibility of fixing the self in print, the work also gave Sterne an opportunity for elaborate games with identity in life itself. Tristram became an *alter ego* that Sterne exuberantly performed in London society. He then extended the performance back to Yorkshire, where his house became 'Shandy Hall', and on to Paris, where he reappeared in enlightenment salons as the 'Chevalier Shandy'. True to his sense of identity as protean, Sterne also adopted another role from *Tristram Shandy*, that of the sentimental Parson Yorick, in which persona he conducted two love affairs and scandalously published his sermons as *The Sermons of Mr Yorick* (1760–9). In 'A Poetical Epistle to Doctor Sterne, Parson Yorick, and Tristram Shandy', the young Boswell was a fascinated observer of the display, to which Sterne then gave a further twist by resuming a mutated version of the Yorick role in his last work, *A Sentimental Journey through France and Italy, By Mr Yorick* (1768). This novel too is autobiographical, both in the basic sense that it reworks authorial experience (Sterne's recent continental tours) and in the deeper sense that it wrestles and plays once more with problems of self-definition. 'There is not a more perplexing affair in life to me, than to set about telling any one who I am', Yorick laments, 'for there is scarce any body I cannot give a better account of than of myself.'[21]

Serialized in roughly annual instalments (with much improvisation, though clearly an overarching plan), *Tristram Shandy* articulates a predicament that was also Sterne's own, afflicted as he was by a tubercular condition that killed him in 1768. Tristram is evidently dying as he writes, and by serializing the work Sterne lent drama to the impasse of representation faced by his narrator, staging a protracted and increasingly urgent performance of digressive writing and progressive disease in which Tristram fails to record his life in the past while watching it fade in the present. The book begins with high expectations of the capacity of language to define and transcribe the self, which for Tristram is a complex entity constituted not only by prior experience but also by present reflection – by 'opinions' as well as by 'life'. If this immensely delicate task is to be prosecuted with rigour, however, both components of selfhood must be accommodated in all their plenitude, and the proliferation of material that results – all of it demanding exhaustive circumstantial documentation – soon involves Tristram in panic. Perplexed throughout by 'what he is to put in,——and what he is to leave out' (3.23.244), he finds himself assailed by too much matter for even the most capacious text; and this discovery is compounded by his Lockean realization that in their very nature 'tall, opake words' are unable to fix experience securely on the page (3.20.235). Misguidedly beginning '*ab Ovo*' ('from the egg' (1.4.5):

the novel opens with a farcically botched conception scene), Tristram finds his narrative line forever forced sideways and back. A year after serialization had begun, and with his second two-volume instalment nearly used up, his narrative is still becalmed on the day of his birth, the consequence being that he has 'three hundred and sixty-four days more life to write just now, than when I first set out' (4.13.341). Thereafter things only get worse, until the work abruptly halts at the end of its delayed and abbreviated fifth instalment, at which point Tristram is narrating another scene of comic mis-begetting (this time involving the impotent Shandy bull) but one occurring five years earlier than his own. Given Tristram's now galloping consumption – the fourth instalment sees him desperately fleeing Death, 'for I have forty volumes to write, and forty thousand things to say and do, which no body in the world will say and do for me' (7.1.576) – Sterne's implication is that this wittily counter-climactic ending also marks his narrator's death.

The symmetries and structures here are highly wrought, but much of Sterne's creative energy thoughout *Tristram Shandy* is spent in the fabrication of textual chaos. Preoccupied as he is by what we now might call the split subject (the disjuncture between the narrated self of the past and the narrating self in the present; between life and opinions) Tristram fails to progress beyond a sense of identity as enigma. His bafflement emerges beautifully from a casual declaration:

——My good friend, quoth I——as sure as I am I——and you are you——
——And who are you? said he.——Don't puzzle me; said I.　　　(7.33.633)

Structurally, this bafflement plays endless havoc with Tristram's text, in ways capriciously indicated by the page of marbled paper inserted at one point as a 'motly emblem of my work' (3.36.268). The marbled page invites and resists multiple interpretations, but its fluid swarm of colour is often read as emblematic of the Humean subject, a 'collection of different perceptions . . . in a perpetual flux'. Indeed, *Tristram Shandy* may be seen as working out, with oddly mingled exuberance and despair, the consequences for autobiography of a scepticism that Hume had pragmatically evaded when contributing to the genre himself. In place of Hume's determination 'to live, and talk, and act like other people', Sterne poses the countervailing case of one who will 'neither think nor act like any other man's child' (1.3.4) – and one who, in attempting to render this uniqueness marmoreal in his text, encounters inevitable defeat. Hume may have thought the matter beyond jest, and could only summon faint praise. As he noted in 1773, 'the best book, that has been writ by any Englishman these thirty Years (for Dr Franklyn is an American) is *Tristram Shandy*, bad as it is'.[22]

Shandean Romanticism

Where *Tristram Shandy* reflects self-consciously on the autobiographer's dilemma, and satirically tests the endeavour for representational completeness beyond its limits, *A Sentimental Journey* pursues a practical alternative course. Presented as bursts of consciousness in discontinuous sequence, Yorick's narrative achieves something of the effect that Tristram attributes to Locke's *Essay*, 'a history-book . . . of what passes in a man's own mind' (2.2.98), and was later co-opted by Virginia Woolf as heralding her own innovations. Both novels were widely imitated at the time, but some of the most interesting appropriations, of *Tristram Shandy* especially, came in the form of serialized 'process poems'. Charles Churchill's *The Ghost* (1762–3) was greeted by reviewers as 'a kind of *Tristram Shandy* in *verse*',[23] and several other improvisatory, associative, formally disrupted poems composed within Churchill's 'Nonsense Club' circle achieve a similar effect. Decades later, Byron identified his unfinished *Don Juan* (1818–23) as 'a poetical T Shandy',[24] and his comment nicely indicates the intertwined self-consciousness about textuality and subjectivity that suffuses the poem as it progresses and digresses. Anne K. Mellor describes Byron as a writer 'engaging in continuous self-creation, [who] deliberately blurred the lines between his "real" self and his "artistic" self', and his narrative poems in general use both characters and narrators to project alternative (even antithetical) senses of Byronic identity, romantic and satiric by turns.[25]

For the poet-narrator of *Childe Harold's Pilgrimage* (1812–18), identity is inconstant or evanescent ('I am not now / That which I have been', he finally declares), but the act of writing sets down a trace of self which, despite its artificial shape, also offers transcendence:

> 'Tis to create, and in creating live
> A being more intense, that we endow
> With form our fancy, gaining as we give
> The life we image, even as I do now.
> What am I? Nothing; but not so art thou,
> Soul of my thought![26]

But *Childe Harold* later resumes this language of inward intensity to concede that 'our outward sense / Is but of gradual grasp', and 'what we have of feeling most intense / Outstrips our faint expression' (iv.1414–17). Similar apprehensions about poetic self-construction, though in a more exuberant key, predominate in the later poem. In the dizzying world of *Don Juan*, where both hero and narrator are ostentatiously mobile in shape, uncertainty is so endemic that flippancy and paradox seem the only response: 'So little do we know what we're about in / This world, I doubt if doubt itself be doubting.'

In this context, even the poem's most energetic passages lend it no more staying power than 'A versified Aurora Borealis, / Which flashes o'er a waste and icy clime'.[27] Meanings will never truly fix, so the poem seeks no closure. Just as an infinity of subjective experience makes Tristram reconceive his projected pair of volumes a year as a volume a month, or again as a forty-year task – 'the more I write, the more I shall have to write' (4.13.342) – so Byron's narrator first extends his twelve-book epic to twenty-four books, and then envisages a hundred. Only through endless writing can his agile subjectivity continue to unfold, with its endless shifts and endless deferrals, and as a process, not as a product.

Not all Romantic poets shared Byron's willingness to revel in the Shandean bind. Wordsworth certainly knew *Tristram Shandy*, having incongruously claimed in 1791 to have read no modern English literature except 'three volumes of *Tristram Shandy*' and some *Spectator* papers, and he probably re-read Sterne's work in 1796 and again in 1806.[28] However, when working from 1798 on what he called the poem 'on the growth of my own mind' or 'on my own life' (posthumously published as *The Prelude* in 1850, but now usually read in its first full manuscript state of 1805), Wordsworth had different priorities to sustain. *The Prelude* is a strenuous, unflinching attempt to discover and trace an integrated organic self and body it forth in language. Finding in nature not only the formative experiences that constitute the author's 'single self' or 'true self',[29] but also the metaphors through which to record its seamless flow and growth, the poem calls on memory to bind its disparate materials as a continuous whole. Stylistically, its distinctive appropriation of Miltonic blank verse provides a register commensurate with the task, a language precise and capacious enough to encompass an argument that is no less heroic, Wordsworth insists, than that of traditional epic.[30] Here the analytic and expressive powers he finds at his disposal promise successful transcendence of the Shandean impasse. 'The earth is all before me' (i.15), he writes in contemplating his task in the opening book, and he closes the book by repeating the point: 'the road lies plain before me' (i.668).

Wordsworth is far too intelligent a poet, however, not to reflect self-consciously on the obstacles impeding his route. A Shandean subtext lurks beneath, and occasionally breaks, the sublime surface of his poem, and one of *The Prelude*'s greatest achievements is to make eloquent within itself a critique of its own ambitions. The initial echoes of Milton's closing lines in *Paradise Lost* – 'The world was all before them . . .' – are ominous in context, recalling as they do the expulsion of Adam and Eve as wanderers in a fallen world of doubt and error. In succeeding books the anxiety becomes explicit, as the poem's road begins to fragment in Shandean detours which, in their various 'broken windings' (ii.289) and 'motions retrograde' (ix.8), threaten the linear coherence of self-analysis. Even if structure can be kept in place, it becomes unclear that adequate language exists to fulfil *The Prelude*'s introspective ambitions, so that one memorable renunciation of 'outward things' as the poem's subject – 'my theme has been what passed within me' – generates immediate anxiety that this new terrain 'lies far hidden from the reach of words' (iii.174–85). Though working hard to unite past and present selves in seamless organic development, the poem is repeatedly invaded by a sense of disjuncture – 'often do I seem / Two consciousnesses' (ii.31–2) – and intimates that the earlier consciousness is only dimly recoverable beneath the projections of the later. 'I cannot say what portion is in truth / The naked recollection of that time', as Wordsworth writes of one reconstructed memory, 'And what may rather have been called to life / By after-meditation' (iii.645–8).

In one of *The Prelude*'s most sustained encounters with its own inherent problems, Wordsworth worries that his analytic resources will never touch the fluidity they seek to define (ii.203–37). 'But who shall parcel out / His intellect, by geometric rules, / Split, like a province, into round and square?' he interrupts his narrative to ask, and a further reference to those who seek 'to class the cabinet / Of their sensations' suggests the same mismatch between rudimentary measurement and immeasurable life. Here one thinks of the natural historian who, in his rage for taxonomy, kills and impales what he seeks to know, preserving only the husk. In perhaps his most telling lines, Wordsworth recognizes the danger of attributing truth to one's own categorical fictions – to the work of 'that false secondary power, by which / In weakness we create distinctions, then / Deem that our puny boundaries are things / Which we perceive, and not which we have made'.

Here, as ever, Wordsworth strives towards a conviction that indeterminacy will be surmounted by the rigour of his own practice, or by his 'best conjectures' (ii.238). Self-evident truths of the kind proclaimed by Bunyan can no longer obtain in *The Prelude*'s secularized world, but it remains no more than a 'Hard task to analyse a soul' (ii.232) – not, that is, an impossible task.[31] The textual history of *The Prelude*, however, tells a tale of ongoing disruption. As Stephen Gill writes, one of the poem's fascinations lies in Wordsworth's 'evasion of memories that threaten to overwhelm or subvert the interpretative pattern being created'.[32] Nothing better illustrates this drama than the excision of an unusually vivid and violent memory from the poem's first drafts, which Wordsworth then published separately, in 1800, as 'Nutting'. By making so clear the gulf between narrated and narrating selves (by making it so great, indeed, that the very notion of continuous selfhood is put at risk), 'Nutting' also makes acute the need to reunite these two selves. It thus becomes, though absent from the text (or present, strictly speaking, in one faint trace at lines i.510–11), *The Prelude*'s exemplary moment. Wrecking a tree to plunder its nuts, the young Wordsworth conspicuously lacks the reverence for nature that defines his mature counterpart, and at the climax of the poem the written self revels in a 'merciless ravage' that is lamented by the writing self. Brilliantly, Wordsworth ends by bridging the gap (even as he exults, the boy feels a pain that presages his mature identity), but then worries aloud that continuous selfhood has been redeemed here not so much by memorial recovery as by wilful projection: 'unless I now / Confound my present feelings with the past . . .' Later Wordsworth spoke of 'Nutting' as 'intended as part of a poem on my own life, but struck out as not being wanted there', and it is hard not to feel that it exposes the evasions of the larger poem too awkwardly to have survived.[33]

Even after amputations of this kind, and in its 1805 state, *The Prelude* struggles with the extent to which, through seven years of composition, the subject it sought to fix has continued to move. As writing goes on, the space between present consciousness and past experience has continued to widen, further alienating the poet from his memories and heralding a future when days he sees 'by glimpses now, when age comes on / May scarcely see at all' (xi.336–8). Already the poem looks divided against itself, the voice of 1798–9 speaking in tones distinctly different from that of 1804–5; and this powerful internal challenge to Wordsworth's notion of a single self only intensifies thereafter. Though Wordsworth announced *The Prelude* as 'long finished' in his preface to a related poem of 1814 ('A drowsy frowzy poem, call'd the "Excursion," / Writ in a manner which is my aversion', as Byron riffed),[34] the poem refused to settle in definitive form. Nor could it, when the subject it sought to resolve was still in formation.

At least three subsequent stages of revision were undergone, in 1819, 1832, and 1839, as Wordsworth sought to render the text conformable to his present, though still unfinished, sense of self. Vexed in its original state by the potential gulf between the written subject of the past and the present writing subject, the poem was thus further vexed between composition and publication by the intrusion of the revising subject. The more Wordsworth revised, in effect, the more he had to revise. As in *Tristram Shandy*, only the death of the author-narrator could halt an otherwise interminable process, leaving behind a deeply fissured final version that renders the mobility of identity over time as both its explicit subject and its textual condition. Sterne's claim that each individual 'may be as unlike . . . the man he was twenty or thirty years ago, as he ever was from any thing of his own species' (*Sermons*, p. 104) is nowhere more magnificently illustrated than by Wordsworth's ongoing struggles to assimilate to his Tory maturity the poem of his radical youth. The repressed inevitably returned, so that even after its last great textual overhaul Macaulay could read *The Prelude* as 'to the last degree Jacobinical, indeed Socialist. I understand perfectly why Wordsworth did not choose to publish it in his lifetime.'[35]

Having witnessed the composition of what he called Wordsworth's 'divine Self-biography',[36] its addressee Samuel Taylor Coleridge experimented with the genre himself in *Biographia Literaria* (1817). This work is more overtly hospitable to Shandean themes. At an early stage of composition Coleridge spoke of writing 'an Autobiographia literaria, or Sketches of my literary Life & opinions', and the Shandean subtitle survives in the published text.[37] It was later alleged by Hazlitt that 'only two or three passages . . . relate to the details of the author's life', the work dissolving instead 'in the multiplicity of his speculative opinions',[38] and the *Biographia* is indeed a kaleidoscope of disparate materials in which philosophy, religion and criticism are more conspicuous than personal narration. Yet Hazlitt's attack underestimates the extent to which the book was shaped – or unshaped – not only by publishing considerations (extraneous matter was imported at a late stage to bulk out the second volume) but also by Coleridge's conscious attraction to Sterne as a creative antithesis to his own organicist ideals. In notes for a lecture of 1818, he praises Sterne as a writer whose 'digressive spirit' is 'the *very form* of his genius', or again as one who 'delight[s] to end in nothing, or a direct contradiction',[39] and in the *Biographia* Sterne becomes the model for comparable impulses of his own.

The *Biographia* makes one explicit reference to *A Sentimental Journey*, but implicit allusions to *Tristram Shandy* run right through the text. As an 'immethodical . . . miscellany' by a writer for whom 'metaphysics and psychology have long been my hobby-horse',[40] the *Biographia* is replete with mock-laments at the disruption of narrative by opaque words or invasive opinion, and with peremptory dialogues about structure and meaning with wrong-headed inscribed readers. The book even boasts a missing chapter as a mark of its fragmented condition, and elsewhere reworks Tristram's wry claim that his work 'is more perfect and complete by wanting the chapter, than having it' (4.25.372) when urging readers to respect the integrity of another chapter because 'the fairest part of the most beautiful body will appear deformed and monstrous, if dissevered from its place in the organic Whole' (1: 234). Finally, and like Sterne again, Coleridge pointedly ends in nothing, or in contradiction. He closes his autobiography by acknowledging that it has in fact been no such thing, and promises a compensatory further attempt while at the same time quietly undercutting his promise with Shandean phrasing. 'For *write* it I assuredly shall, should life and leisure be granted me', he affirms (II: 237), ironically recalling Tristram's vain hope of completing his own *Life and Opinions* in 'forty years, if it pleases the fountain of health to bless me so long with life and good spirits' (1.22.82).

Much of the philosophical digression in *Biographia Literaria* concerns personal identity and consciousness, as Coleridge takes issue with Hume and his contemporary David Hartley on the processes of mental association, while also pondering the split between analysed and analysing subject – between 'Ego contemplatus' and '*Ego contemplans*' (1: 72n.). The impossibility of conventional autobiography for Coleridge, however, arises as much from personal inhibitions about disclosure as from philosophical constraints. Like Wordsworth in *The Prelude*, Coleridge is shifty in treating his political apostasy and, as Rosemary Ashton writes, 'could hardly have written with composure . . . about his unhappy and now broken marriage and his all-consuming obsession, the opium addiction'.[41]

Perhaps the astutest contemporary observer of these suppressions and evasions was Coleridge's sometime acolyte Thomas De Quincey, and when writing his own autobiography in the *Biographia*'s immediate wake De Quincey made pointedly central to his text exactly the condition that Coleridge had hidden. Indeed, *Confessions of an English Opium-Eater* (1821) plainly alludes to Coleridge as the 'celebrated man of the present day' who has indulged, but not recorded, an addiction yet more excessive than De Quincey's own.[42] As Nigel Leask has suggested, it is as though De Quincey invites us to read the *Confessions* as the *Biographia*'s otherwise invisible subtext, with Coleridge the ghostly double who haunts his self-representation. Early readers saw the link, as when Henry Crabb Robinson called the *Confessions* 'a fragment of autobiography in emulation of Coleridge's diseased egotism'.[43] Yet Coleridge is only one of several influences to mediate De Quincey's self-representation. Other models include Rousseau, whose title De Quincey revives, and Wordsworth, whose poems not only weigh down De Quincey's pockets in the narrative but also structure his recollections in a *Prelude*-like sequence of formative 'spots of time'. For all the rootedness of the *Confessions* in unique experience, the work repeatedly casts its subject in moulds created for others – a recognition with which De Quincey seems to flirt when writing a notable passage about 'counterfeiting my own self' (p. 25). By the end of the work the autobiographical subject seems yet more thoroughly displaced. 'Not the opium-eater, but the opium, is the true hero of the tale; and the legitimate centre on which the interest revolves', De Quincey insists (p. 78).

In fact the pharmacological and autobiographical strains of the *Confessions* work in tandem, not competition. If autobiography had come to emulate the novel's quest to expose the 'inmost recesses' of the mind, no resource could do so more profoundly than opium as De Quincey describes it, and here we may truly talk of the unconscious in something like its Freudian sense as entering the genre. Far from being narcotic, opium vividly intensifies for De Quincey the experience of subjectivity, and strips away the 'veil between our present consciousness and the secret inscriptions on the mind' (p. 69). At best it confers on the faculties 'the most exquisite order, legislation, and harmony' (p. 40); but as De Quincey moves on to the nightmarish downside of addiction his text correspondingly fragments. The tumultuous dreams to which he devotes the climax of the work promise new territory for the autobiographer in his quest to fix personal identity; but at the same time these dreams resist rational and connected prose, and De Quincey despairs 'of either recalling, or constructing into a regular narrative, the whole burthen of horrors which lies upon my brain' (p. 62). Here the autobiography unravels in a chaos of jerky time-shifts, improvisatory digressions, and hectoring imperatives to the reader. As in *Biographia Literaria*, the Shandean resonances are studiously contrived, and at one point De Quincey even evokes the famous blank page in which Tristram had despaired of ever catching in language the appearance of a character from his past. 'No', De Quincey writes: 'paint me, if at all, according to your own fancy' (p. 61).[44] Once again, *Tristram Shandy* becomes the natural resource for expressing the autobiographer's bind. In dreams, the *Confessions* insist, we do indeed approach an authentic self, but a self that resists representation.

De Quincey was to pursue his efforts sporadically for decades more, returning in *Suspiria de Profundis* (1845) to write a supplement to the *Confessions*, and expanding the original text in 1856. The mind, as *Suspiria de Profundis* optimistically declares, is a palimpsest from which 'everlasting layers of ideas, images, feelings', though buried or erased, may nonetheless be uncovered by opium and dreaming (p. 144). Yet this later work abruptly halts without ever reaching its dreams, still scratching at the surface strata.

NOTES

1. *Monthly Review*, 2nd series 24 (1797), 375; Thomas Carlyle, *Sartor Resartus*, ed. Rodger L. Tarr (Berkeley: University of California Press, 2000), p. 73.
2. Robert Montgomery, *The Age Reviewed: A Satire*, 2nd edn (1828), p. 172 n.; Robert Southey, in *Annual Review* 5 (1807), 298. Southey knew of *The Prelude* by this date.
3. William Taylor, in *Annual Review* 5 (1807), 562, quoted by James M. Good, 'William Taylor, Robert Southey, and the Word "Autobiography"', *Wordsworth Circle* 12 (1981), 125–7 (p. 126).
4. John Sturrock, *The Language of Autobiography* (Cambridge: Cambridge University Press, 1993), p. 4.
5. Jean-Jacques Rousseau, *Confessions*, ed. J. M. Cohen (Harmondsworth: Penguin, 1953), p. 574.

6. John Bunyan, *Grace Abounding and The Pilgrim's Progress*, ed. Roger Sharrock (London: Oxford University Press, 1966), pp. 5–6, 7, 43.

7. *A Short Account of God's Dealings with the Reverend Mr George Whitefield* (1740), pp. 6, 72.

8. Samuel Richardson, *Pamela*, ed. Thomas Keymer and Alice Wakely (Oxford: Oxford University Press, 2001), pp. 271, 8.

9. Daniel Defoe, *Roxana*, ed. John Mullan (Oxford: Oxford University Press, 1996), p. 213; *Moll Flanders*, ed. G. A. Starr (Oxford: Oxford University Press, 1980), p. 7. On the domino figure, see Terry Castle, *Masquerade and Civilization: The Carnivalesque in Eighteenth-Century English Culture and Fiction* (London: Methuen, 1986), pp. 58–9, 77–8.

10. Samuel Richardson, *Clarissa*, ed. Angus Ross (Harmondsworth: Penguin, 1985), pp. 987, 1017, 974, 1194.

11. Thomas Amory, *The Life of John Buncle, Esq.*, 4 vols. (1756–66), I: v.

12. Felicity Nussbaum, *The Autobiographical Subject: Gender and Ideology in Eighteenth-Century England* (Baltimore: Johns Hopkins University Press, 1989), p. 23.

13. Edward Gibbon, *Memoirs of My Life*, ed. Georges A. Bonnard (London: Nelson, 1966), p. 2.

14. *Boswell's Life of Johnson*, ed. George Birkbeck Hill, rev. L. F. Powell, 6 vols. (Oxford: Clarendon Press, 1934–64), I: 30.

15. *Boswell's Column, 1777–1783*, ed. Margery Bailey (London: Kimber, 1951), p. 325.

16. David Hume, *A Treatise of Human Nature*, ed. L. A. Selby-Bigge, rev. P. H. Nidditch (Oxford: Clarendon Press, 1978), pp. 251–3.

17. Patricia Meyer Spacks, *Imagining a Self: Autobiography and Novel in Eighteenth–Century England* (Cambridge: Harvard University Press, 1976), p. 13.

18. *The Sermons of Laurence Sterne: The Text*, ed. Melvyn New (Gainesville: University Press of Florida, 1996), pp. 300, 39, 32.

19. Laurence Sterne, *The Life and Opinions of Tristram Shandy, Gentleman*, ed. Melvyn New et al. (Gainesville: University Press of Florida, 1978–84), 1.23.83. References are given by book, chapter, and page.

20. *Letters of Laurence Sterne*, ed. L. P. Curtis (Oxford: Clarendon Press, 1935), p. 90 (30 January 1760).

21. Laurence Sterne, *A Sentimental Journey through France and Italy*, ed. Melvyn New and W. G. Day (Gainesville: University Press of Florida, 2002), p. 112.

22. Alan B. Howes (ed.), *Sterne: The Critical Heritage* (London: Routledge, 1974), p. 147 (letter of 30 January 1773).

23. *Monthly Review* 27 (October 1762), 316.

24. *Byron's Letters and Journals*, ed. Leslie A. Marchand, 12 vols. (London: John Murray, 1973–82), X: 150 (14 April 1823).

25. Anne K. Mellor, *English Romantic Irony* (Cambridge: Harvard University Press, 1980), p. 31.

26. Byron, *Complete Poetical Works, Volume II*, ed. Jerome J. McGann (Oxford: Clarendon Press, 1980), iv.1662–3; iii.46–51.

27. Byron, *Complete Poetical Works, Volume V*, ed. Jerome J. McGann (Oxford: Clarendon Press, 1986), ix.135–6; vii.11–12.

28. Duncan Wu, *Wordsworth's Reading, 1770–1815*, 2 vols. (Cambridge: Cambridge University Press, 1993–5), I: 132–3; II: 205.

29. William Wordsworth, *The Prelude: The Four Texts (1798, 1799, 1805, 1850)*, ed. Jonathan Wordsworth (London: Penguin, 1995), iii.356; x.915.

30. Ibid., iii.184; here Wordsworth's term 'heroic argument' echoes *Paradise Lost* (ix.13–14), where Milton alludes in turn to the *Iliad*.

31. Here again Wordsworth reinforces his point by echoing *Paradise Lost*, where Raphael finds it 'Sad task and hard', but achievable nonetheless, to 'relate / To human sense . . . invisible exploits' (v.564–5).

32. Stephen Gill, *William Wordsworth; The Prelude* (Cambridge: Cambridge University Press, 1991), p. 3.

33. Michael Mason (ed.), *Lyrical Ballads* (Harlow: Longman, 1992), pp. 298 ('Nutting', lines 44, 47–8), 377 (authorial comment of 1843).

34. Byron, *Don Juan*, iii.847–8, in *Complete Poetical Works, Volume V*.

35. Journal entry of 28 July 1850, quoted by Stephen Gill, *Wordsworth and the Victorians* (Oxford: Clarendon Press, 1998), p. 29.

36. *Coleridge's Notebooks: A Selection*, ed. Seamus Perry (Oxford: Oxford University Press, 2002), p. 53 (4 January 1804).

37. *The Collected Letters of Samuel Taylor Coleridge*, ed. Earl Leslie Griggs, 6 vols. (Oxford: Oxford University Press, 1956–71), IV: 578–9 (29 July 1815).

38. J. R. de J. Jackson (ed.), *Coleridge: The Critical Heritage* (London: Routledge, 1970), p. 295 (in *Edinburgh Review*, August 1817).

39. Howes (ed.), *Sterne: The Critical Heritage*, pp. 358, 353.

40. Samuel Taylor Coleridge, *Biographia Literaria*, ed. James Engell and W. Jackson Bate (Princeton: Princeton University Press, 1983), I: 88; I: 85.

41. Rosemary Ashton, *The Life of Samuel Taylor Coleridge* (Oxford: Blackwell, 1996), p. 305.

42. Thomas De Quincey, *Confessions of an English Opium-Eater and Other Writings*, ed. Grevel Lindop (Oxford: Oxford University Press, 1996), p. 2.

43. Edith Morley (ed.), *Henry Crabb Robinson on Books and Their Writers*, 2 vols. (London: Dent, 1938), I: 267; quoted by Nigel Leask, '"Murdering One's Double": De Quincey's *Confessions of an English Opium Eater* and *Biographia Literaria*', *Prose Studies* 13 (1990), 78–98 (p. 83).

44. See *Tristram Shandy*, 6.38.566: 'Sit down, Sir, paint her to your own mind . . . please but your own fancy in it.'

FURTHER READING

Baxter, Edmund, *De Quincey's Art of Autobiography*, Edinburgh: Edinburgh University Press, 1990.

Conrad, Peter, *Shandyism: The Character of Romantic Irony*, Oxford: Blackwell, 1978.

Cox, Stephen D., *'The Stranger Within Thee': Concepts of the Self in Late Eighteenth-Century Literature*, Pittsburgh: University of Pittsburgh Press, 1980.

Garber, Frederick, *Self, Text, and Romantic Irony: The Example of Byron*, Princeton: Princeton University Press, 1988.

Kearns, Sheila M., *Coleridge, Wordsworth, and Romantic Autobiography: Reading Strategies of Self-Representation*, Madison: Fairleigh Dickinson University Press, 1995.

Keymer, Thomas, *Sterne, the Moderns, and the Novel*, Oxford: Oxford University Press, 2002.

Leader, Zachary, *Revision and Romantic Authorship*, Oxford: Oxford University Press, 1996.

Mellor, Anne K., *English Romantic Irony*, Cambridge: Harvard University Press, 1980.

Nussbaum, Felicity, *The Autobiographical Subject: Gender and Ideology in Eighteenth-Century England*, Baltimore: Johns Hopkins University Press, 1989.

O'Neill, Michael, *Romanticism and the Self-Conscious Poem*, Oxford: Clarendon Press, 1997.

Perry, Seamus, *Coleridge and the Uses of Division*, Oxford: Oxford University Press, 1999.

Spacks, Patricia Meyer, *Imagining a Self: Autobiography and Novel in Eighteenth-Century England*, Cambridge: Harvard University Press, 1976.

Sturrock, John, *The Language of Autobiography: Studies in the First Person Singular*, Cambridge: Cambridge University Press, 1993.

II

JON MEE

Blake and the poetics of enthusiasm

Academic accounts of the differences between eighteenth-century and Romantic poetry are often over-stated, sometimes accepting on trust self-interested narratives of the renaissance of a pure poetry of imagination and feeling such as Wordsworth's 'Essay, Supplementary to the Preface' (1815). The rebirth of 'PURE POETRY' was being declared as early as Joseph Warton's *Essay on the Writings and Genius of Pope* (1756), and even some decades before.[1] Warton wrote against satire and what he saw as the versified morality of the Scriblerians, yet he could still find in Pope's *Eloisa to Abelard* (1717) at least signs of the raptures of the true poet: 'Poetry, after all, cannot well subsist, at least is never so striking, without a tincture of enthusiasm' (1: 320). Shaun Irlam's recent study of mid-century poetry describes the emergence of a 'poetics of enthusiasm'. Joseph Addison, John Dennis, and Shaftesbury are identified as the critical progenitors and James Thomson and Edward Young the major poets of this cultural transformation. Others that Irlam would include in his line of enthusiasm include Mark Akenside, William Collins, Thomas Gray, Christopher Smart, and Joseph and Thomas Warton.[2] My essay too will offer an account of relations between earlier eighteenth-century poets and their Romantic successors, but with an emphasis on the delicate question of regulation. Prior to the process of its rehabilitation described by Irlam, the word 'enthusiasm' was primarily identified with religious excess and the passions of the crowd more generally. Anxieties about how far enthusiasm could be allowed free rein even within the aesthetic sphere remained in play even very late into the Romantic period. The primary meaning of 'enthusiasm' in society more generally retained its older pejorative sense well into the nineteenth century. This persistence was influenced by the continuation of the phenomenon of popular religious enthusiasm that had always provided the basic connotation of the word 'enthusiasm'. The spectre of a degenerate form of enthusiasm in the passions of the crowd complicates the narrative of rehabilitation offered by critics such as Irlam. Furthermore, popular versions of the idea of the republic of letters were taken by some to imply that that 'there is nothing to stop anyone who can feel from springing into verse'.[3] Many of those who desired the power of enthusiasm sought to disavow these democratic implications, but for others – William Blake among them – poetry was defined by its association with an enthusiasm that might manifest itself even in the humblest breast.

For all that it was strongly associated with the zeal of the sects in the English civil war, the classical origins of the word enthusiasm always kept open the possibility of thinking of a noble inspiration connected with the greatness of the Ancients. One of the boldest early attempts to reclaim this classical inheritance was made in the third Earl of Shaftesbury's *Characteristics* (1711). John Locke, who, ironically, had been Shaftesbury's tutor, had added a chapter 'On Enthusiasm' to his *Essay concerning Human Understanding*, but what Locke disparaged as 'the Conceits of a warmed or over-weening Brain', Shaftesbury glorified as an innate moral sense of the harmonious whole that was the Creation.[4] Shaftesbury was concerned that Locke reduced human beings to mere machines. Shaftesbury agreed with Locke that enthusiasm could be and had been dangerous, but viewed it not only as inescapable but also as fundamental to what it was to be human. Enthusiasm in Shaftesbury's lexicon named a passion that urged human beings to feel benevolence towards their fellows and ultimately join with their Creator:

> So far is he from degrading enthusiasm or disclaiming it in himself that he looks on this passion, simply considered, as the most natural, and its object as the justest, in the world.[5]

Those parts of Shaftesbury that addressed the glories of nature remained popular even early into the next century, anthologized, for instance, in Anna Laetitia Barbauld's *The Female Reader* (1811), and reaching a readership far beyond the original limits of Shaftesbury's aristocratic sphere. The ascents of the soul celebrated by Shaftesbury were 'natural' enthusiasm, but he did concede that they could be debased into the form feared by Locke. True enthusiasm had to be cultivated and regulated if it was not to degenerate into the vulgar spasms of the crowd. Whereas Locke's view of enthusiasm had been proscriptive, Shaftesbury's was regulative. Natural enthusiasm, this noble passion, was the product of a species of self-fashioning. The only way to deal with the 'combustible matters' which 'lie prepared and within ready to take fire at a spark, chiefly in a multitude of the same spirit' (p. 23) is to subject them to self-regulation before they come close to the dangerous crowd. Shaftesbury recommends soliloquy as a technology of discipline, testing the passion to communicate against one's own understanding before it is brought before the public. He suggests that authors ought to retire to solitary places, 'woods and river banks', to test their work against themselves so that the 'fancy' may 'evaporate' and the 'vehemence' of the 'spirit and voice' may be reduced (p. 73). Retirement is no end in itself for Shaftesbury, it is unnatural not to be sociable, in fact the withdrawal of the hermit is another form of vulgar enthusiasm, but retirement in its proper place is a necessary preparation for integration into the polite world. Regulation rather than persecution was also Shaftesbury's recommended response to social as well as personal manifestations of enthusiasm. His recommendation of raillery and ridicule as a corrective to religious excess – which earned both him and followers such as Akenside the disapprobation of the Church – is the corollary of the toleration of religious dissent in the Whig state. To a century obsessed with ideas of sympathy and conversation, regulation offered a way of confirming the fundamental importance of sociability without abandoning society to the crowd, but the nature and extent of the regulation was endlessly contested as groups well beyond those Shaftesbury himself imagined capable of self-regulation clamoured to be let into the polite public sphere. It was a discourse that embraced the human possibilities created by the going-out-of self, but remained anxious that without discipline such transports could be destructive of the very identity they promised to fulfil.

Mediated perhaps through the influence of Addison's essays on 'the Pleasures of the Imagination' in the *Spectator*, the idea of poetry as a sphere in which the emotions could be regulated into a natural harmony became widespread in the eighteenth century, but Shaftesbury's ideas had a direct influence on James Thomson and Mark Akenside, two poets whose importance was acknowledged in turn by several of their Romantic successors. Wordsworth's 1815 'Essay', for instance, offered a survey of the development of English poetry and its failure to live up to the inspired example of the elder poets Shakespeare and Milton which identified Thomson's *The Seasons* (1730) as an early sign of a renaissance in English taste: 'It is a work of inspiration; much of it written from himself and nobly from himself.'[6] Just before he begins his discussion of Thomson, Wordsworth mentions Shaftesbury's opinion of the uninspired nature of English poetry at the beginning of the eighteenth century. Wordsworth describes Shaftesbury in passing as 'an author at present unjustly deprecated'. Thomson himself, in fact, had directly praised Shaftesbury in *The Seasons*:

> The generous ASHLEY thine, the Friend of Man;
> Who scann'd his Nature with a Brother's Eye,
> His Weakness prompt to shade, to raise his Aim,
> To touch the finer Movements of the Mind,
> And with the *moral Beauty* charm the Heart.[7]

Thomson saw in nature a version of Shaftesbury's 'moral beauty'. The second edition of *Winter* in 1727 came with a Preface that makes the nature of Thomson's poetic ambitions very clear:

> . . . let POETRY, once more, be restored to her antient Truth, and Purity; let Her be inspired from Heaven, and, in Return, her Incense ascend thither; let Her exchange Her low, venal, trifling, Subjects for such as are fair, useful, and magnificent; and, let Her execute these so as, at once, to please, instruct, surprize, and astonish: and then, of Necessity, the most inveterate Ignorance, and Prejudice, shall be struck Dumb; and POETS, yet, become the Delight and Wonder, of Mankind. (p. 304)

Against a worldly poetry, concerned with 'low, venal, trifling, Subjects', Thomson proposes a poetic concerned with the revelation of a divine order. Notably like Shaftesbury, Thomson's poem deistically sees this order not in terms of a transcendent God, but rather an immanent one embodied in his Creation:

> I know no Subject more elevating, more amusing; more ready to awake the poetical Enthusiasm, the philosophical Reflection, and the moral Sentiment, than the *Works of Nature*. (p. 305)

Throughout Thomson's poem, retirement in the bosom of nature brings with it an 'unworlding' awakening that discloses a higher truth to the poet and a moral sense within the self that shakes us out of worldly self-interest.[8] Thomson's poem is full of the kind of apostrophes that litter Shaftesbury's *Characteristics*, those moments of revelation when immersion in nature reveals a deeper truth. Yet Thomson's 'finer movements of the mind' were also based on a recognition and regulation of their combustible potential. The same process revolves around the so-called spots of time in Wordsworth's *Prelude*: they are moments of transport that allow a glimpse of a higher order, but they must be safely regulated and turned back into a continuous sense of self-identity.

Irlam sees a tension within Thomson's poem between the detailed accounts of the natural world for which it was and is justly famous and these apostrophes. The outcome is a kind of 'stammering' (p. 125) wherein the visionary perspective often seems to be disavowed even as it is proclaimed. Not least, for all Thomson's veneration of 'Society divine' (*Winter*, line 541), noble enthusiasm, he implies, must be distinguished from the spasming of the 'degenerate crowd' (*Autumn*, line 965). Although Thomson's Patriot poetics mean that he is committed to taking his enthusiasm back out into the public world, specifically in the attacks on the corruption of the Walpole regime more obvious in poems such as *Liberty* (1735), a commitment in tune with the Whig version of the dialectic of retirement and commitment inherited from Shaftsbury, these differing impulses remain in an uneasy tension throughout *The Seasons*. Certainly there is no smooth progress from retirement to public life in the poem as a whole, nor – unlike Wordsworth's *The Prelude* – is there the sense of a continuous subjectivity developing through the quasi-religious immersion in nature.

Similar tensions can be seen within the work of others poets practising a poetics of enthusiasm in mid century. Akenside's *Pleasures of Imagination* (1744) is another poem with specific debts to Shaftesbury. What Akenside adopts from Shaftesbury is not just the idea that the poetic imagination can glimpse in the transports of its enthusiasm the harmony of a universal order, but also the assumption that in the space of retirement the combustible matters within us can be let loose with relative safety. Having worked upon them in private, the poet can return to society and the active life. As Kelvin Everest has put it in his discussion of the influence of Akenside and others on Coleridge's 'conversation poems': 'Retirement conventionally pointed back to society'.[9] Indeed Akenside had an influence on those who came after him not just as a poet of Nature and 'metaphysics', but also as a 'Patriot' poet, someone for whom the virtues discovered by the affections in private were to be the basis of the public man going out and acting in the nation's interest. Anna Laetitia Barbauld, for instance, eventually edited Akenside's poem in 1795 with an introductory essay, where she made it clear that his influence was not only to do with 'ideas of the fair and beautiful in morals and in taste, gathered from the writings of SHAFTESBURY, HUTCHINSON', but also what she saw as the poet's 'high sense of liberty'. Coleridge too in praising Akenside's 'metaphysics' at around the same time was doing so in the context of a debate with John Thelwall about the nature of political poetry.[10] The 'high sense of liberty' (p. xvi) praised by Barbauld in Akenside's poetry was hated by Tories such as Samuel Johnson, who wrote of Akenside's 'unnecessary and outrageous zeal for what he called and thought liberty', even though much earlier in his career Johnson had written poems such as 'London' (1739) in much this vein.[11] Yet Akenside himself seems to have retreated from the more public implications of his idea of Patriot virtue when he revised his poem (issued posthumously in 1772; Barbauld chose to edit the original). This draws attention to an arresting feature of the poetry of enthusiasm that followed Shaftesbury, that is, retirement increasingly came to play the predominant part, and the melancholic idea of 'literary loneliness' – a cousin in *diminutio* of Shaftesbury's more dialectical idea of retirement – becomes a powerful element in mid eighteenth-century verse.[12]

As well as praising his politics, Barbauld's essay on Akenside also distinguished his liberal religious sentiments from 'the deepest gloom' of another blank verse meditative poem, Edward Young's *Night Thoughts*:

> The religion of the other, all at least that appears of it, and all indeed that could with propriety appear in such a Poem, is the purest Theism; liberal, cheerful, and sublime; or, if admitting any mixture, he seems inclined to tincture it with the mysticism of PLATO, and the gay fables of ancient mythology.   (p. xiv)

For much of her career, Barbauld was distancing herself from what she perceived as the gloominess of her own Presbyterian forebears in Dissent. The Warrington Academy where she was brought up was the clearinghouse of new ideas of Dissent that sought a union with a broader Anglican culture of politeness. Young's poem is often perceived now as an exercise in stale eighteenth-century moralizing, but Barbauld obviously perceived something darker there that is not easily squared with W. J. T. Mitchell's description of the poem as 'stoic, latitudinarian morality, stale Greek mythology, and urbane social flattery'. Young's *Conjecture's on Original Composition* (1759), after all, as Simon Jarvis's essay in this volume implies, had been a key text in the redefinition of poetry in terms of impassioned enthusiasm.

Critics often overlook the eager desire for rapturous affirmations of God's power in much of the eighteenth century's directly religious poetry. Isaac Watts was an influential figure in this respect, praising Elizabeth Rowe's *Devout Exercises* (1737) for its 'sacred Zeal' and 'Rapture'.[13] Christopher Smart's *Jubilate Agno* is another powerful example of this poetry of divine plenitude from the mid century, although, as Harriet Guest has shown, Smart was more concerned than Watts to convert the private raptures of Dissent into the more public devotionalism of the Anglican confessional state. Finding a form that could revive devotion and remain accessible to a broad public was no easy task for Smart: he suffered the fate 'either of remaining unpublished, or of becoming a byword . . . for its inaccessibility'.[14] The problem of controlling the effects of the religious sublime were widely felt. Even the very public success of Young's *Night Thoughts* was ringed with anxieties as to the unworlding power of its apocalyptic vision.[15] John Wesley brought out an abridged edition of Young's work in 1770. While he was trying to reach a popular readership with a cheap abridged edition, he was also eager 'to *explain* the words which are *obscure*, not in themselves, but only to common readers'. The disciplinary aspect of his enterprise is heard in his judgement that Young 'takes words in a very *uncommon*, not to say, *improper* sense'.[16] Other editors of the poem seem to have been even more troubled by the extent that Young's poem offended against good taste in its apocalyptic ecstasies. An edition of the poem illustrated by Blake's friend Thomas Stothard in the 1790s noted that 'one of Young's most conspicuous faults, is the crowding his images too fast on the imagination'.[17] Wesley had particular reason to be worried about the obscurities caused by such crowding as he was taking the text to a readership that was widely regarded as incapable of regulating responses to the rousing of its religious passions. Throughout the mid century Wesley was accused again and again of stirring feelings among the populace that he could not control. Unworlding apocalypticism in this sort of context was widely regarded as dangerously destructive of proper domestic and social ties and not merely an offence against poetic decorum. Perhaps seeking to confirm the prejudices of elite readers, at least one 'Methodist' autobiography from the period illustrated the practical effects of Young's unworlding on an 'uneducated' reader. Written after their author had become disaffected from the Methodist movement, James Lackington's *Memoirs* (1791) recalls being so rapt at the sight of Young's book in a shop window – he does not say whether or not it was Wesley's abridgement – that he sacrificed his last few pence and his family's Christmas dinner to purchasing the poem:

> Down I sat, and began to read with as much enthusiasm as the good doctor possessed when he wrote it: and so much did it excite my attention as well as approbation, that I retained the greatest part of it in my memory.[18]

Lackington may provide us with a way of thinking about Blake's relationship to the poetics of enthusiasm in the mid century. For it reveals that readers in the eighteenth century could see something much more intense in Young's poem than critics now usually allow. Blake's illustrations to Young's poem represent a response to its zeal that disavows many of the criteria of taste and politeness that organized the mainstream poetics of enthusiasm.

Blake was born the year after Warton's essay on Pope was published. Wesley's abridgement of Young and Akenside's posthumous *Poems* (1772) appeared while he was in his teens. Blake's own earliest poetry betrays the influence of both Collins and Gray. Gray's 'The Bard' (1757) obviously appealed to the side of his imagination taken with the distant British past and the idea of poetry as involved in a struggle for liberty against a despotic state. James Macpherson's pseudo-translations from the ancient Caledonian bard 'Ossian' provided a similar impetus for Blake's poetry, especially where it pushed against conventional metre towards the 'formlessness' of his late prophecies.[19] Yet perhaps the most sustained relationship with an eighteenth-century predecessor was with the work of Young, an engagement that manifested itself most productively in the 256 watercolours made over 1795–7 to illustrate *Night Thoughts*. Of these engravings some 43 were selected by Blake's publisher Richard Edwards to illustrate the first volume of a projected de luxe edition of Young's entire poem. Significantly, however, no further volumes followed the first, perhaps because of the decline in the luxury book trade during the French Wars, but perhaps also because of the publishers' anxieties about the 'propriety' of Blake's illustrations. For Blake's illustrations take the poem even further from the polite liberality looked for by Barbauld in her comparison of Young and Akenside. The question here is not one of the Romantic completion of an unfinished eighteenth century project. I have already suggested that the poetics of enthusiasm were in no sense resolved by those Romantic poets who inherited earlier eighteenth century concerns about the limits of its unworlding effects, but what Blake's designs do is exaggerate rather than resolve the sources of these anxieties.

Essential to the unworlding rhetoric of Young's poem is the contrast between the transitoriness of earthly things and the eternal life promised by Christ. Stephen Cornford has placed this aspect of the poem in the context of the more general melancholia of mid-century poetics: 'Like Gray's *Elegy* and Robert Blair's *The Grave, Night Thoughts* sees death as the great leveller. There is no hierarchy or social distinction (vi. 287); the slave and monarch are alike in death (vi. 550–5; viii.433–5). None can escape the implications of immortality' (13). I have already suggested that this aspect of mid-eighteenth-century poetics was often itself in an uneasy tension with a 'Patriot' discourse. Such was certainly the case with Gray as well as both Akenside and Thomson; and the possibility of a radical understanding of the unworlding of the state of things-as-they-are certainly forms part of the attraction of poems such as 'The Bard' for Blake. To this extent Blake was participating in a broader social formation of those whose aspirations had been fired by a literalist 'misreading' of the idea of the republic of letters. For this kind of reason the plebeian radical Thomas Spence reprinted Gray's *Elegy* in his periodical *Pig's Meat*, and the London Corresponding Society made use of Thomson's poetry in the 1790s.[20] Several of Blake's illustrations obtrude the contemporary political situation on to the eye of the reader in a way that converts the perspective from eternity into a form of social criticism. Young addresses 'Death' from a perspective that questions of permanence of the world-as-it-is:

> Great Proprietor of all! 'Tis thine
> To tread out Empire, and to quench the Stars;
> The Sun himself by thy permission shines,
> And, one day, thou shalt pluck him from his sphere
>
> (i. 204–7)

(15)

Of sweet domestic Comfort, and cuts down
The fairest bloom of sublunary Bliss.

Bliss! sublunary Bliss! proud words! and vain:
Implicit Treason to divine Decree!
A bold invasion of the rights of Heaven!
I clasp'd the Phantoms, and I found them Air. 200
O had I weigh'd it e'er my fond Embrace!
What darts of Agony had miss'd my heart?
Death! Great Proprietor of all! 'Tis thine
To tread out Empire, and to quench the Stars;
The Sun himself by thy permission shines,
And, one day, thou shalt pluck him from his sphere.
Amid such mighty Plunder, why exhaust
Thy *partial* Quiver on a-Mark so mean?
Why, thy *peculiar* rancor wreck'd on me?
Insatiate Archer! could not One suffice?   210
Thy shaft flew thrice, and thrice my Peace was slain;

1   And

Figure 5 William Blake's watercolour illustration for Night I of the Richard Edwards edition (1797) of Edward Young's *Night Thoughts*: 'Thy shaft flew thrice . . .'

Blake illustrates Young with the figure of Death treading crowned (possibly decapitated) heads under foot (fig. 5). Compare the 1793 edition of the poem, edited by the Church and King polemicist Charles De Coetlogon, and one sees that it is Death who wears the crown and treads mere mortals between his feet (fig. 6).[21] Faced with another illustration prophesying the doom of tyrants (Blake picks on a passing reference of Young to Belshazzar's feast), the publisher felt it expedient to point out 'the propriety with which the story is alluded to by the poet and delineated by the artist'.[22]

Blake's defiant misreading of the poetics of enthusiasm is not only to do with politics. The apocalypticism of Young's poem is taken in other directions that transgress the ideas of politeness that Barbauld used to separate the liberality of Akenside from the gloom of Young. Although we do not have much direct information about the reception of the illustrations for *Night Thoughts*, comments on his illustrations to Robert Blair's *The Grave* help us see where contemporaries drew the line about the licence that could be granted to those charged with the task of representing spiritual matters. Robert Hunt's review of Blake's illustrations in the *Examiner* protested loudly at what he perceived as their grotesque connection between the spiritual and the physical worlds. Where a polite distinction between body and spirit was not properly respected, Hunt fears 'an appearance of libidinous intrudes itself upon the holiness of our thoughts, and counteracts their impression'.[23] The same concerns seem to have dogged whoever provided the notes to the Edwards edition of *Night Thoughts*:

> The folly and danger of pursuing the pleasures of sense as the chief objects of life illustrated by the figure of Death just ready to throw his pall over a young and wanton female.   ('Explanation to the Engravings')

The description scarcely does justice to an illustration which rather seems to represent 'the figure of Death' as a blind, repressive force seeking and perhaps failing to smother a liberated young women (who judging by the anklet may have broken away from slavery). Far from an image of 'wanton' sensuality, she seems a typically Blakean representation of sexual freedom. For her the body seems part of a visionary joy. Blake's designs may represent a kind of defamiliarization, but their unworlding does not leave the things of the flesh behind. In general terms Blake makes little distinction between spiritual and corporeal forms in the *Night Thoughts* illustrations. Many of his figures are naked and overtly eroticized. Even where they are draped, the musculature suggests a corporeal presence of the sort that Hunt believed inappropriate to intellectual or spiritual allegories:

> That work was a futile endeavour by bad drawings to represent immateriality by bodily personifications of the soul, while it's partner the body was depicted in company with it, so that the soul was confounded with the body, as the personifying figure had none of the distinguishing characteristics of allegory, presenting only substantial flesh and bones.   (p. 216)

Figure 6 Engraving of the same lines from the Charles De Coetlogon edition (1793) of *Night Thoughts*; this printing 1806.

The attack on Blake in the *Examiner* coincided there with a series of articles attacking Methodism as the latest manifestation of the popular malady of religious enthusiasm. The author of these articles, Leigh Hunt, responded to Methodism as offending against taste where it refused to regulate the intensity of its religious feelings:

> People of exuberant fancies and uncultivated minds cannot think too highly of themselves, when they hear the refuse of society claiming familiarity with all the persons in the Trinity and talking of going to heaven as they would of the one-shilling gallery: they are led on therefore from familiarity to confidence, and from confidence to a sense of equality, and thus become gods themselves.[24]

'Uncultivated minds' cannot regulate their feeling into a polite form, from this point of view, and are apt to run over in antinomian excesses that allow them to substitute their own passions for true spirituality. Editors of *Night Thoughts*, as we have seen, were alert to the dangers of Young's poetic enthusiasm transgressing these barriers in its own intensity. The anonymous editor of the edition illustrated by Stothard strives to distinguish Young's poetic feelings from 'the "wildfire of the soul", which, disregarding both reason and revelation, leads its subjects into extravagancies inconsistent with both, cannot be too cautiously avoided, or too pointedly condemned. – Enthusiasm, in its original import, implies inspiration: when the spirit is from GOD, it is divine: when from the opposite quarter – diabolical' (*Night Thoughts* (1798), p. 344). Edwards declared that his edition was being published 'to solicit the attention of the great for an enforcement of religious and moral truth' (*Blake Records*, p. 56). Given that his illustrator believed the Bible to be 'filld with Imaginations & Visions from End to End & not with Moral Virtues' (E664), it is not surprising that his project collapsed. Throughout his career Blake seems to have disavowed many of the criteria that were taken to distinguish the poetic from more dangerous strains of enthusiasm, including those respected by his Romantic contemporaries, at least those who wrote from within the elite culture.

In 1769 the President of the Royal Academy Sir Joshua Reynolds warned an audience of aspiring painters that 'mere enthusiasm will carry you but a little way'.[25] William Blake responded with characteristic bluntness in his annotations to the published version of the lectures: 'Meer Enthusiasm is the All in All!' (E645). Blake's attitude disavows the discourse of regulation that defined most literary attitudes to enthusiasm in the period. Whereas these attitudes usually assumed the necessity but not the sufficiency of enthusiasm, Blake insisted that 'Enthusiastic Admiration is the first Principle of Knowledge & its last' (E647). In *Jerusalem*, Los labours so that 'Enthusiasm and Life may not cease.' (*J*. 9.31: E152). Earlier in the poem Blake had framed his entire project in terms of his enthusiasm, although he engraved the plate in question with many of the key words (indicated here in italics) gouged out:

> The Enthusiasm of the following Poem, the Author hopes [*no Reader will think presumptuousness or arroganc[e] when he is reminded that the Ancients acknowledge their love to their Deities, to the full as Enthusiastically as I have who Acknowledge mine for my Saviour and Lord, for they were wholly absorb'd in their Gods.*] I also hope the Reader will be with me, wholly One in Jesus our Lord, who is the God [*of Fire*] and Lord [*of Love*] to who the Ancients look'd and saw his day afar off, with trembling & amazement.

(J. 3: E145)

The iconoclasm of Plate 3 may represent a bitter recognition of the limits that were imposed on enthusiasm generally within the aesthetic and religious spheres, but also more particularly in the attacks of the *Examiner* that Blake suffered with the Methodists. The rents in the text are perhaps the most extreme signs of Blake's refusal to recuperate his transports into a unified form. Blake's enthusiasm lies unregulated on the surface of the published book that is 'a broken text'.[26] M. H. Abrams defined Wordsworth's smoothing over of the 'right-angled' turns of prophetic inspiration into a coherent sense of personal and textual identity as a defining feature of Romanticism.[27] Blake's prophetic form was based on a much more literal and interruptive sense of inspiration made manifest in its most extreme form by Plate 3. Rather than a product of recollection in tranquillity, *Jerusalem* seems to have been composed and printed in spates as inspiration came to Blake.[28] The poem may have been composed over a long period, but inspiration rather than evolution seems to be its dominant mode. Not that the text was unrevised, rather Blake chose to dispense with the appearance of unified form through the revisions he made. The result was a text that most readers of Blake's time would have regarded as distracted and incomplete in its commitment to continual annihilation of what Blake calls the 'Selfhood'. To play down the disorientation readers still experience when reading *Jerusalem* is posthumously to regulate Blake's enthusiasm into a more acceptably poetic form. Poets from Joseph Warton and Mark Akenside to Coleridge and Wordsworth all in different ways practised a poetics of enthusiasm in the eighteenth century. For all their differences, the common tendency was to be much more cautious than Blake. To declare one's complete absorption into the divine was to open up the fear of a transport which might leave one unhooked from a determinate self. Poetic celebrations of enthusiasm most often sought to be invigorated not distracted by enthusiasm. Blake's poetics of distraction puts the self into hazard in a way that I think would have alarmed most practitioners of this poetics. The abrogation of such regulation in textual form was generally taken to be a sign that authors had been swallowed up by the combustible matter within themselves. *Jerusalem*'s textual dissolution should perhaps be seen as the corollary of the thematics of self-annihilation within the poem. For the latter brings forward as a positive principle the kind of distraction of the self often feared as a consequence of enthusiasm within elite poetic culture.

My account of Blake's relationship to the poetics of enthusiasm is not framed in terms of a Romantic completion of an unfinished eighteenth-century project. Rather I would suggest that his career ought to be seen as a particularly spectacular manifestation of a broader formation that understood or mis-read the poetics of enthusiasm in a much more literal sense than most of the elite. Both Wordsworth and Coleridge were closer to Reynolds than to Blake on this matter. None of the first three thought that enthusiasm could be the 'last word' on anything. Blake seems to have been more open to the currents of dangerous secular and religious enthusiasms circulating in the London of his time that so alarmed his polite contemporaries, but he was also alert to the possibilities within the emergent poetic tradition that included Young and others. In this respect his position is not unlike that of the labouring-class poets discussed in the final chapter of the present volume. For most of his life, of course, Blake was thought of by his contemporaries as a copy engraver, that is, not as someone securely placed within the category 'artist'. Blake's enthusiasm certainly looked to Robert Hunt and many other contemporaries very like the uncouth variant disavowed both by the elite, but the poetics of the elite was itself not altogether dismissive of the possibility of a public form of enthusiasm, however wary its was of bringing such combustible mater into crowded spaces. Its poetics of unworlding was not simply unworldly then. Indeed, in some respects, earlier eighteenth-century versions of the poetics of enthusiasm, such as those practised by Akenside and Thomson, not to mention Barbauld, were more committed to a dialectic of retirement and engagement than some of Blake's Romantic contemporaries, for whom 'recollection in tranquility' seems almost to be given more important role than the oppositional possibilities of 'the spontaneous overflow of powerful feeling'.

NOTES

1. Joseph Warton, *Essay on the Writings and Genius of Pope* (1756), I: iv.
2. Shaun Irlam, *Elations: The Poetics of Enthusiasm in Eighteenth-Century Britain* (Stanford: Stanford University Press, 1999), p. 6.
3. Judith Pascoe, *Romantic Theatricality: Gender, Poetry, and Spectatorship* (Ithaca: Cornell University Press, 1997), p. 79.

4. John Locke, *An Essay concerning Human understanding*, ed. Peter H. Nidditch (Oxford: Oxford University Press, 1979), p. 699.
5. Anthony Ashley Cooper, Third Earl of Shaftesbury, *Characteristics of Men, Manners, Opinions, Times*, ed. Lawrence E. Klein (Cambridge: Cambridge University Press, 1999), p. 353.
6. W. J. B. Owen and Jane Worthington Smyser, eds., *The Prose Works of William Wordsworth* (Oxford: Oxford University Press, 1974), III: 74.
7. *The Seasons*, ed. James Sambrook (Oxford: Oxford University Press, 1981), *Summer*, lines 1551–5.
8. I take the useful term 'unworlding'; from Irlam's discussion in *Elations*. 'Otherworldliness' was a term applied pejoratively by George Eliot to Young. Irlam uses 'otherworldliness' in the specific sense of 'the direct outgrowth of a putatively epiphanic experience'. Its 'negative preliminary' for Irlam is 'unworlding', that is, 'a molting process characteristic of narratives of conversion' (pp. 7–8). 'Unworlding' in the poetry of the mid century does not always seek an otherworldly escape from the world, but often uses unworlding as the prelude to some kind of socio-political intervention.
9. Kelvin Everest, *Coleridge's Secret Ministry: The Context of the Conversation Poems 1795–1798* (Hassocks: Harvester, 1979), p. 192.
10. See Barbauld's 'Essay on Akenside's Poem on the Pleasures of Imagination', in Mark Akenside, *The Pleasures of Imagination* (1795), p. viii. For the context of the exchange between Coleridge and Thelwall on Akenside, see Jon Mee, *Romanticism, Enthusiasm, and Regulation: Poetics and the Policing of Culture in the Romantic Period* (Oxford: Oxford University Press, 2003), pp. 149, 154, and 155.
11. *Lives of the English Poets*, ed. G. B. Hill, 3 vols. (Oxford: Oxford University Press, 1905), III: 411.
12. See John Sitter, *Literary Loneliness in Mid Eighteenth-century England* (Ithaca: Cornell University Press, 1982). For his part, Everest notes (p. 192) that 'increasingly as the eighteenth century wore on, the poet in nature seems to embrace an exhausted tranquillity that comforts the defeated moralist'.
13. Isaac Watts, 'Preface' in Elizabeth Rowe, *Devout Exercises of the Heart in Meditation and Soliloquy, Prayer and Praise* 2nd edn (1738), pp. xxiv and xxii.
14. Harriet Guest, *A Form of Sound Words: The Religious Poetry of Christopher Smart* (Oxford: Oxford University Press, 1989), p. 68.
15. Edward Young, *Night Thoughts*, ed. Stephen Cornford (Cambridge: Cambridge University Press, 1989), p. ix.
16. *An Extract from Dr Young's Night-Thoughts on Life, Death, and Immortality* (Bristol, 1770), p. vi.
17. Edward Young, *Night Thoughts* (London: T. Heptinstall, 1798), p. 333.
18. James Lackington, *Memoirs of the First Forty-five Years of the Life of James Lackington* (1791), p. 136.
19. For a discussion of the influence of Gray and especially Macpherson in this respect, see Jon Mee, *Dangerous Enthusiasm: William Blake and the Culture of Radicalism in the 1790s* (Oxford: Oxford University Press, 1992), ch. 2.
20. See *Pig's Meat*, 3rd edn (1795 [?]), II: 124–8, and the discussion of Thomson in John Barrell and Harriet Guest, 'Thomson in the 1790s', in Richard Terry (ed.),

James Thomson: Essays for the Tercentenary (Liverpool: Liverpool University Press, 2000), pp. 226–9.

21. See Edward Young, *Night Thoughts on Life, Death, and Immortality . . . with notes Critical and Illustrative by the Rev C. E. De Coetlogon* (London: Chapman, 1793).

22. See 'Explanation of the Engravings' included in Edward Young, *The Complaint, and the Consolation; or, Night Thoughts* (London: Edwards, 1797), n.p.

23. Robert Hunt in the *Examiner* for Sunday 7 April 1807, reprinted in G. E. Bentley, Jr, *Blake Records* (Oxford: Clarendon Press, 1969), p. 197.

24. [Leigh Hunt], *An Attempt to Shew the Folly and Danger of Methodism* (1809), p. xiii.

25. Sir Joshua Reynolds, *Discourses on Art*, ed. Robert R. Wark, 3rd edn (New Haven: Yale University Press, 1997), p. 31.

26. On *Jerusalem* as a deliberately 'broken text', see Jerome McGann, *Towards A Literature of Knowledge* (Oxford: Oxford University Press, 1989), p. 12.

27. Abrams, *Natural Supernaturalism: Tradition and Revolution in Romantic Literature* (New York: Norton, 1971), p. 113.

28. Joseph Viscomi, *Blake and the Idea of the Book* (Princeton: Princeton University Press, 1993), notes that even the 60-plate version Cumberland saw in 1807 'seems to have been printed in various sessions and not systematically' (p. 313). The rest, Viscomi suggests, was 'written and rewritten no doubt as inspiration struck . . . not laboured on year in and year out' (p. 339).

FURTHER READING

Clark, Timothy, *The Theory of Inspiration: Composition as a Crisis of Subjectivity in Romantic and Post-Romantic Writing*, Manchester: Manchester University Press, 1997.

De Bolla, Peter, *The Discourse of the Sublime: Readings in History, Aesthetics, and the Subject*, Oxford: Blackwell, 1989.

Guest, Harriet, *A Form of Sound Words: The Religious Poetry of Christopher Smart*, Oxford: Oxford University Press, 1989.

Hawes, Clement, *Mania and Literary Style: The Rhetoric of Enthusiasm from the Ranters to Christopher Smart*, Cambridge: Cambridge University Press, 1996.

Heyd, Michael, *'Be Sober and Reasonable': The Critique of Enthusiasm in the Seventeenth and Early Eighteenth Centuries*, Leiden: E. J. Brill, 1995.

Irlam, Shaun, *Elations: The Poetics of Enthusiasm in Eighteenth-Century Britain*, Stanford: Stanford University Press, 1999.

Jones, Chris, *Radical Sensibility: Literature and Ideas in the 1790s*, London: Routledge, 1993.

Knapp, Steven, *Personification and the Sublime: Milton to Coleridge*, Cambridge, MA: Harvard University Press, 1985.

Mee, Jon, *Romanticism, Enthusiasm, and Regulation: Poetics and the Policing of Culture in the Romantic Period*, Oxford: Oxford University Press, 2003.

Meehan, Michael, *Liberty and Poetics in Eighteenth Century England*, Beckenham: Croom Helm, 1985.

Morris, David B., *The Religious Sublime: Christian Poetry and Critical Tradition in Eighteenth-Century England*, Lexington, KY: University Press of Kentucky, 1972.

Rivers, Isabel, *Reason, Grace, and Sentiment: A Study of the Language of Religion and Ethics in England, 1660–1780*, 2 vols., Cambridge: Cambridge University Press, 1991–2000.

Roston, Murray, *Poet and Prophet: The Bible and the Growth of Romanticism*, London: Faber and Faber, 1965.

Sitter, John, *Literary Loneliness in Mid Eighteenth-century England*, Ithaca: Cornell University Press, 1982.

Whelan, M. Kevin, *Enthusiasm in the English Poetry of the Eighteenth Century (1700–1774)*, Washington, DC: Catholic University of America, 1935.

12

JUDITH PASCOE

'Unsex'd females': Barbauld, Robinson, and Smith

In the 1815 collection *Poetic Trifles*, a poem entitled 'What came of firing a Gun' describes the unfortunate victim of a boy's killing spree, a bird knocked out of the sky in the poem's first lines:

> Ah! there it falls, and now 'tis dead;
> The shot went through its pretty head,
> And broke its shining wing!
> How dull and dim its closing eyes!
> How cold, and stiff, and still it lies!
> Poor harmless little thing!

Without knowing anything about the author, we might be tempted to attribute this poem to a woman writer on the basis of its similarity to other sympathetic animal poems such as Anna Barbauld's 'The Mouse's Petition', Mary Robinson's 'The Linnet's Petition', and Charlotte Smith's elegy on the death of a pet dormouse.[1] Male writers, of course, also wrote sentimental animal poems – William Cowper's 'On a Goldfinch Starved to Death in His Cage' is one example – but recent feminist criticism has encouraged us to view women writers' animal petition poems as a distinct genre, and to read these poems as veiled critiques of masculine power structures. Marlon Ross and Mitzi Myers, for example, both read Barbauld's poem as a political intervention, with the poem's trapped mouse standing in for disempowered peoples.[2] 'What came of firing a Gun' concludes:

> Poor little bird! – if people knew
> The sorrows little birds go through,
> I think that even boys
> Would never call it sport and fun,
> To stand and fire a frightful gun,
> For nothing but the noise.[3]

Following the prevailing critical trend, we might read the blaming of the bird's death on the careless brutality of boys as a coded rebuke to masculine violence or as a guarded allusion to governmental abuse of power. Continuing in this vein, we might see the poem's last lines as an attempt to reveal the blustery hollowness of power with their suggestion that the gun is fired merely to create a loud noise.

The problem with this approach is not only that the poem is too slight to bear the weight of this critical scaffolding, but also that it was written by Richard Polwhele, an author not known for his feminist or revolutionary sympathies. Polwhele, celebrated in his own day for his 1786 translation of Greek pastoral poetry, penned topographical histories and religious tracts, as well as *Poetic Trifles*. However, Polwhele has earned his most enduring fame as the author of *The Unsex'd Females* (1798), his excoriation of Mary Wollstonecraft and the women writers he perceived as her literary heirs. Wollstonecraft incited Polwhele's wrath with her critique of the ways in which women were infantilized in British society. In her *Vindication of the Rights of Woman* (1792), she argued that women should be granted expanded educational and work opportunities so that they could achieve their full human potential, and she decried the ways in which women were acculturated to become decorative dilettantes, to be creatures of passion rather than rationality. Polwhele's disparaging comments on Anna Barbauld, Mary Robinson, and Charlotte Smith stemmed from their success as embodiments of the Wollstonecraftian ideal woman: a woman who used her intellect to challenge unfair societal norms. In her writings of the 1790s, Barbauld pushed for the abolition of slavery and for the repeal of laws limiting the political participation of religious dissenters. In the same decade, Robinson and Smith gained reputations as prolific novelists who infused the novel of sensibility with elements of Wollstonecraftian critique. Robinson's *Vancenza; or, the Dangers of Credulity* (1794) features a virtuous heroine who regrets an education focused primarily on the elegant rather than the useful, which thereby limits her capacity to live independently. The ten novels written by Charlotte Smith from *Emmeline* (1788) to *The Young Philosopher* (1798) portray strong heroines who persevere in the face of persecution – young women who, like the self-educated Emmeline, are known for both sensibility and intelligence.

Polwhele's disparaging comments on Barbauld, Robinson, and Smith have served feminist critics in recent years as examples of the chauvinism these authors confronted when they ventured into print, or as humorous evidence of a prevailing hostility toward female education. After all, Polwhele is the moralizing mocker of female botanists who 'With bliss botanic as their bosoms heave / Still pluck forbidden fruit, with mother Eve'.[4] He alleged that women were only interested in the study of botany for the access it provided to illicit sexual knowledge, and he linked women's 'botanizing' with unseemly political involvement. Fired by Thomas Mathias's blistering attack, in his *Pursuits of Literature* (1798), on 'unsex'd female writers [who] now instruct, or confuse, us and themselves, in the labyrinth of politics, or turn us wild with Gallic frenzy', Polwhele used Mathias's phrase and conservative sentiments to launch his own poetic rebuke of women who, in his view, shared Wollstonecraft's radical ideas or scandalous lifestyle.[5]

Ironically, Polwhele has lately been riding the coat-tails of the very writers he faulted for their affinities to Wollstonecraft, writers who have become a focus of critical interest largely because of their perceived feminism. Polwhele's diatribe helps modern critics demonstrate how impossible it was for late eighteenth-century women writers to be received in gender-neutral terms; according to Polwhele, Wollstonecraft and her followers were unsexed, or stripped of desirable and necessary feminine attributes, by virtue of their radical enthusiasms. But, at the same time, it is the gender of writers like Barbauld, Robinson, and Smith that provides an impetus for, and focus of, new critical considerations of their poetry. Feminist attention to past inequities in the treatment of women writers has led to a critical renaissance for these authors – you do not see anyone championing Polwhele as a neglected male poet – but it has also, I will argue, caused them to be read too exclusively in gendered terms, terms that have come to seem a little repetitive. Mitzi Myers, writing of 'The Mouse's Petition', notes that 'The gender-coded animal is everywhere in Georgian female writing' ('Of Mice and Mothers', p. 275). While this is undoubtedly true, the ease with which it is possible to slot a poem written by an outspoken conservative male writer into a subgenre of poetry – the animal protest poem – lauded as a signal innovation of women writers should cause us to tread cautiously when we read women's poetry chiefly as feminist *cris de coeur*. In reading women poets primarily through the ways in which their poetry negotiates gender we do not attend carefully enough to other kinds of affiliation. If Barbauld, Robinson, and Smith were not female they would not be receiving as much critical attention as they currently enjoy; but it is also the case that if they were not female they might be getting critical attention of less restricted kinds. Polwhele, with his blinkered focus on the political self-positioning of women writers, unfortunately stands as the precursor to, as well as the antagonist of, recent critics who dwell too exclusively on the political or feminist leanings of women poets.

Polwhele begins his poetic screed with this invitation to readers:

> Survey with me, what ne'er our fathers saw,
> A female band despising NATURE's law,
> As 'proud defiance' flashes from their arms,
> And vengeance smothers all their softer charms.
>
> (p. 6)

The female band that Polwhele depicts responding to Wollstonecraft's warrior call smother their softer charms out of fealty to Wollstonecraft's critique of sensibility and its disabling effect on women. Polwhele saw reason – championed by Wollstonecraft as the antidote to excessive emotionality – as a false idol which had precipitated the Reign of Terror, and which continued to threaten Christian values and national loyalty. Once Barbauld, according to Polwhele, 'caught the strain' of Wollstonecraft's clarion call, she 'deem'd her songs of Love, her Lyrics vain' (p. 15). Robinson 'to Gaul her Fancy gave' (p. 16), and Smith 'resign'd her power to please, / Poetic feeling and poetic ease' (p. 17). Polwhele would not have known, when he wrote these lines, of Barbauld's poem 'The Rights of Woman', seemingly written as a rebuttal of Wollstonecraft's *Vindication of the Rights of Woman*, but not published until 1825; he allied her with Wollstonecraft because of her publication of political tracts and 'Epistle to William Wilberforce' (1791).[6] Polwhele seems to have associated Robinson with Wollstonecraft primarily on the basis of her scandalous personal life; her most overtly feminist work, *A Letter to the Women of England on the Injustice of Mental Subordination*, was not published until a year after *The Unsex'd Females* appeared. Smith, more directly than the other two women, had endorsed the revolutionary ideals of liberty and freedom in her 1793 poem *The Emigrants*, but she did so in measured terms, careful to differentiate those ideals from their violent realizations. In grouping these three women together because of their supposed rejection of 'nature's law', that is, their support for Wollstonecraft's radical ideas or bohemian lifestyle, Polwhele linked writers who differed from each other in significant ways.

John Rieder entitles an essay 'The Institutional Overdetermination of the Concept of Romanticism'; one could as easily assay 'the institutional overdetermination of the concept of Romantic women poets'.[7] The designation of certain poets as Romantic is, as Marilyn Butler points out, a twentieth-century development, in no way reflecting the self-identification of these poets, or even the characterizations of their contemporary critics, who called them 'Lakeists' or 'Cockneys' or 'Satanists'.[8] While it may have been much harder for women poets to avoid thinking of themselves as women poets, and while this was certainly the designation thrust upon them by critics of the period, the assumption of a common female experience rests upon considerable historical imprecision. Barbauld's, Robinson's, and Smith's 'femaleness' was refracted through entirely disparate upbringings and circumstances. Barbauld spent her formative years on the campuses of dissenting academies where her father taught; she also benefited from his private tuition in the study of Latin and Greek. Charlotte Smith received painting lessons as a small child from the landscape artist George Smith at her father's estate in the Sussex countryside, and, upon moving to her father's London house at age eight, impressed her Kensington schoolmates with her original ideas, which were deemed 'full of wit and imagination' (Fletcher, p. 14). Robinson, the daughter of a philandering ship captain whose failed scheme to establish fishing camps on the coast of Labrador precipitated his family's decline in fortune, caught brief glimpses of the intellectual realms Barbauld and Smith inhabited. She attended a boarding school run by Hannah More's sisters in the mid-1760s and, after her family's move to London from Bristol, enrolled briefly at a Chelsea boarding school. But Robinson grew up in an atmosphere of financial and social insecurity, while Barbauld and, to a lesser extent, Smith enjoyed comparative domestic placidity. Barbauld, additionally, enjoyed the company of intellectual radicals (like Joseph Priestley and his wife) who inspired a strong sense of religious and political calling.

If Barbauld, Robinson, and Smith shared anything in common as they were growing up it may have been a common literary bent and a precocious poetic fluency – qualities not directly linked to gender. If we look beyond childhood, however, Smith's and Robinson's experiences seem to converge. Both entered young into marriages motivated largely by financial concerns; both of them compiled their first collections of poetry while in debtor's prison with their husbands. But Smith, even as she launched her *Elegiac Sonnets* from the environs of the King's Bench Prison, was careful to label her poems as the productions of 'Charlotte Smith of Bignor Park, in Sussex', in this way gesturing toward her genteel upbringing even as she faced financial ruin. Robinson, with no such dignifying pedigree, dedicated her first volume of poems to Georgiana, Duchess of Devonshire, a notorious Foxite lobbyist and sentimental novelist whose name stood as shorthand for the fashionable London circles in which Robinson was already enmeshed. Robinson and Smith, that is, situated themselves in distinctly different circles. And if we turn to the most invasive aspect of uniquely female experience – the experience of childbirth and motherhood – Charlotte Smith, with her twelve children, came to reside in an entirely different country from Robinson with her single daughter, but also from Barbauld with her lone adopted son.

So why do we assume that these three women writers share a common poetic aesthetic? Largely because the three of them floated across our field of vision at the same time, part of a group of eight hundred women who, according to J. R. de J. Jackson's helpful reckoning, published volumes of poetry during the years between 1770 and 1835.[9] 'We have had two hundred years to discover a discourse of and strategies for reading male poets', Isobel Armstrong writes of the problem that newly discovered women's poetry presents to existing modes of interpretation. 'They belong to a debate, a dialectic; we know how to think about politics, epistemology, power, and language, in productive ways that . . . make these poets *mean* for us.' Not so, with the women poets: 'We are discovering who they are, but there are few ways of talking about them.'[10] Armstrong wrote these words in 1995, and in the years before and since then critics have striven to describe this poetry's distinct characteristics. Since the women poets arrived on the literary-critical scene en masse, in a cascade of new editions and anthologies,[11] and since the impulse to resurrect them was a feminist one, it should come as no surprise that critical discussions of their work have focused on how the poems elucidate a uniquely female experience, or on how they participate in a covert form of resistance to patriarchal oppression, or on how patriarchal oppression stopped these women poets from getting their critical due. Critics have attempted to articulate what makes women Romantic poets different from male Romantic poets, or to argue that these differences necessitate a reconceptualization of Romantic aesthetics. Anne K. Mellor explained 'Why Women Didn't Like Romanticism', and Marlon Ross dubbed women writers of the Romantic period 'partial dissenters' from prevailing Romantic discourse, claiming that early nineteenth-century female poets represent 'a distinct class, with its own ideological patterning, rather than merely a species of the overarching class of romantic poets'.[12]

Women poets have been characterized, by this writer among others, as victims of a hostile literary climate or as plucky guerrilla girls launching acts of literary resistance, but almost always they have been characterized as women poets, as if that category had or has a fixed and knowable valence. A 1776 essay in the *Westminister Magazine* purporting to set forth 'Observations on Female Literature' described Anna Barbauld as being 'not only *poetically enchanting*, but personally attractive', before crediting her poems with a 'masculine force, which the most vigorous of our poets has not excelled'. '[T]here is nothing, indeed, feminine belonging to them, but a certain gracefulness of expression . . . that marks them for the productions of a Female Hand.'[13] While recent critics have refrained from ranking women poets in terms of their personal attractiveness, they have felt similarly compelled to distinguish women's writing from men's writing, to assess women's poetic practices predominantly as examples of women's poetic practices, that is, as inextricably linked to gender concerns.

Commentators on eighteenth-century and Romantic women's poetry tend to extrapolate from particular poems by women writers a shared female aesthetic, an exercise that inevitably results in generalizations so broad as to practically compel the finding of exceptions. William McCarthy, Barbauld's most knowledgeable editor and an astute analyst of her poems, notes the ironic contrast between William Woodfall's 1773 observation that the poems in Anna Barbauld's just-published first collection were insufficiently 'feminine', and labeling of Barbauld as disappointingly 'unfeminist' by more recent commentators. But rather than rejecting the limitations of either standard, he goes on to 'decode' the ways in which Barbauld's early poems 'document her resentment of woman's restricted fate, her imaginative resistance to that fate, and her efforts to conceive a more satisfying idea of her gender'.[14] McCarthy goes on to highlight the 'sensory delight' inherent in Barbauld's earliest poems, suggesting that her desires take the form of compensatory fantasies enacted in her verse. Margaret Anne Doody, in an essay on eighteenth-century women's poetry, places a similar emphasis on the evocation of sensual experience by women writers, suggesting that these writers as a group seek to find out what we have in common with other life forms.[15] Pointing to the poetic tendency of women to identify self and emotion with animals or birds, Doody goes on to read Barbauld's poem 'The Caterpillar' as an example of the common emphasis on animal dignity and sensory pleasure by eighteenth-century women poets.

Interestingly, both of these critics, in attributing to women poets, as represented by Barbauld, a heightened sensitivity to the material world and a gendered willingness to flaunt (or at least to encode) that sensitivity in poems, participate in the debate over sensibility that fuelled Polwhele's dispute with Wollstonecraft. Polwhele castigates the Wollstonecraftian 'school' for its abdication of appropriate female emotionality. Whereas Wollstonecraft sees heightened sensibility as shackling women to lives as quivering barometers of fine feeling, Polwhele sees refined sensibility as a defining attribute of women, one that can only be disavowed at a risk to societal institutions. Polwhele contrasts Wollstonecraft's supposed proponents with women moved to write by a different form of muse; he waxes nostalgic, writing:

> Ah! once the female Muse, to NATURE true,
> The unvalued store from FANCY, FEELING drew;
> Won, from the grasp of woe, the roseate hours,
> Cheer'd life's dim vale, and strew'd the grave with flowers.
>
> (p. 11)

It is easy to get entangled in Polwhele's poetic syntax, especially in the phrasal inversion of this passage's second line, but he seems to be endorsing a school of female poetry that draws feeling from fancy in order to produce a cheering and decorative kind of verse. In the passage of the poem that faults Barbauld, Robinson, and Smith, Polwhele seems most disturbed by their rejection of a charming style of verse full of 'poetic feeling and poetic ease'; he bemoans Barbauld's supposed rejection of lyrics and songs of love as vain exercises. In their efforts to associate Barbauld's depictions of sensual pleasure to a female poetics, McCarthy and Doody, as well as other critics who claim for women poets as a group a finer attentiveness to the natural world or a heightened emotional responsiveness, weigh in on Polwhele's side of the late eighteenth-century debate over sensibility; Wollstonecraft would have been uneasy with any attempt to compose a sisterhood from women's superior sensitivity.

In Polwhele's effort to delineate a suitable demeanor for women writers, he was, himself, sensitive to genre distinctions, and his notes to *The Unsex'd Females* register his admiration for the poetic gifts of even those women poets whose politics he condemns. He calls Barbauld's poetry 'chaste and elegant'; he attributes to Robinson's poetry 'a particular delicacy'; and he enthuses at length on the 'sweetly picturesque' quality of Smith's sonnets and the 'new and charming' aspect of her images. He is most enamoured of the young Barbauld, 'Miss Aikin', classifying her 'among the gods', calling her 'the favourite of my earlier years', and even favouring her poetry over that of Elizabeth Carter, one of the coterie of women writers he sets in contrast to Wollstonecraft's nefarious league (*Unsex'd Females*, pp. 16–18). That is, once Polwhele begins talking about poetics instead of politics, the evil alliance which he has so vehemently attacked begins to dissolve. In his celebration of the early Barbauld, and in his emphasis on the elegance of her verse, he gestures toward formal qualities that her poetry shares with women writers on either side of his political divide, but also with the most influential male writers of her day. Barbauld as poet is as much a product of her aesthetic moment as she is a participant in contemporary debates over the status of women.

While Polwhele's comments on the aesthetic qualities of three women's poetry may not seem entirely divorced from his awareness of their gender – 'chaste and elegant' is a phrase he probably would not have applied to a male writer's work – they hearken back to the particular cultural moment in which these three writers served their poetic apprenticeship. The mid-century lyrics of William Collins provided a poetic bellwether for poets of the 1770s and 1780s, the decades in which Barbauld, Robinson, and Smith published their first volumes. Barbauld described the Collinsonian aesthetic in her 1797 Preface to his *Poetical Works*, in which she delineates two types of poetry, 'Didactic or Dramatic poetry' and 'pure Poetry'. The latter preferred kind of poetry depends 'on a felicity of expression, rather than a fullness of thought', and 'like a delicate piece of silver filigree receives in a manner all its value from the art and curiosity of the workmanship'.[16] Barbauld celebrates lyric poetry for being, in a manner of speaking, all style and no substance. She writes, 'The substratum, if I may so express myself, or subject matter, which every composition must have, is, in a Poem of this kind, so extremely slender, that it requires not only art, but a certain artifice of construction, to work it up into a beautiful piece' (vi).

Applied to the poetry of Barbauld, Robinson, and Smith, this conceptualization helps us to appreciate certain features of their early poems, whose
charms owe at least as much to the ability to filigree as to the substantiality
of subject matter. It is worth recalling the predominance of pastoral verse in
Barbauld's and Robinson's first volumes, something it is easy to forget given
the tendency among recent editors to omit these poems.[17] It is not easy to
extrapolate a political or feminist reading from poems chronicling the trials
and tribulations of shepherds and shepherdesses cavorting in bucolic realms
where tending sheep never gets in the way of tendering heartbreak, and this
partly explains their current lack of appeal.

'Song III', just one of many pastoral poems in Barbauld's 1773 volume,
proceeds as a dialogue between Sylvia and Corin whose amorous misunderstandings commence as follows:

> Sylvia. LEAVE me, simple shepherd, leave me;
> Drag no more a hopeless chain:
> I cannot like, nor would deceive thee;
> Love the maid that loves again.[18]

In the opening poem of Robinson's 1775 collection, 'A Pastoral Ballad', an
aggrieved female narrator calls together the shepherds 'who sport on the
plain', in order to recount the disappointing behavior of her former lover:

> But alas! t'other day at the fair,
> (Sad story for me to relate,)
> He bought ribbons for Phillis's hair,
> For Phillis, the nymph that I hate.[19]

Feminist critics have rightly made much of Barbauld's role as a mentor
for subsequent women poets.[20] Robinson writes in her *Memoirs* of having received the works of Miss Aikin 'with rapture', thinking them 'the most
beautiful poems' she had ever seen, and considering the 'woman who could
invent such poetry, as the most to be envied of human creatures'.[21] But
even as Robinson emulates Barbauld in this volume, she creates a slightly
warped version of Barbauld's sincere pastoral mode. Pastoral romance, in
Robinson's version, is depicted in terms of giving and getting; Robinson's
narrator measures her success with her shepherd in commodity terms, the
number of ribbons he has bought for her rival's hair. She also states her feelings so baldly that she nearly punctures the rarefied bubble of lofty feeling
that keeps pastoral verse afloat.[22]

Even as Barbauld and Robinson operate in the same generic mode – a
mode, it should be noted, they shared in common with Richard Polwhele,
hard at work translating Greek pastoral poetry for his *The Idyllia, Epigrams*

and Fragments of Theocritus, Bion, and Moschus (1786) – their very different social circumstances intrude upon their poems. Already singled out by David Garrick, whose attentions ensured her the kind of publicity upon which fashionable success depended, Robinson operated at the center of the ostentatious and shallow London social circles of the 1770s. Her first volume of poetry, following Barbauld's, sings the praises of pastoral seclusion, but in 'Letter to a Friend Upon Leaving Town', her narrator describes all the features of the city life she plans to eschew at such length that the joys of rural life get lost in the flurry of metropolitan detail. Robinson writes:

> No more the Mall, can captivate my heart,
> No more can Ranelagh, one joy impart.
> Without regret I leave the splendid ball,
> And the inchanting shades of gay Vauxhall,
> Far from the giddy circle now I fly,
> Such joys no more, can please my sicken'd eye.
>
> *(Selected Poems, p. 72)*

Sickened her eye may be, but it still tends to linger over the pleasure gardens, fashionable avenues, and gala dances of London.

If Robinson practices a cynical version of pastoral poetry, Charlotte Smith, in her enormously popular *Elegiac Sonnets* (1784) begins to develop a clinical version of that mode. Sonnet II, 'Written at the close of spring', begins:

> The garlands fade that Spring so late wove,
>   Each simple flower which she had nursed in dew,
> Anemonies, that spangled every grove,
>   The primrose wan, and hare-bell mildly blue.[23]

Smith provides the scientific name for the wood anemone in a note to the poem; here the pastoral verse tradition collides with Linnaean science, but in her attention to botanical exactitude, Smith still manages to serve the ideal of a highly decorative and carefully crafted style of poetry that Barbauld endorses in her preface to Collins's verse. Smith marks her allegiance to Collins in the conclusion to Sonnet xxx, 'To the River Arun':

> Banks! which inspired thy Otway's plaintive strain!
>   Wilds! – whose lorn echoes learn'd the deeper tone
> Of Collins' powerful shell! yet once again
>   Another poet – Hayley is thine own!
> Thy classic stream anew shall hear a lay,
> Bright as its waves, and various as its way!
>
> *(Poems of Charlotte Smith, p. 33)*

Smith pays tribute to her patron William Hayley in these lines, depicting the river Arun as the muse to a distinguished poet lineage that links Collins to Hayley, and, quietly, to Smith herself, as the latest poet to take the river as her inspiration. But she also adheres to the poetic model celebrated by Barbauld. Smith's scientific adaptation of pastoral verse is featured in this poem's second stanza where she describes rocks covered with the 'mantling bindwith', a plant which inspires this detail-laden note:

> The plant Clematis, Bindwith, Virgin's Bower, or Traveller's Joy, which towards the end of June begins to cover the hedges and sides of rocky hollows with its beautiful foliage, and flowers of a yellowish white of an agreeable fragrance; these are succeeded by seed pods that bear some resemblance to feathers or hair, whence it is sometimes called Old Man's Beard. (p. 33 n.)

We might read this note in the context of Barbauld's celebration of artful filigree in verse; scientific details provide Smith with another mode of decoration. The note allows her to exhibit her knowledge of natural history, but those seed pods also represent a poetic opportunity.

Although Smith published a novel more or less annually during the 1790s, including *Desmond* (1792) and *The Old Manor House* (1793), Barbauld, in her edition of *The British Novelists*, advances Smith's reputation as a poet rather than a novelist: 'Possessed of a fine imagination, an ear and a taste for harmony, an elegant and correct style, the natural bent of Mrs. Smith's genius seems to have been more to poetry, than to any other walk of literature' (*Selected Poetry and Prose*, p. 437). Smith may have shared Barbauld's vision of pure poetry, but she could not afford to devote herself primarily to this mode of rarefied craftsmanship. Both she and Robinson – who published both *The False Friend* (1799) and *The Natural Daughter* (1799) in the year before her death – put considerable creative energy into writing novels because of the greater potential for monetary reward. Smith's biographer notes her many complaints about the burdens of the novelist's wretched trade; Walter Scott, recalling Smith after her death, wrote, 'Nothing saddens the heart so much as the sort of literary labour which depends on the imagination, when it is undertaken unwillingly, and from a sense of compulsion' (Fletcher, p. 318). The poetry publishing careers of Barbauld, Robinson, and Smith in the aftermath of their first volumes of poetry provide a telling study in contrasts. A large number of Barbauld's poems were not published in her lifetime. These include 'An Inventory of the Furniture in Dr Priestley's Study'; 'To Dr Aikin on his Complaining that she neglected him'; 'Epistle to Dr Enfield on his Revisiting Warrington in 1789'; and 'Lines To Be Spoken by Thomas Denman', a recitation piece for a four-year-old pupil that features a grim ogre with 'seven league boots upon his giant legs / [who]

swallows little children like poached eggs' (*Selected Poetry and Prose*, p. 109). Barbauld's circle of academic compatriots provided an audience for sparkling occasional verse. Robinson and Smith also penned this kind of poetry, for example, Robinson's 'Impromptu Sent to a Friend Who Had Left His Gloves, by Mistake, at the Author's House on the Preceding Evening' and Smith's 'To Mrs. O'Neill, with Some Painted Flowers' (and, we should recall, the genre was not the exclusive purview of women – see Polwhele's 'A Poetical Address to a Widow Lady, Over a Dish of Tea in Her Hermitage'). But Barbauld could be satisfied with the select audience for which her poems were originally intended. Robinson, by contrast, published her glove poem in the *Morning Post* on 29 December 1797, reprinted it in her *Memoirs*, and probably had it slated to appear in the collected works she was compiling before she died; her daughter carried out final editing duties for this collection, which was published posthumously in 1806. Robinson did not have the luxury of letting poems land exclusively on a friend's drawing room table; poems were saleable commodities which earned her money in her capacity as newspaper poet, and which she used to fill out the pages of her memoir and novels. It is not unusual for a Robinson poem to be published in four different venues.

One can contrast Barbauld's 'The Caterpillar', a poem she wrote in the aftermath of her very successful 'The Mouse's Petition', with Smith's proliferation of animal poems in her *Conversations Introducing Poetry: Chiefly on Subjects of Natural History* (1804). Smith's 'The hedge-hog seen in a frequented path' familiarly depicts the animal's vulnerability to 'man or thoughtless boy' who may its 'harmless life destroy'. Smith writes:

> Poor creature! to the woods resort,
> Lest lingering here, inhuman sport
> And whelming water, deep and cold,
> Make thee they spiny ball unfold,
> And shew thy simple negro face.
> (*Poems of Charlotte Smith*, p. 183)

Just as Smith worked as many changes as possible on the sonnet form after the success of her first edition of the *Elegiac Sonnets*, in the *Conversations* she writes a number of poems in what had come to be a familiar animal poem mode – the hedgehog, like the mouse and linnet that came before it, is presented as an appealing victim and one whose plight can be associated with downtrodden others – its 'simple negro face' conjures up the slave trade. Barbauld's narrator, rather than being a straightforward advocate for the caterpillar, acts instead as a spokesperson for a range of responses to the creature. She begins by demonstrating her acute sensibility, describing in minute detail the caterpillar's beauty ('the azure and the orange that divide /

Thy velvet sides'), as well as its sensual quiddity (its 'velvet sides' and 'hairy feet' experienced as it inches up her arm). But even as she resolves not to kill it, she recalls former acts of mass caterpillar destruction:

> . . . recent from the slaughter am I come
> Of tribes and embryo nations: I have sought
> With sharpened eye and persecuting zeal,
> Where, folded in their silken webs they lay
> Thriving and happy; swept them from the tree
> And crushed whole families beneath my foot;
> Or, sudden, poured on their devoted heads
> The vials of destruction.
>
> (*Selected Poetry and Prose*, p. 180)

Barbauld's narrator compares the lack of pity she has felt when confronted with trees full of caterpillars to the warrior who 'o'erwhelming cities, fields, / And peaceful villages', 'shouts triumphant', but who is halted in his relentless carnage by the sight of a 'single sufferer from the field escaped'. The poem concludes with this comment on the 'sympathy spontaneous' elicited by one sufferer, even when hordes of like sufferers evoke no similar feeling: "Tis not Virtue, / Yet 'tis the weakness of a virtuous mind.' Barbauld's poem might well be a commentary on poems that her 'Mouse's Petition' helped to popularize, poems which allow the reader to congratulate herself on her sympathetic response to one singled-out creature, while larger horrors go on around her. 'The Caterpillar' explores the inconsistencies of human sympathy rather than merely providing the reader a safe point of smug identification with a virtuous narrator.

It is patently unfair to compare this poem to Smith's hedgehog poem, since the latter is aimed at a juvenile audience and so would not aspire to the kind of philosophical complexity that Barbauld's poem enacts. My point in placing them side by side is to point out the comparable inappropriateness of talking about these poems as representing a shared female sympathetic response to animal nature. Smith, partly from dire personal circumstances, is working changes on a successful poetic formula in the *Conversations*, producing animal petition poems in volume because they were suitable for the marketable children's book she was compiling. Barbauld, because of her radically different personal circumstances, had no need to extrapolate on her former success, and, in fact, freed of any pressing need to please a buying audience, could use her caterpillar poem to explore limitations of the response the animal petition poem solicited. By the time she wrote 'The Caterpillar', which has been speculatively dated to around 1816, Barbauld had long outlived both Robinson and Smith, and we might contrast those poets' deathbed efforts to see volumes of poetry into press with Barbauld's comparative poetic reticence in her final years, a silence which some critics have ascribed to vicious reviews, but which might also be attributed to the inevitable loss of the scintillating circle of friends she had sought to amuse with her earlier verse.

That Richard Polwhele was able to paint writers of such different personal dispositions and literary careers as Barbauld, Smith, and Robinson as being of the same deviant stripe suggests the broadness of his critical brush and its remove from these writers' actual artistic ambitions. Ten years before he wrote his diatribe against the 'unsex'd' followers of Wollstonecraft, Polwhele wrote two addresses to be spoken by the most famously unsexed woman of his era, the actor Sarah Siddons, whose performance as Lady Macbeth ('Come, you spirits / That tend on mortal thought, unsex me here', she famously proclaims[24]) caused spectators to marvel at the masculinity of her performance. Polwhele wrote opening and closing night addresses for Siddons's 1789 performances in Exeter, apparently untroubled by her much-noted androgynous tendencies. Siddons spectacularly unsexed herself on stage; Barbauld, Robinson, and Smith may have had no desire to do the same, but until literary critics unsex their poetry, their poems will seem to have far too much in common, and their individuality will be lost.

NOTES

1. Smith's biographer cites this early poem as one she still recollected vividly in her fifties; it no longer survives. See Loraine Fletcher, *Charlotte Smith: A Critical Biography* (London: Macmillan, 1998), p. 13.
2. Barbauld's editors William McCarthy and Elizabeth Kraft provide a history of critical response in their headnote to the poem, *Anna Laetitia Barbauld: Selected Poetry and Prose* (Peterborough, Ontario: Broadview Press, 2002), pp. 69–70. Marlon Ross describes the poem as a political letter 'which targets the heart of established power by directly addressing the monarch and parliament': 'Configurations of Feminine Reform: The Woman Writers and the Tradition of Dissent', in Carol Shiner Wilson and Joel Haefner (eds.), *Re-Visioning Romanticism: British Women Writers, 1776–1837* (Philadelphia: University of Pennsylvania Press, 1994), p. 98. Mitzi Myers writes that 'the animal victim was widely deployed by humanitarian writers for the young . . . but it was especially adaptable to women's concerns and their critique of masculine values': 'Of Mice and Mothers: Mrs. Barbauld's "New Walk" and Gendered Codes in Children's Literature', in Louise Wetherbee Phelps and Janet Emig (eds.), *Feminine Principles and Women's Experience in American Composition and Rhetoric* (Pittsburgh: University of Pittsburgh Press, 1995), p. 275.
3. Richard Polwhele, 'What came of firing a Gun', in *Poetic Trifles, or Pretty Poems, for Young Folks* (Banbury, 1815), p. 4.

4. *The Unsex'd Females: A Poem, Addressed to the Author of Pursuits of Literature* (London, 1798), p. 8.
5. Polwhele quotes these lines from the seventh edition of Mathias's poem as an epigraph to *The Unsex'd Females*.
6. McCarthy and Kraft suggest that 'the Rights of Women' is tonally complicated, and possibly ironic (*Anna Laetitia Barbauld*, p. 130).
7. John Rieder, 'The Institutional Overdetermination of the Concept of Romanticism', *Yale Journal of Criticism* 10 (1997), 145–63.
8. Marilyn Butler, 'Romanticism in England', in Karl Kroeber and Gene W. Ruoff (eds.), *Romantic Poetry: Recent Revisionary Criticism* (New Brunswick: Rutgers University Press, 1993), 8.
9. James Robert de J. Jackson, *Romantic Poetry by Women: A Bibliography, 1770–1835* (Oxford: Clarendon Press, 1993). See also Stuart Curran's pathbreaking essay 'Romantic Poetry: The "I" Altered', in Anne K. Mellor (ed.), *Romanticism and Feminism* (Bloomington: Indiana University Press, 1988), pp. 185–207.
10. Isobel Armstrong, 'The Gush of the Feminine: How Can We Read Women's Poetry of the Romantic Period?', in Paula R. Feldman and Theresa M. Kelley (eds.), *Romantic Women Writers: Voices and Countervoices* (Hanover, NH: University Press of New England, 1995), p. 15.
11. See especially the anthologies by Ashfield, Breen, Feldman, Lonsdale, and Wu listed below under 'Further reading'.
12. Anne K. Mellor, 'Why Women Didn't Like Romanticism: The View of Jane Austen and Mary Shelley', in Gene W. Ruoff (ed.), *The Romantics and Us: Essays on Literature and Culture* (New Brunswick: Rutgers University Press, 1990), pp. 274–87; Marlon B. Ross, *The Contours of Masculine Desire: Romanticism and the Rise of Women's Poetry* (New York: Oxford University Press, 1989), pp. 4 and 6.
13. 'Observations on Female Literature in General, Including Some Particulars Relating to Mrs. Montagu and Mrs. Barbauld', *Westminster Magazine* (June 1776), 284.
14. '"We Hoped the *Woman* Was Going to Appear": Repression, Desire, and Gender in Anna Laetitia Barbauld's Early Poems', in Feldman and Kelly (eds.), *Romantic Women Writers*, p. 116.
15. Margaret Anne Doody, 'Sensuousness in the Poetry of Eighteenth-Century Women Poets', in Isobel Armstrong and Virginia Blain (eds.), *Women's Poetry in the Enlightenment: The Making of a Canon, 1730–1820* (London: Macmillan, 1999), pp. 3–32.
16. Anna Laetitia Barbauld, 'Preface', *The Poetical Works of William Collins* (1797), pp. iv–v.
17. The Barbauld poems in her 1773 volume which are most heavily invested in pastoral convention are not among the poetry and prose selected by McCarthy and Kraft for their excellent Broadview edition; similarly, what seemed like poem after identical poem about pouting shepherds in Robinson's 1775 volume caused me to cull just three poems from that collection for the Broadview Robinson edition. See Judith Pascoe (ed.), *Mary Robinson: Selected Poems* (Peterborough, Ontario: Broadview, 2000).
18. Anna Laetitia Aikin, *Poems* (1773), p. 72.

19. Mary Robinson, *Poems* (1775), p. 2.
20. See especially Stuart Curran's 'Romantic Women Poets: Inscribing the Self', in Armstrong and Blain, *Women's Poetry in the Enlightenment*, pp. 145–66.
21. Mary Robinson, *Memoirs of the Late Mrs. Robinson, Written by Herself*, 4 vols. (1801), 1: 102.
22. I am indebted to Jacqueline Labbe for her eye-opening comments on the anti-pastoral aspects of Robinson's verse.
23. Stuart Curran (ed.), *The Poems of Charlotte Smith* (Oxford: Oxford University Press, 1993), p. 13.
24. *Macbeth*, I.v.39–40.

FURTHER READING

Armstrong, Isobel, and Virginia Blain (eds.), *Women's Poetry in the Enlightenment*, London: Macmillan, 1999.
Ashfield, Andrew (ed.), *Romantic Women Poets 1770–1838: An Anthology*, Manchester: Manchester University Press, 1995; *Romantic Women Poets Volume 2: 1788–1848*, Manchester: Manchester University Press, 1998.
Breen, Jennifer (ed.), *Women Romantic Poets, 1785–1832: An Anthology*, London: Dent, 1992.
Feldman, Paula (ed.), *British Women Poets of the Romantic Era: An Anthology*. Baltimore: Johns Hopkins University Press, 1997.
    and Theresa M. Kelley (eds.), *Romantic Women Writers: Voices and Countervoices*, Hanover, NH: University Press of New England, 1995.
Fletcher, Loraine, *Charlotte Smith: A Critical Biography*, London: Macmillan, 1998.
Jackson, James Robert de Jager, *Romantic Poetry by Women: A Bibliography, 1770–1835*, Oxford: Oxford University Press, 1993.
Keach, William, 'Barbauld, Romanticism, and the Survival of Dissent', *Essays and Studies* 51 (1998), 62–77.
Lonsdale, Roger (ed.), *Eighteenth-Century Women Poets: An Oxford Anthology*, Oxford: Oxford University Press, 1989.
McGann, Jerome, *The Poetics of Sensibility: A Revolution in Literary Taste*, Oxford: Clarendon Press, 1996.
Ross, Marlon B., *The Contours of Masculine Desire: Romanticism and the Rise of Women's Poetry*, New York: Oxford University Press, 1989.
Ty, Eleanor, *Unsex'd Revolutionaries: Five Women Novelists of the 1790s*, Toronto: University of Toronto Press, 1993.
    Empowering the Feminine: The Narratives of Mary Robinson, Jane West, and Amelia Opie, 1796–1812, Toronto: University of Toronto Press, 1998.
Wilson, Carol Shiner, and Joel Haefner (eds.), *Re-Visioning Romanticism: British Women Writers, 1776–1837*, Philadelphia: University of Pennsylvania Press, 1994.
Wu, Duncan (ed.), *Romantic Women Poets: An Anthology*, Oxford: Blackwell, 1997.

13

PAUL MAGNUSON

The Lake School: Wordsworth and Coleridge

The group of poets who gathered first in Bristol in 1795 and later in the Lake District introduced new accounts of the relationship of the mind to nature, new definitions of imagination, and new lyric and narrative forms. Their theories of creativity emphasized the individual imagination, but their practice of writing tells another story, one of collaborative writing. This practice originated in imagining a social community that Samuel Taylor Coleridge and Robert Southey called pantisocracy, or government by all. Coleridge and Southey met in June 1794, planned to emigrate to Pennsylvania with a few friends to set up an ideal community based on abandoning private property, and together composed poetry and delivered public lectures to raise money for their emigration. Pantisocracy proved utterly impractical, and Southey withdrew from the plan in the summer of 1795. Their plans for a community of writers with shared property changed to a practice of collaborative writing, dialogic creativity, and joint publication. When Coleridge met William Wordsworth in September 1795, the two began a dialogue in their poems. Their attempts at joint composition were successful only in minor poems, but their best poems were generated in response to others by members of their circle, and were often addressed to them. Their individual poetic voices were generated in a process of poetic statement and counterstatement within a social context that came to be known to the public as the Lake School.

In his *Lectures on the English Poets* (1818), William Hazlitt placed Wordsworth as the leader of the Lake School of poetry and located 'its origin in the French revolution, or rather in those sentiments and opinions which produced that revolution', which were 'imported into this country in translations from the German about that period':

> According to the prevailing notions, all was to be natural and new. Nothing that was established was to be tolerated. All the common-place figures of poetry, tropes, allegories, personifications, with the whole heathen mythology, were instantly discarded; a classical allusion was considered as a piece of antiquated

foppery; capital letters were no more allowed in print, than letters-patent of nobility were permitted in real life; kings and queens were dethroned from their rank and station in legitimate tragedy or epic poetry, as they were decapitated elsewhere; rhyme was looked upon as a relic of the feudal system, and regular metre was abolished along with regular government. . . . The object was to reduce all things to an absolute level.[1]

Hazlitt echoed Francis Jeffrey's review of Southey's *Thalaba* (1802) in the Whig *Edinburgh Review*, which opened with the declaration that 'poetry has this much, at least, in common with religion, that its standards were fixed long ago, by certain inspired writers, whose authority it is no longer lawful to call in question' and included Southey as a member of a '*sect* of poets', who were '*dissenters* from the established systems in poetry and criticism'. Their dissent originated in the 'distempered sensibility of Rousseau' and the harsh versification of William Cowper and John Donne. To these sources, Jeffrey also added 'the simplicity and energy . . . of Kotzebue and Schiller'. Jeffrey denied that common people were fit subjects for poetry: 'The poor and vulgar may interest us, in poetry, by their *situation*; but never, we apprehend, by any sentiments that are peculiar to their condition, and still less by any language that is characteristic of it'. He added, 'A splenetic and idle discontent with the existing institutions of society, seems to be at the bottom of all their serious and peculiar sentiments.'[2]

Hazlitt's parallel between political and poetic revolution and Jeffrey's between religious and poetic dissent were anticipated by attacks in the *Anti-Jacobin* on the Bristol poets in the mid 1790s. The *Anti-Jacobin, or Weekly Examiner* began publication in November 1797, under the direction of William Gifford and George Canning, to correct what they saw as lies and misrepresentations in the opposition press. Its Tory authors parodied the Jacobin poets, Southey, Coleridge, Charles Lloyd, and Charles Lamb. In 'New Morality', published 9 July 1798, they caricatured the Jacobin poets as praising Louis La Révellière Lepaux, a member of the French Directory:

> And ye five other wandering Bards, that move
> In sweet accord of harmony and love,
> C—dge and S—th—y, L—d, and L—be, and Co.
> Tune all your mystic harps to praise Lepaux.
>
> (lines 333–7)

In Bristol, Joseph Cottle became their patron by publishing Southey's and Coleridge's works and paying them more than they could get from London booksellers or subscription lists. Cottle himself had published the anti-war poem 'War. A Fragment' in his *Poems* (1795). The 'Co.' in the lines quoted above from 'New Morality' may be a veiled allusion to Wordsworth, but the reference is more likely to Cottle. Coleridge and Southey wrote a play, *The Fall of Robespierre*, published in 1794 at Cambridge. Coleridge assisted in revisions of the first four books of Southey's epic *Joan of Arc* (1796), which portrayed Joan's battles for liberty and equality against English tyranny. Coleridge included some poems by Charles Lamb and some sonnets jointly authored by Southey and himself in his *Poems* (1796), and included more poems by Lamb and Charles Lloyd in his second volume of 1797.

Coleridge and Wordsworth met in the early fall of 1795 in Bristol. Wordsworth had received a legacy at the death of his friend Raisley Calvert and the use of Racedown in Dorset, the Pinney's country house, where William and Dorothy lived from the summer of 1795. With financial help from Cottle and Thomas Poole, who arranged for Coleridge to take a cottage in Nether Stowey in late December 1796, Coleridge published *The Watchman*, a short-lived political journal, and his first volume of poems. Although Coleridge and Wordsworth did not meet often while Wordsworth was at Racedown, they read each other's poems. Wordsworth sent his anti-war poem 'Salisbury Plain' to Cottle, who forwarded it to Coleridge in March 1796. Coleridge interleaved the copy, wrote an extensive commentary, and reported to John Thelwall that Wordsworth was 'the best poet of the age' and that Wordsworth admired parts of his 'Religious Musings', the concluding work in *Poems* (1796).[3] In early June 1797, Coleridge visited Racedown for several weeks. Wordsworth read his play 'The Borderers' and 'The Ruined Cottage', later published in Book I of *The Excursion* (1814), the story of Margaret, whose husband was forced by famine to join the army and who lost her children and sank into despair while her cottage fell into ruin. Coleridge read his play 'Osorio', later produced and published as *Remorse* (1813). The Wordsworths returned to Nether Stowey with Coleridge, and, with the assistance of Thomas Poole, leased Alfoxden, a house a few miles from Nether Stowey, where they moved in July. In the following year, Coleridge, Wordsworth, and Dorothy Wordsworth were in each other's company daily. Dorothy's journals record, not only their daily rambles, but her keen observations of nature, many of which Coleridge and Wordsworth incorporated into their poetry. She also acted as a copyist of their poems and as their first reader, so she was an essential presence at the origin of their poems and in the process of revision.

In early November, Coleridge and Wordsworth attempted together to write 'The Wanderings of Cain', in three cantos. As Coleridge explained, in one evening Wordsworth was to write the first part; Coleridge, the second; and whoever finished first was to write the third. Coleridge fulfilled his assignment, but Wordsworth wrote nothing, and the whole ridiculous scheme 'broke up in a laugh: and the Ancient Mariner was written instead'.[4] 'The

Ancient Mariner' was started on a walking tour beginning on 12 November, when they planned to write a ballad to pay the cost of the tour. Wordsworth later recalled that 'much the greatest part of the story was Mr Coleridge's invention', but that he had suggested some details, such as the killing of the albatross and the 'spectral persecution, as a consequence of that crime and his own wanderings'.[5] Wordsworth offered another account to Crabb Robinson in which he said that he suggested 'much of the plan'.[6] Coleridge's narrative strongly resembles Wordsworth's expansion of his earlier 'Salisbury Plain', to include the narrator, a sailor who, depressed by war and injustice, kills a stranger and wanders aimlessly without seeing 'one chearful sun'. Later, nature restores a 'second spring' to his mind, but terror returns with reminders of his crime.[7] Coleridge transformed Wordsworth's Spenserian stanzas into a medieval ballad borrowing language from Percy's *Reliques of Ancient English Poetry* (1765). 'The Ancient Mariner' is a multi-layered work, which has been read as a narrative of a crime against imagination and imagination's restoration through the blessing of the water snakes, an interpretation suggested by the marginal gloss, which Coleridge added when it was republished in *Sibylline Leaves* (1817). The mariner is a prophetic figure teaching human love, like his prototype the Wandering Jew. It has also been read as the description of a psychological nightmare, a world without any moral order, in which the mariner must endlessly repeat his trauma. It may also be read as a veiled reaction to the French Revolution. As Wordsworth noted, the mariner does not initiate action, but is acted on by natural and supernatural forces. A storm, a term commonly used to describe revolutionary violence, drives the ship to the South Pole. In *Conciones ad Populum. Or Addresses to the People* (1795), Coleridge wrote that the European ministers and monarchs 'can "Ride in the whirlwind and direct the storm," or rather like the gloomy Spirits in Ossian, "sit on their distant clouds and enjoy the Death of the Mariner"'.[8]

Wordsworth withdrew from writing 'The Ancient Mariner,' since, as he said, 'our respective manners proved so widely different that it would have been quite presumptuous in me to do anything but separate from an under-taking upon which I could only have been a clog'. Wordsworth explained that after the failure of their joint effort on 'The Ancient Mariner', they began to talk of a volume of poetry on the supernatural and on common life (*LB*, 348). In December, Wordsworth was in London, and in January and February, Coleridge was away at Shrewsbury. When they returned in the spring, Coleridge wrote poems that responded to the French invasion of Switzerland and to rumors of a planned French invasion of England circulated almost daily in the Ship News column of the *Morning Post*. Wordsworth composed short ballads, many of which were included in *Lyrical Ballads*

(1798): 'Anecdotes for Fathers', 'We Are Seven', 'The Thorn', 'Simon Lee', and 'Goody Blake, and Harry Gill', among others. The Wordsworths discovered in March that their lease of Alfoxden would not be renewed, because the local people suspected that they were Jacobins, so they decided to travel to Germany to study German and perhaps to avoid joining the local militia drilling in the threat of invasion. Coleridge turned again to Joseph Cottle with proposals for publication to earn money for the trip. He offered several possibilities: the joint publication of their plays and Wordsworth's 'Salisbury Plain' along with 'The Ruined Cottage'.

Nothing came of these plans, but when Cottle visited them in late May, they agreed on the contents of *Lyrical Ballads* (1798), which was to begin with Coleridge's 'Rime of the Ancient Mariner' and include 'The Female Vagrant', a portion of Wordsworth's earlier 'Salisbury Plain'. In the *Biographia Literaria* (1817) Coleridge offered a retrospective analysis of their different modes in *Lyrical Ballads*. He wrote poems of the supernatural 'so as to transfer from our inward nature a human interest and a semblance of truth sufficient to procure for these shadows of imagination that willing suspension of disbelief for the moment, which constitutes poetic faith' (*BL*, II: 6). In a later comment, Coleridge defended 'The Ancient Mariner' from the charge that it had no moral: 'The fault of the Ancient Mariner consists in making the moral sentiment too apparent and bringing it in too much as a principle or cause in a work of such pure Imagination'.[9] Wordsworth wrote poems of common life to add 'the charm of novelty to things of every day, and to excite a feeling analogous to the supernatural, by awakening the mind's attention from the lethargy of custom' (*BL*, II: 7).

Lyrical Ballads concluded with 'Tintern Abbey', written in July 1798 after the contents of the rest of the volume had been settled. 'Tintern Abbey' traces the growth of Wordsworth's imagination and human sympathy from the simple sensations and physical exuberance of childhood, to the love of nature, and finally to the maturity of his self-conscious imagination in which emotions are tempered to insight into the 'life of things' (line 50). Emotion is tempered by the 'still, sad music of humanity' (line 92), which resonates with the social themes of the earlier poems in the volume. Wordsworth thought of 'Tintern Abbey' as an ode, and it is strongly influenced by the structure of Coleridge's meditative blank verse poems. Coleridge annotated one copy of *Sibylline Leaves* with a note to 'The Eolian Harp' claiming to have originated the style. He 'first introduced this species of short blank verse' poem, of which Southey, Lamb, and Wordsworth, 'have since produced so many exquisite specimens'.[10] Coleridge's blank verse poems, commonly called 'Conversation Poems', derived from the tripartite structure of the classical ode as adapted by Collins and Gray, with its contrasting strophe and antistrophe and concluding epode. The blank verse was adapted from Cowper's conversational style in *The Task* (1785). Coleridge's 'The Eolian Harp', 'Reflections on Having Left a Place of Retirement', 'This Lime-Tree Bower My Prison', 'The Nightingale', and 'Frost at Midnight' all share a similar structure. Coleridge addresses a family member or close friends, while he is tuned to the landscape or his immediate surroundings. His imagination moves outward in space or back in time to speculate on a scene that reveals both an active energy in nature and a human community. In the epode, he returns to the present with a heightened awareness of nature as a form of divine energy and natural language. 'Tintern Abbey', like 'Frost at Midnight', begins in the present with images of solitude and seclusion in a landscape that appears an articulate unity. Both poets turn to a recollection of a personal past to recover a generous sociality and the sources of imagination. In the epode, both turn to others for assurance of their future. Coleridge turns to his son Hartley; Wordsworth, to his sister.

In the mid sections of Coleridge's poems, nature's animating energy is represented by the image of the eolian harp, a stringed instrument over which a breeze blows to produce music. In 'The Eolian Harp', as published in *Poems* (1796), Coleridge asks whether nature may be

> organic Harps diversly fram'd,
> That tremble into thought, as o'er them sweeps
> Plastic and vast, one intellectual Breeze,
> At once the Soul of each, and God of All?
> (lines 37–40)

Coleridge added lines to 'The Eolian Harp' in *Sibylline Leaves* (1817), in which the breeze is the 'one Life, within us and abroad, / Which meets all Motion and becomes its soul' (lines 26–7). He thought of 'the one Life' as a combination of the neo-platonic idea of a shaping immaterial nature from Ralph Cudworth's *True Intellectual System* (1678) and Joseph Priestley's scientific materialism in *Disquisitions Relating to Matter and Spirit* (1777), in which matter is not merely impermeable solidity, but points of attraction and repulsion, a form of energy. Coleridge transformed Cudworth's and Priestley's account of an unconscious energy as a medium of God's purpose in nature to an agency that possessed and created human consciousness. In a letter of 1802, Coleridge explained, 'Nature has her proper interest; & he will know what it is, who believes & feels, that every Thing has a Life of its own, & that we are all *one Life*' (*CL*, II: 864), but he was always cautious about the pantheistic implications of the figure of the harp and the implied passivity of the mind. In early 1798 Wordsworth used the phrase the 'one Life' in an extension of 'The Ruined Cottage' now called 'The Pedlar'. The Pedlar sympathizes with Margaret because in his youth in 'all things / He saw one life, and felt that it was joy'.[11] For Wordsworth the 'one life' signified variously a figure of nature's active energy, an image of human community, and a source of sublime emotion. The 1805 version of Wordsworth's *Prelude*, known in the Wordsworth circle as the poem to Coleridge, begins with 'a blessing in this gentle breeze', and Wordsworth 'felt within / A corresponding mild creative breeze'.[12]

Lyrical Ballads was published anonymously in September 1798 because, as Coleridge explained, 'Wordsworth's name is nothing – to a large number of persons mine *stinks*' (*CL*, I: 412). At the same time, Coleridge published *Fears in Solitude*. Coleridge's volume included 'France: An Ode', which recanted his earlier prophecy of the fall of Britain in the 1796 version of 'Ode on the Departing Year', and 'Frost at Midnight', in which domestic tranquility implied a loyal nationalism. *Fears in Solitude* was published by Joseph Johnson, who in July had been found guilty of seditious libel for publishing a pamphlet by Gilbert Wakefield and awaited sentencing to the King's Bench Prison, so the volume stood as a public defence of both Johnson and Coleridge. In March 1798, just before writing 'Fears in Solitude' and 'France: an Ode', Coleridge wrote to his brother, the Reverend George Coleridge, 'I have snapped my squeaking baby-trumpet of Sedition' (*CL*, I: 397), but he continued to publish poetry and articles in the *Morning Post* that opposed the government.

Weeks before the publication of *Lyrical Ballads* and *Fears in Solitude*, Coleridge, Wordsworth, and Dorothy left for Germany. Coleridge went to Göttingen to attend lectures at the university, and Wordsworth travelled to Goslar, where he and Dorothy were isolated in inexpensive lodgings for the winter. Wordsworth returned to the blank verse mode of 'The Pedlar' and 'Tintern Abbey' and drafted lyric fragments on his childhood, which later were included in the first book of *The Prelude*. In March 1798 Wordsworth had announced a long poem to present 'pictures of Nature, Man, and Society. Indeed I know not any thing which will not come within the scope of my plan'.[13] As his plans became more ambitious to finish the poem eventually called 'The Recluse', his ability to complete it became more uncertain. *The Prelude* was to be an introduction to 'The Recluse', a magisterial work of three parts of which only one part, *The Excursion*, was completed, along with fragments of a second part, 'Home at Grasmere'. The Preface to *The Excursion*, perhaps written between 1800 and 1802, announces Wordsworth's 'high argument' (line 71). He dismisses Milton's muse and fabled paradise for the 'simple produce of the common day' (line 55) and proclaims that his subject is 'the Mind of Man – / My haunt, and the main region of my song'.[14]

The 1798 drafts of *The Prelude* contain some of Wordsworth's finest lyrics, the stolen boat episode and the skating scene of Book I of the 1805 version in which nature's spirits 'intertwine for me / The passions that build up our human Soul' and purify the soul 'by pain and fear, until we recognize / A grandeur in the beatings of the heart' (*1805*, i.433–4, 440–41). Wordsworth evokes the aesthetic doctrine of the sublime articulated by Edmund Burke's *A Philosophical Inquiry into the Sublime and Beautiful* (1756). Burke explains that fear and terror are the strongest human emotions and that they are evoked by objects in nature or art that are great or obscure, such as huge mountains, storms at sea, and the darkness of night, which suggest infinity and power. There is a subtle shift in Wordsworth's and Coleridge's ideas of nature from an active energy that impresses itself on the mind and creates a consciousness, represented by the figure of the breeze and the harp, to a source of sublimity in which both the mind and nature cooperate in the generation of emotion.

Wordsworth had difficulty in forming the 1798 lyric memories into a continuous narrative. While a moment of childhood was 'a visible scene / On which the sun is shining', he also acknowledged that those moments were 'islands in the unnavigable depth / Of our departed time'.[15] The light of memory and imagination 'created a memorial which to me / Was all sufficient' and 'seemed to speak / An universal language,' but he admitted that 'I deemed that I had adequately cloathed / Meanings at which I hardly hinted' (*1799*, p. 163). When Wordsworth returned to England in April 1799, he wrote a version of *The Prelude* in two parts. The first ended with the 'spots of time' that 'retain / A fructifying virtue', which nourishes and repairs the 'imaginative power' (*1799*, i.288–93). The second part, resembling Book II of later versions, contained the blessed babe passage, reviewed Wordsworth's life through his school days, and concluded with an address to Coleridge as 'one, / The most intense of Nature's worshippers, / In many things my brother' (*1799*, ii.506–8).

Coleridge moved his family to Greta Hall, Keswick in the Lake District in the summer of 1800, where, in 1803, Southey's family joined them. In late summer and early fall 1800, Coleridge and Wordsworth prepared a second edition of *Lyrical Ballads*. Wordsworth was disappointed with the reviews and sale of the first edition and blamed its reception on 'The Ancient Mariner', which began the volume. Southey called it a 'Dutch attempt at German sublimity', and other reviewers thought it nonsense.[16] Sara Coleridge, perhaps representing the common reader, wrote to Thomas Poole in March 1799 that 'the Lyrical Ballads are laughed at and disliked by all with very few excepted'.[17] Wordsworth published the second edition in two volumes under his own name. He moved 'The Ancient Mariner' toward the end of the first volume and added a note explaining, in his view, its defects. The second volume began with Wordsworth's 'Hart-leap Well', and included 'The Brothers', 'There was a Boy', 'Ruth', 'Nutting', and five poems with the general title 'Poems on the Naming of Places', along with the Lucy poems: 'Strange Fits of Passion', 'She Dwelt Among the Untrodden Ways' and 'A Slumber Did My Spirit Seal'. The second volume was to conclude with 'Christabel'. Coleridge wrote the first part of 'Christabel' in the spring of 1798 and completed the second part in August 1800 but was unable to finish it. On October 6, after Wordsworth had finished writing the Preface to *Lyrical Ballads* (1800), Dorothy recorded in her journal that they had decided to omit 'Christabel', and Wordsworth wrote 'Michael' to take its place. A few days later Coleridge wrote that 'Christabel' was excluded because it was contrary to the purpose of *Lyrical Ballads*, 'an experiment to see how far those passions, which alone give any value to extraordinary Incidents, were capable of interesting, in & for themselves, in the incidents of common Life' (*CL*, I: 631).

In the autumn of 1800, misunderstandings and disagreements began to divide Coleridge and Wordsworth. In September, when Coleridge was struggling to finish 'Christabel', he wrote to James Webbe Tobin, 'I abandon Poetry altogether – I leave the higher & deeper Kinds to Wordsworth, the delightful, popular & simply dignified to Southey; & reserve for myself the honorable attempt to make others feel and understand their writings' (*CL*, I: 623). Southey published volumes of poetry in 1798 and 1799 containing some poems that obviously derived from Coleridge's and Wordsworth's poetry. For example, Southey's 'The Ruined Cottage' derived from Wordsworth's unpublished 'The Ruined Cottage', although Southey's poems lack the emotional intensity and figurative complexity of *Lyrical Ballads*. When the final sheets for *Lyrical Ballads* (1800) were sent to the printer in December 1800, Coleridge remarked to John Thelwall, 'As to Poetry, I have altogether abandoned it, being convinced that I never had the essentials of poetic Genius, & that I mistook a strong desire for original power' (*CL*, I: 656). The following March, Coleridge suggested a kind of epitaph for himself: 'Wordsworth descended on him like the Γνῶθι σεαυτόν [know thyself] from Heaven; by shewing to him what true Poetry was, he made him know, that he himself was no Poet' (*CL*, II: 714).

After 1800 Coleridge's poetry was sporadic, and only occasionally responsive to Wordsworth's poetry. His metaphysical studies, the 'abstruse research' of 'Dejection: An Ode', and literary criticism occupied his mind. He encouraged Wordsworth to write the great philosophical poem, which Wordsworth was temperamentally unsuited to write. He also urged Wordsworth to write the Preface to *Lyrical Ballads*, which Coleridge claimed was 'half a child of my own Brain' (*CL*, II: 830). Reviewers and satirists regarded the Preface as the manifesto of their poetic creed and achievement. The Preface's most contested claim was that poetry should treat of incidents from 'common life', described in a 'selection of language really used by men'.[18] Wordsworth explained that 'low and rustic life was generally chosen because in that situation the essential passions of the heart find a better soil in which they can attain their maturity, are less under restraint, and speak a plainer and more emphatic language' (*PW*, I: 124). The Preface thus rejects the prevailing notion that literature should present noble actions and characters and that only great objects can be sublime. The Preface also rejects the conventions of poetic diction, the use of an exclusively poetic language. In an 1802 addition to the Preface, Wordsworth argued further that 'there neither is, nor can be, any *essential* difference between the language of prose and metrical composition' (*PW*, I: 135).

Yet the Preface is more than a reaction to worn out literary fashions. It elaborates an expressionistic aesthetic, which traces the 'manner in which we associate ideas in a state of excitement' (*PW*, I: 123–4). Poetry is defined, not by a theory of imitation, or by a didactic purpose, but rather by a self-conscious exploration of creativity. Poetry arises from the 'spontaneous overflow of power feelings' (*PW*, I: 127). 'Spontaneous', as Wordsworth uses the word, means self-generated and not stimulated by external agency. Creativity begins with 'emotion recollected in tranquility' (*PW*, I: 148). In Wordsworth's first drafts of *The Prelude*, those recollected emotions are the child's fear and terror, which through the adult's process of memory and imagination, are transformed into awe and wonder. The emotion in which creation begins is 'kindred' to the recollected terror, and that awe generated poetry. In its discussion of an expressionistic aesthetic, the Preface applies more to *The Prelude* drafts of the previous year than it does to the poems in *Lyrical Ballads*.

Lyrical Ballads (1800) was published in London by Longman and Rees, who had purchased Cottle's copyrights when Cottle's business failed, although the copyright of *Lyrical Ballads* was considered of no value. Coleridge encouraged Wordsworth to send presentation copies to half a dozen eminent persons including Charles James Fox, William Wilberforce, and Anna Laetitia Barbauld. Wordsworth's letter to Fox lamented that industrialization was dissolving 'the bonds of domestic feeling among the poor', yet he illustrated those domestic affections by 'The Brothers' and 'Michael', which portrayed 'small independent *proprietors* of land here called statesmen, men of respectable education who daily labour on their own little properties'. They are 'proprietors of small estates, which have descended to them from their ancestors' (*WL*, I: 313–4). In the Lake District, a 'statesman' is someone who owns his land in fee simple (absolutely and without restriction).

From the publication of the second edition of *Lyrical Ballads* until 1813–14, Wordsworth, Coleridge, and Southey were regarded in the public sphere as a school of poets, despite their private disavowals of shared principles. Wordsworth's reputation rested on *Lyrical Ballads* (1800) and *Poems in Two Volumes* (1807). *The Prelude* remained a private poem unpublished until after Wordsworth's death in 1850, with the exception of two fragments that Coleridge published in *The Friend* (1809), the skating episode from Book I and a fragment on the French Revolution beginning 'Bliss was it in that dawn to be alive'. 'There was a Boy', later included in Book V, was published in *Lyrical Ballads* (1800). In the winter of 1801–1802, Wordsworth worked on a third book of *The Prelude* and 'The Pedlar', but he made little progress on *The Prelude*. In the spring of 1802 he turned to shorter poems, and on 29 July Coleridge wrote with evident disappointment at Wordsworth's inability to continue work on *The Prelude*: Wordsworth 'has written lately a number of Poems (32 in all) some of them of considerable Length / . . . the greater number of these to my feelings very excellent Compositions / but here & there a daring Humbleness of Language & Versification, and a strict adherence to matter of fact, even to prolixity, that startled me' (*CL*, II: 830).

Coleridge returned to the Lake District from London in March 1802, stopping on the way to visit Sara Hutchinson, the sister of Mary Hutchinson, whom Wordsworth was to marry. Coleridge had become estranged from his wife and conceived a deep affection for Sara Hutchinson. His visit occasioned some pain between them. Earlier in March he had projected 'a lively picture of a man, disappointed in marriage, & endeavoring to make a compensation to himself by a virtuous & tender & brotherly friendship with an amiable Woman – the obstacles – the jealousies – the impossibility of it. – Best advice that he should as much as possible withdraw himself from pursuits of morals &c – & devote himself to abstract sciences.'[19] On 26 March Wordsworth wrote 'The Rainbow', which was to form the epigraph to the 'Immortality Ode'. The following day Dorothy wrote in her journal that Wordsworth had written 'part of an ode'.[20] In response, Coleridge wrote Sara Hutchinson a long verse letter dated 4 April, the first version of 'Dejection: An Ode'. Coleridge's verse letter is deeply personal and registers his own domestic unhappiness and creative failures as well as his hopes for Sara's comfort as a member of the Wordsworth household. His letter echoes the first four stanzas of Wordsworth's ode, which end with the question, 'Whither has fled the visionary gleam?' Wordsworth probably did little more on the ode until 1804, when he finished it and attributed his loss of visionary insight to the process of growing up. During the summer Wordsworth wrote 'Resolution and Independence', and Coleridge revised his verse letter to 'Dejection: An Ode', published with some omissions in the *Morning Post* on Wordsworth's wedding day, 4 October 1802. These poems form a dialogue on creativity and personal loss. Coleridge's verse letter marks his turn from poetry to 'abstruse research', the kind of philosophical study of Descartes and Locke that he undertook in the early months of 1801. The opening of Wordsworth's 'Ode' locates his troubled creativity in a blindness, the loss of celestial light, and Coleridge's 'Dejection' answers Wordsworth's question with the recognition that whatever we see in nature is a projection of our own mind: 'we receive but what we give, / And in our life alone does Nature live' (lines 47–8). 'Resolution and Independence' answers Coleridge's emotional vacillation from ecstatic joy to abject depression by offering the leech gatherer as an emblem of stoic fortitude.

Coleridge's depression deepened from illness, opium, and domestic unhappiness, so he planned, in the late fall of 1803, to travel to Malta for his health. He asked Wordsworth to prepare a manuscript of his unpublished poems, which he could take with him. Coleridge left the Lake District in late December. In early 1804 Wordsworth returned to *The Prelude* and projected a five-book poem that would include his years at Cambridge with their summer holidays and conclude with a vision from Mt. Snowdon, in which imagination resides both in nature and in the human mind and heart. Early in March he dropped his plans for a five-book poem and began to expand *The Prelude* to cover the years in London and the French Revolution. Completed in 1805, the expanded *Prelude* constructed a full spiritual and poetic autobiography that included his childhood experiences in nature, a set of separation crises from nature and his home that led him to despair over the failure of the Revolution, and a restoration of his imagination through memory. In reconstructing the poem, he moved the 'spots of time' (line 258) episodes from Book I to Book XI of the 1805 version, where they illustrate a restoration of imagination after his return from France and involvement in the debates over the Revolution. Although Wordsworth continued to evoke nature as an inspiring muse and moral guide, he revised the 'spots of time' so that 'the mind / Is lord and master, and that outward sense / Is but the obedient servant of her will' (*1805*, xi.270–2). He also moved the Snowdon episode from the end of the five-book poem to the concluding book, where it exemplifies the mutual influence of mind and nature. Yet in the early months of his work on the expanded *Prelude*, he drafted a passage on the crossing of the Alps on his walking tour of 1790, which argued that the highest moments of vision come when the light of sensation from nature is extinguished following a disappointment in nature's ability to fill his imaginative expectations. Coleridge heard Wordsworth read *The Prelude* in late 1806 and responded with 'To William Wordsworth'. He praised it as a 'prophetic Lay' (line 3) and praised its expression

> of moments awful,
> Now in thy inner life, and now abroad,
> When power streamed from thee, and thy soul received
> The light reflected, as a light bestowed.   (lines 16–19)

Thus *The Prelude* offers contrary accounts of the mind's relation to nature, yet for all the instability of its narrative and equivocation on the influence of nature, it stands as one of the earliest and most insightful portraits of the artist.

Wordsworth's *Poems in Two Volumes* (1807) included 'Resolution and Independence', 'The Solitary Reaper', 'Stepping Westward', and 'Elegiac Stanzas Suggested by a Picture of Peele Castle', and concluded with the 'Immortality Ode'. It included a collection of 'Sonnets Dedicated to Liberty' and another called 'Moods of My Own Mind'. In spite of the presence of these justly admired poems, the reviewers were particularly harsh. Jeffrey's notice in the *Edinburgh Review* ridiculed both the common diction and the excessive emotion generated by trivial events, but the reviewers were not the only ones to criticize. *The Simpliciad* (1808), attributed to Richard Mant, printed a satire on the 'New School' of poetry on the upper half of the page with quotations from Wordsworth, Coleridge, and Southey as examples of imbecility on the lower half. Byron's review in the *Monthly Literary Recreations* (July 1807) agreed with Jeffrey's complaints about the unworthy subjects and childish language, and he repeated his criticism in *English Bards and Scotch Reviewers* (1809). The 'simple Wordsworth' is the 'mild apostate from poetic rule', who 'both by precept and example, shows / That prose is verse, and verse is merely prose'. And Leigh Hunt's *Feast of the Poets* (1815) parodied Wordsworth contemplating a straw and then gazing on 'nothing'.[21] The high church Bishop Mant, the Whig Byron, and the radical Hunt agreed that the public poetry of the Lake School was childish, yet aside from Jeffrey's naming them dissenters, there was little explicit political criticism of them from 1800 to 1813.

In 1815 Coleridge hoped to publish a volume of his poetry with a preface on philosophical criticism in poetry. The preface grew into the *Biographia Literaria*, his autobiography as a poet and philosophic critic to match Wordsworth's poetic autobiography, *The Prelude*. The *Biographia* explains the philosophical bases of self-consciousness and imagination by refuting materialist accounts of the association of ideas and illustrates Coleridge's 'practical criticism' (*BL*, II: 19) with a criticism of Wordsworth's poetry. At the same time that Coleridge defended Wordsworth as a great poet, he was eager to distance himself from Wordsworth's poetic system, as it was understood in the public press. There had been a serious quarrel between the two in 1810, when Coleridge and Basil Montagu traveled from the Lake District to London where Coleridge was to live with Montagu. Montagu told Coleridge that Wordsworth had warned Montagu about Coleridge's use of opium and alcohol and said that he had given up hope for Coleridge. Coleridge bitterly accused the Wordsworth circle of causing his anguish, and the Wordsworths resented being thought responsible for Coleridge's failures. Henry Crabb Robinson patched up the quarrel, but the relationship was never as close as it had been.

Chapters 17 through 20 of the *Biographia* address Coleridge's disagreements with the Preface to *Lyrical Ballads*, which Wordsworth wrote to justify his own poetry, not Coleridge's. One of the aims of the *Biographia* was to distance both himself and Wordsworth from the public's impression of their poetry as silly and childish, low subjects expressed in a vulgar language. Earlier in 1802, a few months before Jeffrey's review of *Thalaba*, Coleridge had expressed his doubts about Wordsworth's 'daring Humbleness of language'. Coleridge added, 'I rather suspect that some where or other there is a radical Difference in our theoretical opinions respecting Poetry' (*CL*, II: 830). In the *Biographia*, Coleridge observes that in the best of Wordsworth's poems, 'The Brothers', 'Michael', and 'Ruth', rustic language is not used. He argues against the use of rustic life because for 'the human soul to prosper', 'a certain vantage-ground is pre-requisite' in 'education, or original sensibility' (*BL*, II: 44–5). The language of the uneducated is 'distinguished from the diction of their superiors in knowledge and power, by the greater *disjunction* and *separation* in the component parts' of their discourse, while the educated are able to 'subordinate and arrange the different parts according to their relative importance, as to convey it at once, and as an organized whole' (*BL*, II: 58). Coleridge adopts 'with full faith the principle of Aristotle, that poetry as poetry is essentially *ideal*, that it avoids and excludes all *accident*' (*BL*, II: 45–6). Coleridge also objects to Wordsworth's claim that there is no essential difference between the language of poetry and prose, and argues that 'I write in metre, because I am about to use a language different from that of prose', more ordered, more impassioned, and more highly figurative (*BL*, II: 69). In later chapters, Coleridge applies these principles to a practical criticism of Wordsworth's poetry that draws on previous reviews and satires. Wordsworth's poetry often is inconsistent in style, sinking from meditative pathos to bathetic literalism and trivial facts, and displaying an emotion disproportionate to the objects or events of the poem. These defects are amply illustrated with reference to Wordsworth's *Poems* (1815). When

Wordsworth re-issued the poems in 1820, he revised most of the poems Coleridge criticized. In effect, Wordsworth's later versions of poems have been edited by Coleridge's *Biographia* to remove many of the lines considered in the public sphere from 1800 to 1814 to be the essential Wordsworth. Yet the *Biographia* praised Wordsworth as a poetic genius particularly for his fidelity to nature, his depth of imagination and sentiment, the clarity and order of his language, and, above all, for his imagination.

The *Biographia* had a further purpose as a defence of Coleridge, Southey, and Wordsworth in the court of public opinion, which in the previous three years had shifted its definitions of the group. From seeing them as practising a misguided allegiance to poetic simplicity, they were now seen as a group of political apostates. In the years since *Lyrical Ballads*, Coleridge had continued to publish newspaper verse and editorials. On 21 October 1802 he contributed an article under the title 'Once a Jacobin Always a Jacobin' to the *Morning Post* announcing his support for war with France and defending private property. Coleridge's editor at the *Post* had been Daniel Stuart, who on 11 January 1811 wrote an editorial in the *Courier* denying that he had ever taken government money for any of his newspapers. He claimed there that the change of policy at the *Post* in 1802 had reflected a general revulsion for the imperial pretensions of Napoleonic France. Yet the *Courier* was receiving government money in 1811, and in spite of misgivings, Coleridge contributed in support of ministerial policy. Wordsworth was appointed to a government sinecure as distributor of stamps for the counties of Cumberland and Westmorland in the spring of 1813. Southey held a government pension from 1807 and wrote articles in 1811 and 1812 in the Tory *Quarterly Review* that argued strongly against reform and invoked the fear of violent revolution. When Southey was appointed poet laureate in September 1813, Leigh Hunt's *Examiner* parodied Southey's laureate verse and, in 1814, included Coleridge in his ridicule. The final chapter of the *Biographia*, written in the spring of 1817, defended *Christabel* (1816) from Hazlitt's harsh review in the *Examiner*. Coleridge feared that it had been called the 'most obscene poem' in the language (*CL*, IV: 918), but insisted that it was no more than a common fairy tale.

The opening stanza of Byron's Dedication to *Don Juan*, written in 1818 but not published with the first edition, addresses Southey, 'What are ye at / With all the Lakers in and out of place?' (*Poetical Works*, V: 'Dedication', lines 5–6). Byron's term 'Lakers' itself suggests a dislocation of the poets, since it refers, not only to the poets, but also to silly tourists, who were not native to the Lake District. Byron notes that the poets are out of place in the Lake District, because they aspire to government office and patronage. They are placemen defined in the public sphere by their location as government servants. But by holding such places, they are in places where they do not belong, and hence they are misplaced. Without a location, they have no legitimacy. Their changing locations is also changing their coats, and the charge against them is not only apostasy but also venality. There is little that is new in Byron's satire, except the comedy of his word play. Many of his accusations had been made before in the *Examiner* and the *Edinburgh Review*, and they were the kinds of accusations that the poets faced when they prepared editions of their works. Since their characters, motives, and political principles were all under attack, their works had to stand in defence of their public names. It was not, nor could it be, a simple matter of covering up or ignoring their earlier radicalism. Their later publications were often designed to legitimate their names and works.

NOTES

1. William Hazlitt, 'On the Living Poets', in *Selected Writings of William Hazlitt*, ed. Duncan Wu (London: Pickering and Chatto, 1998), II: 314–15.
2. *Edinburgh Review* 1 (October 1802), 63–4, 66, 71.
3. *Letters of Samuel Taylor Coleridge*, ed. E. L. Griggs (Oxford: Clarendon Press, 1956), II: 215–16 (hereafter *CL*); *Biographia Literaria*, ed. James Engell and W. J. Bate (Princeton: Princeton University Press, 1983), I: 79 (hereafter *BL*).
4. Coleridge, *Poetical Works*, ed. J. C. C. Mays (Princeton: Princeton University Press, 2001), I: 360.
5. Isabella Fenwick, note in *Lyrical Ballads and Other Poems, 1797–1800*, ed. James Butler and Karen Green (Ithaca: Cornell University Press, 1992), p. 347 (hereafter *LB*).
6. *Diary, Reminiscences, and Correspondence of Henry Crabb Robinson*, ed. Thomas Sadler (1869), III: 85.
7. *The Salisbury Plain Poems of William Wordsworth*, ed. Stephen Gill (Ithaca: Cornell University Press, 1975), p. 115.
8. Coleridge quotes from Addison's *The Campaign* and Macpherson's *Fingal*. Coleridge, *Lectures 1795 On Politics and Religion*, ed. Lewis Patton and Peter Mann (Princeton: Princeton University Press, 1971), p. 69 and note.
9. Coleridge, *Table Talk*, ed. Carl Woodring (Princeton: Princeton University Press, 1990), I: 149 (30 May 1830).
10. Mary Lynn Johnson, 'How Rare Is a "Unique Annotated Copy" of Coleridge's *Sibylline Leaves*?', *Bulletin of the New York Public Library* 78 (1975), 472.
11. Wordsworth, *The Ruined Cottage and The Pedlar*, ed. James Butler (Ithaca: Cornell University Press, 1979), p. 177.
12. William Wordsworth, *The Thirteen-Book Prelude*, ed. Mark Reed, 2 vols. (Ithaca: Cornell University Press, 1991), i.42–3. Hereafter cited in the text as *1805*.
13. *Letters of William and Dorothy Wordsworth*, ed. Ernest de Selincourt and Chester L. Shaver, 2nd edn (Oxford: Clarendon Press, 1967), I: 212 (hereafter *WL*).

14. *The Poetical Works of William Wordsworth*, Vol. v, ed. E. de Selincourt and Helen Darbishire (Oxford: Oxford University Press, 1959), lines 40–1.
15. Wordsworth, *The Prelude, 1798–99*, ed. Stephen Parrish (Ithaca: Cornell University Press, 1977), p. 81 (hereafter abbreviated *1799*).
16. *Critical Review* (Oct. 1798), p. 201.
17. *Minnow among Tritons: Mrs. S. T. Coleridge's Letters to Thomas Poole, 1799–1834*, ed. Stephen Potter (London: Nonesuch Press, 1934), p. 4.
18. *The Prose Works of William Wordsworth*, ed. W. J. B. Owen and Jane Worthington Smyser, 3 vols. (Oxford: Clarendon, 1974), I: 123–4 (hereafter *PW*).
19. *Notebooks of Samuel Taylor Coleridge*, ed. Kathleen Coburn (Princeton: Princeton University Press, 1957), I: 1065.
20. *Journals of Dorothy Wordsworth*, ed. Mary Moorman (Oxford: Oxford University Press, 1971), p. 106.
21. Lord Byron, *The Complete Poetical Works*, ed. J. J. McGann, 7 vols. (Oxford: Oxford University Press, 1980–93), I: 236, lines 236–7, 241–2, and Leigh Hunt, *The Feast of the Poets* (1815), pp. 14–15.

FURTHER READING

Abrams, M. H., *The Mirror and the Lamp: Romantic Theory and the Critical Tradition*, Oxford: Oxford University Press, 1953.
    Natural Supernaturalism: Tradition and Revolution in Romantic Literature, New York: Norton, 1971.
Beer, John, *Coleridge the Visionary*, London: Chatto and Windus, 1959.
Butler, Marilyn, *Romantics, Rebels, and Reactionaries: English Literature and Its Background, 1760–1830*, New York: Oxford University Press, 1981.
Hartman, Geoffrey, *Wordsworth's Poetry, 1787–1814*, New Haven: Yale University Press, 1964.
Lindenberger, Herbert, *On Wordsworth's 'Prelude'*, Princeton: Princeton University Press, 1963.
McFarland, Thomas, *Coleridge and the Pantheist Tradition*, Oxford: Oxford University Press, 1969.
    Romanticism and the Forms of Ruin: Wordsworth, Coleridge and Modalities of Fragmentation, Princeton: Princeton University Press, 1981.
Magnuson, Paul, *Coleridge and Wordsworth: A Lyrical Dialogue*, Princeton: Princeton University Press, 1988.
    Reading Public Romanticism, Princeton: Princeton University Press, 1998.
Newlyn, Lucy, *Coleridge, Wordsworth, and the Language of Allusion*, Oxford: Oxford University Press, 1986.
Roe, Nicholas, *Wordsworth and Coleridge: The Radical Years*, Oxford: Oxford University Press, 1988.
Ruoff, Gene, *Wordsworth and Coleridge: The Making of the Major Lyrics, 1802–1804*, London: Harvester, 1989.
Wordsworth, Jonathan, *William Wordsworth: The Borders of Vision*, Oxford: Oxford University Press, 1982.

14

KATHRYN SUTHERLAND

Jane Austen and the invention of the serious modern novel

To Caroline Spurgeon, Shakespeare scholar, 'every scrap of information and every ray of light on Jane Austen are of national importance' – an assertion which might be completed by G. K. Chesterton's observation that 'Jane Austen, of course, covered an infinitely smaller field than any of her later rivals [the Brontë sisters and George Eliot]; but I have always believed in the victory of small nationalities'.[1] Spurgeon was writing in 1927, Chesterton in 1913, and between them stretched the 'Great' War of 1914–18. Jane Austen, too, was a wartime writer whose perspectives and philosophies can, with justice, be described as determined by Britain's wars with revolutionary and Napoleonic France, a backdrop against which her short adult life was lived. In thinking about how and why certain works of literature gain status as cultural capital (as 'Literature'), war as the real test of value has always been important. By the same argument, literary history (the practice by which we discuss, enforce, and occasionally revise the traditional curriculum of works that form the literary canon) is itself inseparable from the formation of nations and nationalities through the recognition and celebration of collective practices and shared accomplishments which distinguish 'us' from 'them'. We write our own history – the history of our particular moment in cultural and personal time – across the body of the works we read and, in recent times, repackage as texts in other forms – screenplay, audio-cassette, even the slogan across tee-shirt or coffee mug. Taken together, the high and low cultural labour of production and distribution – as critical commentary, classroom set text, BBC screenplay, Miramax film, and consumer tat – declares decisively that for the Western, English-speaking world Jane Austen was *the* twentieth-century novelist. The twentieth century's concerns were marketed or branded as hers.

Despite later enthusiastic appreciation, after her death in 1817 and for much of the nineteenth century Austen's novels languished in relative popular neglect, overshadowed by the larger-scale fictional histories of the individual in society inaugurated by her contemporary Walter Scott and successfully continued in the novels of Dickens and Eliot. What changed things was the publication in 1870 of her nephew James Edward Austen-Leigh's *Memoir of Jane Austen*. Issued only a year later in a more substantial second edition, to which were appended previously unpublished manuscript writings (*Lady Susan*, *The Watsons*, and a highly edited version of *Sanditon*), this family Memoir effected a small revolution in reception. To Henry James the change was for the worse, transforming Jane Austen almost overnight from a select coterie writer, appreciated by the discerning few, into an object of sentimental gush and popular worship, a phenomenon which Leslie Stephen in 1876 labelled 'Austenolatry', 'perhaps the most intolerant and dogmatic of literary creeds'.[2] In the early years of the twentieth century and in the wake of the First World War, this mass appreciation was given critical direction through the emergence of English Studies as a school and university discipline. Jane Austen's reception at that time as *the* quintessential English novelist cannot be divorced from a mood of national unity, first celebratory and latterly defensive. Her virtues were discerned to be a fortuitous blend of our best national characteristics, a paradoxical but potent amalgam of the domestic and the classical, the exquisitely self-referential and the universal. Since then the contest has been redrawn in surprising ways; far from narrowing, the essential differences between worshippers and critics have mutated into more and shriller contrasts. The traditional opposition between amateur Janeites and the academy, over ownership of the novelist all know but very few appreciate in the approved way, was extended after 1970 to include the recognition of her capacity for sisterhood: Austen's ability, newly perceived by some readers, for escaping the bounds of the novel into history, ideas, and, above all, sexual politics. Ensuing interpretations divided readers not only into politicized and non-politicized camps, but also between conservative and conservative-critical representations of her feminist politics. More recently, the stand-off between different Anglo-Saxon attitudes appears to contest the very terms of Austen's Englishness – an English-national or, more correctly, an English-speaking Jane Austen? So we find, since the 1980s, the emergence of a range of blatantly transgressive readings, on paper and on film – eroticized, queer, and post-colonial critiques – whose origin can be traced to an American rather than British reception tradition. The disruptive and cheerfully extravagant impulse behind this transatlantic critical fashion, and the howls of local protest some of its interpretations have produced, especially on her native soil, has made even more explicit the respectful, insular, and nostalgic agenda of most British readings.

One reason why the history of Jane Austen's conflicted twentieth-century reception is so instructive is that it charts the rise and fall of the mission for national cultivation through a professionalized English Studies. At the same time, Austen's canonical eminence in the twentieth century has made it more difficult to trace her contemporary allegiances, her relation to the novel in her own time. We might speculate whether the slimness and sameness of her production (only six relatively short finished novels) contributed to her success: would a male author gain entry into the canon in terms of how little space he occupied? But it is certain that since her brother Henry wrote the first 'Biographical Notice' (1818) of the novelist, within a few months of his sister's death, the conditions on which Austen's novels have been admired have been oddly negative and firmly isolationist. Henry writes there of the modesty of her art, even its artlessness, and of her disengagement from the contemporary literary scene – 'so much did she shrink from notoriety', 'her power of inventing characters seems to have been intuitive', 'every thing came finished from her pen'; and he quotes only two extracts from her correspondence, one of which emphasizes her Christian submissiveness to death, and the other the self-confessed narrowness of her scope ('a little bit of ivory, two inches wide, on which I work with a brush so fine as to produce little effect after much labour').[3] Even before this posthumous 'Notice', Walter Scott, the most successful romance writer of the age, had contributed to John Murray's periodical *The Quarterly Review* the first major assessment of Austen's work. The occasion was the appearance of *Emma* (1816), the fourth novel and first to be published under Murray's prestigious imprint. Eager to serve Murray's interests as well as to praise a novelist he admired, Scott commends Austen for something new in the novel at that time – acute social criticism independent of sensational incident and improbable event. But he couches his appreciation in ambiguous terms. Accordingly, '*Emma* has even less story than either of the preceding novels' (Scott refers to *Sense and Sensibility* and *Pride and Prejudice*), and the young reader, for whose moral welfare critics were commonly anxious at that time, may take up the book 'without any chance of having his head turned by the recollection of the scene through which he has been wandering'.[4] The implication is that Austen's novels are so like life that they cannot seduce like fiction; further, that their excellence can be ascribed to the narrow limits within which they exert their powers and to their essential difference from the contemporary novel. It is a backhanded compliment that resurfaces regularly throughout the history of their reception. For A. C. Bradley in an important lecture of 1911, generally regarded as the beginning of a serious academic criticism, Austen is a safe read because 'she troubles us neither with problems nor with painful emotions, and if there is a wound in our minds she is not likely to probe it';[5] while more recently Claudia Johnson has argued for her greatness on the grounds that she depolemicizes the art of 'her more conspicuously political sister-novelists'.[6] No doubt because she was a woman writer and a novelist (working, that is, within a suspiciously democratic form), the business of canonization has served Austen with a double dose of mystification and decontextualization. What is even more curious is the extent to which this was already at work in the reception of her novels during her lifetime.

Difficult to determine in Austen's case is the ground between a historically sensitive understanding of reception, the kinds of readings we now find in her fiction, and the social contexts for literature out of which these novels emerged. By social contexts for literature, I mean any and all of the following: conditions of publication, the contemporary market for and expectations of the novel as a genre, its polemical engagements, its readership, and the impact of these on the formation of the writer's self-consciousness as she shapes her narrative. Some general points are worth emphasizing: in the course of Jane Austen's lifetime (1775–1817) literature became increasingly subject to particular modes of marketing and consumption that helped consolidate its functions, whether for entertainment or instruction, within a domestic and therefore feminized space. At the same time, the proliferation of varied methods of access, through circulating libraries, subscription libraries, and reading clubs, and in the pages of magazines as well as in volume format, contributed to blur previous distinctions between the public-political and private-unpoliticized space of reading, between kinds of literature, and specifically between 'high' and 'low' genres and the tastes and capacities of socio-economically diverse audiences. Like the periodical press, which exploded into activity in the early nineteenth century, the circulating library both cheapened literature and branded readers as group-identified, sociable consumers. Above all, the statistical rise of the novel from the 1780s ensured that, despite occasional troughs in output (most interestingly in the middle years of the 1810s, when Austen was publishing), by the end of the 1820s it was the dominant literary form; and it remained so for the rest of the nineteenth century.[7] In its internal organization and its textual affectiveness, the novel became at this time the genre which best engages with both public and private norms by domesticating the political and politicizing the domestic. It became the genre most likely to reproduce complex social reality and therefore most likely to contain or inflame social grievances. In other words, it became dangerous, and it did so by harnessing the political potential of the domestic in the form of its conventional subject matter and context for reading. It follows that if the novel became powerful at this time, so too did women writers and women readers, both groups defining and dominating the form for much of the period.

Austen grew up in a family of talented amateur writers who were also avid novel readers. In a letter of December 1798 to her sister Cassandra she records with some relish the prospect of a fresh supply of novels, in the shape of a new circulating library in their part of Hampshire: 'As an inducement to subscribe Mrs Martin tells us that her Collection is not to consist only of Novels, but of every kind of Literature, &c &c – She might have spared this pretension to *our* family, who are great Novel-readers and not ashamed of being so.'[8] Her father, a country clergyman who took in paying pupils, owned a private library which by 1801 ran to some 500 volumes and included novels (*Letters*, p. 74). Jane's own copy of volume two of Johnson's *Rasselas* survives, with her name written on the title-page in a childish hand; the name of 'Miss J. Austen, Steventon' is also printed in the list of subscribers to Fanny Burney's *Camilla*, which she has clearly read by September 1796 (*Letters*, p. 6), less than two months after publication. We know she read Fielding but preferred Richardson, whose *Sir Charles Grandison* (1753–4) was so familiar to her that she could recount 'all that was ever said or done in the cedar parlour'.[9] The flamboyantly bad novelist Egerton Brydges was among her early neighbours at Steventon, and her mother's cousin Mrs Cooke of Bookham published a novel, *Battleridge, an Historical Tale founded on facts* (1799). Mrs Cooke was not only intimate with the Austens (her husband was Jane's godfather) but she knew the immensely successful Burney, who was during the period of *Camilla*'s composition and publication her near neighbour. The connection is suggestive – explaining Austen's subscription to Burney's novel and the way Burney's example seems to have worked on her fictional consciousness in the period 1796–7 when she was drafting *First Impressions*, the work her father offered in November 1797 to the great London publisher Thomas Cadell (incidentally, one of those involved in the *Camilla* subscription). 'I have in my possession', George Austen wrote, 'a manuscript novel, comprising 3 vols., about the length of Miss Burney's "Evelina".'[10] Cadell rejected the manuscript unseen, and it was only published after revision in 1813 as *Pride and Prejudice*. But Burney's influence remains visible, in its new title, which echoes a phrase from the final chapter of her *Cecilia* (1782), and in the social spread, which is also a moral spectrum (from vulgar social-climbing relatives to the snobbish minor scions of a sterile aristocracy), which the heroine must negotiate in her journey to self and social understanding.

Between 1811 and 1817, in a remarkable burst of creativity in her thirties, Austen completed six novels: *Sense and Sensibility* (1811), *Pride and Prejudice* (1813), *Mansfield Park* (1814), *Emma* (1816), and, appearing posthumously in a four-volume set, *Northanger Abbey* and *Persuasion* (1818). But she was already writing from as early as 1787 (aged 12) truncated experimental fictions which she copied into three manuscript notebooks, portentously inscribed, as part of a sustained bookmaking joke, 'Volume the First', 'Volume the Second', and 'Volume the Third'. Running through these anarchic, often violently energetic comic pieces is a pronounced thread of critical comment on contemporary fiction. It seems likely from the immense fertility of their intertextual parody that Austen was by her early teens widely and deeply read in eighteenth-century English fiction. What these early pieces show is how extensively the activity of critical reading disciplines her function as a writer. The habit was endemic to composition for her; subsequently all her full-length novels imply a critical perspective on fiction which drives through their narratives the contemporary debate over the status of the genre and the dangers and profits of its reading. In her novels, the novel itself is assumed as the common ground or shared locus of illusion on which all readers can draw.

In the earliest pieces, the names of her characters suggest familiarity with a fashionable fictional directory of sentimental pairings – 'Frederic and Elfrida', 'Edgar and Emma', and the vulgar 'Jack and Alice' (compare the published titles *Laura and Augustus* (1784), *Damon and Delia* (1784), *Edward and Sophia* (1787), *Alfred and Cassandra* (1788)). But unlike their popular models, Austen's apprentice tales of apparently ideal moral creatures lurch alarmingly towards greed, self-centredness, and naked aggression. What begins in fun – the self-conscious appropriation and display of the sentimental clichés of circulating-library fiction – can end in something altogether more disturbing in its savage excess. 'Henry and Eliza', the adventures of a female foundling, owes more than a gestured debt to the picaresque construction of Fielding's *The History of Tom Jones, a Foundling* (1749), a novel in six volumes. What is on trial in Austen's 'novel' in six pages is the extreme fictional expression of the fashionable liberation ethics of some eighteenth-century thinkers, who proposed a self-regulating society in which the interests of individual and group can be harmonized. In 'Henry and Eliza' we discover the ego run amok, action without motive, and the appearance of virtue without its substance – a chaotic disaggregation of self and society. 'Beloved by Lady Harcourt, adored by Sir George & admired by all the World, [Eliza, the foundling] lived in a continued course of uninterrupted Happiness, till she had attained her eighteenth year, when happening one day to be detected in stealing a banknote of 50£, she was turned out of doors by her inhuman Benefactors.'[11] Abandoned to her fate in a perilous world, the heroine swiftly latches onto a new patron, elopes with the lover of this patron's daughter, acquires children, becomes a widow, is imprisoned, escapes, and returns to her original patrons, who in a final twist suddenly call to mind that they are her natural parents, having abandoned her at birth in a haycock. Not only does reward not eventually attach itself to virtue, but the reader is left with the more disturbing sense that this tale of moral disequilibrium is constructed from a profounder dissociation, in which language too is irresponsible for the effects it describes, as when Eliza's babies display their hunger by 'biting off two of her fingers' (*Minor Works*, p. 37). Significantly, Henry (the tale is 'Henry and Eliza') makes only the briefest appearance and is quickly dismissed as surplus to the needs of heroine and plot. This, too, is a swipe at the fashionable novel of the late 1780s and 1790s, whose focus on the plight of woman in society is engineered through the absence or withdrawal of male support.

'Henry and Eliza' was written before Austen was fifteen, but its implied critique of the novel of incident, in which the protagonist's encounter with a series of improbable obstacles to fortune stands in place of psychological complexity and progression, is the basis for all her mature fictions. Their declared narrowness of scope – '3 or 4 Families in a Country Village' (*Letters*, p. 275) – rejects the abductions, sudden moral or financial reversals, surprising revelations, and loose episodic structure of many contemporary novels in favour of an alternating concentration on limited social and inward developments – a blend of behaviour minutely observed and subsequent moral reflection, usually centred in the consciousness of the heroine. What Austen does not reject in the fashionable tales of her sister-novelists – of Gothicists like Charlotte Smith and Ann Radcliffe, of novelists of manners like Burney and Maria Edgeworth, of writers of national, regional, and historical tales like Edgeworth (again), Sydney Owenson (Lady Morgan), Jane West, and Elizabeth Hamilton, and of programmatic moral educators like Mary Brunton and Amelia Opie – is the sense that fiction is a legitimate variation on the philosophical and political discourse of ideas. Denied access to serious institutions of learning, women discovered in the novel at this time a space for informed social comment and polemical engagement, as well as for entertainment. If Austen's fiction is a sustained dialogue with and allusive critique of the contemporary novel, it is so on terms which endorse the genre's high social and moral purpose even as they satirize its more extravagant effects.

The most obvious example is *Northanger Abbey*, the first of the novels accepted for publication. It was in draft as early as 1798 and sold under the title 'Susan' to the small-scale publishers Crosby and Co. in 1803, though it did not appear in print until 1818 and then from the house of Murray. One of the earliest finished and the latest published of her fictions, this is, as its final title implies, Austen's Gothic novel. Its heroine Catherine Morland, as socially vulnerable and insecure as any 'orphan' of Charlotte Smith's imagining, is misled and ultimately vindicated by the fictions she devours. The most important parts of the novel, Catherine's courtship by Henry Tilney, centre on themes of reading and (female) writing and they signal Austen's intention to be considered among a group of serious women novelists; at the same time the surface texture of the narrative bristles with clues, jokes, and allusions at the expense of the naive romance reader. Reading novels, it becomes clear, is a skilled occupation which, if misapplied, can be our worst preparation for society, but, properly understood, it is also our best; for it includes the interpretation of dress, conversation, behaviour, and motive – of people in their social and psychological entirety. Hence, the narrator's famous defence of the modern novel as 'some work in which the greatest powers of the mind are displayed, in which the most thorough knowledge of human nature, the happiest delineation of its varieties, the liveliest effusions of wit and humour are conveyed to the world in the best chosen language' (*Northanger Abbey*, p. 38). Two points are worth emphasizing from this much quoted passage – that the novels chosen to exemplify the genre's power are Burney's *Cecilia* and *Camilla* and Edgeworth's *Belinda* (1801) (female-authored and with female subjects); and that what they challenge for cultural eminence is the pre-digested anthology of male writings, at this time the conventional staple of the schoolroom. Austen writes: 'And while the abilities of the nine-hundredth abridger of the History of England, or of the man who collects and publishes in a volume some dozen lines of Milton, Pope, and Prior, with a paper from the Spectator, and a chapter from Sterne, are eulogized by a thousand pens, – there seems almost a general wish of decrying the capacity and undervaluing the labour of the novelist.' In other words, Austen is here reversing the assumed hierarchies of pedagogy and entertainment, of canonical and contemporary writing, and of male and female writers, all with the purpose of vindicating the novel.

Versions of three of Austen's novels belong to the 1790s, a decade remarkable for female intellectual and creative intervention in the ferment of ideas following the French Revolution. These drafts, whose outlines can be traced in the thematic preoccupations and ideological oppositions of their subsequently published forms, associate Austen's early fiction with the writings of both conservative and radical contemporary female social commentators. *Sense and Sensibility*, in draft before 1797 as 'Elinor and Marianne', shares with progressive novels of the 1790s a criticism of the patriarchal family and of the vulnerability within its structures of the romantic and dependent young woman. Not only Marianne but Elinor, too, is a victim to romantic love; but only Marianne inhabits her passion and its rejection obsessively and to the verge of 'self-destruction' (*Sense and Sensibility*, p. 105). Aptly named, Marianne is fictional cousin to Wollstonecraft's Maria, the heroine of *The Wrongs of Woman* (1798), who 'wished to be only alive to love',[12] and to Mary Hays's outspoken Emma from *The Memoirs of Emma Courtney* (1796). If *Pride and Prejudice* and *Northanger Abbey* also bear traces of the 1790s debates between the sexes, *Mansfield Park* and *Emma*, conceived and executed between 1811 and 1815, are, by contrast, coloured by

the conformism which marked British thinking in the later stages and immediate aftermath of the European war against Napoleon, and by the shift
in the novel at that time towards a more complex siting of the individual
in society. Austen shares with Scott, whose best-selling first novel *Waverley*
appeared in 1814, the same year as *Mansfield Park*, a sense that the social
medium is not simply an obstacle and antagonist but the context in which
the individual finds her identity.

Mansfield Park contains in Maria Bertram a reconsideration of the turbulent heroines of 1790s radical romance, but this time as a more cynical
study, without the painful social innocence of her rebellious and outspoken
forebears. This later Maria is a fortune-hunter, playing a game she thinks
she understands and for which she has been trained from birth, by education and her father's social anxiety; but what neither she nor her family
takes into account is the strength of her own passions. What ensues is a grim
'self-revenge' (*Mansfield Park*, p. 202) in which she is self-taunted to her
own destruction. There is something unremittingly bleak in *Mansfield Park*'s
programmatic study of family abuse which finally defies the optimistic solutions of Austen's earlier fiction to the general failure and individual tragedy it
uncovers. In Fanny Price the reader meets a new kind of heroine, whose lack
of status and family recognition, familiar enough from the feisty heroines
of Defoe or Richardson, is transformed into pathology. Fanny's is a psychic
rather than a physical existence, and the shift implies a new role for the novel
in delineating how we know and confront reality. *Emma* is far less savage
but no less constricted in its human dealings: its minute exploration of the
small disturbances which cause shock waves through a village community is
a complex study of individual egotism and social complacency. An equivocal
celebration of the virtues and security of English provincial life, *Emma* is also
Austen's response to the regional or national tale enjoying popular success in
the 1810s. Edgeworth, Owenson, and Scott were using the novel to read the
landscapes of Ireland and Scotland in particular ways and to mount arguments for cultural specificity. Highbury, with 'so many good-looking houses'
is a model of settled, English respectability, but it takes no more than the
anticipation of a dance at the Crown Inn to reveal the anxieties beneath the
surface as to the 'difficulty in every body's returning into their proper place
the next morning' (*Emma*, p. 198).

Only with *Persuasion* and *Sanditon*, the novel Austen was writing in the
last months of her life, do we sense the reawakening of an optimistic attitude
to risk. *Persuasion* is about being given and seizing second chances, the economic and moral bankruptcy of old families, and the appeal of meritocracy,
in the form of the riskiest of all professions, the navy. Set precisely in 1814–
15, between Napoleon's abdication and just before his final overthrow at

Waterloo, its private core, the revived courtship of Anne Elliot and Captain Wentworth (previously considered 'a very degrading alliance' (*Persuasion*, p. 26)), is played out in opposition to established structures and in defiance of the endogamous marriage settlements which secure the gentry societies of *Mansfield Park* and *Emma*. By contrast, Sir Walter Elliot is a grotesque commentary on Regency manners; a parodic invention, untainted by the psychological realism that distinguishes Sir Thomas Bertram's social anxiety, he recaptures some of the energy and exuberance of the juvenile writings. This same spirit of parody invests *Sanditon*, whose lightly sketched domestic entanglements are set against the risks associated with property speculation and the hazardous fortunes of yet another fashionable seaside resort, with its brand new Trafalgar House and its plans for a Waterloo Crescent. This is a society as unsettled as it is possible to imagine, washed up fortuitously and temporarily on the southern English coast. It is difficult to guess how Austen might have developed her plot, not only because of the novel's fragmentary condition but because of its return to the formal daring and sheer oddity of her early fiction. This in itself is a puzzle – why would she at this particular moment risk her mounting success and respect as a serious novelist of everyday life to disinter the freaks and extravagances of her juvenilia? But this is exactly what she does – in the interfering hypochondriac Miss Diana Parker, who 'Two years ago' cured Mrs Sheldon's coachman of a sprained foot by rubbing his ankle 'with my own hand for six Hours without Intermission' (*Minor Works*, p. 386); and in the absurdly posturing Sir Edward Denham, whose passion for Scott's verses leads him to declare, somewhat enigmatically, 'That Man who can read them unmoved must have the nerves of an Assassin! – Heaven defend me from meeting such a Man un-armed' (*Minor Works*, pp. 396–7). Moved centre-stage, such dysfunctional characters bring a challenging whiff of freedom, which in her published studies of banal and oppressive societies was more cautiously censored. There is even a disturbing sexual energy in Miss Parker and the prolonged action of her hands on the coachman's foot. With *Sanditon*, it seems, Austen was taking the novel of everyday social observation into new and dangerous waters.

Specific features mark Austen's contribution to the novel as a serious modern literary form. Among these is her ability to reproduce conversation as the probable exchanges of morally fallible human beings, as distinct from the lofty and sententious group monologues to be found in the writings of her contemporaries. 'Seldom, very seldom, does complete truth belong to any human disclosure; seldom can it happen that something is not a little disguised, or a little mistaken' (*Emma*, p. 431) – these words signal a revolution in thinking about the way people interact in novels. In circumscribing the novelist's imagination within the probable range of ordinary human behaviour, the reproduction of something as near as possible to real conversation (with its own peculiar deceits and fictions), Austen also allows for the introduction of something more like real morality. Fiction now has a vehicle by which it can grow beyond the stereotyped boundaries of the circulating library and engage with real human dilemmas. For Scott, the author of *Emma* heads a 'style of novel' new 'within the last fifteen or twenty years' and whose chief characteristic is its 'art of copying from nature as she really exists in the common walks of life'.[13] Even Coleridge, whose open contempt for the popular novel of the day is well known, gestured his exception for Austen's novels as 'perfectly genuine and individual productions',[14] noting elsewhere that 'Women are good novelists . . . because they rarely or never thoroughly distinguish between fact and fiction. In the jumble of the two lies the secret of the modern novel.'[15] The comment is the basis of a far better insight than he intended. Like her contemporaries, Austen constructed the space of each novel as a confrontation between previous fictions (of whose artifices this new novel will be both digest and critique) and everyday life (whose dimensions the new novel will reproduce and enlarge). But what is really new to Austen is the inwardness of the heroine, whose complex life of the mind replaces the less probable adventures in the body of her conventional counterpart. In Austen, in other words, the 'jumble of fact and fiction' finds its keenest expression as the constituents of a mental landscape which we recognize as the natural longing of human beings to be and not be themselves. This, too, is presented as a kind of conversation – the conversation of the self with itself. One of Austen's greatest contributions to the novel as fiction and ethic is her deployment, deepened from novel to novel, of a narrative method inflected by the personal subjectivity of a self-conversing heroine.

There survives a short sequence of four letters, written to her twenty-one year old niece Anna Austen between July and September 1814, in which Austen shares her views on novel writing (see especially *Letters*, pp. 267–78). The occasion is Anna's sending drafts of a novel, tentatively entitled 'Which is the Heroine?', for her aunt's inspection. From its description (the novel was never finished) it appears to be a sprawling romance of fashionable life, peopled by improbably named characters – St Julian, Devereux Forester, and Lady Clanmurray – whose adventures are to take them from London's Berkeley Square to Ireland. As the sections of manuscript arrive by post Austen reads them aloud to her sister Cassandra and their mother, sending the ensuing comments in her letters back to Anna. This was a method that worked for Austen's own early drafts, which were, at least during the Steventon years, routinely tested by ear on a family audience – something which in no small part explains the aural or spoken conviction their final forms retain. As working drafts and as finished novels they are predicated on conversation as critical exchange. What dominates Austen's reading of Anna's manuscript is the importance she places on consistency ('Remember she is very prudent; – you must not let her act inconsistently'); on naturalness ('I do not like a Lover's speaking in the 3d person; – it is too much like the formal part of Lord Orville [in Burney's *Evelina*]'); on conciseness ('we have thought the sense might be expressed in fewer words'); on writing from experience ('we think you had better not leave England. Let the Portmans go to Ireland, but as you know nothing of the Manners there, you had better not go with them . . . Stick to Bath . . . There you will be quite at home'); and on observing social proprieties ('when Mr Portman is first brought in, he wd not be introduced as *the Honble – That* distinction is never mentioned at such times'). While Aunt Cassandra 'does not like desultory novels, & is rather fearful yours will be too much so', she, on the other hand, can 'allow much more Latitude . . . & think Nature & Spirit cover many sins of a wandering story'. In any case, 'People in general do not care so much about it'. Austen advises against overwriting – 'your descriptions are often more minute than will be liked. You give too many particulars of right hand & left' – and she argues the advantages of extensively editing the manuscript at a late stage – 'I hope when you have written a great deal more you will be equal to scratching out some of the past'. But her chief criticism is reserved for 'thorough novel slang': 'Devereux Forester's being ruined by his Vanity is extremely good; but I wish you would not let him plunge into a "vortex of Dissipation". I do not object to the Thing, but I cannot bear the expression; – it is such thorough novel slang – and so old, that I dare say Adam met with it in the first novel he opened'. Finally, she commends the concentrated study of social relations over the 'wandering' style she earlier excused: 'You are now collecting your People delightfully, getting them exactly into such a spot as is the delight of my life; – 3 or 4 Families in a Country Village is the very thing to work on'. She was at the time engaged on *Emma*.

The hagiographic critics of the mid twentieth century did not care to notice how shrewdly Austen judged and adapted fashion in launching her novels, treading a line between marketing her fictions commercially and writing only for the market. She was deeply immersed in the contemporary novel and followed its fads critically and anxiously. The criticism is implied in her advice to Anna and in the hilarious 'Plan of a Novel', which she wrote in response to the well-meaning but pompous interference of the Prince Regent's librarian, James Stanier Clarke, with whom she negotiated in 1815 over the royal dedication of *Emma*. Between them, the comments to Anna and 'Plan' contain Austen's 'art of fiction', written at a stage in her own publishing career when she can express with some confidence what she believes the novel should do. The 'Plan' is ostensibly written 'according to hints from various quarters', and Austen's surviving manuscript gives references for several of her sources, which range from her niece Fanny Knight to William Gifford, the editor of Murray's *Quarterly Review*, who probably corrected *Emma* for the press. Only a few pages long, it sets in a ludicrous light many of the devices of commercial fiction: an extraordinarily virtuous and talented heroine; her near-incestuous relationship to a sickly father, who is impoverished and a general liability but possessed of an intriguing past (which he relates at interminable length); the heroine's need to earn her living, which she does in desperate circumstances; her vigorous pursuit by an unprincipled and worthless lover; the distant and respectful admiration of an ideal but ineffectual lover; her terrible ordeals and adventures; the death of her father; her narrow escape from the villainous anti-hero; her sudden reunion with the hero. Austen observes: the father and daughter 'are to converse in long speeches, elegant Language – & a tone of high, serious sentiment'; 'Heroine & her Father never above a fortnight together in one place'; 'All the Good will be unexceptionable in every respect – and there will be no foibles or weaknesses but with the Wicked, who will be completely depraved & infamous, hardly a resemblance of Humanity left in them.' She concludes, 'name of the work *not* to be *Emma*' (*Minor Works*, pp. 428–30). The 'Plan' has several specific targets among the day's bestsellers – the textually and geographically wandering romances of Jane and Anna Maria Porter, Sophie Cottin's *Elizabeth; or, Exiles of Siberia* (1806), translated into English for the powerful Minerva Press Library in 1807, Fanny Burney's *The Wanderer* (1814), and Mary Brunton's *Self-Control* (1810). Of these Brunton is the most interesting, and also Austen's most persistent target.

Mary Brunton's success clearly worried Austen. *Self-Control* appeared as she was seeing *Sense and Sensibility* through the press. She reports to Cassandra from London: 'We have tried to get Self-controul, but in vain. – I *should* like to know what her Estimate is – but am always half afraid of finding a clever novel *too clever* – & of finding my own story & my own people all forestalled' (*Letters*, p. 186). More than two years later, putting the finishing touches to *Mansfield Park*, she writes, 'I am looking over Self Control again, & my opinion is confirmed of its' being an excellently-meant, elegantly-written Work, without anything of Nature or Probability in it. I declare I do not know whether Laura's passage down the American River, is not the most natural, possible, every-day thing she ever does' (*Letters*, p. 234). Another year passes, and in November 1814, in the middle of writing *Emma*, she repeats in a letter to Anna the unfavourable opinion of a reader of *Mansfield Park*, observing: 'I will redeem my credit with him, by writing a close Imitation of "Self-control" as soon as I can; – I will improve upon it; – my Heroine shall not merely be wafted down an American river in a boat by herself, she shall cross the Atlantic in the same way, & never stop till she reaches Gravesent' (*Letters*, p. 283). Then, some time between November 1815 and April 1816, during the writing of *Persuasion*, comes a final swipe in 'Plan of a Novel'.

Self-Control was a runaway success – three editions in the first six months, a total of about 3,000 printed copies – contributing significantly to the vogue for moral-domestic novels between about 1808 and 1819, very roughly the span of Austen's own professional career. It was a fashion the conservative polemicist Hannah More began with her improbable best-seller, *Coelebs in Search of a Wife. Comprehending Observations on Domestic Habits and Manners, Religion and Morals* (1808). Brunton's three editions and 3,000 copies in six months compare with two editions of *Mansfield Park* (May 1814 and February 1816), perhaps 2,000 copies in all, of which nearly 500 were remaindered in January 1820.[16] Ludicrous it may be, but 'Plan of a Novel' is a recognizable reduction to formula of Brunton's tale. *Self-Control* is the story of Laura Montreville, who resolves to resist the demands of a lecherous lover, the libertine Colonel Hargrave, while failing to understand the sober and virtuous passion of the worthy De Courcy. Left penniless in London she determines to earn a living for herself and her invalid father by selling her amateur sketches: 'Could she but hope to obtain a subsistence for her father, she would labour night and day, deprive herself of recreation, of rest, even of daily food, rather than wound his heart, by an acquaintance with poverty.'[17] Of course, her father dies, and Laura is cast upon an unscrupulous female relation, who connives at her seduction by her worthless lover. Laura's many sufferings culminate in kidnap, a perilous sea-crossing to Canada, and eventual escape by canoe from a wilderness confinement among American Indians. The contexts are improbable, the narrative loose and redundant, the dialogue stilted and spoken at the top of the voice, yet *Self-Control* is an intense and absorbing anticipation of the self-embattled studies of female psychology that Charlotte Brontë will later develop. Its appeal is un-Austenian and still today it makes compelling reading. For a start, Laura's impossible virtue is complicated by the fact that she too defines as love the sexual predatoriness of her would-be seducer Hargrave – so much so that she has power (only just) to resist him but not reason enough to recognize as love the companionate and rational proposals of De Courcy. Her dilemma makes this an erotic tale of virtuous conduct, somewhat in the manner of Richardson's *Pamela* (1740). Secondly, Laura's is a recognizable proto-feminist voice for economic opportunities for women, sounding a note often heard in the female polemical writings of the 1810s but scarcely ever in Austen, unless we count Jane Fairfax's complaint against the trade in governesses (*Emma*, p. 300). In contrast to this double dose of sensation – sexual and economic – Austen's narratives appear tame.

Austen begins the process by which the novel explains us imaginatively to ourselves in something like a direct correlation with probable reality. But fiction has also, both in her age and ours, worked effectively in other ways – distributing the balance between probability and improbability differently. Almost her exact contemporary, Brunton (1778–1818) situates her improbable improving tales at the far end of the same moral-domestic spectrum. *Discipline* (1815), her second novel, presents in the lively Ellen Percy and her sober and didactic older suitor, Mr Maitland, a model for the more muted relationship between Emma and Mr Knightley. Austen's spare conversational narratives read like nothing her contemporaries produced. They represent her ambition to take the novel in a new direction, but this does not mean she was not anxious for immediate success and approval or that she underrated the appeal of more sensational fiction. Instead, we see her attempting to moderate its power by containing it critically within her own quieter art. Her novels are written as elaborate patterns of difference and opposition in which the discordant elements vitally contribute to each other's construction, with the result that meaning never finally settles but remains at play across a range of possibilities. In *Mansfield Park*, for example, Fanny Price exists as contrast to, and finds her behaviour implicated in, the kind of moral judgement made against her cousin Maria Bertram, the passionate heroine of a far different romance. When Fanny refuses Henry Crawford (in a courtship whose emotional undertow owes much to the Laura–Hargrave relationship in *Self-Control*) Sir Thomas describes her conduct as 'wilful and perverse', imbued with 'that independence of spirit, which prevails so much in modern days' (*Mansfield Park*, p. 318). The charge appears unjust – more apt as anticipatory verdict on Maria's elopement than on the shrinking conduct of Fanny. Nevertheless, it provides a clue to the way in which the life of the mind is so powerfully developed in Austen's characters that it assumes an alternative existence. Beneath her modesty, Fanny Price is indeed as 'wilful and perverse' as the adulterous Maria, after her fashion, is paradoxically conformist. By a similar process, *Emma* is both a study in provincial limitations and the altogether more impetuous romance of improbable liaisons that Emma herself writes from the same local materials. If Austen's concentration on the everyday, in contrast to what Wordsworth called the fashion for 'frantic novels',[18] challenged the form to become a more complex critical medium for our romantic imaginings, it did so by driving those longings deeper (in psychological and structural terms) into the fabric of her texts. Her stories and her style of telling them are suggestive compounds of elements identified and denied, or as W. J. Harvey put it in a mid twentieth-century essay on *Emma*, 'the written novel contains its unwritten twin whose shape is known only by the shadow it casts.'[19]

The determination with which Austen perfected the equivocal art of the critical novel was occasionally shaken: she was fearful that her style would strike the reader as too economical, and she jokes uneasily about padding out future narratives with that conventional novel staple, the digression. She writes of the newly published *Pride and Prejudice*, 'it wants to be stretched out here & there with a long Chapter – of sense if it could be had, if not of specious nonsense – about something unconnected with the story; an Essay on Writing, a critique on Walter Scott, or the history of Buonaparte – or anything that would form a contrast . . .' (*Letters*, p. 203). The joke conceals an anxiety about the intensity and singularity of her focus in contrast to the less demandingly diffuse style of much circulating library fiction. But this economy also contributes directly to her serious status – to the portability of her fictions (that is, their capacity to live independently of contemporary contexts) and to their availability for re-reading. '[R]ead again and for the third time at least Miss Austen's very finely written novel of *Pride and Prejudice*,' records Scott in his journal on 14 March 1826. 'That young lady had a talent for describing the involvements and feelings and characters of ordinary life which is to me the most wonderful I ever met with.'[20]

It would be wrong to imply that Austen was not writing for the moment, but it was a special moment in the history of the novel. Her writing career coincided precisely with the establishment of the British novel as a serious literary form, a legitimate vehicle for moral knowledge, and an accounting for and representation of experience that might compel respect. Since the mid eighteenth century critics and practitioners had been writing up the novel's status as an intellectually serious and aesthetically rigorous form. It could even be argued that the striving for psychological truth and probability, a feature of contemporary poetry (Wordsworth's *Lyrical Ballads* (1798/1800)) and drama (Joanna Baillie's *Plays of the Passions* (1798–1812)) witnessed to an interest in motive and human conduct that the novel, over any other genre, is best placed to trace. At the same time, a new fashion among publishers for uniform collections of novels, taking advantage of the breaking of perpetual copyright in 1774, encouraged critics and readers to think of the form as less ephemeral – something solid, and with a genealogy and traditions of its own. Particularly significant in this early phase of canon formation was Anna Laetitia Barbauld's *British Novelists* (1810). Issued in fifty volumes by a conger of booksellers, who banded together to spread the costs and the risk, the collection went farther than any other – in its comprehensive attention to the generic integrity of modern fiction, in its presentation of the novel in nationalist, war-time terms, and in its critical observations on women as writers and consumers. The chosen works of each novelist are prefaced by a biographical and critical introduction and the whole collection is fronted by an essay 'On the Origin and Progress of Novel-Writing'. Barbauld's survey follows a characteristic enlightenment trajectory, one employed by Warton, Beattie, and Hurd in their earlier literary histories of vernacular poetry and romance, where 'progress' is discernible as a shedding of non-native (typically oriental and European) superstition, fantasy, and improbability, in a steady march towards a superior and exclusive native manufacture. According to Barbauld, the novel emerges from eastern origins, through medieval European romance, to its highest evolution as a substantial British work of moral instruction, in which 'the interest, even of the generality of readers, is most strongly excited when some serious end is kept in view'.[21] Her conviction of the value of fiction lies in its capacity to educate and to represent reality, and in its cultivation of the domestic imagination. In all these, she maintains, the modern female novelist reigns supreme – Burney and Edgeworth receive high praise, and of the twenty-one British novelists represented, eight are women.

Published on the eve of her professional career, *British Novelists* did not prescribe how Austen would write, but it is fair to say that the collection provides a history and textual authority for the novels she does write and publish at this time. Over the next decade, in a critical ghosting of that career, the special business of the novel will be defined more precisely than before as the delineation and exploration of the ordinary. Such ordinariness amounted to a recalibration of the standard for seriousness and truth to life that the novel had earlier achieved in the hands of Richardson, who now seemed to many readers merely contrived. For Hazlitt in 1815 there is 'an artificial reality about [Richardson's] works'; 'he does not appear to have taken advantage of any thing in actual nature.' Despite this, 'standard novels and romances' have the power, unlike poetry, 'to examine the very web and texture of society, as it really exists, and as we meet with it when we come into the world'. In reading them we 'have our moral impressions far more frequently called out, and our moral judgements exercised, than in the busiest career of existence'.[22] The contemporary novel has a new role in explaining reality. Hazlitt's praise for this modern discourse of morality includes by implication Austen's critical fictions, with their basis in probable psychology and motive.

NOTES

1. In B. C. Southam (ed.), *Jane Austen: The Critical Heritage*, 2 vols. (London: Routledge, 1968–87), II: 292 and 240.

2. In Southam (ed.), *Jane Austen: The Critical Heritage*, II: 47.
3. Henry Austen, 'Biographical Notice of the Author', in R. W. Chapman (ed.), *The Novels of Jane Austen*, 3rd edn, 5 vols. (Oxford: Oxford University Press, 1965–6), V: 7–8. All subsequent references to Austen's novels will be to this standard edition and included in the body of the text.
4. Extracted in Southam (ed.), *Jane Austen: The Critical Heritage*, I: 65 and 68.
5. A. C. Bradley, in Southam (ed.), *Jane Austen: The Critical Heritage*, II: 235.
6. Claudia Johnson, *Jane Austen: Women, Politics, and the Novel* (Chicago: University of Chicago Press, 1988), pp. xxiv–xxv.
7. Peter Garside, 'The English Novel in the Romantic Era: Consolidation and Dispersal', in Peter Garside, James Raven, and Rainer Schöwerling (eds.), *The English Novel 1770–1829: A Bibliographical Survey of Prose Fiction Published in the British Isles*, 2 vols. (Oxford: Oxford University Press, 2000), II: 72–6.
8. Deirdre Le Faye (ed.), *Jane Austen's Letters*, 3rd edn (Oxford: Oxford University Press, 1995), p. 26.
9. James Edward Austen-Leigh, *A Memoir of Jane Austen and Other Family Recollections*, ed. Kathryn Sutherland (Oxford: Oxford University Press, 2002), p. 71.
10. Ibid., p. 105.
11. 'Henry and Eliza', in Jane Austen, *Minor Works*, ed. R. W. Chapman, rev. B. C. Southam (Oxford: Oxford University Press, 1972), p. 34.
12. Mary Wollstonecraft, *Maria, or The Wrongs of Woman*, ed. Moira Ferguson (New York: Norton, 1975), p. 142.
13. In Southam (ed.), *Jane Austen: The Critical Heritage*, I: 63.
14. Samuel Taylor Coleridge, *Table Talk*, ed. Carl Woodring, 2 vols. (Princeton: Princeton University Press, 1990), II: 80 n.
15. Samuel Taylor Coleridge, *Lectures 1808–1819 on Literature*, ed. R. A. Foakes, (Princeton: Princeton University Press, 1987), p. 193.
16. David Gilson, *A Bibliography of Jane Austen*, corrected edn (Winchester: St Paul's Bibliographies, 1997), p. 60.
17. Mary Brunton, *Self-Control* (London: Pandora Press, 1986), p. 140.
18. 'Preface' (1800) to *Lyrical Ballads*, in *The Prose Works of William Wordsworth*, ed. W. J. B. Owen and Jane Worthington Smyser, 3 vols. (Oxford: Clarendon Press, 1974), I: 128.
19. W. J. Harvey, 'The Plot of *Emma*', *Essays in Criticism* 17 (1967), 55.
20. W. E. K. Anderson (ed.), *The Journal of Sir Walter Scott* (Oxford: Clarendon Press, 1972), p. 114.
21. Anna Laetitia Barbauld, 'On the Origin and Progress of Novel-Writing', in *The British Novelists*, 50 vols. (1810; new edition, 1820), I: 57.
22. 'Standard Novels and Romances' (*Edinburgh Review*, February 1815), in *The Complete Works of William Hazlitt*, ed. P. P. Howe, 18 vols. (London: J. M. Dent, 1930–33), XVI: 15–16 and 5.

FURTHER READING

Butler, Marilyn, *Jane Austen and the War of Ideas*, 2nd edn, Oxford: Clarendon Press, 1987.
Copeland, Edward, and Juliet McMaster (eds.), *The Cambridge Companion to Jane Austen*, Cambridge: Cambridge University Press, 1997.

Duckworth, Alistair M., *The Improvement of the Estate: A Study of Jane Austen's Novels*, 2nd edn, Baltimore: Johns Hopkins University Press, 1994.

Fergus, Jan, *Jane Austen: A Literary Life*, Basingstoke: Macmillan, 1991.

Grey, J. David (ed.), *Jane Austen's Beginnings: The Juvenilia and Lady Susan*, Ann Arbor: UMI Research Press, 1989.

Johnson, Claudia L., *Jane Austen: Women, Politics, and the Novel*, Chicago: University of Chicago Press, 1989.

Kelly, Gary, *English Fiction of the Romantic Period, 1789–1830*, London: Longman, 1989.

Lascelles, Mary, *Jane Austen and Her Art*, Oxford: Clarendon Press, 1939.

Lynch, Deidre (ed.), *Janeites: Austen's Disciples and Devotees*, Princeton, NJ: Princeton University Press, 2000.

Park, You-me, and Rajeswari Sunder Rajan (eds.), *The Postcolonial Jane Austen*, London: Routledge, 2000.

Sales, Roger, *Jane Austen and Representations of Regency England*, London and New York: Routledge, 1994.

Tanner, Tony, *Jane Austen*, Basingstoke: Macmillan, 1986.

Todd, Janet (ed.), *Jane Austen: New Perspectives* (Women and Literature, NS 3), New York: Holmes and Meier, 1983.

Tuite, Clara, *Romantic Austen: Sexual Politics and the Literary Canon*, Cambridge: Cambridge University Press, 2002.

Waldron, Mary, *Jane Austen and the Fiction of her Time*, Cambridge: Cambridge University Press, 1999.

Wiltshire, John, *Recreating Jane Austen*, Cambridge: Cambridge University Press, 2001.

15

GREG KUCICH

Keats, Shelley, Byron, and the Hunt circle

One of the longstanding stereotypes of British Romanticism features the Romantic poet as a solitary genius, an outcast bard like Blake's Rintrah in *The Marriage of Heaven and Hell*, either communing with Nature in sublime isolation or delving into the inner reaches of the imagination for visionary prophecies of a new millennial order. Exemplified in the vatic utterances of Wordsworth's 'Prospectus' to *The Recluse* (a fragment first published in his 1814 preface to *The Excursion*), this model of the Romantic poet gained widespread prevalence through M. H. Abrams's landmark study *Natural Supernaturalism*.[1] However, more recent scholarship on Romanticism, much of which attends more closely to the social contexts of literary experience, places new emphasis on the group interactions and collaborative dynamics that generated a significant amount of the era's major poetry. Jack Stillinger, for instance, qualifies the Romantic 'myth of solitary genius' in his important analyses of the 'multiple consciousnesses' in Wordsworth's *Prelude* and the various 'helpers' involved in the production of Keats's *Isabella* (1818).[2] Such approaches to collective endeavour can run the risk of promoting reductive versions of the conventional division of Romanticism into two generations, usually defined by way of contrasts between distinctive groups: the Lake poets Wordsworth, Coleridge, and Southey, versus the younger London writers Hunt, Keats, Shelley, and Byron. That paradigm, though still useful, remains limited: some writers, like Charles Lamb, enjoyed strong ties with members of both generations; Blake, in particular, but also most women writers, do not fit the chronological or ideological contours of either group; significant aesthetic divergences, such as Byron's scorn for Keats's disapproval of Pope, qualify the internal coherence of both generational bodies.[3] Nevertheless, the increasing attentiveness to social contexts in recent studies of Romanticism, particularly of the Hunt circle, has opened up rewarding new ways to comprehend the period's second-generation writers in terms of a series of creative interactions with one another informed by specific socio-political circumstances.[4]

Although the younger Romantics did not necessarily shun solitary composition – Keats, for instance, did leave his circle in London to be alone on the Isle of Wight when he took on the challenge of writing *Endymion* (1818) – a brief survey of their reading and writing practices shows that collaboration and group encounters played a central role in their creative acts. Byron read Hunt's *The Story of Rimini* (1816) in manuscript and offered stylistic corrections. Hunt did the same for Keats's efforts to imitate *Rimini* in 'Specimen of an Induction to a Poem' and 'Calidore'. Keats and Hunt co-authored an essay for Hunt's periodical *The Indicator,* titled 'A Now', which draws on the imagery of Keats's ode 'To Autumn' as well as the language from his Byronic parody 'The Jealousies'.[5] Keats also teamed up with his friend Charles Brown in 1819 to produce a tragedy, *Otho the Great.* Shelley's conversations with Byron about Wordsworth's merits directly inspired the sublime nature scenes of *Childe Harold's Pilgrimage*, Canto III (1816). Two years later, Shelley chronicled in *Julian and Maddalo* the complicated history of his intellectual exchanges with Byron. Shelley's epic poem of 1817, originally titled *Laon and Cythna*, underwent a revision by committee (including Mary Shelley, Claire Clairmont, Charles Ollier, Thomas Love Peacock, and Thomas Jefferson Hogg) in order to produce a less radical version entitled *The Revolt of Islam.* Shelley also worked together with Mary Shelley on the travel narrative *History of a Six Weeks' Tour* (1817), the mythological plays *Proserpine* and *Midas* (1820); and the production of a preface and final text for *Frankenstein* (1818). Hunt at one time or another collaborated with nearly every major figure of second-generation Romanticism, through his periodical ventures, the *Examiner*, the *Reflector*, the *Indicator*, and the *Liberal*, the last of which he produced in Pisa with Byron and Mary Shelley. He also staged poetry-writing contests among the members of his circle and took the lead in a coterie practice indulged in frequently by them all, exchanging and annotating each other's books.

Scholars of second-generation Romanticism have focused on many of these discrete scenes of collective literary experience, particularly the dynamic between Mary Shelley and Percy Shelley, the interactions between Byron and Shelley, and the convergences and tensions between Keats and Shelley. Within the last several years, however, Hunt has attracted growing critical interest for his magnetic ability to bring together such a disparate array of personalities and talents. It has been persuasively argued, in fact, that Hunt's circle, in its various print forms and social locations, provided one of the most important cultural environments, if not a kind of central training ground, for the artistic development of second-generation Romanticism.[6] Hunt's so-called 'Cockney School' was not a formal association with a clearly established set of principles; and there were pronounced tensions, different aesthetic investments, and shifting alliances among its members. Keats, an early devotee to Hunt, would grow more distant, though the split between them has been exaggerated; Byron and Hunt, once close in London, fell out much to Hunt's embitterment when thrust upon each other in Italy. Nevertheless, a number of shared political and literary priorities emerged within the Hunt circle, which helped condition the writings of the individual poets in significant ways. Rather than viewing Hunt as the dominant influence on such complex and very different writers, we can view the circle he mobilized as the common ground where they shared and experimented with political values and literary practices to form a crucial foundation from which their distinctive literary trajectories developed. The history of Keats, Shelley Byron, and Hunt in the Cockney School can thus reveal how a number of the major concerns of second-generation Romanticism evolved, particularly regarding the political functions of literature, a topic which remains today one of the more intensely contested areas of debate among scholars of the period.

Several years older than most of the other writers of this generation, Hunt became a lion of the intellectual left just as his younger peers were entering the literary scene. He had gained notoriety as both a poet and as the radical editor of the *Examiner*, relentlessly battering away at government corruption and injustice until he was finally imprisoned in 1813 for his blistering criticism of George, the Prince Regent. Sentenced to two years in gaol, Hunt did not acquiesce passively. Instead he transformed his prison cell into a magical bower of aesthetic bliss decorated with wall paper of trellised roses; a sky-blue painted ceiling dotted with meandering clouds; Venetian blinds over the barred windows; a lute, a piano forte, busts of poets, bookcases, couches, and ubiquitous flowers. 'There was no other such room', Lamb declared, 'except in a fairy tale.'[7] This astonishing scene became an irresistible attraction for liberal writers and politicians, a kind of outrageous salon that drew such prominent figures as Bentham, Brougham, Godwin, Byron, Haydon, Hazlitt, Moore, Edgeworth, the Lambs, John Scott, and Sir John Swinburne, along with an unending procession of friends and relatives. They dined, drank, performed concerts, recited poetry, all in a flamboyant display of insolence toward state authority. Hunt's impertinence continued in print as well, for he kept producing *Examiner* critiques of government and controversial poems like *The Descent of Liberty* (1815) while also working on the scandalous *Story of Rimini*, which retells Dante's episode of the illicit love of Paolo and Francesca in a way that endorses social rebellion, erotic love, and incest. This improbable haven of radical politics, transgressive

aesthetics, and incorrigible sociality, thriving within the very center of institutional constraint, established the foundations of what later became known
as the upstart Cockney school of politics and poetry.

Several months after his release from the dungeon salon in February 1815,
Hunt transported its subversive environment to the cottage in Hampstead,
where he took up residence in October (a blue plaque now marks the site).
Here, amid the same aesthetic objects that graced the dungeon, the literary
and musical soirées revived and expanded into picnics on Hampstead Heath.
Although some critics have seen Hunt grow more quiescent politically at this
moment, the aesthetic and political radicalism of the prison years actually
flourished anew in the pages of the *Examiner* and with the publication of
Rimini (1816). The circle from the prison salon also expanded considerably
to include Keats, the Shelleys, John Hamilton Reynolds, Horace Smith, the
musician Vincent Novello, and the comic actor Charles Mathews, among
many others. Considering those who were connected to the Hampstead
group through its various offshoots – such as the Shelley-Byron entourage in
Geneva; the party gathered around the Shelleys at Marlowe, which included
Peacock and Hogg; the Pisa setting where the group eventually reconvened
to produce the *Liberal* – the Hunt circle emerged as a pivotal centre bringing
together most of the major writers of second-generation Romanticism. The
Examiner, moreover, became the print vehicle for this community of writers, regularly featuring their work (Keats's first publication, 'O Solitude! if I
must with thee dwell', appeared here, as did poems by Shelley and Byron
of this period) and announcing their advent as a new school of poets in
Hunt's famous 'Young Poets' review of Keats, Shelley, and Reynolds (*Selected
Writings*, II: 72–5).

Many took notice, including conservative periodical writers appalled by
the diabolical blend of Jacobinism, radical aesthetic experimentation, and
erotic license promulgated in Hunt circle writings. In October 1817 *Blackwood's Edinburgh Magazine* launched its notorious series of attacks, 'On
the Cockney School of Poetry' (written by John Gibson Lockhart under the
signature of 'Z'), exploiting Hunt's London background and lack of university training to condemn the group as a motley crew of lower-class, vulgar, immoral, and seditious Cockney outcasts.[8] The Cockney label, though
far from accurate given Hunt's professional class standing and education
at Christ's Hospital School, was actually incited by Hunt, who deliberately adopted Cockney personae and Cockney phrasings in his poetry and
journalism in order to destabilize conventional aesthetic and social standards. The circle, itself, actively manifested such subversions through its
gender and class inclusiveness, which figured forth, albeit not without fric-
tion, a kind of new egalitarian community. Many talented women actively

participated – Mary Shelley, Mary Lamb, Claire Clairmont, Mary Sabillia Novello, Marianne Hunt (Hunt's wife), and her sister Elizabeth Kent – and principal group members represented a wide range of class identities, such as the aristocratic Shelley and the middle-class Keats. Proud of this brilliant, new society and its ability to disconcert established political, literary, and social institutions, Hunt would celebrate years later his membership in the 'illustrious . . . Cockney school of poetry' (*Autobiography*, p. 414).

How much involvement in this community meant to the younger poets of the second generation is registered in the zeal of their initial attraction to it and the great pleasure they took in memorializing its activities in their verse. Byron acknowledged that Hunt's first volume of poetry, *Juvenilia* (1801), had inspired him at Harrow to try his hand at poetry (Hunt, *Autobiography*, p. 314), and he trekked to visit 'the wit in the dungeon' (Byron, *Letters and Journals*, III: 49) with obvious enthusiasm. In 1815 he pored over the manuscript of *Rimini*, which Hunt dedicated to him, and later expressed gratitude that Hunt was one of the few public men to defend him when he separated from his wife amid scandal and left England for the continent early in 1816. (He would never return and thus did not take part physically in the events Hunt hosted in Hampstead.) Shelley first communicated with Hunt through a letter to gaol offering financial assistance, which Hunt diplomatically refused. When Shelley returned from Geneva to England in 1816, he actively sought out Hunt's company at Hampstead. The next year he brought the Hunt family to live with him at Marlowe. Later, he would dedicate *The Cenci* (1820) to Hunt, declaring himself 'Your affectionate friend', and arranged for the Hunt family to join him in Italy.[9] Keats eagerly read the *Examiner* at Enfield School, pumped his friend, the headmaster's son Charles Cowden Clarke, for details of his visits to Hunt in prison, and wrote early poems in honour of Hunt. Having nicknamed Hunt 'Libertas' ('To Charles Cowden Clarke') in recognition of his principled stand against state injustice, and after imitating *Rimini* in 'Specimen' and 'Calidore', Keats finally exclaimed when Clarke arranged an introduction: 'seeing Mr Hunt . . . will be an Era in my existence'.[10]

Keats and Shelley celebrated in verse their experiences at the Hampstead cottage, both in the immediacy of the moment, as recorded by Keats in 'Sleep and Poetry' (1817) when spending the night there – 'a poet's house who keeps the keys / Of pleasure's temple' (lines 454–5) – and for years afterward, as Shelley recalled the same location in his *Letter to Maria Gisborne* (1820) – 'his room . . . adorned . . . With graceful flowers tastefully placed about; / And coronals of bay from ribbons hung' (lines 212–15). Shelley finally issued the most memorable portrait of the key canonical figures associated with the Hunt circle in his famous elegy on Keats, *Adonais* (1821), which transplants those spirited Cockney gatherings into allegorical space with Byron, as 'The Pilgrim of Eternity' (line 266), Hunt as 'the gentlest of the wise' (line 312), and himself, as 'a Power / Girt round with weakness' (lines 281–2), all gathering both to mourn Keats and to stake their allegiance with him among a higher coterie of time's immortal poets.

To comprehend precisely why this generation of poets so valued their experience in Hunt's 'temple' and carried shared memories of it throughout their careers, we must go back to the origins of the Cockney school and its founding priorities in Hunt's cell. The immediate circumstance of Hunt's incarceration was his indignant response to a sycophantic burst of adoration for the Prince Regent in the 19 March 1812 issue of the pro-government newspaper the *Morning Post*: 'You are the glory of the People . . . you conquer all hearts, wipe away tears, excite desire and love, and win beauty towards you – You breathe eloquence – You inspire the Graces – You are an Adonis in loveliness!'[11] Incensed by this fulsome hagiography for a notoriously self-indulgent, untrustworthy libertine, Hunt lashed out in the *Examiner*:

> What person, unacquainted with the true state of the case, would imagine, in reading these astounding eulogies, that this *Glory of the People* was the subject of millions of shrugs and reproaches! . . . That this *Conqueror of Hearts* was the disappointer of hopes! That this *Exciter of Desire* . . . this *Adonis in Loveliness*, was a corpulent gentleman of fifty! In short, that this *delightful, blissful, wise, pleasurable, honourable, virtuous, true*, and *immortal* PRINCE, was a violator of his word, a libertine over head and ears in debt and disgrace, a despiser of domestic ties, the companion of gamblers and demireps, a man who has just closed half a century without one single claim on the gratitude of his country or the respect of posterity! *(Selected Writings*, I: 221)

It was the extremity of this diatribe that enabled the government, after several previous failed attempts at prosecuting the *Examiner*, to win a case of political libel that landed Hunt in gaol.

The most significant feature of this episode, in relation to Hunt's impact on the younger writers of the second generation, lies with the intense sense of betrayal that spurred his tirade. His *Examiner* writings frequently seethed with indignation against government corruption, but this level of personal invective grew unusually sharp because of the Regent's recent history of political backtracking on the liberal causes Hunt passionately endorsed, particularly Catholic Emancipation and parliamentary reform.[12] Before assuming the Regency in early 1811, when his father was declared mentally unfit to rule as king, George had backed the Whig opposition to government and the same liberal causes that Hunt supported. The Tory Prime Minister, Spenser Perceval, fully expected to be supplanted by a new liberal government. To the horrified astonishment of his former Whig associates, however, George chose to retain his father's Tory administration while abandoning his liberal friends. This political turnaround was cemented when George came into his full powers early in 1812 and confirmed his repudiation of reform by maintaining Perceval's Tory administration and policies. Having urged George against such a course of action for over a year in the pages of the *Examiner*, Hunt's experience of betrayal ran deep. It was heightened, moreover, by the specific occasion behind the *Morning Post* article, a London gathering of Irish politicians in celebration of St Patrick's Day at which George received mixed reactions in the traditional toast. The eulogies of the *Post* came in direct reply to that ambiguous reception, which, given George's backtracking on Irish rights as well as other liberal causes, seemed egregiously hypocritical to Hunt. It was political apostasy, then, at the highest levels of government that triggered the extremity of his attack on the Regent and loomed as the dominant factor in his incarceration.

This experience of political betrayal, and the resulting alienation from government, took on increasing intensity throughout Hunt's prison years and profoundly affected his views of the relationship between literature and politics. In May of 1812, several months before Hunt's trial, Perceval was assassinated by a bankrupt merchant embittered over his harsh economic policies. George then appointed an even more staunchly conservative administration – headed by Liverpool as Prime Minister, Castlereagh as Foreign Minister, and Sidmouth as Home Secretary – which would solidify conservative rule throughout the remainder of the Romantic period. This administration worked tirelessly to close down radical print culture and reform movements through aggressive legislation such as the suspension of Habeas Corpus and the Gagging Acts of 1817, and through the kind of state violence against citizen protesters that became infamous at the Peterloo Massacre of 1819, when the mounted yeomanry of Manchester attacked a peaceful protest gathering at St Peter's Field, killing eleven and wounding hundreds of civilians.

The shadow of such an organized backlash against the reform politics Hunt espoused actually spread throughout Europe during his prison years. When Napoleon abdicated, first in 1814, and then after his brief return to power and final defeat at Waterloo in 1815, the victorious European powers – Britain, Austria, Prussia, and Russia – initially promised a new dawn of global freedom and the encouragement of national liberation movements that had developed in the wake of the Napoleonic wars, especially in the Italian provinces rebelling against Austrian occupation. Instead, the Allied Powers who redrew the map of Europe at the Congress of Vienna in 1814–15 repudiated national independence movements throughout Europe and restored the old despotic regimes of monarchial absolutism that had ruled before the French Revolution. A hypocritical 'Holy Alliance' of Russia, Austria, and Prussia exploited Christianity as an ideological weapon for consolidating government tyranny. Hunt learned about most of these dispiriting betrayals in his cell and reviled them in the pages of the *Examiner* (*Selected Writings*, I: 329–36).

His experience of political apostasy escalated to a new level, deeply affecting his views of literature's role in the current European crisis, when Southey and Wordsworth assumed government positions in 1813–14 and brought the weight of their cultural power as leading poets into the services of what Hunt viewed as state despotism. After the death of poet laureate Henry Pye in August 1813, Southey accepted the laureateship, a paid government position, and eventually began producing panegyrics on leading government figures, policies, and military triumphs, most notably his *Carmen Triumphale, For the Commencement of the Year 1814*. Wordsworth followed a somewhat less publicly visible but similar track in accepting a government position as Distributor of Stamps for Westmorland in 1813 and began issuing his own poetry in celebration of England's European victories, particularly his Waterloo sonnets of 1816 and his controversial *Ode: 1815*, which in the original version allegorically figures the 'Carnage' on the field of Waterloo as the 'daughter' of God.

Hunt fired numerous *Examiner* broadsides against these publications, and the political reversals they confirmed, attacking Southey 'for apostasy' and 'plung[ing] into the very thick of . . . corruption', and Wordsworth for consenting to become 'a pathetic court poet' (*Selected Writings*, I: 297 and II: 207). The maddening repetition in these lapses of the widespread political apostasy Hunt had been lamenting since 1812 explains why he sustained his rage at Southey and Wordsworth for years, mocking Southey as 'Robert Southey, Esq. P. L.' (meaning '*Precious Looby*') in an 1819 *Examiner* review castigating Wordsworth's *Peter Bell* (*Selected Writings*, II: 189). Hunt's bitter recognition of the insidious collaboration here between poetry and oppressive state power would inspire him to formulate various types of resistance, including the radical aestheticism of his prison antics. However, the powerful collusion between poetical reaction and political tyranny, whose iron grip he experienced along his own pulses in jail, could also leave him feeling severely alienated from cultural as well as political life. Several months after his release from prison, and just as he was meeting with Byron and beginning to establish the new circle at Hampstead, he commenced a lengthy series of *Examiner* articles entitled 'Gloomy State of Things in France' that ran until the spring of 1816.

It would be an exaggeration to claim that Hunt's influence alone conditioned a deep sense of cultural alienation among the younger second-generation poets; gloominess was shared by many liberals in 1815, and Byron had already produced the first two cantos of his tale of alienated wandering, *Childe Harold's Pilgrimage*. Still, the impact of this dimension of Hunt's writing during the prison years can be traced throughout the younger poets' works of 1815–17. Despite the sprightly rhythms, rural beauties, and consoling pathos of *Rimini*, Hunt's narrative sadly emphasizes the tragic deaths of two incestuous lovers betrayed by their avaricious parents and destroyed by oppressive legal and social codes beyond their control. Its medieval context thus disturbingly approximates the 'Gloomy State' of apostasy and repression throughout contemporary Europe in a symbolic pattern adapted throughout the works of the younger second-generation poets around this time. Keats's brief imitations of *Rimini* in 'Specimen' and 'Calidore' are much more upbeat, yet even they contain unsettling traces of grisly power – 'bloody field', 'proud [and] lonely turret', 'threatening portcullis', 'dismay and terror and alarm' ('Specimen', line 40; 'Calidore', lines 38–9, 79, 145) – which recur more prominently throughout the early poems: the 'sceptred tyrants' of 'On Peace' (line 10); the 'Minion of grandeur' and 'wretched crew' of 'Written on the Day that Mr Leigh Hunt Left Prison' (lines 5, 14); the 'foulest shame' of 'Infatuate Britons' in 'Lines Written on 29 May, the Anniversary of Charles's Restoration' (lines 1–2); the 'startle[d] princes' of 'To My Brother George' (line 76); the Polish patriot Kosciusko's 'horrid suffrance' in 'Sleep and Poetry' (line 388); the '*gloominess*' (my italics) and 'dreadful cares' engendered by religious superstition in 'Written in Disgust of Vulgar Superstition' (line 3).

When Keats advanced beyond these shorter efforts in 1817 with his first major poem, *Endymion*, even though he self-consciously aimed for independence from Hunt by this stage, he still followed the narrative and ideological patterns of cultural dislocation in *Rimini*. *Endymion*, though set in a mythological landscape quite different from the chivalric ambience of Hunt's poem, tracks a related history of separated lovers and social alienation, punctuated by such authorial pronouncements as the condemnation of 'thrones', 'crowns', and 'empurpled vests', 'belabour'd drums' and 'sudden cannon' wreaking their havoc upon the 'blear-eyed nations' (iii.11–18). Shelley's epic venture of the same year, parts of which were written in the company of Hunt at Marlowe, adopts a different allegorical register for a similar political history. *The Revolt of Islam* opens with a preface echoing Hunt's *Examiner* writings of 1814–17 on the failures of the French Revolution, the revival of old despotisms throughout Europe, and the 'infectious gloom' shadowing the nations.[13] The epic initially presents a narrator despondent over the 'trampled' hopes of France (line 127) and then moves into an allegorical history of two lovers (incestuous siblings in the original version of the poem) who are divided by political tyranny. Their wanderings, joyous reunion, eventual betrayal and execution by the agents of a resurgent despotism present a story like the tale of Paolo and Francesca that even more vividly depicts the gloomy state of post-Waterloo Europe. Byron's verse drama of 1816, *Manfred*, frequently read as a mental drama of the poet's own tortured psyche, offers yet another formulation of this political outlook. Here, again, we find a narrative of social alienation and incestuous lovers torn apart, which is also set within a metaphorical landscape pointedly associated with the recent political betrayals of reactionary Europe. Thus pronounces the figure of Nemesis: 'I was detain'd repairing shattered thrones, / Marrying fools, restoring dynasties . . .'[14]

If the younger poets of the second generation shared with Hunt this spirit of alienation in a bleak time, they also partook of the Cockney school's defiance toward authority and its vigorous commitment to social transformation. Hunt's relentless forays against Southey and his more nuanced critiques of Wordsworth offered important models for their own forms of resistance. High-spirited mockery of Southey in the *Examiner's* demolition of *Carmen Triumphale* begins with a parodic invocation – 'Robert Southey, Esquire, Poet Laureat, (alas, for plain ROBERT!) has published his Ode for the New Year, – and such an Ode!' (*Selected Writings*, I: 310) – that anticipates Byron's more well-known mock dedication of *Don Juan*: 'Bob Southey! You're a poet – poet Laureate, / And representative of all the race . . .' (lines 1–2). Hunt would also turn Southey's own voice against himself, by publishing in the *Examiner*, for instance, an early poem of Southey's repudiating '*Preferment's pleasant path*' at the very moment of his installation as poet laureate (*Selected Writings*, I: 296). And this, too, set an example for Byron, who published *The Vision of Judgment*, a brilliant parody of Southey's eulogy to King George III, *A Vision of Judgment*, in the first issue of the *Liberal* (1822).

Wordsworth came in for a different type of critique in Hunt's writings, which Keats and Shelley would extend. While Hunt pulled no punches in assailing the reactionary politics of the 'pathetic court poet', he retained high praise for Wordsworth's creative gifts as a poet of nature and the imagination, which he celebrated in *The Feast of the Poets* (1815 revised edition) and the Preface to *Foliage* (1818). Byron had little patience for such distinctions, emphatically rejecting Hunt's positive comments on Wordsworth (*Letters and Journals*, IV: 324–5 and VI: 46–7) and delivering rapier strikes against the Lake poet throughout *Don Juan*: 'We learn from Horace, Homer sometimes sleeps; / We feel without him: Wordsworth sometimes wakes . . .' (iii.873–4). Yet even Byron, influenced by the joint counsel of Hunt and Shelley, could recognize enough of value in Wordsworth to experiment with his mode of natural sublimity in Canto III of *Childe Harold's Pilgrimage*. The overall mixture of disdain, betrayal, and admiration in Hunt's ongoing response to Wordsworth comes closer to the ambivalent tone of Shelley's 1816 sonnet 'To Wordsworth'. That ambivalence also approximates the complex reactions of Keats, who ranked Wordsworth's *Excursion* as one of the 'three things to rejoice at in this Age' (*Letters*, 1: 203) in 1818 but lamented in the same year that 'Lord Wordsworth' had turned a Tory at last: 'Sad – sad – sad' (1: 299).

Along with the continuing sense that something of value could be salvaged from the ruinous apostasy of the first generation came a strong conviction in the Hunt circle that redemptive cultural and political transformations could still be effected, even in such an iron time of retrenchment. One of the most important ways of fighting the good fight against their time's decay involved social and imaginative acts that bodied forth, in the material human settings of the prison and Hampstead gatherings as well as in multiple poetic landscapes, a new society conditioned by political liberty for all, social equality across class and gender lines, erotic freedom from outworn moral and religious codes, and the replacement of 'sudden cannon' by the intellectually liberating powers of music, poetry, and the fine arts as the new driving forces of social organization. Besides creating the material environments for such a new society, Hunt also furnished a poetic model in *The Descent of Liberty*, composed in prison on the occasion of Napoleon's first abdication (April 1814). Imagining from behind bars the triumph of liberty throughout the world, Hunt concludes the masque with Liberty's ringing announcement of a cosmic transformation:

> All is finished. Now I rise
> Back to my wide-breathing skies,
> Where there is no hindering
> To the heart or to the wing;
> But the planets, round and free,
> Lapse about eternally,
> And the space through which they burn
> Fills a thrill at my return,
> And the never-tiring Joy,
> Rosy and heart-dancing boy,
> On continual errand runs
> In and out a thousand suns.
>
> (lines 744–54)

Readers of Shelley will be struck by the similarity of vision as well as poetic phrasing that informs Shelley's own masque of universal change in Act IV of *Prometheus Unbound*. Composed in 1819, it features such lyrical celebrations of cosmic joy as the Moon's love song to the Earth:

Thou art speeding round the Sun,
Brightest World of many a one,
Green and azure sphere, which shinest
With a light which is divinest
Among all the lamps of Heaven
To whom life and light is given;
I, thy chrystal paramour,
Borne beside thee by a power
Like the polar Paradise;
Magnet-like of lovers' eyes.

(iv.456–66)

Several years before Shelley composed these lines, he and Keats were both venturing out from the ideal sociality of the Hampstead gatherings to produce their own visions of social transformation and cosmic harmonies at the end of *The Revolt of Islam* and *Endymion*. Tracking the apocalyptic joy of *Prometheus Unbound* back through those works, the Hampstead foundation, and still earlier to *The Descent of Liberty* and Hunt's cell, shows how fruitfully both Keats and Shelley adapted and extended what they gained from the association. Such a lineage also shows how the most visionary of second-generation Romantic poems do not merely aspire to escapist fantasy, but rather emanate from material social conditions and strategic imaginative procedures for effecting political change in a gloomy world.

The most elaborate and controversial strategy toward this end involved the development in poetry of what we might call a Cockney aesthetics of insider insolence. Here again, the practice originated in prison, where Hunt cultivated that impertinent flamboyance within the confines of institutional power. The act of intruding on authority from within took on an aesthetic dimension when Hunt strategically fused high art – recitals of Mozart, readings of Ariosto and Spenser, celebrations of Milton – with his lowly dungeon setting and a self-conscious Cockney idiom deployed at the same time in the pages of the *Examiner*.[15] Hunt's aim was not so much to parody lofty poetic traditions, but rather to destabilize class and cultural hierarchies by flagrantly inserting an upstart Cockney presence into the most sacred bastions of art. This manoeuvre assumed its most substantial poetic formulation in *Rimini*. Into this serious tragedy based on the high traditions of Dante and medieval romance, Hunt strategically insinuates a series of impertinent Cockney phrasings: the bantering tone of what Z called 'a Cheapside shopkeeper'[16] in Hunt's quips about 'The two divinest things this world has got, / A lovely woman in a rural spot' and Francesca's having 'stout notions on the marrying score' (iii.557–8; ii.27); the cheeky vulgarity of dropping a 'g' in 'emerging' to make it rhyme with Virgin' (iii.498–9); and the propensity to rhyme words ending in long 'e', such as 'canopy', with long 'i' sounds, such as 'reply'. The socially destabilizing strategy of such infiltrations registered powerfully with conservative reviewers like Z, who condemned 'the spoken jargon of Cockneys' in Hunt's circle as one of the more dangerous cultural vehicles of the upsetting politics of Cockneyism.[17]

Keats was the immediate object of this indictment by Z, and he certainly went furthest among the younger poets in adapting the insolent Cockney politics of style. Considerable critical attention has focused in recent years on his incorporation of Cockney stylistics throughout his early poetry. Roe, tracing what he calls the 'insolent volubility of Keats's poetry', cites these jaunty rhymes in 'Sleep and Poetry': 'pleasant sonnet' / 'think upon it'; 'pleasant flow' / 'portfolio'.[18] William Keach shows how the breakdown of couplet barriers in Keats's early poetry, also learned from Hunt's precedent in *Rimini*, acts as a Cockney aesthetics of stylistic subversion that advances a parallel politics of reform seeking to undermine class and social divisions.[19] I have argued elsewhere for the infusion of Hunt's Cockney 'jargon' in Keats's later as well as early poetry, and Roe and Cox have pursued at greater length these intriguing signs of continuing Cockneyism throughout Keats's great poetic output of 1818–19, when he produced the works that placed him 'among the English Poets' (*Letters*, I: 394).[20] Similar arguments could be made for Shelley's 1819 satire on Wordsworth, *Peter Bell the Third*, which he sent to Hunt in England. His *Letter to Maria Gisborne* not only relishes the memory of Hampstead gatherings but also echoes the Cockney rhymes of *Rimini*: 'mince-pies' / 'luxuries' (lines 305–6). Even the quintessentially Byronic wizardry of rhyme in *Don Juan* probably owes a certain debt to those days working on the manuscript of Hunt's poem.

Locating the various inflections of Hunt circle practices in these later works will qualify scholarly arguments for the political withdrawal of second-generation poets and show, instead, how they integrated stylistic and political matters in their ongoing efforts to counter the reactionary backsliding of their day. Their multiple adaptations of Hunt's most sophisticated cultural theory about politics and literature offer the strongest signs of their abiding commitment, however many different forms it assumed, to that cause. From 1813, when Southey and Wordsworth publicly aligned literature with the force of political reaction, Hunt began assembling a counter-tradition of poets past and present, with Milton at the forefront, who stood for liberty (*Selected Writings*, I: 296–300). As government repression solidified during the ensuing years, and the likelihood of a change in Liverpool's aggressively conservative administration all but disappeared, it became clear to Hunt that reform would have to come through a change in public opinion engineered by the modern continuers of England's progressive literary traditions. If poetry like Southey's and Wordsworth's could bolster a retrograde government, a counter-poetics dedicated to imaginative empathy, social freedom, and political progress could advance the march of reform. Thus a new kind of culture war opened up, and opinion was the prize to be fought for on the battlefield of literary endeavour. Armed with that conviction, Hunt approached the writing, reviewing, and editing of literature as so many vital contributions, aided by the power of the printing press, to the cause of swaying opinion toward a progressive future. He remained optimistic, in the face of brutal government reaction, about the inexorable march of this intellectual progress, proclaiming in the *Examiner* in 1819 that the 'gigantic . . . sovran Lord' of knowledge 'has awaked for the first time in the known history of the world, and is stretching his earth-thrilling limbs from Caucasus to the Andes' (*Selected Writings*, II: 175).

The extent to which this notion informed Keats's major writings may be suggested by Hunt's own reading in the *Indicator* of *Hyperion* as a dramatic rendering of the intellectual progress of liberty (*Selected Writings*, II: 296–306), and by Keats's last known poetic composition, a revisionary Spenserian stanza that celebrates the power of Typographus, or poetry and the printing press, to strike down tyrannical authority. Writing in 1821, Shelley rather strikingly echoes Hunt's vision of an 'awakened' lord of knowledge in the famous conclusion to *A Defence of Poetry*, which celebrates the 'awakening' of 'the spirit of good' to advance inexorably and work a beneficial change in human society through the ministrations of 'Poetry'.[21] Shelley acted on his conviction of that power when he composed *The Mask of Anarchy* right after the Peterloo Massacre of 1819 and sent it to Hunt in hopes of swaying opinion toward a peaceful revolution by publishing it in the *Examiner*.[22] Byron, too, aspired to this form of impact when, just as Hunt joined him in Pisa in 1822, he committed *Don Juan* more directly to the cause of reform by switching to a liberal publisher (Hunt's brother, John) and issuing a Preface to Cantos VI–VIII denouncing Castlereagh and the Liverpool administration's foreign policy.

As a final measure of how much this and the other lessons they shared in the Hunt circle meant to the younger poets of second-generation Romanticism, some of the most poignant experiences of their final days revolved around their group activities. Keats stayed with Hunt near the end of his time in England, when dying of tuberculosis and planning a desperate trip to Italy in hopes of recovering his health. There, in the Hunt family home at Kentish Town, he resorted to an old habit from the days of Hampstead collaborations and marked in Charles Brown's copy of Spenser his favourite passages for his beloved Fanny Brawne (*Letters*, II: 302).[23] Shelley, soon after welcoming Hunt to Italy in 1822, drowned with Hunt's copy of Keats's 1820

Lamia volume open in his coat pocket. Byron's last significant collaborative project, before he set off for his ill-fated participation in the Greek war of independence, involved him with Hunt, Mary Shelley, and others from the old circle who contributed to the *Liberal*. Perhaps Hunt most eloquently summed up the significance of it all when years after Shelley's death he came across a passage in Shakespeare's *Richard II* (in a volume originally presented to him by Shelley as a 'Votive offering') that reminded him of a humorous escapade travelling with Shelley and, in good coterie fashion, annotated the text: 'Dear S'.[24]

NOTES

1. M. H. Abrams, *Natural Supernaturalism: Tradition and Revolution in Romantic Literature* (New York: Norton, 1971).
2. Jack Stillinger, *Multiple Authorship and the Myth of Solitary Genius* (New York: Oxford University Press, 1991).
3. *Byron's Letters and Journals*, ed. Leslie Marchand, 12 vols. (London: John Murray, 1973–82), VIII: 104.
4. See Nicholas Roe, *John Keats and the Culture of Dissent* (Oxford: Clarendon Press, 1997); Jeffrey N. Cox, *Poetry and Politics in the Cockney School: Keats, Shelley, Hunt, and Their Circle* (Cambridge: Cambridge University Press, 1998); Nicholas Roe (ed.), *Leigh Hunt: Life, Poetics, Politics* (London: Routledge, 2003).
5. *Indicator*, 28 June 1820; reprinted in *The Selected Writings of Leigh Hunt*, 6 vols. (London: Pickering and Chatto, 2003), Volumes I–II, ed. Jeffrey N. Cox and Greg Kucich, II: 268–72.
6. See Roe, *John Keats*, pp. 116–33, and 'Introduction' in *Leigh Hunt*, pp. 1–18; Cox, *Poetry and Politics*; also Cox and Kucich's 'Introduction' in *Selected Writings of Leigh Hunt*, I: xxi–xlv.
7. Hunt recalled this comment in *The Autobiography of Leigh Hunt* (London: Cresset Press, 1948), p. 243.
8. *Blackwood's* 'Cockney School' reviews went on for several years, and the label as a term of derision was picked up by other conservative periodical writers. For a selection from *Blackwood's* 'Cockney School' reviews, see Donald H. Reiman (ed.), *The Romantics Reviewed* (New York: Garland, 1972), part C, vol. I.
9. Shelley, 'Preface' to *The Cenci*, in *The Poems of Shelley*, ed. Kelvin Everest and Geoffrey Matthews, 2 vols. (London: Longman, 1989–2000), II: 726.
10. *The Letters of John Keats*, ed. Hyder Edward Rollins, 2 vols. (Cambridge, MA: Harvard University Press, 1958), I: 113.
11. *Morning Post*, 19 March 1812.
12. Hunt recalled in his *Autobiography* that one of 'the main objects of the Examiner newspaper [was] to assist in producing Reform in Parliament' (p. 175).
13. Not surprisingly, Hunt commends this Preface and quotes extensively from it in his review of Shelley's poem (*Selected Writings*, II: 154–6).
14. Byron, *Manfred*, II.iii.62–3, in *Complete Poetical Works*, ed. J. J. McGann, 12 vols. (Oxford: Clarendon Press, 1980–93), VI.

15. See Greg Kucich, '"The Wit in the Dungeon": Leigh Hunt and the Insolent Politics of Cockney Coteries', *European Romantic Review* 10 (1999), 242–53.

16. 'On the Cockney School of Poetry. No. I', *Blackwood's Edinburgh Magazine* (October 1817), 39.

17. 'On the Cockney School of Poetry. No. IV', *Blackwood's Edinburgh Magazine* (August 1818), 521.

18. Roe, *John Keats*, p. 13.

19. William Keach, 'Cockney Couplets: Keats and the Politics of Style', *Studies in Romanticism* 35 (1986), 182–96.

20. Greg Kucich, 'Cockney Chivalry: Hunt, Keats and the Aesthetics of Excess', in Roe (ed.), *Leigh Hunt*, ch. 7; see also Roe, *John Keats*; Cox, *Poetry and Politics*.

21. *Shelley's Poetry and Prose*, ed. Donald H. Reiman and Neil Fraistat (New York: Norton, 2002), p. 535.

22. Given the incendiary quality of Shelley's masque and the government's aggressive prosecution of radical journalists in the wake of Peterloo, Hunt felt publication in the *Examiner* to be too risky. He did not publish it until 1832.

23. For a discussion of these markings, see Greg Kucich, '"A Lamentable Lay": Keats and the Marking of Charles Brown's Spenser Volumes', *Keats–Shelley Review* 3 (1989), 1–22.

24. *Richard II*, III.ii.155–6. Hunt's annotated copy of *Richard II* is now in the Huntington Library. For details on the episode with Shelley, see *Letters*, I: 140, n.1.

FURTHER READING

Bate, Walter Jackson, *John Keats*, London: Chatto & Windus, 1979.

Bennett, Betty T. and Stuart Curran (eds.), *Mary Shelley in Her Times*, Baltimore: Johns Hopkins University Press, 2000.

Brewer, William D., *The Shelley–Byron Conversation*, Gainesville: University Press of Florida, 1994.

Chandler, James, *England in 1819: The Politics of Literary Culture and the Case of Romantic Historicism*, Chicago: University of Chicago Press, 1998.

Cox, Jeffrey N., *Poetry and Politics in the Cockney School: Keats, Shelley, Hunt and their Circle*, Cambridge: Cambridge University Press, 1998.

Curran, Stuart, *Shelley's Annus Mirabilis: The Maturing of an Epic Vision*, San Marino: Huntington Library, 1975.

Fogle, Richard Harter, *The Imagery of Keats and Shelley: A Comparative Study*, Chapel Hill: University of North Carolina Press, 1949.

Gilmartin, Kevin, *Print Politics: The Press and Radical Opposition in Early Nineteenth-Century England*, Cambridge: Cambridge University Press, 1996.

Holmes, Richard, *Shelley: The Pursuit*, London: Penguin, 1974.

Mahoney, Charles, *Romantics and Renegades: The Poetics of Political Reaction*, New York: Palgrave, 2003.

Marchand, Leslie A., *Byron: A Biography*, 3 vols., New York: Alfred A. Knopf, 1957.

McGann, Jerome J., *The Romantic Ideology: A Critical Investigation*, Chicago: University of Chicago Press, 1983.

Mellor, Anne K., *Mary Shelley: Her Life, Her Fiction, Her Monsters*, New York: Methuen, 1988.

Motion, Andrew, *Keats*, London: Faber and Faber, 1997.

Reiman, Donald H., *Shelley and his Circle, 1773–1822*, 10 vols., Cambridge, MA: Harvard University Press, 1961–2002.

Robinson, Charles E., *Shelley and Byron: The Snake and Eagle Wreathed in Flight*. Baltimore: Johns Hopkins University Press, 1976.

Roe, Nicholas, *John Keats and the Culture of Dissent*, Oxford: Clarendon Press, 1997.

(ed.), *Keats and History*, Cambridge: Cambridge University Press, 1995.

(ed.), *Leigh Hunt: Life, Poetics, Politics*, London: Routledge, 2003.

Rollins, Hyder Edward (ed.), *The Keats Circle*, 2 vols., Cambridge, MA: Harvard University Press, 1965.

Ryan, Robert M. and Ronald A. Sharp (eds.), *The Persistence of Poetry: Bicentennial Essays on Keats*, Amherst: University of Massachusetts Press, 1998.

Sperry, Stuart, *Keats the Poet*, Princeton: Princeton University Press, 1973.

Shelley's Major Verse: The Narrative and Dramatic Poetry, Cambridge, MA: Harvard University Press, 1988.

Stillinger, Jack, *Multiple Authorship and the Myth of Solitary Genius*, New York: Oxford University Press, 1991.

Wheatley, Kim, *Shelley and His Readers: Beyond Paranoid Politics*, Columbia: University of Missouri Press, 1999.

16

JOHN GOODRIDGE AND BRIDGET KEEGAN

Clare and the traditions of labouring-class verse

Like the thresher poet Stephen Duck a century earlier, John Clare (1793–1864) has always had a place in the literary histories, if only as a biographical footnote. Clare's confinement in the Northampton Asylum in 1841, and Duck's apparent suicide by drowning in 1756, helped to turn these authors, and many like them, into object lessons on the perils of a literary career for those from humble backgrounds. What the tendency to moralizing anecdote has obscured is that Duck and Clare were just two among more than a thousand poets from economically disadvantaged social backgrounds who wrote and published between 1700 and 1900. It is the purpose of this chapter to consider how Clare's poetry responds to the variety and complexity of a *tradition* of British labouring-class poetry. The sheer number of poets from labouring-class backgrounds, the common themes and styles evident in their verse, and their self-conscious response and resistance to trends within polite and popular poetry, demonstrate that these authors comprise a parallel tradition in British literature, one to which Clare is a significant and self-aware contributor.

Clare indeed is the crucial hinge between the labouring-class poetry of the eighteenth century and early Romantic period on one hand, and the later Chartist and Victorian working-class poetry on the other. His poetry might be read as both a culmination and a transformation in the tradition, responding to themes and issues from earlier labouring-class verse, but also introducing new topics or significantly altering the discourse devoted to familiar themes. Clare's writing, for example, embodies a poignant struggle to reconcile the two identities of village labourer and poet. The struggle between occupation or social station and vocation or aspiration is a key topic in the history of eighteenth-century plebeian poetry. As William Christmas writes, 'Clare's innovative, politicized, and radically self-reflexive poetry represents a potential end to [the history of plebeian poetic endeavour] as it also suggests a new beginning'.[1]

Clare also both responds to and resists the polite poetic discourses available to him, as many of his predecessors had done, drawing on mainstream eighteenth-century poems like Gray's *Elegy* or Pomfret's *The Choice*, but often transforming them to answer his own needs. In an early sonnet, for example, he turns Gray's famous 'Full many a flower is born to blush unseen / And waste its sweetness on the desert air' into something rather less passive:

> Full many a flower, too, wishing to be seen,
> Perks up its head the hiding grass between.[2]

Clare also shows his affinity with eighteenth-century poets from socially marginalized positions (such as Thomas Chatterton and the mariner poet William Falconer), and his responses often exhibit what Margaret Doody describes as the distinctive feature of eighteenth-century poetry overall, 'a *doubleness* that makes us hear two languages at work'. Doody notes that for three poets from the lower classes, Chatterton, Burns, and Falconer, as opposed to poets such as Pope, 'the move into other languages was made literally. The latter part of the eighteenth century saw the production of works which required glossaries to explain foreign or exotic words from another language or sub-language.'[3] Chatterton's pseudo-medieval 'Rowleyese', Falconer's nautical vocabulary, and Burns's Scots vernacular all required 'translations' – and they, like most editions of Clare's poetry from the earliest to the most recent, included glossaries.

Although Doody claims this double-voicedness for a majority of eighteenth-century poetry, it takes on particular characteristics for labouring-class poets, who were deemed most interesting when they wrote and spoke in 'other' languages. However, when plebeian poets attempted the refined idiom of polite poetry, they were implicitly speaking a tongue that was perceived as being foreign *to them*. A critical and linguistic double standard was at work, and the 'bilingual' aspect of labouring-class poetry was often a one-way street. For polite audiences, dialect poetry was 'interesting', whereas publishing poetry in polite idioms was presumptuous, or even politically suspect. Robert Southey lamented the 'almost inevitable' process whereby both Duck and the shoemaker poet James Woodhouse abandoned 'their own language' in favour of forming their style 'upon some approved model'.[4] Clare's first reviews – which rehearse much the same postures as those used towards Duck a century before, repeated for many others in the interim – often praise him for his quaintness, but tend to condemn anything that indicates aspirations beyond the linguistic reflection of 'rural simplicity'. His friend Octavius Gilchrist, for example, cautiously admits that it 'would be presumptuous' to 'pronounce that Clare's genius is not framed for sustained or lofty flights', but nevertheless confirms that what he has read of Clare supports this view, and moves rapidly on to praising the 'minute observation of nature, delicacy of feeling, and fidelity of description' – the fine particularity regularly imposed as the critical benchmark for Clare by his critics.[5]

Donna Landry has theorized the paradoxes of 'two languages' in relation to eighteenth-century plebeian women writers, and this may apply to labouring-class poets of both genders. For Landry, imitations of polite discourse were not primarily a way for poets to adopt pretensions, but also one of 'many forms of elaborately coded class opposition'. Building upon Doody, she identifies labouring-class impersonations as a kind of ventriloquism that repeats but simultaneously 'challenges the verse forms and values of mainstream culture', as 'a way of speaking out, and of altering social discourse'. This is 'ventriloquism with a subversive twist. It is as if the dummy did not merely serve to demonstrate the master's skill at speaking through another's body, but took on a life of its own, began to challenge the master by altering the master's texts.'[6]

Clare frequently attempts to draw together popular and literary discourse, taking the position of an oral bard and composer of popular ballads, as well as that of a refined poet of nature such as Thomson, and we can see in his poetic bilingualism a challenge to the notion that poets of particular classes can speak only in certain ways. Such a struggle is clear in Clare's vocational poem, 'The Village Minstrel' (1821). Although the 'Minstrel' identifies himself with a rural and predominantly oral, 'primitive' poetic tradition (Clare's first title for the poem was 'The Peasant Boy'), in the poem we see that Lubin (Clare's alter ego) is much less interested in the popular culture that surrounds him than in the more transcendent poetry of nature that belonged to Thomson and Wordsworth. Lubin's choice of the latter poetic, by the end of the poem, exposes him to the scorn of the polite world to which he attempts to attach himself. A similar story is offered in 'The Fate of Genius', a kind of coda to Gray's *Elegy*, in which the poet's choice is presented as literally fatal.[7]

It might be argued that Clare's cross-cultural trespassing, his refusal to be confined by his class to a particular idiom and his appropriation of the refined poetic discourse of the age on his own terms, is a form of what the post-colonial critic Homi Bhabha has defined as 'sly civility', the speech of the subaltern, always 'splitting, doubling, turning into its opposite'.[8] Subaltern 'sly civility' is a response to problems of address that are mirrored within Clare's poetry: to whom, and for whom, does the subaltern, or the labouring-class poet, speak? The duplicity of their discourse confirms that, as Bhabha puts it, 'two attitudes towards external reality persist; one takes reality into consideration while the other disavows it and replaces it by a product of desire that repeats, rearticulates "reality" as mimicry' (p. 91). Is it any surprise that Clare, like Chatterton before him, would compose literary 'forgeries'?[9] Clare's later adoption of the persona and even the identity of Lord Byron is an extreme response to the splitting of poetic identity, between peasant and poet, subject and subaltern, exemplified in a double-tongued discourse that is found throughout Clare's work and in the body of eighteenth-century plebeian poetry that precedes him.

The predominant themes and recurring forms of eighteenth-century labouring-class poetry offer a fertile background against which to understand Clare's works. These themes include the question of the nature of the poet (as a 'genius' who wrote effortlessly and 'naturally', or as an erudite, polished craftsperson); the role of religion, particularly Methodism, as a source of political empowerment as well as oppression; and a relationship to the natural world, informed at once by picturesque ideals and by first-hand practical interaction with land and water, flora and fauna. In all of these areas, labouring-class poets demonstrated that – all claims for 'natural genius' aside – their limited formal education by no means meant they were not each deeply steeped in literary tradition. Labouring-class poets maintained lively connections to popular, oral literary forms, as well as aspiring to broaden their understanding and command of polite conventions, and throughout the eighteenth and early nineteenth centuries exhibited a dual emphasis in the interplay of 'popular' and 'polite', 'rustic' and 'refined'. The doubleness is played out in form, language, and subject matter.

The first full-scale account of the English labouring-class poets, published in 1831 by Robert Southey, established Stephen Duck as a key figure in the history of the phenomenon. In 'The Thresher's Labour' (1730) Duck had used refined couplets to treat the subject of his rustic labour, embellishing his account of the threshers' attempts at oral songs with erudite allusions to classical mythology. His poetry remains an attractive starting place to discuss the tradition, since he exemplifies the dualities of labouring-class poetry clearly. However, Duck was by no means the first poet to make manual labour his poetic theme or to make a name for himself by calling attention to his humble origins. In the late seventeenth century, poets such as the bargeman John Taylor (discussed by Southey), or the shoemaker Richard Rigbey, published poetry announcing their labouring-class origins. Indeed two canonical poets of the early modern era have links to manual occupations: John Bunyan began as a tinker and Ben Jonson as a bricklayer. In the early eighteenth century, prior to Duck, the tavern-keeper Edward Ward and the Irish bricklayer Henry Nelson composed poetry in popular styles. Several anonymous poets in Dublin had regularly celebrated the feast days of their guild's patron saint in verse. Even the footman, Robert Dodsley, who went on to become the publisher for Duck and numerous other mid-eighteenth-century poets, had published his first poem, *Servitude*, in 1729.

Yet it was Duck's poem that captured the interest of a wide audience, and altered the critical discourse within which these poets were read. It attracted a spate of imitators (as well as parodists, such as the Irish poet, John Frizzle). Attracted by Duck's success, labouring-class poets like John Bancks and Robert Tatersal borrowed his formula to versify their respective occupations. The gardener Peter Aram and the servant Mary Masters published poems, and Dodsley was encouraged to bring out his collection, *The Muse in Livery*, in 1732. The best-known response to Duck for modern readers is Mary Collier's witty feminist response to 'The Thresher's Labour', *The Woman's Labour*, published in 1739.

After 1740 labouring-class poets less frequently made their primary occupations the focus of their poems, though some might allude to it alongside other themes. The georgic level of detail found in Duck and Collier was largely absent, and often the only mention made of a trade was on the title page or within prefaces or advertisements. Indeed, from the mid eighteenth century onwards, many labouring-class poets actively worked to erase their labouring identity from their publications. The Irish bricklayer poet Henry Jones, for example, one of the more prolific poets of this period, ceased to call himself a bricklayer in his published work soon after he moved to London in 1748 with the help of his patron Lord Chesterfield. For almost the last twenty years of his career, Jones would often excuse his efforts citing his poor education, but never again used the sobriquet 'The Bricklayer Poet'. Like Jones, Clare would rapidly regret marketing himself as a 'peasant poet', on seeing that the drawbacks outweighed the benefits, after his first collection was published in 1820.

From the mid eighteenth century, labouring-class poets appear to have shifted towards identifying their subject position as much from their impoverished formal education as their day job. Southey's term (used in his title), *The Uneducated Poets*, is interesting in this respect; and labouring-class poets have also often been termed 'self-taught' or 'autodidact' authors, and still are today. However, although these poets might marshal their lack of classical knowledge as a dodge against potentially harsh critics, it is wrong to assume that 'self-taught' indicates an absence of knowledge, classical or otherwise. That the poets got whatever poetic education they had by themselves invited patrons, readers, and often the poets themselves to see in their productions the product of 'natural' or 'original' genius. The notion that artistic talent derives from innate gifts is a theory at least as old as Plato, and the mid-eighteenth century witnessed a vogue for the philosophical and aesthetic concept of genius. The bibliography of eighteenth-century treatises and poems devoted to the topic is lengthy, but it is generally agreed that Addison's 1711 *Spectator* essay on 'Genius' is the earliest contribution, and one of the most influential. Addison is careful to distinguish between those geniuses who 'were never disciplined and broken by Rules of Art' and those 'that have formed themselves by Rules, and submitted the Greatness of their natural Talents to the Corrections and Restraints of Art';[10] and it was the former rather than the latter type which fascinated eighteenth-century readers and theorists. In the words of Mark Akenside, 'Nature's kindling breath / Must fire the chosen genius'.[11] By the mid century, treatises such as Edward Young's influential *Conjectures on Original Composition* (1759) had begun to privilege a genius untainted by the intervention of any education or training.

The search for natural genius also fired the patrons of many eighteenth-century labouring-class poets. Some, like the Oxford Professor of Poetry, Joseph Spence, roamed the countryside searching for untaught geniuses languishing in obscurity. Spence was among Duck's earliest promoters and later went on to write about and encourage Thomas Blacklock and James Woodhouse, among others. Betty Rizzo has suggested that the patrons most interested in labouring-class natural genius were often those who sought to gain from challenging the presumed polished Augustan standards of polite gentleman poets.[12] It is true that several middle-class women, with literary aspirations of their own, were instrumental in seeing labouring-class poets into print. Bridget Freemantle assisted Mary Leapor, and it was the self-made printer Samuel Richardson who helped to produce Leapor's second posthumous volume. Elizabeth Montagu hired James Woodhouse after his first patron, William Shenstone, died, and Montagu also later helped Hannah More in the latter's infamously ill-fated sponsorship of Ann Yearsley.

Yet it was not simply those who felt themselves to be outsiders in their own right who subscribed to or even more liberally supported the poetry of labouring-class authors. Members of the literary establishment also took an active interest in specimens of genius that they happened to encounter. Pope and Swift, despite their scathing dismissals of Duck's abilities, both subscribed to his 'official' 1736 debut collection. In the later eighteenth century, Joseph and Thomas Warton appear to have taken time off from creating the canon of English poetry, to support the likes of the soldier poet William Vernon and the shoemaker poet John Bennet. Reading the subscription lists from the myriad collections of labouring-class poetry of the eighteenth century offers insights into a far more subtle level of literary politics at work.

The fact that Poets Laureate and other leading cultural figures – like David Garrick or Edmund Burke – can be found on these subscription lists suggests that labouring-class poetic production may have been a less minor phenomenon than the literary histories have suggested.

Despite its potential promotional value, being identified as a 'natural' genius was clearly as much a curse as a blessing, not least because many of the poets were at great pains to demonstrate their hard-won talents. For many of them writing poetry was not effortless or easy, as the theory of natural genius would seem to suggest. The advertisements and prefaces introducing labouring-class collections very often stress the poets' pursuit of knowledge under difficulties. They have rather more in common with their Augustan predecessors than might be expected, in that many of them are intensely conscientious about explicitly demonstrating their familiarity with poetic traditions, both classical and English. Later in his career Stephen Duck developed his skills as a classicist; William Vernon carefully imitated Horace, albeit from translations; and many poets took pains to include allusions to classical mythology – from Duck and Collier, comparing their labours to those of Sisyphus and the daughters of Danae, to Anne Wilson making reference to Andromache in her poem on the river Tees (1778). Each successive lifetime edition of William Falconer's popular poem *The Shipwreck* (1762, 1764, 1769) is more overlaid than the last with recondite classical allusions. In terms of awareness of *neo*-classical poetry and poetics, the influence of Pope upon eighteenth-century labouring-class poets was extensive. Reverential invocations and imitations of Pope can be found, for example, in the works of Henry Jones, Mary Leapor, and the itinerant player and poet Cuthbert Shaw. The impact of Miltonic themes and verse forms is central too. Stephen Duck, as Spence characterized it, studied *Paradise Lost* 'as others study the Classics'.[13] John Bennet's long poem *Redemption* (1796) demonstrates Milton's centrality to religious themes in labouring-class poetry. Both Mary Leapor and the shoemaker poet N. Elliot invoke Butler's *Hudibras*, and the weaver poet Samuel Law modelled his poetry of natural description on Thomson. The shoemaker poet James Woodhouse enjoyed a close working relationship with William Shenstone at the start of his career. Another shoemaker, Joseph Blacket, made reference to the full canon of British poetry in his 'The Bards of Britain'.[14]

But despite the evidence of erudition in much labouring-class poetry, the myth of genius remained a powerful, if powerfully deceiving, rubric within which to read it. As part of this rubric, rural geniuses were frequently presented as solitary figures, and yet there is evidence that labouring-class poets often enjoyed convivial relations with and helped one another. Robert Dodsley was instrumental in publishing fellow labourer poets like James

Woodhouse; Stephen Duck went on to subscribe to Mary Leapor's poems. Several later poets invoked Duck in either cautionary or reverential terms, most famously George Crabbe, who, if not quite part of the tradition we are discussing here, was certainly to a large degree 'self-taught'. Cuthbert Shaw parodied Duck, Henry Jones, Robert Dodsley and Samuel Derrick in his Popean satire *The Race* (1766). James Maxwell joined many of his fellow weaver poets from Paisley in writing about Robert Burns (though he was one of the few who responded negatively to Burns's lifestyle). Indeed, labouring-class poets in the eighteenth century often demonstrated an awareness of each other in terms of the category of 'genius'. Gestures to Stephen Duck's unhappy end provide a good example. It would seem to have been almost a condition of genius that it carried with it both the promise of talent and of tragedy. The death of Chatterton, and the rapid mythologization of his supposed suicide at the age of seventeen (routinely blamed on that arbitrary literary power-broker Horace Walpole), showed that public interest in the idea of natural genius had not waned over the century. Clare was well aware of the power of this aesthetic concept, and sketched in one notebook a series of rustic memorial stones, bearing the names of Chatterton, Keats, Bloomfield, and himself.

Labouring-class poets like James Maxwell, and the shoemakers John Lucas and John Bennet, saw their poetic genius as a direct gift from God, viewing their creative urges in theological terms, and there are other important religious themes in labouring-class poetry. These have largely been ignored by modern critics, perhaps because the pious poetry produced by labouring-class poets appears to express a submissive acceptance of social realities, or even, in ways comparable to Hannah More's *Cheap Repository Tracts* of the 1790s, to enforce social subjugation repressively and actively. For a good deal of labouring-class religious poetry this view is not necessarily wrong. But it is an oversimplification that, along with the idea that religious verse is uninteresting, has tended to justify the wholesale dismissal of a large proportion of labouring-class poets' literary production. Surveying the collections of labouring-class poets from 1740 to 1830, it is rare to find one that does not include poems on pious topics. Several of the poets went on to become preachers or to fulfil other occupations within the Anglican or nonconformist churches. Thomas Olivers was a Methodist preacher and later an editor for Wesley's press, and N. Elliot was an 'Overseer for the Poor' at St Peter le Bailey in Oxford. Many shoemaker poets were also actively involved within non-conformist denominations.[15]

The influence of religion on labouring-class poetry is evident in terms not only of subject matter but also of preferred forms and genres. Labouring-class poets frequently versified scriptures, and composed hymns, prayers, and meditations. Religious books were of course more accessible to labouring-class authors than classical works, which may help explain this. While many poets had some access to classics in translation, it was more often *Paradise Lost* or the puritan classic Foxe's *Book of Martyrs* (both of which are in Clare's surviving library) that are cited among poets' earliest reading materials. Religious poetic forms and versifications of scripture are recurring formal types. Indeed, it might be argued that religious poetry is precisely where the 'sly civility' or double-voicedness of labouring-class poetry often lies. A good proportion of what we would today identify as political expression in labouring-class poetry is couched in religious language, and framed as religious rather than overtly political discourse. The poet's right to write, particularly if presented as driven by divine inspiration, could be presented in similar terms to the right of all souls to salvation. The links between the rise of denominations that were perceived as socially levelling, such as Methodism, and the increase in the number of labouring-class poets, may not be a coincidence. Even the simple ability to read and write, on which labouring-class poetry was founded, derived to a great extent from evangelical movements of the eighteenth century. Without the Sunday School movement, many members of the lower classes might never have learned to read at all.[16] But the political danger of literacy was underscored too, even late in the eighteenth century, by Hannah More's warning that while the poor might *read*, they should be prevented from learning to *write*.[17]

Yet write they did, and they often turned to religion as a vehicle through which to explore issues that might also be called political. Although there are examples of overtly political writing in this tradition, such as the labouring-class contributions to the debate on abolition recently catalogued by Tim Burke, politics in labouring-class verse is more often submerged, hidden behind the choices of scriptures to versify and Biblical stories to adapt.[18] Old Testament stories were popular, such as those of the Shunamite (versified by Duck), Deborah and Barak, and especially Job: exemplars whose sufferings were ultimately repaid with liberation. Mary Collier in 1739 cleverly retells the story of the 'Three Wise Sentences' from the Apocryphal book of Esdras. Three of King Darius's bodyguards debate the question of what is the strongest force in the world. One says 'wine', another 'the king', but the king gives the prize to the third who combines feminism and piety by saying that women are the strongest force, 'but truth is victor over all things'. The former servant Elizabeth Hands used the far darker story of 'The Death of Amnon' (1789) to place gender issues on the agenda. John Lucas in 'The Fall of Pharoah' (1781) disguises a potentially dangerous political story about rebellion against tyranny, by transposing the setting to ancient Egypt and recasting the labouring classes as Hebrews suffering under the oppressive Pharaoh.[19]

Clare's own connections to radical religion and Methodism are well documented. As he notes in his autobiographical writings, he had early tendencies to deism, and briefly 'turned a methodist'.[20] But while he notes that he is theologically closest to the Methodists, he rejected fully identifying himself with the denomination because he found many fellow believers to be too ignorant and narrow minded. Clare's free-thinking religious propensities were viewed as dangerous in a poet of such powerful talents, as evident in the way in which he was treated by his patrons Lord Radstock and Eliza Emmerson. It will surprise no one familiar with the characters of these two figures that the vast majority of religious tomes in Clare's library were given by Lord Radstock. Happily for posterity, Clare eschewed the literary influence of these dull collections of sermons. This is not to say, however, that religious discourse and style are nowhere found in Clare's poetry. They appear, for example, in the eschatological tone of much of the asylum poetry. Clare owned much religious literature of various styles, from Milton's *Paradise Lost* to Bunyan's *Pilgrim's Progress*. He had a copy of his friend H. F. Cary's translation of Dante's *Divine Comedy*. And – unsurprising given Clare's affinity for songs of all kinds – he had collections of both Watts's and Wesley's hymns.

Religion is not the only place in Clare's poetry or in labouring-class poetry in general that politics appears. Abolitionism has been mentioned. Clare is prominent for the powerful anti-enclosure rhetoric of his poetry, for example in 'Remembrances' (1832), drawing imagery from the dark days when Boney was a figure of fear and the sight of hanging 'traitors' a familiar one:

> Inclosure like a Buonaparte let not a thing remain
> It levelled every bush and tree and levelled every hill
> And hung the moles for traitors – though the brook is running still
> It runs a naked brook cold and chill[21]

Beyond the proto-Marxist politics ascribed to the poets in studies of labouring-class poetry written in the 1960s and 1970s, there is a wider variety of political concerns expressed in labouring-class poetry than has been documented. In addition to the abolition debate, poets also take strong stands on issues of war and its impact on the poor. Although there are nationalistic poems supporting British conquests, both the journeyman woolcomber poet Christopher Jones, and the Scottish domestic servant Christian Milne, protest in their poetry against the practice of press-ganging. While a good deal of labouring-class poetry seems merely to replicate the political agenda of the ruling classes, some argues against imperialism, both within and outside the United Kingdom. Anne Wilson, for example, uses the locodescriptive genre of riparian or river poetry to make a subtle critique of the English assimilation of Scottish culture, transposing contemporary tensions into legendary narratives of the goddess Britannia's refusal to allow Uther Pendragon to reside in the North with his beloved enchantress Genuera. Wilson's double-voicedness allows the poet to speak within and against the dominant discourses of a nationalism that had used Arthurian legend to erase regional distinctions. The Welsh poet and stonemason Edward Williams ('Iolo Morganwg') very substantially contributed to the revival of interest in Welsh history, poetry, and folklore.[22]

The politics of landscape, as evidenced in Wilson, has long been a theme of Clare criticism, but by reading Clare within the longer labouring-class tradition, both his innovations and his debts, not only to the canonical loco-descriptive poets (such as Thomson) but to his labouring-class forbears, can be better understood. For Clare is not the only labouring-class poet with debts to Thomson, nor is he the first to have written critically about the enclosure movement (by which common land and open fields were appropriated into private farms and estates) and other forms of agricultural 'improvement'. James Woodhouse, whose earliest poetry participates in the enthusiasm for landscape design of his patron William Shenstone, later offers a scathing critique of enclosure in his monumental verse autobiography *The Life and Lucubrations of Crispinus Scriblerus* (1814/1896). Nathaniel Bloomfield's anti-enclosure poem 'Honington Green a ballad', published a decade earlier, had, when first read in manuscript by his more famous brother Robert, 'melted me into salt water'. Much has been written recently about Mary Leapor's 'double-voiced' relation to the country-house tradition of nature writing, in her poem 'Crumble Hall'.[23] Labouring-class poets responded variously to privileged poetic spaces, for example the landscape of Clifton in Bristol: Henry Jones, Thomas Chatterton and Ann Yearsley each wrote long poems about this celebrated area. Just as for Clare, poetic regionalism also had political implications in the poetry of Samuel Law, Anne Wilson, and many of the Scottish labouring-class poets with whom Clare was familiar.

John Clare's position within the labouring-class tradition is in some ways more complex than that of any other poet. Prodigiously talented, prolific and (to his own surprise) fairly long-lived, Clare faced all the issues that had confounded so many of his predecessors, survived a relentless series of personal and socio-economic catastrophes (of which the enclosure of his native Helpston between 1809 and 1820 was only the most acute), and lived on, though locked away in an asylum, into an age in which the model of the 'natural genius' or 'peasant poet' had long been superseded by the less vulnerable, more self-reliant figure of the Victorian self-taught or self-made author. His 'double voicedness' manifests itself, above all, in his struggle to bring together the oral tradition of narrative and song that was his natural background, and the world of polite poetry that had ruled his imagination from the moment he first set eyes on a battered copy of Thomson's *Seasons* at the age of thirteen. A key moment in his literary education, described in his unfinished autobiography, was the process of reading some of his first verses aloud to his parents, disguising his own authorship of them so as to get an unbiased opinion from these revered representatives of a generation steeped in storytelling and song.

In trying to draw his native culture into the world of polite, printed literature, Clare had few enough examples to follow. He was himself, for example, one of the earliest collectors of English regional folksong, though he was certainly aware of Scottish ballad and song collecting (in 1826, for example, his publisher John Taylor presented him with a copy of Allan Cunningham's *The Songs of Scotland*). He eagerly seized on evidence of earlier literary visits to the oral well, delighting to find in Thomas Percy's *Reliques of Ancient English Poetry* (1765), for instance, 'all the stories of my grandmother and her gossiping neighbours'.[24] If the 'doomed poets' of his tombstone drawings offered a gloomy warning about the 'fate of genius' when it came from humble life, they also offered invaluable literary precedents, particularly Robert Bloomfield, whose narrative poems of rural life, published during Clare's childhood, had achieved considerable success in precisely the cross-pollination of folk and literary materials that Clare so greatly wished to emulate. His own narrative poems, though they have received less attention than his descriptive and anti-enclosure verses, represent a considerable achievement in finding appropriate written verse forms for popular oral narrative. Clare is particularly adept at framing narratives, setting up his stories in the context of labour or leisure, very often with a charismatic female narrator. Bloomfield offered important precedents for these techniques, especially in his riotous feast-day poem 'The Horkey' (1806).

But there is an even more pervasive labouring-class influence on Clare's poetry than Bloomfield. If critics have so far discovered little evidence, beyond the vital figure of Bloomfield, for direct labouring-class influence on Clare's poetry, it may be because they have been looking on the wrong side of the Tweed. For although the English self-taught tradition, as we have been arguing, is a distinctive one in eighteenth-century English poetry, the Scottish influence that kicks in especially after 1786 would become central to the English tradition. Robert Burns was the most influential single figure on English and Scottish labouring-class poets for most of the nineteenth century. Even before Burns, however, the Scottish influence was highly significant. As Hamish Henderson has remarked, Scotland was the engine of eighteenth-century British balladry and folksong.[25] It fed into the work of English 'peasant poets' like Bloomfield and Clare through printed and oral channels.

The outlines of John Clare's Scottish influence are familiar. Its roots lie with his absent Scottish grandfather John Donald Parker, the hundred or more ballads his father could sing or recite 'over his horn of ale with his merry companions at the Blue bell public house which was next door', and early encounters with Allan Ramsay's poems, Percy's *Reliques*, and later with Burns, Hogg, Scott, Robert Tannahill, and Allan Cunningham (who befriended Clare). Its branches are the very many poems he wrote that were Scottish in diction and form, particularly in the asylum (what Ronald Blythe calls his 'Scottish Period').[26] But we would argue that Clare's absorption of eighteenth-century Scottish poetry had an even more profound and fundamental influence on his development as a poet. Just as Scotland provided him with an ideal of freedom, encapsulated in the Miltonic 'mountain liberty' Clare saw in the faces of the Scottish drovers as they moved through the static Northamptonshire landscape, so its songs and poems offered (to borrow a term from Anne Janowitz) a 'communitarian' kind of poetry, less marked by distinctions of high and low class and culture, more concerned with singing and storytelling as social activities.[27]

For Clare the labouring-class tradition is filtered through Bloomfield and through the Scottish poets, and appropriately his most impassioned statement about the subject position of the 'peasant poet' occurs in a letter to the Scottish labouring-class poet Allan Cunningham, enclosing a sample of Robert Bloomfield's handwriting. It opens with a stirring greeting of solidarity, and in warm praise of Bloomfield, who had just died:

> Brother Bard and Fellow Labourer,
> I beg your acceptance according to promise of this autograph of our English Theocritus, Bloomfield. He is in my opinion our best Pastoral Poet. His 'Broken Crutch', 'Richard and Kate', &c. are inimitable and above praise.

George Crabbe, by contrast, 'writes about the peasantry as much like the Magistrate as the Poet', and Clare declares that he 'never forgave' Byron's 'sneering mention' of Bloomfield in his satire *English Bards and Scotch Reviewers* (1809). This is clearly written in distress at Bloomfield's recent miserable end, and Clare goes on both bitterly to satirize the fetishizing of peasant poets through the use of occupational sobriquets, and to seize again the idea of a solidarity between labouring-class poets, as a consolation and a source of strength:

I should suppose, friend Allan, that 'The Ettrick Shepherd' [James Hogg], 'The Nithsdale Mason' [Cunningham], and 'The Northamptonshire Peasant' [Clare himself], are looked upon as intruders and stray cattle in the fields of the Muses (forgive the classification), and I have no doubt but our reception in that Pinfold of his lordship's 'English bards' would have been as far short of a compliment as Bloomfield's. Well, never mind, we will do our best, and as we never went to Oxford or Cambridge, we have no Latin and Greek to boast of, and no bad translations to hazard (whatever our poems may be), and that's comfort on our side.[28]

Proudly seizing the badge of cultural and educational exclusion, as Clare does here, is one response to the pressures of 'peasant poethood'. Another is to take over the persona of 'his lordship' himself, which Clare duly did both in his satirical poems of 1841, 'Don Juan' and 'Child Harold', and in his asylum claims actually to *be* Lord Byron. The myriad self-presentational strategies Clare developed, in his poetry as in his madness, are evidence of the enormous difficulty of trying to cope with being 'stray cattle in the fields of the Muses', and of the sly ingenuity by which poets like Clare *did* cope.

Clare is, as has often been noted, a poet of the margins, and was himself marginalized by literary history until very recently. Those who have worked so hard over the last century to bring him into the mainstream might perhaps consider that to place him again with the 'peasant poets' is to retreat from the task of reading Clare's poetry on its own terms. But the labouring-class tradition in poetry is an unavoidable, central context for understanding Clare's achievement, in that it shaped so many of his literary strategies, from the exuberant rewritings of Thomson and Gray at the start of his career, to the retreat into anonymous Scottish balladry in some of the asylum poetry. A fuller understanding of this tradition can only strengthen our ability to read Clare, both for his own special qualities, and as a representative of this important and historically undervalued tradition.

NOTES

1. William J. Christmas, *The Lab'ring Muses* (Newark: University of Delaware Press, 2001), p. 282.
2. John Clare, 'Sonnet XXVIII. In Hilly Wood', lines 9–10, in *The Village Minstrel, and Other Poems* (1821), II: 176; cf. Gray's *Elegy*, lines 55–6.
3. Margaret Anne Doody, *The Daring Muse: Augustan Poetry Reconsidered* (Cambridge: Cambridge University Press, 1985), pp. 225, 227.
4. Robert Southey, *The Lives and Works of the Uneducated Poets [1831]*, ed. J. S. Childers (London: Oxford University Press, 1925), p. 118.
5. Mark Storey (ed.), *Clare: The Critical Heritage* (London: Routledge, 1973), p. 40.
6. Donna Landry, *The Muses of Resistance* (Cambridge: Cambridge University Press, 1990), pp. 5, 6.

7. *The Early Poems of John Clare 1804–1822*, ed. Eric Robinson, David Powell and P. M. S. Dawson, 2 vols. (Oxford: Oxford University Press, 1984), II: 666–70.

8. Homi Bhabha, *The Location of Culture* (London: Routledge, 1994), p. 97.

9. John Goodridge, 'Identity, Authenticity, Class: John Clare and the Mask of Chatterton', *Angelaki* 1 (1993), 131–48.

10. Donald F. Bond (ed.), *The Spectator*, 5 vols. (Oxford: Clarendon Press, 1965), II: 127, 129 (No. 160, 3 September 1711).

11. Mark Akenside, *The Pleasures of Imagination* (1744), i. 37–8.

12. Betty Rizzo, 'The Patron as Poet Maker: The Politics of Benefaction', *Studies in Eighteenth-Century Culture* 20 (1990), 241–66.

13. Stephen Duck, *Poems on Several Occasions* (1736), p. xiv.

14. Samuel Jackson Pratt (ed.), *The Remains of Joseph Blacket* (1811).

15. Bridget Keegan, 'Cobbling Verse: Shoemaker Poets of the Long Eighteenth Century', *The Eighteenth Century: Theory and Interpretation* 42 (2001), 195–217.

16. See David Vincent, *Bread, Knowledge and Freedom: A Study of Nineteenth-Century Working Class Autobiography* (London: Methuen, 1981), an invaluable source on the emergence of labouring-class writing and reading in the eighteenth as well as nineteenth centuries.

17. Quoted in Landry, *Muses of Resistance*, p. 123.

18. Tim Burke, '"Humanity is Now the Pop'lar Cry": Laboring-Class Writers and the Liverpool Slave Trade, 1787–1789', *The Eighteenth Century: Theory and Interpretation* 42 (2001), 245–63.

19. See Elizabeth Hands, *The Death of Amnon. A Poem. With an Appendix: containing Pastorals, and other Poetical Pieces* (Coventry, 1789); also Landry, *Muses of Resistance*, pp. 38–43. For John Lucas, see *The Fall of Pharoah; and Philo's Apology. Two Poems* (Salisbury, 1781).

20. John Clare, *By Himself*, ed. Eric Robinson and David Powell (Manchester and Ashington: Carcanet, 1996), p. 133.

21. John Clare, *Poems of the Middle Period 1822–37*, ed. Eric Robinson, David Powell, and P. M. S. Dawson, 2 vols. (Oxford: Oxford University Press, 1998), III: 133, lines 67–70. We have corrected 'naker' to 'naked' and replaced ampersands.

22. See Wilson's *Teisa: A Descriptive Poem of the River Teese, Its Towns and Antiquities* (Newcastle upon Tyne, 1778), lines 713–1009. On Williams, see Prys Morgan, *Iolo Morganwg* (Cardiff: University of Wales Press, 1975), and 'From Death to a View: The Hunt for a Welsh Past in the Romantic Period', in *The Invention of Tradition*, ed. Eric Hobsbawm and Terence Ranger (Cambridge: Cambridge University Press, 1992), pp. 43–100.

23. See Nathaniel Bloomfield, *An Essay on War . . . and Other Poems on Various Subjects* (1803); *Selections from the Correspondence of Robert Bloomfield*, ed. W. H. Hart (1870), no. 11; Jeannie Dalporto, 'Landscape, Labor, and the Ideology of Improvement in Mary Leapor's "Crumble Hall"', *The Eighteenth Century: Theory and Interpretation* 42 (2001), 228–44.

24. *The Letters of John Clare*, ed. Mark Storey (Oxford: Oxford University Press, 1985), pp. 386 and 82. See also Clare, *By Himself*, pp. 192–3.

25. Hamish Henderson, *Alias MacAlias: Writings on Songs, Folk and Literature* (Edinburgh: Polygon, 1992).

26. Ian Bowman, 'John Clare – The Scottish Connection', *Scots Magazine* (March 1988), 580–5; Ronald Blythe, 'John Clare in Scotland', *John Clare Society Journal* 19 (2000), 73–81; Clare, *By Himself*, p. 2.
27. Anne Janowitz, *Lyric and Labour in the Romantic Tradition* (Cambridge: Cambridge University Press, 1998). See also John Clare, *The Shepherd's Calendar*, ed. Eric Robinson, Geoffrey Summerfield and David Powell (Oxford: Oxford University Press, 1993), p. 77 ('July', line 218); cf. Milton, 'L'Allegro', line 36.
28. Clare, *Letters*, pp. 302–3.

FURTHER READING

Christmas, William J., *The Lab'ring Muses: Work, Writing, and the Social Order in English Plebeian Poetry, 1730–1830*, Newark: University of Delaware Press, 2001.

(ed.), *The Eighteenth Century: Theory and Interpretation* 42.3 (Fall 2001), Special Issue: Eighteenth-Century Laboring-Class Poets.

Fairer, David, *English Poetry of the Eighteenth Century, 1700–1789*, London: Longman, 2003.

Goodridge, John, *Rural Life in Eighteenth-Century English Poetry*, Cambridge: Cambridge University Press, 1995.

(general ed.), *Eighteenth-Century English Labouring-Class Poets*, 3 vols., London: Pickering and Chatto, 2003; *Nineteenth-Century Labouring-Class Poets*, 3 vols., London: Pickering and Chatto, 2004.

(ed.), *The Independent Spirit: John Clare and the Self-Taught Tradition*, Helpston: The John Clare Society, 1994.

and Simon Kövesi (eds.), *John Clare: New Approaches*, Helpston: The John Clare Society, 2000.

Greene, Richard, *Mary Leapor: A Study in Eighteenth-Century Women's Poetry*, Oxford: Clarendon Press, 1993.

Haughton, Hugh, Adam Phillips, and Geoffrey Summerfield (eds.), *John Clare in Context*, Cambridge: Cambridge University Press, 1994.

Klaus, H. Gustav, *The Literature of Labour: 200 Years of Working-Class Writing*, Brighton: Harvester, 1985.

Kövesi, Simon (ed.), The John Clare Web Page, <http://human.ntu.ac.uk/clare>.

Landry, Donna, *The Muses of Resistance: Laboring-Class Women's Poetry in Britain, 1739–1796*, Cambridge: Cambridge University Press, 1990.

Unwin, Rayner, *The Rural Muse: Studies in the Peasant Poetry of England*, London: George Allen and Unwin, 1954.

INDEX

literacy 4, 43
Literary Journal 128
Literary Magazine 11, 163
Liverpool, Robert Jenkinson, Lord 269,
    275, 276
Lloyd, Charles 228, 229
Locke, John 33, 34, 45, 57, 178, 195
    *Essay Concerning Human
        Understanding* 180, 184, 195
Lockhart, John Gibson 56, 266
London Corresponding Society 50,
    201
Longinus 33
Longman's British Theatre 114, 116
Lovat, Simon Fraser, Lord 167
Lowth, Robert 34–5
Lucas, John 287
    'The Fall of Pharoah' 288
Luther, Martin 175
lyric 115, 217, 218, 227, 234

Macaulay, Thomas Babington 157, 188
    Minute on Indian Education 61–2, 70–1
McCarthy, William 216, 217
McGann, Jerome 88
Mackenzie, Henry 82, 87, 88, 93
    Julia de Roubigné 86, 89, 90
    Lounger 93
    The Man of Feeling 19, 80, 81, 88, 91, 93,
        96
    Mirror 5, 91
Mackenzie, Niall 160
Macklin, Charles 108, 109
Macpherson, James xiii, 88, 130, 200
magazines, *see* periodicals
Maginn, William 128
Magnuson, Paul 44
Malone, Edmond 27
Malthus, Thomas 11
Mandeville, John 63
Mant, Richard 239
    The Simpliciad 239
Martin, Philip 166
Marvell, Andrew 160–1
Marx, Karl 34
Mary, Queen of Scots 87, 123, 165,
    167
Masters, Mary 284
Maundrell, Henry 63, 71
masquerades 113, 177
Mathews, Charles 266
Mathias, Thomas
    Pursuits of Literature 213

Maturin, Charles Robert 127
    Melmoth the Wanderer 131–2
Maxwell, James 287
Meeke, Mary 125
Mellor, Anne K. 184, 216
memoirs, *see* autobiography
Methodism 176, 179, 200, 205, 206, 283,
    287, 288, 289
Michie, Allen 152
Mill, John Stuart 44
Millar, Andrew 15
Milne, Christian 289
Milton, John 27–8, 36, 37, 124, 196, 233,
    251, 274, 275, 286, 292
    Paradise Lost 185, 192, 286, 288, 289
Minerva Press 16, 18, 125, 256
missionaries 70
Mist's Weekly Journal 158
Mitchell, W. J. T. 199
Monboddo, James Burnet, Lord 168
Montagu, Basil 240
Montagu, Elizabeth 285
Montagu, Lady Mary Wortley 64
Montaigne, Michel de 181
Montesquieu, Charles de Secondat, Baron de
    Montesquieu 66
    Persian Letters 64
Montgomery, Robert 173
Monthly Magazine 11, 54
Monthly Review xiv, 11
Moore, Edward 144
Moore, Thomas 72, 265
    Lalla Rookh 65
Moore's Almanack 4
More, Hannah 113, 157, 285, 288
    Cheap Repository Tracts 51, 287
    Coelebs in Search of a Wife 257
    Sensibility 45, 85, 91, 96
Morier, James
    Adventures of Hajji Baba 65
Morgan, Lady, *see* Owenson, Sydney
Morning Post 230, 233, 238, 241, 268,
    269
Mort Castle 121
Mozart, Wolfgang Amadeus 274
Munro, Alexander
    *Structure and Function of the Nervous
        System* 83
Murphy, Arthur 164
Murray, James 161
Murray, John 12, 246, 250
    see also Quarterly Review
Myers, Mitzi 211, 213

CAMBRIDGE COMPANIONS TO LITERATURE

CAMBRIDGE COMPANIONS TO CULTURE